Penguin Books
Prick Up Your Ears

John Lahr was born in Los Angeles in 1941 and was
educated at Yale and Oxford. He became the theatre
columnist for the *Village Voice* and a contributing
editor to *Evergreen Review*, and was the youngest recipient of
the George Jean Nathan Award for Dramatic Criticism
(1969). He has also been Literary Adviser to the Repertory
Theater of Lincoln Center in New York and the
Tyrone Guthrie Theater in Minneapolis.

As well as the acclaimed biography of his father, *Notes on a
Cowardly Lion*, John Lahr has written three books of
theatrical criticism and two novels.

He now lives in London with his wife, Anthea, and son,
Christopher.

Penguin Books

John Lahr

PRICK UP YOUR EARS

The Biography of Joe Orton

Penguin Books Ltd, Harmondsworth, Middlesex, England
Penguin Books, 625 Madison Avenue,
New York, New York 10022, U.S.A.
Penguin Books Australia Ltd, Ringwood, Victoria, Australia
Penguin Books Canada Ltd, 2801 John Street,
Markham, Ontario, Canada L3R 1B4
Penguin Books (N.Z.) Ltd, 182–190 Wairau Road,
Auckland 10, New Zealand

First published by Allen Lane 1978
Published in Penguin Books 1980

Copyright © John Lahr, 1978

Entertaining Mr Sloane first published by Hamish Hamilton 1964;
subsequently by Eyre Methuen 1973
Copyright © 1964 by Joe Orton
Loot first published by Methuen & Co. 1967
Copyright © 1967 by Joe Orton
What the Butler Saw first published by Methuen & Co. 1969;
the revised version first published by Eyre Methuen 1976
Copyright © 1969, 1976 by the Estate of Joe Orton, deceased
Funeral Games and *The Good and Faithful Servant* first published
by Methuen & Co. 1970.
Copyright © 1970 by the Estate of Joe Orton, deceased
Extracts from the private diaries of Joe Orton copyright ©
1976 by the Estate of Joe Orton, deceased

All rights reserved

The publishers wish to emphasize that the material quoted
in this volume from Orton's private diaries is fully
protected by copyright and that no further use whatsoever
may be made of this material without the express permission
in writing of the Estate of Joe Orton, c/o Margaret
Ramsay Ltd, 14a Goodwin's Court, London wc2.

Reproduced, printed and bound in Great Britain by
Cox & Wyman Ltd, Reading
Set in Monotype Bembo

Except in the United States of America, this book is sold
subject to the condition that it shall not, by way of trade
or otherwise, be lent, re-sold, hired out, or otherwise
circulated without the publisher's prior consent in any form
of binding or cover other than that in which it is published
and without a similar condition including this condition
being imposed on the subsequent purchaser

To ANTHEA and CHRISTOPHER:
Gravity's angels

CONTENTS

LIST OF ILLUSTRATIONS

... Cleanse my heart,
give me the ability to rage
correctly.

Joe Orton, *Head to Toe*

... Edna Welthorpe writes 'The people here
leave a lot to be desired and flaunt their prefer-
ences for what they cryptically call "bits of the
other" at every café. I might have been assaulted
through the ears on many occasions – by *words*
only,' she adds.

Joe Orton to Kenneth Williams in a letter
from Morocco

ACKNOWLEDGEMENTS

'Life being what it is, one seeks revenge,' Paul Gauguin wrote. The comedian gets even with laughter: a hostile sharpshooter using his wit to kill the past and defend himself from the present. Joe Orton was the first person to make me laugh in the theatre the way my father did. In their unique ways, both men created the purest of theatrical experiences: joy. In *Notes on a Cowardly Lion*, I had the good fortune to chronicle at first hand the life and laughter of Bert Lahr. *Prick Up Your Ears* is an extension of my inquiry into the nature of comedy. I consider Joe Orton to be as great a comic playwright as Bert Lahr was a comic actor. They shared, as all comic spirits must, the capacity for being at once mischievous, irreverent, truthful, outrageous, infantile, vulgar, and brilliant. Comedy challenges romantic formulations about creativity, making something beautiful and positive out of a variety of murky emotions. For those unfamiliar with Orton's special brand of humour, a paperback volume of his collected plays is published in England by Eyre Methuen and in America by Grove Press.

Prick Up Your Ears has taken a long time to write – some would say too long. In the biography of Bert Lahr, I had a career of over fifty years with which to deal and access to the beloved grouch himself. With Orton, things were different. Killed in his prime, Orton barely had time to establish himself in public life. His sexual life was anonymous; and his social life was just beginning to be studded with the familiar names in the aristocracy of British show-biz success of which he was a new and glittering member. No one knew him well, or for long. The biography became a mosaic, pieced painstakingly together with his own words and the observations of those whose path he crossed.

In search of the man and a sympathetic interpretation of his work, the biographer throws a wide net. He relies on the wisdom of friends and the kindness of strangers. Fred Jordan, then of Grove Press, first told me of Orton's diaries in 1970. Peggy Ramsay, who as Orton's agent had suggested he keep a diary as early as 1965, gave me the run of her office and a great deal of time and initial encouragement. She provided me with Orton's diaries (two covering the last six months of his life and a childhood diary), his clipping books, the various drafts of his plays and the unpublished novels. She also gave me entrée to London's theatre world and Orton's family. James Price, then head of Allen Lane, commissioned the book but left before I delivered it. Kenneth Williams talked with illuminating candour and affection about both Halliwell and Orton. He trusted my biographical approach, giving me a great deal of his time and allowing me to quote from his diaries. Bob Gottlieb of Knopf and Paul Sidey of Penguin Books have been superb editors of the biography, giving it many careful readings and offering editorial suggestions which have, I hope, rid it of prolixity.

The early period of both Orton's and Halliwell's life required a lot of sleuthing. Orton was then known as John Orton and few people I interviewed connected him at first with Joe Orton the playwright. Halliwell, like Orton, kept to himself. Finally, a network of informants from Leicester and the Wirral emerged. The Orton family was crucial to my research. William Orton, Douglas Orton, Marilyn Orton Lock, and especially Leonie Orton Barnett with her perceptive and affectionate regard for Joe were a great help. As were: Mrs C. A. Bish, David Bowers and Joyce Holmes Bowers, David Campton, Bruce Cleave, Mrs Sheila Cook, Mr and Mrs S. Coppack, Dorothy Dalby, J. P. Howarth, Mr and Mrs Noel Lacey, L. Moore-Tucker, Roy Mothersole, Millicent Overon, John Pooley, Dorothy Root, Ada Rothery, Edna and Harold Rowson, Joanne Runswick, Sylvia Sargeant, Michael

Steele, Eric Swift, B. H. T. Taylor, Bernard Widdowson, Trevor Williams.

For information about Orton's and Halliwell's theatrical and literary life prior to Orton's success I am grateful to: Gene Baro, Richard Brain, Max Burten-Shaw, Hugh Cruttwell, C. A. Elliott, Lawrence Griffin, June Clark Howarth, Rosalind Knight, Keith Lyon, John Moffat, Charles Monteith, Richard O'Donoghue, Jack Payne, Mary Phillips, Sidney Porrett, Barbara Rowlands, Diana Scougall, Claire Tompkins, Margaret Whiting.

Orton's success was meteoric. While Orton rarely had a nice word to say about anybody, his producers have been as loyal to the memory of his talent as they were to his work. Michael Codron let me snoop through his production files of *Entertaining Mr Sloane* and *Loot* in Harrods' cavernous storage rooms. Oscar Lewenstein, who produced the successful version of *Loot* and *What the Butler Saw*, and later in 1975 as artistic director of the Royal Court mounted a revival of Joe Orton's three full-length plays, was a great source of information. In building up a picture of Orton's professional and private life during this period, I would like to thank: Lindsay Anderson, Sheila Ballantine, Michael Bates, Stanley Baxter, Miss D. I. Boynes, Coral Browne, Robert Chetwyn, Mr and Mrs H. Corden, Adrienne Corri, Kenneth Cranham, Martin Drew, Patrick Dromgoole, Martin Esslin, Crispin Evans, James Fox, Peter Gill, Penelope Gilliatt, Sheila Hancock, Barry Hanson, Julian Holloway, Dr Douglas Ismay, Colin Jeavons, Nigel Logan, Glenn Loney, Frank Marcus, Charles Marowitz, Geraldine McEwan, David Mercer, Lee Montague, Braham Murray, Timothy O'Brien, James Ormerod, Harold Pinter, Sir Terence Rattigan, Peter Reeves, Karel Reisz, Madge Ryan, Mr and Mrs Aldo Salvoni, Alan Schneider, Dudley Sutton, John Tydeman, Simon Ward, Michael White, Peter Willes, David William, Peter Wood.

And for various services rendered – either stimulating discussion, advice, enthusiastic support or technical assistance – the biography cannot go to press without acknowledging the generosity of: Paul Barker, Alan Bennett, Georges and Anne Borchardt, John Connell,

Tish Dace, Tom Erhardt, Sir John Foster, Stephen Frears, Ray Gosling, Peter Grose, Vaughn Grylls, John Hirsch, Martha Kaplan, Robert J. Lifton, Kit Lukas, Raymond Mander and Joe Mitcheson, Martin Paisner, Richard Seaver, Geoffrey Strachan, Annette Taylor, Christopher Tugendhat, E. Willats.

In this book, as in all my writing, Anthea Lahr has been my intimate collaborator. Her editorial acumen, her sound judgement, and her insight into the neurotic patterns of Orton and Halliwell are present on every page. She has blue-pencilled my excesses, answered my endless questions, and with typical patience and generosity listened as I read her each day's writing. The debt which authors always acknowledge to their wives has become a publishing cliché. In my case, reader, believe it. Without Anthea, this book and my writing career would not exist.

London
October 1977

1

JOKERS ARE WILD

> Murder is negative creation, and every murderer
> is therefore the rebel who claims the right to be
> omnipotent. His pathos is his refusal to suffer...
>
> W. H. Auden, *The Dyer's Hand*

> MISS PRISM. The good ended happily, and the
> bad unhappily. That is what Fiction means.
>
> Oscar Wilde, *The Importance of Being Earnest*

Joe Orton and Kenneth Halliwell were friends. For fifteen years, they lived and often wrote together. They wore each other's clothes. Their wills each named the other as sole beneficiary. They shared everything except success. But on 9 August 1967, murder made them equal again.

The note was found on top of the red-grained leather binder which held Orton's diary. The words, fastidiously written, had none of the horror that the scene did:

> If you read his diary all will
> be explained.
>
> KH
> PS. Especially the latter part

Halliwell lay nude on his back in the centre of the room, three feet from Orton's writing desk. The backs of his hands, the top of his chest, and his bald head were splattered with blood. Except for his arms, rigor mortis had set in. Halliwell's gory pyjama top was draped over the desk chair. On the linoleum floor near him was a glass and a can of grapefruit juice which had speeded the twenty-two Nembutals into his blood, killing him within thirty seconds. Halliwell had died sooner than Orton, whose sheets were still warm when the police discovered him in bed, his head cratered like a burnt candle.

At forty-one, Halliwell was no stranger to horrific death. When he was eleven, his doting mother had been stung in the mouth by a wasp and within minutes had choked to death before his eyes. Twelve years later, Halliwell came downstairs for breakfast to discover his father with his head in the oven, dead from asphyxiation. Halliwell was haunted by his father's death. While studying at RADA in 1953, he told an actress who had tried to rally him out of one of his frequent depressions: 'I'll end up just like my father and commit suicide.' Halliwell had no reason to trust life.

'God laughs and snaps his fingers,' he and Orton wrote in an unpublished novel, *The Boy Hairdresser* (1960). 'The only thing for man to do is to imitate God and snap his fingers too.' Halliwell's final fillip was nine hammer blows to Orton's head, a last crazy gesture of omnipotence in a life which from the time of his parents' deaths had been out of control. The hammer lay above the bed-cover on Orton's chest. Halliwell, who had once taken Marlowe as his stage surname, had dispatched Orton with a frenzied brutality typical of that Elizabethan playwright's blood-lust. He had walloped Orton's head so furiously that the vault of his skull had been bashed open and several lacerations on the scalp held the shape of the hammer. Orton's face was caked with dried blood. His brain had been splattered on wall and ceiling.

It was Orton's mind – the gorgeous, wicked fun it poked at the world – which made him irresistible and obsessed Halliwell. He had known that brain before it had been tutored by him in literature. He'd nurtured it, enjoyed it, provoked it to defy convention, edited its excesses. 'Marriage excuses no one the freaks' roll-call.' Halliwell and Orton both shared a trickster's suspicion of normality, but only Orton could give the anarchic instinct memorable shape in a sentence. His curious chemistry of anger, optimism, and erudition blessed him with a comic style unique to his era. The mind that was meant to be Halliwell's cultivated and constant companion had acquired an independent life and vision. Often during the last months of their lives, Orton tried to reason Halliwell into a life of his own:

When we got home we talked about ourselves and our relationship. I think it's bad that we live in each other's pockets twenty-four hours a day three hundred and sixty-five days a year. When I'm away Kenneth does nothing, meets nobody. What's to be done? He's now taking tranquillizers to calm his nerves. 'I need an affair with somebody,' he says. He says I'm no good. I'm only interested in physical sex, not love. 'Your attitude to sensitive people is Victorian,' he said. 'Basically, it's Dr Arnold's "get on the playing fields. You won't be so sensitive then."' 'All you need is a field of interest outside me. Where you can meet people away from me . . .'

(30 April 1967)

Halliwell's threats in the last year always tried to manoeuvre Orton back into the cosy unit he'd outgrown:

Kenneth H had a long talk about our relationship. He threatens, or keeps saying, he will commit suicide. He says, 'You'll learn then, won't you?' and 'What will you be like without me?' We talked and talked until I was exhausted . . .

(1 May 1967)

Had Halliwell killed Orton and himself four years earlier, their deaths would have been another short item in the local paper. Instead, they were headline news. Between 1963, when his first play was accepted, and 1967, when he died, Orton became a playwright of international reputation. His œuvre was small, but his impact was large. By 1967, the term 'Ortonesque' had worked its way into the English vocabulary, a shorthand adjective for scenes of macabre outrageousness. Orton wrote three first-class full-length plays – *Entertaining Mr Sloane*, *Loot* and the posthumously produced *What the Butler Saw* – and four one-act plays. In his short career, two films were made from his plays; and *Loot* was voted the *Evening Standard*'s Best Play of 1966. Orton's plays often scandalized audiences, but his wit made the outrage memorable. Orton's laughter bore out Nietzsche's dictum that 'He who writes in blood and aphorisms does not want to be read, he wants to be learned by heart.' Orton brought the epigram back to the contemporary stage to illuminate a violent world: 'It's life that defeats the Christian Church, she's always been well-equipped to deal with death' (*The Erpingham Camp*); 'All classes are criminal today. We live in an age of equality' (*Funeral Games*). Orton's laughter created a 'panic'. His stage gargoyles tried to frighten their audience into new life.

Orton's death – laced as it was with the irony of his fascination with the grotesque – had special public interest. No playwright in living memory had met a more gruesome end. The news was reported on the front page of *The Times* and all the major English papers. The *Times* obituary (written by its drama critic Irving Wardle) called Orton 'one of the sharpest stylists of the British new wave . . . a consummate dialogue artist, and a natural anarch'. It was a better review from the paper than Orton ever earned in life. Almost instantly, Orton's death became more famous than his work. Many interpreted his death as retribution for the unrelenting anarchy of his laughter.[1] But Orton was not hounded by society into a self-conscious martyrdom. He was not a victim of the gospel of ecstasy which burned out the lives of so many pop stars of the sixties. A voluptuary of fiasco, Orton died from his short-sighted and indecisive loyalty to a friend.

Halliwell had purchased the second-floor bed-sitting-room at 25 Noel Road, Islington, in 1959, so that he and Orton could have some security while they tried to write. But it was finally Orton who persevered, sitting at their glossy white desk and writing while Halliwell looked on. Even the financial balance which had given Halliwell so much power over Orton in the early years had shifted dramatically. It was now Orton who had the big bank balance of £20,222 and Halliwell whose inheritance had dwindled in support of them to £5,817. 'Joe has everything, doesn't he?' Halliwell complained to Miss Boynes, the elderly lady who lived beneath them and to whom he went for scraps of conversation during the long days when Orton was absent from the flat. Halliwell, who longed to be an artist, had played midwife to his friend's talent. His creative gesture was the source of his sadness and undoing. There was no visible sign of his contribution; and Halliwell, pathetically, was forced to substantiate his claims in language as if syntax could somehow bind him permanently to Orton's success. He employed the royal 'we' when speaking of Orton and referred to his talent as 'a genius like us'.

At 11.40 a.m. on 9 August a chauffeur arrived at 25 Noel Road to take Orton to Twickenham Studios, where he and his producer, Oscar Lewenstein, were meeting with Richard Lester to talk about Orton's film script *Up Against It*. The chauffeur trudged up the bleak staircase with its linoleum steps smelling of wax and the grey striped wallpaper stained with damp and peeling. He knocked at Flat 4 on the top floor. There was no answer. He checked back with the Lewenstein office and was told to try again. Orton's agent, Peggy Ramsay, had tried to reach him at 8.30 that morning to confirm the lunch date and she too had received no reply. She was worried. The chauffeur tried twice again and on the third reconnoitre squinted through the letter box to make sure nobody was home. 'This time,' he told the Coroner, 'I noticed the light was on in the hall. I thought this was unusual. I could see the top of a man's head. He appeared to be lying on the floor. I could see his face from the nose upwards. His eyes were closed. I knew this was not Mr Orton because this man appeared to be bald-headed. I knew Mr Orton because I had driven him in the firm's car to different destinations.'

Two stools, two chairs, two single divan beds, and now, so the police discovered, two bodies. The only identifying mark on Orton's body was a blue swallow tattooed over his appendix scar. Orton was planning to refurbish the design. He wanted a flock of swallows on the wing arching across his stomach like porcelain ducks over a mantelpiece. The joke imprinted on his body and the ghoulish spectacle of his bludgeoning made a contrast that matched the weird surroundings. Orton and Halliwell's bed-sitter had seemed to visitors like some extraordinary tomb. There was no sense of comfort to the austere room – venetian blinds, electric heater, scrubbed linoleum floor. The ceiling was painted in a chequerboard of pink and yellow. The colours weighed down on the small space. The walls were covered with an elaborate collage which stretched up to the ceiling and in which recognizable shapes merged with mythical beasts, Renaissance high art, and tabloid headlines. 'The room was very arid,' Penelope Gilliatt recalls. 'It made me want to put my elbows out and stretch the walls.'

Above Orton's bed and overlooking his battered body was a Renaissance crucifix pasted on top of a Union Jack. On another wall near Halliwell's corpse was a map of Australia transformed into a tutu. At the bottom of the map was a pair of crossed horse's legs, on top was an ape's body with hands dangling down on to the 'skirt'. A Cro-Magnon head had been mounted on this torso; and blood had been spliced into the image.

The room was Halliwell's theatre and a mosaic of his mind. Its humour was a testament to his fear and loathing. Halliwell's design – in its startling and aggressive flatness – was a collage of fractured images, a series of haunting notions where the past, present and the surreal coexisted but never coalesced to make a coherent whole. The warped images signalled an imagination in retreat:

Which is worse [asks Donelly, the failed artist and Halliwell's fictional *alter ego* in *The Boy Hairdresser* just before he attempts murder], fruitless running or aimless drifting? Evil to look back on, nothing to look forward to, and pain in the present. The faces passing seemed to him pale, with hunger not physical, mixture of brute and human, devouring and defiling: long claws and bird mouths, fat hips and loins.

This description was an accurate account of the panic which plagued and distorted Halliwell's every encounter with the world and which he made explicit in his anarchic wall collages. They were more powerful, precise and disturbing than his writing. Halliwell came to look upon his murals as his art form. He even wrote to Peggy Ramsay asking for her professional opinion of them:

Must make it plain this invite is not from J or anything to do with him or his Works. I should like your opinion of my collage murals. Does my real talent if any lie in this direction, etc. I know how unspeakably more than busy you are so quite understand if you can't spare time for even a cuppa any time. For instance the woman who came to interview J for the *Evening Standard* this afternoon spent her time admiring my murals and saying did they cost a terrific lot of money and how professional they were, etc. This has happened before with all sorts of people. However.[2]

Lost to himself, Halliwell didn't have the self-regard to state any demand directly. He lacked the courage to put forward and promote his art. The hope of glory and the fear of rejection were a paralysing combination. Trying to give Halliwell some interest outside himself, Orton encouraged his murals and in 1967 arranged for an exhibition of fifteen pictures in a Chelsea antique store. A few pictures were sold to Orton's business associates; but the public showed little interest. It was a familiar pattern.

Halliwell had always yearned to be visible. 'Applaud me, but no one applauded,' says Donelly in *The Boy Hairdresser*. 'Instead, in the distance, a child screamed.' Halliwell had worked hard to win the world's attention. He had trained at RADA as an actor but abandoned the profession as a bad bet. He had laboured at writing for a decade, and then given it up. Six novels and one stage adaptation were stashed in the drawer under his bed. They suffered from the same posturing and lack of spontaneity that he did. As late as 1966, Halliwell had sent his stage adaptation, *The Facts of Life*, to Peggy Ramsay, London's most powerful play agent, whose literary instincts are as sharp as her tongue. 'I haven't really got through your adaptation', she wrote him. 'The first scene sent me into such a well of boredom that I had to struggle to continue which I did in a kind of abstract anguish!!!'[3]

Having educated Orton to be his intellectual equal, Halliwell was now drawn into an inevitable and unequal competition with him. Orton radiated a sexuality and warmth that drew people to him. Orton spoke with an appealing working-class accent; his lazy upper lip slurred consonants and made his delivery funny. 'He thought he was really beautiful, Joe did,' says Kenneth Cranham, one of Orton's favourite actors and closest acquaintances. 'The buzz was him himself. When he'd leave a room he would stand in front of a mirror – very upright – and look at himself like he thought he was very butch. If you saw him, it was quite exciting. You knew he was a promising person. You knew he'd say something funny.' Buttocks clenched, pelvis thrust out, army bag slung over his shoulder – Orton strutted through a world he found 'profoundly bad and irresistibly funny'.[4]

Halliwell was more daunting. Seven years older than Orton and totally bald, Halliwell had always been conscious that youthfulness had eluded him. When he applied to RADA in 1950, he confessed to the registrar 'I'm already twenty-three and, God knows, look thirty'.[5] Without his wig, Halliwell was a grave and menacing presence whom people remembered as larger than Orton, although at five foot eight Halliwell was two inches shorter. Orton bought Halliwell the wig in 1964 with the first profits from *Entertaining Mr Sloane*. It was ungraded, and perched ceremoniously on Halliwell's head like a tea cosy. 'Kenneth improved when he began wearing the wig,' Peggy Ramsay says. 'He was very ashamed of his baldness and he kept his hat on everywhere including the theatre. I think that looking in the mirror with it actually altered his personality. He became rather charming and sincere, so that I quite forgot my first alarmed reaction to his personality.' Halliwell vacillated between extraordinary aggressiveness and timidity – a characteristic which their good friend, the comedian Kenneth Williams, found ludicrous. 'Halliwell never seemed to me ever to establish himself,' Williams says. 'He always seemed to melt into the background and simper "I'm not wanted", "I'm not spoken to", "I'm only here because Joe's here". The only time he seemed to me bold

and resolute was in contradicting Joe's apparent errors.' Halliwell
was too defensive about himself to put others at ease. He tried
fiercely to hide his sadness, which only made him sadder and
more isolated. 'It was quite hard to see Joe because you always
risked incurring Kenneth's wrath,' Cranham recalls. 'Joe gave me
an old coat of his and Kenneth got very uptight. He saw me as a
threat. One night they were backstage and Kenneth said, "I thought
you were all beautiful". He turned to me. "Which is very surprising
for you because you're ugly, really."'

Halliwell's pride made it hard for him to command respect, and
he did not welcome sympathy. Always on guard, he lacked any
spontaneity. Even his voice had a pedantic, prissy tone that was
offputting. In *The Boy Hairdresser* they'd analysed the difference in
their personalities. Donelly wistfully considers the charming trucul-
ence of his room-mate Peterson, who, like Orton, was able to
generate easy affection:

There are many kinds of crucifixion: not all involving the use of
wood and nails. Long before Donelly saw Peterson, he heard his
voice and then his laugh. He experienced a feeling of nausea, knowing
each careless phrase, each lie meant to win friendship . . .
Ten minutes on his own and Peterson had picked up somebody;
he had found an audience: it was an enviable habit.

Since childhood, Halliwell's life had been one long adjustment to
anxiety. The pain of failure, the waste of talent, the isolation, and
the sense of betrayal an orphan feels towards those who have 'left'
him bred in Halliwell a festering and terrifying hostility towards
the world. He could love literature but never life or himself. He
tried to examine his battle to contain this rage in *The Boy Hairdresser*. Donelly contemplates suicide and the death of his friend.
He dreams of punishing society for its 'stupidity'. Unable to win
love from the world, Donelly settles for its hate, going berserk and
shooting grapeshot at an indifferent public to make it take notice:
'His vision was now clear: people ran, hiding in doorways, away

from him, out of control.' The spirit of revenge – to impose on others the emptiness one feels in oneself – was something both Orton and Halliwell understood. But only Orton could displace this anger creatively in laughter. Halliwell's instincts lacked Orton's resilient wonder and detachment. 'Life was a joke,' Donelly said. 'Beauty, culture, civilization – death. Spring, the universe, God. – Christ! – who laughs?' Joking took confidence; and Halliwell had lost that strength. He could instruct but not please. He had hoped and worked for the miracle of fame to eradicate the weight of his past; but it was Orton who was being reborn before his eyes. To Halliwell, the situation was typical of his life: a hateful joke that couldn't be revenged in laughter. Obsessed with his anger, he had to use all his energy to control it. His fiction could not convey the overwhelming sense of suffocation and terror that haunted him and that enervated Orton during the last abusive months. Halliwell contained so many 'murdered selves', and they emerged in fits of violent self-loathing during these wrangles. Halliwell hated the lingering pain; but in order to appease these destructive forces and salvage some identity, he became their ally against himself:

Suddenly I realized that Kenneth was looking tight-lipped and white-faced. We were in the middle of talks of suicide and 'you'll have to face up to the world one day'. And 'I'm disgusted by all this immorality.' He began to rail savagely at Tom and Clive and after a particularly sharp outburst, alarmed me by saying 'Homosexuals disgust me!' I didn't attempt to fathom this one out. He said he wasn't going to come away to Morocco. He was going to kill himself. 'I've led a dreadful, unhappy life. I'm pathetic. I can't go on suffering like this.' After talking until about eight he suddenly shouted out and hammered on the wall, 'They treated me like shit! I won't be treated like this.'

(1 May 1967)

Numb to himself and the world around him, Halliwell defended his shrinking ego in the last months by shrinking the circumference of the 'dead' world around him. He stayed at home, venturing out only to shop or accompany Orton:

Dreary day. Kenneth in an ugly mood. Moaning. I said, 'You look like a zombie.' He replied, heavily, 'So I should. I lead the life of a zombie.'

There was truth in Halliwell's observation. Even their room, where their emotional and artistic life had taken place for eight years, was tainted. To Halliwell, the room was a fortress. His personality, so easily dismissed by the outside world, was the pervading presence, pasted on every inch of the wall. He fussed and cleaned and decorated. But Orton had begun to hate the place. 'I really do think I'll have to get something larger soon,' he told the *Evening News* on 9 June 1967, when Halliwell was in Morocco and he had returned to London for the opening of *Crimes of Passion*. 'Just to have a room to work in. I work better when there's someone else wandering around but it's not fair to the other person. They can't read and if they want to type anything the place sounds like a typing pool.' In private, Orton was more scathing. 'Joe wanted to get the hell out of there. He felt confined. He used to talk a lot about how he hated it,' Adrienne Corri recalls. 'Ken didn't want to change. He did most of the housekeeping and it would have changed Ken's whole way of living if they'd left the room.' But Orton was changing; and the room only reinforced his fear of coming to an emotional and creative standstill. He stayed away often for long periods of the day, and Halliwell was painfully aware of the meaning of these absences. In April – perhaps sensing the threat to their relationship – Halliwell had suggested moving to Brighton and keeping the London flat as a *pied à terre*. The move would mean a return to the comfy isolation of their earlier years. Orton saw the house outside London as a means of setting up a home for his friend in much the same way as Halliwell, fifteen years before, had used his inheritance to make a home for Orton. Orton confided the plan to Kenneth Williams. 'I'll pop down on weekends,' he said. Williams was dubious: 'Weekends? That's not much of a life!' Orton didn't reply. He was searching for ways to extricate himself honourably from Halliwell's yapping misery. The Brighton house never materialized, although he and Halliwell spent a day looking at properties. Halliwell continued to push for a new home. He wanted Orton to himself, but Orton had other ideas:

'I hate this time of the year,' Kenneth says. He's been looking through a property paper and has found a 'marvellous' house in East Croydon. He's sulking at the moment because I've said quite firmly that I won't go and live in East Croydon. 'You're so unadventurous,' he said. We went for a walk . . . Kenneth began to carp about the weather and lead by degrees into a tirade against London and a eulogy of the life in the country. I remained unimpressed because although I don't mind moving out of London, I'm not going to be buried in some God-forsaken hole in the wilds. Kenneth sulked a lot more. In the end I said, 'You're getting to be a fucking Mater Dolorosa, aren't you?'

(22 April 1967)

The complaints, the tears, the diatribes, the threats were distress signals which Orton, with a new sense of his worth, could not allow himself to interpret. In their writing Orton and Halliwell had imagined everything about their relationship except success. Now success had put Orton out of touch with his friend's suffering. 'You're turning into a real bully, do you know that?' Halliwell shouted at Orton. 'You'd better be careful. You'll get your deserts.'[6] The balance of their relationship had been tipped irrevocably in Orton's favour. Halliwell was trapped, a prisoner of his neurotic dependency. His life was in Orton's hands, but Orton would not take responsibility for it. Without Orton, Halliwell knew he had nothing; and death would be a welcome release from his punishing sense of failure. Like Donelly contemplating Peterson's death ('his beauty smashed for ever'), Halliwell had an appetite for the death he finally sought:

He wanted to die. To get back to a dim memory of a better place. In his heart each man carries some lost paradise, a ruined world of submerged continents. He wished to return.

The preview of their end was not only in their writing. Six weeks before, during their holiday in Morocco, Halliwell attacked Orton.

The day Halliwell and Orton left for Morocco, Halliwell wrote to Peggy Ramsay urging her to visit them in their large Tangier apartment on the Rue Pizarro, with its 'superb rather Noel Coward rep set salon'. Halliwell dated his high-spirited letter 'hectic last day in hell'. But it was not simply a crowded, dusty city that was torture. He signed himself 'Kenneth Halliwell, Secretary to JOE ORTON'.[7] He was now, for tax, visa, and banking purposes, a 'Personal Assistant', and not even his bravado could deflate the lingering hurt of being officially an appendage. The anxiety was bound to breed disagreement, even in their 'Eden'.

They were occupying the flat in which Tennessee Williams wrote *Suddenly Last Summer*. It was an overpowering apartment, decorated in fustian Second Empire style, with antiques, gilded chandeliers and ornate mirrors. Its main attraction was the terrace that protected them from the 'hellish Tangier wind', which blew sand into Halliwell's wig and kept them from sunbathing. Cypress trees from the courtyard towered twenty feet above their windows, their ghostly rustling lending a curious doom to the place. They were not at ease in the chic spaciousness. The second day of their holiday Orton wrote:

We locked the main salon of the flat which is enormous and gives an impression of millionaire elegance. We'll just pretend that the flat consists of the kitchen, bathroom, and two bedrooms. Kenneth worried. 'It's so dangerous,' he says. 'Look,' I've said, perhaps rashly, 'if there's real nastiness we can just sling him out. We're never having more than one in at a time, our money is locked away and up to date, I've *never* had any trouble with a boy.' 'There's always a first time,' Kenneth said darkly, with which I can't argue.

(8 May 1967)

Orton eyed the prospect of Moroccan boys like Pinocchio at the fair. But sexual abundance was more threatening for Halliwell, who was no longer pretty or sure of the affections of his friend. Halliwell was sexually timid. Orton was brazenly promiscuous. Halliwell had to accept Orton's 'trolling', but he never condoned it. In moments of anxiety his own fear of abandonment and inferiority tried to disguise itself as worry about their well-being. The danger in rough trade, the lack of intimacy in 'tea room' sex, were not what Halliwell craved. He wanted what J. R. Ackerley called 'the sad little wish . . . someone to love me'.[8] Despite the Librium and Valium that Halliwell handed around at meal times he was unnerved by the first few days in Tangier, which were spoiled by his hysterical performances that had begun to constrict and annoy Orton:

I went back and faced Kenneth in such a rage at the Windmill [Orton wrote in his diary, after an expedition to buy hashish]. 'Where've you been? You have been gone an hour and a half. I was nearly out of my mind with worry.' With that, on the terrace of the Windmill, he burst into tears, to my own embarrassment. 'My nerves can't stand you going off without my knowing where you are.' After a great scene he said that Mohammed el Khomsi with the gold tooth, a boy of about eighteen, had been looking for me. 'I've arranged for him to come to the flat tomorrow,' he said. I was rather choked by this as it ties me down. 'Well, you said you wanted to fuck him,' Kenneth said peevishly, 'and he's going to Gibraltar in a fortnight to work as a page boy in a hotel.' He then began complaining about my liking Mohammed (the first one) and how he was a nasty bit of work. 'And you're so mad to go along the beach with him. Absolutely mad.' He then began saying I would get into trouble. 'That boy of yours looks like a nutter to me.' In the end, fed up to the back teeth with nagging, I said, 'Every boy in town is no good except the marvellous one you attach yourself to . . .'

(12 May 1967)

Halliwell did not adjust easily to shifts of locale. His dread of going nowhere and being nobody made it hard for him to relax into the idle rootlessness of a vacation. In the first few days in Tangier, Halliwell jockeyed nervously for Orton's affection and esteem. He needed to feel equal to Orton's sexual enterprise, which inevitably led to sad, fatuous moments of abrasion:

We were hailed with 'Hallo' from a very beautiful 16 year old boy whom I knew (but had never had) from last year. Kenneth wanted him. We talked for about five minutes and finally I said, 'Come to our apartment for tea this afternoon.' He was very eager. We arranged that he should meet us at the Windmill beach place. As we left the boy Kenneth said, 'Wasn't I good at arranging things?' This astounded me. 'I arranged it,' I said. 'You would have been standing talking about the weather for ever.' K. didn't reply . . .

(9 May 1967)

Halliwell feared being excluded from Orton's orbit. Whenever the situation presented itself, Halliwell tried to pander to Orton's enthusiasms. Orton didn't like it:

We had tea and Ken and Lhabi went into the bedroom . . . When Ken came back they had had sex. 'I've arranged for you to have him tomorrow,' Kenneth said in a confidential tone when the boy was out of the room. 'I've already arranged to have Mohammed tomorrow,' I said. 'I really wish you wouldn't play the procuress quite so much. I'm quite capable of managing my own sex! . . .'

(10 May 1967)

The bickering gradually abated; and by 17 May Orton could report in his diary 'Kenneth in his element and holding forth. I'm glad he's happy for a change.' So was Orton. 'My life beginning to run to a time table no member of the Royal Family would tolerate. Life is perfect,' he wrote to Kenneth Williams, 'and the pleasures of the senses never pall and have never been better.'[9]

The combination of sex, hashish and sun fulfilled the Dionysian intention behind his comedies. They celebrate instinct and gratification, and aspire to corrupt his audience with pleasure. 'I always say to myself that the theatre is the Temple of Dionysus, and not Apollo. You do the Dionysus thing on your typewriter, and then you allow a little Apollo in, just a little to shape and guide it along certain lines you may want to go along. But you can't allow Apollo in completely.'[10] Orton was obsessed with the Dionysian theme. In early June of 1967, the Royal Court premiered *The*

Erpingham Camp, his reworking of *The Bacchae*. Along with a new version of his first play, *The Ruffian on the Stair* (1963), they were presented under the title *Crimes of Passion*. It was passion – the thrilling, punishing battle between licence and control – which gave a hard edge to Orton's life and his plays.[11] *What the Butler Saw*, which lay in a drawer beneath his bed in Islington awaiting a final draft, planned comic revenge on Pentheus, the persecutor of Dionysus who is at the same time doomed to suffer from Dionysian passion. At the finale, the figure of control – Sergeant Match – climbs down through the skylight on a rope ladder. With a wink at Euripides, Orton has Match wearing a leopard-spotted dress.[12] Instead of condemning the spectacle, he joins the participants and ascends towards a new light. 'Providing one spends the time drugged or drunk, the world is a fine place,' Orton wrote on 3 June. And, a month later, rewriting the finale of *What the Butler Saw* he worked this observation into the final stage direction: 'They pick up their clothes and weary, bleeding, drugged and drunk, climb the rope ladder into the blazing light.' Orton's vision of suffering had finally merged with his dream of survival.

Like the votaries of Dionysus, Orton was hounded by his passion. In his plays, Orton faced his rage and exorcized it in his lethal wit. Morocco slaked the tension that was always erupting in Orton's life between his emotional needs and the society's social and sexual taboos:

Here and there were numbers of nearly naked young boys [Orton wrote, a month after their return from Morocco, after he had been walking with Halliwell along Brighton Pier]. This made me unhappy. After passing a fifteen year old youth lying face-downward wearing red bathing drawers, I said in a rage, 'England is intolerable. I'd be able to fuck that in an Arab country. I could take him home and stick my cock up him!' 'This is verbal exhibitionism!' Kenneth said, glancing at a number of evil-faced old women in a shelter. 'Look at them – crouching like Norns or the spirit of fucking British civilization,' I said. 'I hate this tight-assed civilization.'

(28 July 1967)

Orton tried to practise the sexual ethic he preached.

You must do whatever you like as long as you enjoy it and don't hurt anybody else. That's all that matters [he told a homosexual friend who felt guilty about his activity]. You shouldn't feel guilty. Get yourself fucked if you want to. Get yourself anything you like. Reject all the values of the society. And enjoy sex. When you're dead, you'll regret not having fun with your genital organs.

(23 July 1967)

But the battle against society was difficult, the social controls impossible to overlook. In England, the strain could create a painful, confusing rage:

I saw a young boy, blond and very healthy-looking filling a bucket with water on the promenade. As he turned the tap off, he looked up. Our eyes met. A great spasm of rage overtook me. I find lust an emotion indistinguishable from anger. Or at least anger predominates when I see something I can't have. I feel I may run mad one day and commit rape.

(26 July 1967)

The startling aggressiveness with which Orton's plays toppled conventional morality helped him get even for his private pain. It gave his comedies their urgency and power. In Morocco, Orton dedicated all his energies to passion and pleasure. Fame seemed a comic memory:

So we had sex, or at least I lay and allowed him to fuck me and thought as his prick shot in and he kissed my neck, back and shoulders, that it was a most unappetising position for an internationally known playwright to be in.

(19 May 1967)

Even ambition became insignificant. The lukewarm reception of *Crimes of Passion* in London could not upset the delicious sexual serenity of his days and nights:

We showered and I gave him five dirham . . . He went off perfectly satisfied, and not for the first time I reflected that having had a boy of his age in England I'd spend the rest of my life in terror of his parents or the police. At one moment with my cock in his arse, the image was, and as I write still is, overpoweringly erotic, and I reflected that whatever the Sunday papers have said about CRIMES OF PASSION was of little importance compared to this.

(11 June 1967)

Orton was a modern Lord of Misrule whose plays were a holiday from the established order. He had realized early in his writing career that for there to be a rebirth in society, there had to be a killing. 'Without cruelty,' wrote Nietzsche, 'no feast.'[13] Comedy could kill and renew. Orton wanted his words 'to vibrate the structure'.[14]

To be destructive, words had to be irrefutable [he wrote in his posthumously published novel Head to Toe (1961)]. And then the book might not be read. He was aware that words and sentences often buried themselves in the reader's mind before exploding and then went off harmlessly. Print was less effective than the spoken word because the blast was greater; eyes could ignore, slide past, dangerous verbs or nouns. But if you could lock the enemy into a room somewhere and fire the sentence at them you would get a sort of seismic disturbance . . .

The 'enemy' rarely showed its face in the casbah; but when it did, Orton would deploy outrage to parry the smug judgements of the straight world. At a pavement café a 'rather stuffy American tourist and his disapproving wife' sat next to Orton and a group of his friends:

They listened to our conversation and I, realizing this, began to exaggerate the content. 'He took it up the arse,' I said. 'And afterwards he thanked me for giving him such a good fucking. They're a most polite people.' The American and his wife hardly moved a muscle. 'We've got a leopard skin rug in the flat and he wanted me to fuck him on that,' I said in an undertone which was perfectly audible to the next table, 'only I'm afraid of the spunk, you see, it might adversely affect the spots on the leopard.' Nigel said quietly, 'Those tourists can hear what you're saying.' He looked alarmed. 'I mean them to hear,' I said, 'they have no right to be occupying chairs reserved for decent sex perverts,' and then with excitement I said, 'He might bite a hole in the rug, and I can't ask him to control his excitement. It wouldn't be natural when you're six inches up the bum, would it?' The American couple frigidly paid for their coffee and moved away. 'You shouldn't drive people like that away,' Nigel said. 'The town needs tourists.' 'Not that kind, it doesn't,' I said. 'This is *our* country, *our* town, *our* civilization. I want nothing to do with the civilization they made. Fuck them! They'll sit and listen to buggers' talk from me and drink their coffee and piss off.' 'It seems rather a strange joke,' Frank said with an old school teacher's smile. 'It isn't a joke,' I said. 'There's no such thing as a joke.'

Nigel who was drinking some strange brandy got very excited by a girl who passed. She looked like a boy. She was German . . . 'Who wants a girl to look like a boy?' I said. 'Or a boy to look like a girl? It's not natural.' 'I really think, Joe,' Nigel said, 'that you shouldn't bring Nature into your conversation quite so often, you who have done more than anyone I know to outrage her.' 'I've never outraged Nature,' I said. 'I've always listened to her advice and followed it wherever it went.'
(25 May 1967)

The American tourists momentarily revived the anxiety of sexual stigma which Orton's laughter kept at bay and which he could forget in Tangier. His diary is otherwise suffused with moments of strange and surprising contentment. The twenty-first of May, he wrote, was 'a day so perfect that sex really seemed irrelevant'. On 22 May Orton found himself standing on a terrace at twilight looking over the city and the bay, the purple glow of the sunset matched by the inner glow of hashish and scotch:

The world became even more wonderful, my limbs felt as if they were made of rubber and catching sight of myself in the mirror I gazed, without self-consciousness, for perhaps five minutes, or so it seemed, into my own eyes . . . I felt elated and danced a wild dance around the hall positively spinning round the urns and hubble-bubbles, like a teetotum. The others came down the stairs talking in mellow English tones, and upon seeing me, Nigel remarked, 'Is this his farewell performance.'

Halliwell reminded Orton of the high price Dionysus paid for ecstasy. Orton knew his friend was right. Neither of them had had much experience of happiness; and they distrusted it. Over tea and hashish cakes in the first month of their vacation, Orton and Halliwell contemplated their pleasure:

Kenneth and I sat talking of how happy we both felt. We'd have to pay for it. Or we'd be struck down from afar by disaster because we were, perhaps, too happy. To be young, good-looking, healthy, famous, comparatively rich *and* happy is surely going against nature, and when to the above list one adds that daily I have the company of little boys who find (for a small fee) fucking with me a delightful sensation, no man can want for more. 'Crimes of Passion will be a disaster,' Kenneth said. 'That will be the scapegoat. We must sacrifice *Crimes of Passion* in order that we may be spared disaster more intolerable.' I slept all night soundly and woke up at seven feeling as though the whole of creation was conspiring to make me happy. I hope no doom strikes.

(25 May 1967)

But it was Orton himself, not his play, who would be sacrificed for his glorious talent. The first hint of Halliwell's rough justice came two days before they were scheduled to return to London.

Although the last two months have been very enjoyable and a great success neither Kenneth nor I will be sorry to leave on Friday [Orton wrote on 25 June]. I feel the need for something fresh. Not work – though undoubtedly I shall finish *What the Butler Saw* – just a change of scene. Even sex with a teenage boy becomes monotonous. Ecstasy is as liable to bore as boredom. I need the atmosphere of London for a month or two in order to stir me from the lethargy into which I am in danger of falling.

Orton was returning to the rewrite of his last and most accomplished farce. His film *Up Against It* was being actively shopped to directors, and his first full-length play, *Entertaining Mr Sloane*, and his newest one-act, *Funeral Games*, were scheduled to be aired on television later in the year. *Loot* was still running on the West End.

Halliwell was returning with no prospects. The anticipation of

the old oppression made him brittle and quarrelsome. Every disagreement was magnified into a threat to his identity. Orton's
disenchantment with him was too close to the surface of their fights
to make it easy for Halliwell to express his anger. Orton's success
made him invulnerable to Halliwell's abuse, which only reinforced
Halliwell's sense of impotence. But, when his anger did erupt, as
on 27 June, he struck out in unexpected fury. 'Kenneth became
violently angry shortly after this and attacked me, hitting me about
the head and knocking my pen from my hand', Orton reported in
his diary.

Overnight, Halliwell's haughty fearfulness had returned. 'In a
growing rage', Halliwell locked out their cleaning woman, who
had disappeared from work leaving her yashmak and slippers in
their house. Halliwell and Orton went out to lunch; and Halliwell,
trying to assert his will, built up the skirmish into a major victory:

> Kenneth in a very loud voice said, 'I've taught our Fatima a lesson.'
> He then told the whole story and ended saying, 'Joe wanted to ignore
> her, but she's got to be made to realise.' Nigel said, 'How right you
> are, dear, it takes a woman to deal with a woman.' 'If I'd said that,'
> I said aside to Kenneth, 'you'd be on a charter flight back to London
> by now.'
>
> (28 June 1967)

Predictably, Halliwell showed his defensiveness by becoming
argumentative and loud:

> Kenneth began an argument. 'He's *awful*,' he said in loud irritating
> tones [Orton wrote in his diary of a blond fourteen-year-old who
> passed their table]. 'If he takes it and he's 14,' I said, 'I can see perfectly
> why the Moroccans are interested and I would be too ...' There
> was a licking of lips all round. 'Well,' Kenneth said in a tight voice,
> 'all I'd like to do to that creature is whip him.' 'You're simply substi-
> tuting violence for sex,' I said. 'Your psychological slip is showing.
> A whip is a phallic symbol. You're doing on a symbolic level exactly
> what I do in reality.'
>
> (28 June 1967)

Orton and Halliwell hoped to return to Tangier in October. As their plane touched down at Heathrow in London on 30 June, Orton said to Halliwell 'The party's over.' But it was clear from the mail that awaited Orton and not Halliwell that there was still the fiesta of Orton's new fame. 'A great many letters', Orton wrote. 'And press cuttings. Invitations to parties I shall not accept. And an invitation to a private viewing at the Drian Galleries of some sculpture. I shall go to this because it might be good for Kenneth's collages.' The routine had started again, and with it, for Halliwell, the same sense of suffocation. 'How dead everyone looks,' he'd remarked to Orton as they stood in Gloucester Road waiting for a taxi to take them from the bus terminal to the home that had become for both of them a kind of purgatory.

The first weeks of July were hot and unusually muggy. London wilted in the unfamiliar heat. Pavements emptied; the city's pace faltered; everything seemed to lose the will to live. And with its dusty, treeless side streets and gnarled thoroughfares choked with traffic exhaust, Islington was particularly unpleasant. Orton was immediately distracted from the stifling weather by the excitement of his rewrites. 'Today I read *What the Butler Saw* and was pleased with it', he wrote on 2 July. 'There are sections that have to be rewritten and others to be clarified. Not a lot of hard graft, though. I shall enjoy this part of the work. It's a final polish.' While Orton made steady progress on his most ambitious and best play, Halliwell was immobilized with a bad attack of hay fever. 'I wish I'd stayed in Morocco,' he moaned. 'Oh, this terrible city.' But Halliwell could not be away from Orton, especially during the final revision of a work, when his own critical ability was needed. Orton's success gave him acute anxiety; but his role as Orton's literary editor was one of the few accomplishments and legitimate sources of pride Halliwell had.

'Telephone off', Orton noted in his diary on 8 July about a fault on their line. 'So no one could contact me . . . Did nothing at all except type *What the Butler Saw*.' All the calls were for Orton. But

Halliwell's only distraction from the heat and hay fever was his friend. In the first two weeks of July, they visited Kenneth Williams; checked up on the cast and the production of Orton's *Loot* at the Criterion Theatre; and with two actors from the *Loot* company spent one delightful afternoon discreetly giggling at the dialogue of *Desert Song*. ('Kenneth Halliwell said that a lot of it reminded him of my writing', Orton wrote in his diary.[15] 'Not surprising really since my writing is a deliberate satire on bad theatre. The plot gave me the idea for my next play.')

On 10 July Halliwell read *What the Butler Saw*:

Kenneth read the script and was enthusiastic. He made several important suggestions which I'm carrying out. He was impressed by the way in which, using the context of a farce, I'd managed to produce a 'Golden Bough' subtext – even (he pointed out) the castration of Sir Winston Churchill (the father-figure) and the descent of the god at the end – Sergeant Match, drugged and dressed in a woman's gown. It was only to be expected that Kenneth would get these references to classical literature. Whether anyone else will spot them is another matter. 'You must get a director who, while making it funny, brings out the sub-text,' Kenneth said. He suggests that the dress MATCH wears should be of something suggestive of leopard-skin – this would make it funny when NICK wears it and get the right 'image' for the Euripidean ending when MATCH wears it.

Halliwell's criticism was as trenchant as his casting suggestions. 'Kenneth says that Alistair Sim would be ideal for Dr Rance. Agree with him. And Arthur Lowe as Dr Prentice', Orton wrote in his diary on 12 July. 'Kenneth also says that we should offer Mrs Prentice to Coral Browne. She'd be rather good – though I doubt whether she'd accept it.' By 16 July, working through the sweltering summer days, Orton finished typing *What the Butler Saw*. Halliwell was 'ill with Hay Fever', Orton's diary reported; meanwhile he himself was invigorated by his accomplishment:

I finished typing *What the Butler Saw*. I added very little on this version (just incorporated Kenneth's suggestions which were excellent) . . . Great relief to have finished *Butler*. I can now give my mind full rein for the historical farce set on the eve of Edward VII's coronation in 1902 and called (at the moment) PRICK UP YOUR EARS. I hope I can write a play worthy of one of Kenneth Halliwell's most brilliant titles. I've already got a quotation from *The Critic* for the play, 'Where history gives you a good heroic outline for a play, you may fill up with a little love at your own discretion: in doing which, nine times out of ten, you only make up a deficiency in the private history of the times.'

On 17 July Orton took *What the Butler Saw* to Peggy Ramsay. Halliwell, who could see the play's excellence and knew that his own suggestions had given it added brilliance, chose this day to quarrel with Orton, their first fight since returning from Morocco. The cycle of Orton's success was sure to begin again; and, as surely, Halliwell's nagging anxiety about his worthlessness would be reactivated.

Kenneth very irritating today. Weather hot again. Blue skies. Kenneth's nerves are on edge. Hay Fever. He had a row this morning. Trembling with rage. About my nastiness when I said, 'Are you going to stand in front of the mirror all day?' He said, 'I've been washing your fucking underpants! That's why I've been at the sink!' He shouted it out loudly and I said, 'Please, don't let the whole neighbourhood know you're a queen.' 'You know I have hay fever and you deliberately get on my nerves,' he said. 'I'm going out,' I said, 'I can't stand much more of it.' 'Go out then,' he said. 'I don't want you in here.'

Halliwell had been masculine and assertive when they'd first met in 1951. But in the three years since the success of *Entertaining Mr Sloane* in 1964, Orton had witnessed Halliwell's gradual and disquieting transformation from partner to sidekick. Orton hated 'the pinafore number' which Halliwell adopted as his new role. 'The virtue of homosexuality, Joe said, was in liking men not girls,' Kenneth Williams recalls. 'So why imitate girls.' Orton's threat to Halliwell was as real as it was intimidating. Halliwell's 'household', like his housewifely role, had become a farce. Orton, who hated fakery of any kind, knew it. The antidote to *Angst* is action – a comic remedy Orton found easier to manage on stage than in life. In *What the Butler Saw*, Dr Rance offers a two-sentence formula for mental health: 'Reject all para-normal phenomena. It's the only way to remain sane.' Orton couldn't completely follow these words of advice. His friendship with Halliwell forced him to keep on pretending. Yet he despised this hypocritical domesticity, and instinctively endangered it, deliberately stalking rough trade:

Took a walk. Nobody around to pick up. Only a lot of disgusting old men. I shall be a disgusting old man myself one day, I thought, mournfully. Only I have high hopes of dying in my prime.

(14 July 1967)

While he waited for the first reactions to *What the Butler Saw*, Orton busied himself with being famous. Within the confines of their flat, Halliwell's abusive frustration continually cast Orton as the heavy; but in the world, Orton was greeted as a luminous, affable good guy:

I went on to a house in Aubrey Walk W.8 to be photographed for *Queen* Magazine. It was all very bright. A lot of clever and attractive young people. A young man said, 'We're doing the "goodies" today.' 'What do you mean?' I said. He showed me a photograph to be included in the same issue as ours. It was a group of about eight people – including Nicholas Tomalin and Cathy McGowan. 'They're the baddies,' he said. 'That'll be on the opposite page to yours.' They're going to contrast various sets of people. The rest of my group were soon assembled – Tom Courtenay, Lucy Fleming, Susannah York, Twiggy, and a Chinese girl and a young man wearing a gold coat and a male mini-skirt. 'Do you go around in that all the time,' I said. 'No,' he said, 'I changed upstairs.'

(18 July 1967)

On 22 July Orton and Halliwell were scheduled to attend a swank party at the home of Peter Willes, the head of drama for Yorkshire Television. Willes had played an important part in Orton's career. Orton showed his gratitude by dedicating *Crimes of Passion* to him.

'He telephoned [me] every day either about his work or mine', Willes wrote in a posthumous collection of Orton's television plays. 'His complete originality ... is what I miss most of all.'[16] Willes's interest in Orton didn't extend to Halliwell, whom he found 'gentle, cloying and wildly dated. He behaved very much like a camp young man of the '30's. He was an oddity, an irritant.' Orton moved more easily than Halliwell through the lords, ladies and theatrical celebrities at Willes's parties. 'The class of my characters has gone up over the years,' Orton quipped, and Willes was in large part responsible for widening Orton's social horizons. Willes was aware of how strained the relationship between Orton and Halliwell had become. In April, at Orton's request, Willes had contacted his own private GP, Dr Douglas Ismay, about his psychological problems. 'Willes suggested that Halliwell come to see me because Orton complained that Halliwell was really getting on his back. It was a method of syphoning off,' Dr Ismay recalls. Halliwell never suspected that he'd been fobbed off; but his own possessiveness of Orton and the threat of Willes's indifference to him made attending Willes's parties difficult. For the July party, Halliwell armed himself with an Eton tie, an emblem of his disdain of Willes's chic milieu, and something, besides Orton's success, to talk about. The attention he got was more than he'd expected:

Went to Peter Willes for dinner. When we got there [a TV producer] stared at Kenneth in horror. 'That's an old Etonian tie!' [the producer] screeched. 'Yes,' Kenneth said, 'it's a joke.' [The producer] looked staggered and wrinkled up his face in an evil sort of way. 'Well, I'm afraid it's a joke against you then. People will imagine you're passing yourself off as an old Etonian. They'll laugh at you.' 'I'm sending up Eton,' Kenneth said. 'Oh, no!' [the producer] cackled with a sort of eldritch shriek. 'You're just pathetic! I mean it's disgraceful wearing that tie.' 'It's a joke!' Kenneth said, looking tight-lipped, a little embarrassed and angry. 'People will know.' 'Not the people I meet,' Kenneth said, 'they'll think it's funny.' 'You're making people angry,' [the producer] said. 'I don't care,' Kenneth said, laughing a little too readily. 'I want to make them angry.' 'But why?' [the producer] said, as we sat down. 'People dislike you enough already. Why make them more angry? I mean – it's permissible, although silly as a foible of youth, but you – a middle-aged nonentity – it's sad and pathetic!' I could see that the conversation had become impossible and that unless something were done the evening would begin in ruins. 'Now stop this both of you!' I said in a commanding voice. 'It's ridiculous to carry on in this way over a wretched tie.' . . . Kenneth laughed. The conversation drifted on in a desultory way, meandering through insults and bubbling over recrimination until Kenneth exploded, 'All you people that are mad on Joe really have no idea what he's like.' [The producer] paled. 'I'm not mad on Joe! Whatever do you mean?' Fortunately before Kenneth could answer this question (and rend our relationship with [the producer] to shreds) the doorbell rang . . . We went out to dinner later . . . Lady Glasgow and Peter Willes discussing the merits or demerits of Kenneth's joke against Eton. 'I always say that my son goes to Slough Grammar School,' Lady G. said. I'd taken two Librium tablets. Lady G. gave two more to me. Producing them gaily from her handbag. 'I have to take tranquillizers when my husband is driving,' she said. 'I simply cannot stand the nervous strain of having him behind the wheel. And prayers are of no avail. It's medical science that calms me down.' . . . We went back to Willes's flat. After a short discussion on the customs of the English gentry towards the end of the 19th century apropos of Willes producing Lady Windermere's Fan for television, Kenneth and I trooped off. 'If only my old aunt were alive,' Wanda, Lady Glasgow, said, with a shake of her head, 'she could really have told us whether or not the footmen would've worn gloves.' Outside on the pavement, Kenneth was still smarting from the 'middle-aged nonentity' line. And quite right too. Kenneth has more talent, although it's hidden, than [the producer] can flash if he had the reflector from Mount Palomar to do it with.

The party episode confirmed what Halliwell feared was the world's low opinion of himself. It left him stunned and dejected. Halliwell's ability was not just hidden from the world by his abrasive defensiveness; it was twisted and weakened by it – and by Orton's brilliant success, which blinded anyone in their company to Halliwell's presence. This incident was the deepest of Halliwell's public rejections, but not the first time he'd felt diminished by Orton's celebrity. He had erupted in a bitter tirade against Orton and the inequality of their social encounters in May after the evening with Clive and Tom when he pounded the walls screaming 'They treated me like shit! I won't be treated like this':

'You had tea, they had tea; you had jam tarts, they had jam tarts. And those photographs of Mustapha – he was so unattractive and because you'd had him they said "what a dish" ' . . . 'Surely you expected this?' I said. 'I expected to be treated with a little more respect.' He began to cry . . . I said . . . 'He's a tuft hunter . . . I saw through it. You saw through it. If I'd been taken in by it then there would have been cause for rage. As it is, it looks like "Hell Hath No Fury" ' . . . 'When I'm not here you won't be able to write in this flip way,' Kenneth said. The inference that I don't know how cruel, despicable and senseless life is hurt me. 'I won't have you monopolizing the agony market,' I shouted at last in a fury. For the best part of a day the to-ing and fro-ing went on. At last, the threats of suicide abated until the last was 'If you have both of them you can say goodbye to me!' And with that we began to pick up the pieces.

(2 May 1967)

Soon afterwards, they departed for Morocco, where Orton's fame was of no importance and victories could be purchased for a few dirham. Momentarily at least, Halliwell could feel equal to his friend. But now back in London, there was no way to sustain the illusion. Orton was the centre of attention; and Halliwell was pushed to the periphery. The day the producer confronted Halliwell with being a 'middle-aged nonentity' Orton received his first delighted feedback about *What the Butler Saw*. 'People must've thought I was mad,' Peggy Ramsay cooed over the phone, calling him early in the morning. 'I simply had hysterics. It's the very best thing you've done so far. And technically in advance of *Loot*.' The next day, 23 July, Oscar Lewenstein rang to invite Orton and Halliwell down to Brighton to discuss production plans; and that afternoon, as Halliwell brooded over the producer's insult, Willes called to gush to Orton about his new play.

'Oh,' he said, 'it's so exciting. It's like a Palais Royale farce. It's simply splendid. And it must be done exquisitely.' 'He only likes it because I said he wouldn't,' Kenneth said, bitterly . . .

(23 July 1967)

The cycle had begun again. Orton's heady success was in the foreground of everybody's mind while Halliwell's leaden sense of failure kept him immobilized. The calls, the meetings, the plans, the letters were for Orton. Soon the interviews would start again, with Halliwell making himself absent while Orton explained his bedsitter life. 'I'm very conscious of what's come before,' he told an interviewer earlier that year. 'I like Lucian and the classical writers, and I suppose that's what gives my writing a difference, an old-fashioned classical education! Which I never received, but I gave myself one, reading them all in English, for I have so little Latin and less Greek.'[17] In private, Orton always acknowledged Halliwell's contribution; but in public he never admitted a teacher or a friend. The press releases said he'd been married and divorced. This was insufficient for Halliwell, who, under this pressure, was forced to make unrealistic demands for himself.

Halliwell wanted a family; Orton wanted freedom – a difference painfully apparent in their attitudes towards sex. On the afternoon of 23 July, they were visited by Kenneth Williams, who recorded their meeting in his diary:

Went up to see Joe Orton and Kenneth. Both were so kind. We talked a lot about homosexuality and the effect the new clause would have (The Humphry Berkeley Bill) not Leo Abse. We all agreed it would accomplish very little, that it was the climate of opinion that really counted more.

Joe walked me all the way to King's Cross. I remonstrated with him, 'No, it's not fair. You must go back to Ken. He's on his own.' He said it didn't matter. Then he said, 'I'll never leave him.'

We talked about his inability to love and his horror of involvement. He said, 'I need to be utterly free.' In the flat K. Halliwell had disagreed with this saying that love was involvement and you cannot live without love.

Williams remembers that when Orton said 'I'll never leave him', Orton stopped on the pavement and looked him in the eye to emphasize his sincerity. 'I hadn't said "leave him". Joe was answering his own question, what was in his mind or what other people said.'

Evidently, Orton was toying with the idea of leaving Halliwell. At one of Adrienne Corri's parties, he had been attracted to a novelist whose accomplishment, university education and poise were the fulfilment of Halliwell's wasted potential. He was flirting with the idea of living with him. In his sickness, Halliwell, who needed love and said so, became increasingly unlovable. His panic to make people draw close only pushed them away, and he broadcast his pleas for attention in his complaints about Orton's 'trolling', his demands on Orton's allegiance and his psychosomatic illnesses. Orton's sexual rapacity was a threatening reminder of Halliwell's emotional dependence. He wanted Orton to share some of his newly-won public life. Orton couldn't. Williams sensed Orton's feisty independence:

I kept saying, 'You better go back, Joe'. Halliwell had asked how long he'd be because he was making the meal. It was just like a wife asking the husband what time he'll be home for dinner. It irked Joe. He kept saying 'Let's go on walking'. He wanted to get away. He was buoyant. He'd become somebody in his own right. It was no longer we', but 'I' – 'I'll find the house. I'll never leave him. Increasingly, it was the sense that I am important.

Orton had sought the advice of Adrienne Corri and Penelope Gilliatt, two women who had survived marital turmoil and could talk intelligently about it. 'I think he was going to leave Halliwell,' Miss Corri says. 'We talked about the ramifications of leaving someone and sorting oneself out. He said that the terrible thing was he didn't know what Ken would do without him.' Miss Gilliatt, who wrote about the problem in *Sunday, Bloody Sunday*, had a similar hunch: 'I had the feeling he wanted to leave Halliwell if he could handle things and introduce some balance into the situation. He wanted always to find out whether it was cataclysmic to leave someone or whether it could be done without such violence as would eventually happen. He was talking mainly about how dependent Halliwell was on him. He wanted advice about how he could lift the weight of this dependence from his shoulders and put it elsewhere.' They argued at length about promiscuity, which upset Halliwell but which Orton claimed stimulated his view of the world. 'He felt very strongly that the energy of making a piece of art came out of the energy of chaos,' Miss Gilliatt says. 'I don't agree with that. We had long arguments about it. He was probably trying to rationalize his own way of life. He was fighting for his life. He was a born writer and he lived in chaotic emotional conditions. He needed time to write. Sometimes he arrived for drinks absolutely worn out from these fights with Halliwell.' The more ferociously Halliwell clung to Orton, the more Orton felt the need to put distance between them. He could not easily face Halliwell with the facts. Orton even asked Miss Gilliatt to plead the case of promiscuity for him. She refused. Orton sought release in rough trade and Halliwell reassurance in involvement.

'Halliwell's argument was that continual immersion of yourself in an anonymous sexual set-up, going with strangers into rooms or alleyways was going to lead to a wastage of aims,' Williams recalls. 'Halliwell was not a fool. He had a very good mind. "Don't you see," he said, "that these sexual experiments can only lead to a dead end?" My immediate response was to agree; but as an actor, I could not help but respond every time Joe told me these anecdotes about his adventures because they were terribly funny and always illuminating.' Orton exploded at Halliwell. 'Look, I've got to do it. I've got to be the fly on the wall!' He'd been equally adamant in talking about promiscuity to Penelope Gilliatt. 'He wanted to know whether I thought it could work in any set-up. He talked about the damage it did; and at the same time he wanted to kick the sides of society apart. He asked if he should deceive Halliwell about it or give it up. And then he said furiously, "No, I can't give up promiscuity! I won't give it up!"'

Orton had a clown's appetite for political anarchy; but for him this was impossible without sexual anarchy. The lavatories were a sordid setting for sexual adventure, and these encounters confirmed his sense of human suffering and outrageousness. They were dangerous and pathetic. Orton knew this and was drawn to them. 'When I meet people casually,' he told Kenneth Williams, 'I always call myself a packer. I make things up. I call myself a packer, a metal worker, a lithographer, a hairdresser's assistant. That way I put people off-guard. Their dialogue is natural. It's also better for sex.' No matter how successful he became, the lavatories confirmed Orton's destiny as an outsider. The encounters also stoked his anger against a society whose taboos forced adults into hidden corners to take their furtive pleasure. As the 'fly on the wall', he paid attention to the detail of character and the stilted language that negotiated these anonymous gropings:

After walking for a while I found a gent's lavatory on a patch of grass near a church, I went in. It was very dark. There was a man there. Tall, grand and smiling. In the gloom he looked aristocratic. When the lights were turned on (after about five minutes) I could see that he was stupid, smiling and bank-clerkish. He showed his cock. I let him feel mine. 'Ooh!' he gasped . . . 'Oo!' I asked if he had anywhere to go back to? 'No,' he said, 'I don't have the choice of my neighbours, you see. They're down on me and I couldn't take the risk.' He nodded to a dwarf skulking in the corner of the lavatory. 'He'll suck you off, though. I've seen him do it.' He made a motion to the dwarfish creature rather as someone would call a taxi and then, I suppose, went back to his neighbours refreshed.

(30 July 1967)

Like the obsessive adulterers in Restoration comedy, which Orton studied with admiration, the spectre of death lurked behind his own pursuit of pleasure. It was impossible to celebrate one without accepting the other. Promiscuity was a submersion in chaos, a flirtation with death, a ritual wasting with its 'magical' corollary of renewed fertility. Orton felt compelled to explore the taboos surrounding life and death. Orton's trips into forbidden territory were the only alternative he saw to the quiet, cosy suffocation of conventional British living that he satirized in his plays, where people ask little of life and receive little in return. Orton had the detachment and brazenness of the dispossessed. He had nothing to lose.

In his laughter Orton could admit the perverse and demystify it by making it delightful. The rewritten opening lines of *The Ruffian on the Stair* (1967) capture a lifetime of impoverishment in the jolt of one exchange:

JOYCE. Have you got an appointment today?
MIKE. Yes. I'm to be at King's Cross station at eleven. I'm meeting a man in the toilet.
JOYCE. You always go to such interesting places.

On 27 July Orton and Halliwell set off with Oscar Lewenstein to his home in Brighton for a long weekend. It was a wet, tense time. They had little in common with Lewenstein besides an enthusiasm for Orton's work. By the time the train pulled into Brighton station, production plans had been mapped out, which left four days of desultory conversation and random reading ahead of them. It was an enervating prospect from which, as usual, only Orton would benefit.

They had been on a Brighton weekend once before, with Sir Terence Rattigan after the success of *Entertaining Mr Sloane* in 1964. Even then Halliwell had appalled rather than impressed. 'He was a bit round the bend,' Sir Terence recalls, noting that Halliwell wore a little bit of 'slap' (rouge). 'He seemed quite determined that Joe should never speak at all. He was desperately trying to give the impression that he wrote all Joe's plays. Joe wasn't denying it.

Joe had very good natural manners. He let Halliwell go on and on. But it was perfectly clear that the man who was overtalking wasn't the man who'd written the plays. It was perfectly plain to me – and this isn't being clever after the event – that Halliwell was wildly jealous of Joe's sexual escapades. He resented Joe's success in that sphere as well. It was one part of Joe's life he couldn't collaborate in.' On the second night of their strained visit, Sir Terence, who had a standing emergency arrangement with his neighbours, the Oliviers, called on them to help weather the boredom of Halliwell's performance. 'Larry and Joan came over,' Sir Terence says. 'You saw the royal pants being bored off Larry. Halliwell lectured him. It was a very depressing evening. Joe didn't seem to mind. He was quite sensitive enough to know what kind of appalling impression Halliwell was making. And also the appalling impression he was giving of Joe. Obviously Joe was going to have to leave this man. He couldn't have lived with him much longer and kept his sanity.'

The Lewenstein weekend was another set-piece for Orton, and Halliwell felt increasingly incidental. Closeted in the company of strangers, obedient to an alien routine, they quickly grew depressed.

'On the way back we tried to avoid looking at the boys and talking about Tangier,' Orton wrote of one of their frequent walks. 'We must get back there as soon as possible,' Kenneth said. 'We could be there now. Instead of this wilderness . . .' They were, as Orton wrote, 'numbed' by the weekend. When they got back to London on 31 July, Halliwell's gloom had not lifted. 'We went to bed early,' Orton noted. 'Kenneth was looking wan.'

The next morning, 1 August, Orton set off to visit his family in Leicester, where the local theatre was mounting *Entertaining Mr Sloane*, the first of his plays to be staged in his home town:

Said goodbye to Kenneth this morning. He seemed odd. On the spur of the moment I asked if he wanted to come home to Leicester with me. He looked surprised and said, 'No.'

Halliwell had never visited Orton's family. Orton's offer was well-meaning but misguided. He couldn't read the signs of Halliwell's depression. Having just left one 'wilderness', Halliwell had no appetite to languish without family or function in another alien territory. Orton had roots and sweet public revenge awaiting him in Leicester. If Halliwell tagged along, he would be just another prop in an Orton production. Life was empty without Orton and insufficient with him. On 3 August, after two days alone, Halliwell's emptiness and fury overwhelmed him. He felt suicidal.

'The number of humiliating admissions I've made. You'd think it would draw me closer to somebody. But it doesn't': Orton's startling line in *The Ruffian on the Stair* pinpointed Halliwell's predicament. No one was really listening or willing to hear. As with his first wig, nobody took much notice. He therefore had to shout louder, which made people listen even less. Halliwell went first to the Samaritans, who couldn't deal with him immediately. He was too desperate to wait, and went instead to Dr Ismay. Even Ismay was unsympathetic to Halliwell. 'I thought he was a bit of a pain in the neck, a bit of a burden. You felt you couldn't get rid of him. It was the holding-on relationship . . . a depressed, deprived person who wants more and more of the doctor or the interviewer.' Halliwell arrived without an appointment. Ismay saw him. 'He told me that following the long holiday, the relationship between him and Orton was not good. He was very depressed about it. He talked about leaving Orton and at the same time committing suicide.' Ismay prescribed an anti-depressant and a small quantity of amphetamines for Halliwell, who made an appointment to see him again the next day.

After seeing the doctor, Halliwell made his way to the one community he had left: the cast of *Loot*. Sheila Ballantine, who played Fay in the London production, found Halliwell sitting on the stage-door steps of the Criterion when she arrived at seven for the performance. He had been there since six, making conversation with the ninety-year-old stage doorman. Halliwell was carrying a book and the manuscript copy of *What the Butler Saw*. 'I brought you the book,' he said, handing her Malcolm Muggeridge's *The Thirties*.

'We'd never discussed Muggeridge,' Miss Ballantine recalls. 'I thought to myself: "I never said anything about this". But I thought he wanted to talk. So we went into my dressing-room while I made up. It had taken me ages to realize that one hardly ever asked Kenneth what he'd been doing. Kenneth was always the one standing alone, listening. People would always be asking Joe things, and he was the one who monopolized conversation. It must have been like that with everybody.' While Halliwell talked to Sheila Ballantine, Kenneth Cranham came into the dressing-room. Halliwell started telling him how ill he was, how he was going to have a nervous breakdown. Cranham remembers that 'Halliwell was very upset about the TV producer's middle-aged nonentity dig. He kept saying "It was me who thought up the title for *Loot*. It was me who got Joe to write".' Neither actor had ever seen Halliwell by himself. Even alone, Halliwell's conversation returned obsessively to Orton. After the show they took him for a drink. He told them about *What the Butler Saw*, making it seem he was letting them in on a secret. 'He was rather suggesting how important he was in the decisions Joe made. He was making a lot of that. It was a bit sad,' Miss Ballantine recalls. 'I knew he was disturbed. I said "Do come and stay with me tonight". "No," he said, "I'll be perfectly all right because Joe's coming back tomorrow".'

Halliwell saw Dr Ismay on 4 August. Even though Orton had returned, his anxiety had not decreased. He wasn't sleeping well and Dr Ismay gave him a small quantity of elixir chloral. Halliwell reiterated his complaints of Orton's rejection and promiscuity, as he would do repeatedly during the last three weeks of his life. 'I never took it too seriously,' Dr Ismay says. Halliwell told him that 'Orton depended on him in phrasing and that he helped him in a very basic way. He wanted to be acknowledged and be included in the glamour and exaltation Joe was receiving with success.' It was an impossible demand. Halliwell's ponderous writing belied his claims to any more substantial role in Orton's plays. 'Halliwell's wit,' Peggy Ramsay says, 'was abrasive, but rather cold and uncreative. It was wit line by line, but it had no vision.' Halliwell saw himself at the fulcrum of Orton's creative life; but this was an over-estimation. Since *Entertaining Mr Sloane*, in which he had been a major influence, Halliwell had become more a sounding board than an inspiration. Even Orton, according to Peggy Ramsay, referred to *Entertaining Mr Sloane* as 'our play'. 'The first time Joe came to see me, he didn't produce Kenneth,' she recalls. 'But the second time he came, he said "Can I bring a friend". Afterwards he always brought Kenneth with him, and Kenneth always attended rehearsals.' But this procedure stopped after *Entertaining Mr Sloane*. Like the influence of any partner in a marriage, Halliwell's contribution to Orton's work and his life had been rich and varied. But Orton did the writing. There was no way to deny him that, except to kill him.

Orton and Halliwell appeared together backstage at the Criterion on 5 August. Orton was effervescent, Halliwell morose. 'Kenneth was very much stranger,' Sheila Ballantine says. 'He had a weird, shut-off presence. Joe was being hilarious describing Kath in the Leicester production and how she had overdone her sexual advances to Sloane. I was being the boy and Joe was being Kath. He was groping me in front of Kenneth. I thought to myself, "He obviously doesn't know how ill Kenneth is or he wouldn't be mucking about with me in front of him." Right in the middle of this, Kenneth started talking about himself: "And I went to the Samaritans. And I . . ." "Yes I know," I said. Joe said "Oh, you told her that, did you?" Then he went on with his description. And I thought "My God, he can't see! He hasn't noticed!"' Simon Ward, who played Dennis in the production, was also puzzled by Orton's indifference to Halliwell's pain. 'Maybe Joe wanted out. It looked as though he were trying for out. No one could be as insensitive as that if you really cared about the person. Ken was looking really bad.'

Halliwell had already attempted suicide once, in 1962. Now Orton was worried about his increasing dependence on anti-depressants and barbiturates, which he mixed together into one large jar. But, as he confided to Adrienne Corri, he didn't think Halliwell would kill himself. On 6 August Orton came backstage without Halliwell during the interval in *Loot*. 'He was a bit skittish. Bright-eyed,' Sheila Ballantine says. ' "I've got somebody with me," he said. I thought to myself, "I must tell him how ill Kenneth is". I didn't. I decided not to interfere.'

On 8 August, the day before Dr Ismay went on holiday, he received an urgent call from Halliwell. He saw him at five p.m. 'He wasn't functioning when he came to see me. He seemed anxious that I was going on holiday. It was serious enough to consider admission to a hospital.' He told Halliwell he should see a consulting psychiatrist and that he would make the proper arrangements. He changed Halliwell's prescription to more powerful anti-depressants. While waiting for Ismay's newest prescriptions to be filled, Halliwell made his way to Peter Willes's nearby apartment to pass the time. 'I'd never been alone with Halliwell,' Willes remembers of Halliwell's rambling, distraught conversation. 'He said "Of course, Joe would miss me more than I'd miss Joe. I've got money. I've got £5,000". I never realized Halliwell had money. I thought he lived off Joe. He said "You should see Joe, he's much different when you're not there and I'm with him. If I say I'm going to leave, he staggers about saying 'You can't destroy me! You can't leave me! I can't bear it!'" I didn't believe any of this, but Halliwell obviously did. When he left, I phoned Joe immediately. I knew Kenneth was very ill.' Earlier in the week Willes had arranged a party for Orton with Dorothy Dickson, the famous musical star of the twenties, so that Orton could meet some of his theatrical admirers – Vivien Leigh, Emlyn Williams, Harold Pinter. Halliwell was not to be invited. Orton had consented. It was, Willes recalls, the first time he'd been disloyal to Halliwell. Now Willes rang up Orton to advise him to be careful. 'I said "Joe, you mustn't leave him for a moment".' Orton agreed to stay at home and watch Halliwell closely.

Orton and Halliwell were last seen together that evening returning from shopping. Halliwell was dressed in a safari jacket, hiding the bags beneath his eyes under sun-glasses. Over the last few weeks, their neighbours the Salvonis had noticed that Halliwell, even on the greyest days, was rarely without the sun-glasses. He seemed withdrawn. He'd stopped greeting people in the street. That night, when Aldo Salvoni stopped and asked them in for a beer, Orton was, as always, boyish and friendly. Halliwell was quiet. They declined the invitation. Orton explained about the meeting with Richard Lester and plans to make a movie of *Up Against It*.

Kenneth Cranham called Orton to ask if he and Halliwell would like to go to a late-night screening of Yoko Ono's film *Bottoms*. Orton said he'd like to come; but he didn't think Halliwell was feeling well. There was a pause on the phone while Orton asked Halliwell, and then Orton said 'No, Kenneth doesn't want to come.' Orton's words to his friends gave no indication of how serious Halliwell's condition was. That night most of the calls were for Halliwell. Dr Ismay called three times. There was always a high incidence of suicide between arranging hospitalization and the patient's actual admission, because of the depressive's feelings of unworthiness and sense of being a burden. Dr Ismay was worried. In the first call, he informed Halliwell that a psychiatrist had been arranged and that he would call at Noel Road in the morning. 'Halliwell told me that I was taking the matter far too seriously and he would make arrangements to see the psychiatrist at a more convenient time.' Dr Ismay then made an appointment for Halliwell on 10 August; and by the last call, Halliwell reported 'I've started taking the new tablets. I feel much better. Thank you for the trouble you've taken.' Perhaps the drugs, which Halliwell could only have acquired three hours before, were beginning to have a soporific effect. Or perhaps the rapid change in Halliwell's temperament which Dr Ismay noticed over the phone was the calm at knowing that neither life nor Orton would punish him much longer.

.   .   .   .   .   .

Orton was killed between two and four in the morning. The Salvonis, whose bedroom was adjacent and who were awake, heard no struggle or argument. Ordinarily even the clatter of Orton's typewriter or Halliwell's sudden bursts into song were audible. The police described Orton's bludgeoning as 'a deliberate form of frenzy'.[18] Halliwell's death note guided police to the diary of the oppressive farce their life together had become:

Exhausting wrangles over trivia. Kenneth, laying in bed, suddenly shouted 'I hope I die of heart disease! I'd like to see you manage then.' He talks a lot of *The Dance of Death*. 'We're living it,' he suddenly said. 'This is Strindberg!' Soothed down the situation only to have it break out later. 'You're quite a different person, you know, since you had your success.'

(18 March 1967)

Halliwell had read and reread the diary. Bruising sentences hinted at the retreat of Orton's affection. 'Arguments continue sporadically, breaking out like sudden flames on a dying fire' (4 April). Orton's pages preserved scenes of Halliwell's aching frustration and failure which Halliwell wanted to forget but which Orton's presence only exacerbated:

When I got back home Kenneth H was in such a rage that he'd written in large letters on the wall 'JOE ORTON IS A SPINE-LESS TWAT'. He sulked for a while and then came around. He'd been to the doctors and got 400 valium tablets. Later we took two each and had an amazing sexual session ... But it didn't work out. 'I'm not sure what the block is,' I said. 'I can fuck other people perfectly well. But up to now, I can't fuck you. This is something quite strange.'

(5 May 1967)

The diary read like a fever chart of Halliwell's depression and a catalogue of the excruciating emptiness of his life. In it, Halliwell could see himself playing an increasingly minor role in the eventful drama of Orton's life. The diary made Halliwell's sense of failure a sideshow; the homicide made it the main attraction. Through murder Halliwell achieved the public association with Joe Orton's career he'd been denied in life. The diary, which ended as exhibit 'A' at their inquest, was entitled 'Diary of a Somebody'.[19]

2

SOMEBODY FROM NOWHERE

> I lived in a normal family. I had no love for my father.
>
> Joe Orton, *What the Butler Saw*

Joe Orton always wanted to shine. He polished the wit of his plays with the same delighted concentration with which he rubbed baby lotion on his face to make it gleam. The result, in both cases, was dazzling. Orton looked on his ascent to wealth and celebrity with amusement, as the title of his diary showed. 'I have often seen reminiscences of people I have never heard of', wrote Charles Pooter, the prim, social-climbing diarist in George and Weedon Grossmith's *Diary of a Nobody*. 'I fail to see why – because I am not a Somebody – my diary should not be interesting.' Pooter's humourless egoism makes his diary a ludicrous catalogue of suburban misadventures, whose situations sometimes paralleled Orton's life:

I have received an invitation to a banquet given by the Lord Mayor of London – just like Pooter Kenneth says . . . It's really absurd, though. The letter says that the banquet is being held 'in honour of those eminent in the arts, sciences, and learning'. 'It's just because of the £100,000,' I said to Peter Willes. 'They've realized that I'm as rich as they are and now they invite me to their rubbishy dinner.' P. Willes looked shocked, 'I really don't think you should talk about the Lord Mayor's banquet like that,' he said. 'I believe they have excellent turtle soup . . .'

(14 March 1967)

Pooter was a Victorian Malvolio lost in a fantasy of his perfection; and Orton was a modern Feste, a realist who was compelled to speak the unspeakable. Like his laughter, Orton's triumph never forgot his past:

We parted having agreed to make a list of possibilities [for casting the Broadway production of *Loot*]. 'Like a nice afternoon gents,' a tout outside a strip club said as we passed. 'Naked ladies. All alive.' 'You look very pretty in that fur coat you're wearing,' Oscar Lewenstein said, as we stood on the corner before going our separate ways. I said, 'Peggy Ramsay bought it me. It was thirteen pounds fifteen.' 'Very cheap,' Michael White said. 'Yes, I've discovered I look better in cheap clothes.' 'I wonder what the significance of that is?' Oscar said. 'I'm from the gutter,' I said. 'And don't you ever forget it because I won't.'

(9 January 1967)

The 'gutter' to which Orton referred was the Saffron Lane Estates in Leicester where he grew up. This was one of the city council's sprawling developments built between 1920 and 1925 on the unfertile boulder clay of Leicester's south side to accommodate the city's growing work force. Leicester's problem during the twenties and thirties was one of growth not depression. The town's unusual prosperity was due to the nature of its major industries. Women like Elsie Orton could find work easily in the hosiery factories, Leicester's oldest and largest industry.[1] Elsie Orton was a machinist. From eight a.m. to six p.m. she stitched underwear, pants, vests, blouses. Her 'villa' was close enough to the factory for her to cook a meal for her children in her lunch-break. Men like William Orton could get work in the footwear business. With both men and women absorbed by light industry, the city fathers could point with self-congratulation to statistics that showed Leicester with the highest per capita income of any city in Britain. Even more astounding, there had been no major labour disputes in the city since 1918.

The Saffron Lane Estates were another sign of Leicester's progress and prosperity. Orton's 'gutter' was not the brutal and bustling industrial landscape of the North, but the drab monotony of a comfortable city whose council housing reflected its unimaginative mediocrity. The bleak adequacy of the Saffron Lane Estates had a deceptive violence. Fayhurst Road, where Orton lived, and the narrow streets around it seemed to have been vaccinated against life, corroborating the claim of a recent city history that 'The dramatic has no place at all in the streets of Leicester'.[2] With its tuft of grass for a front lawn and its maple tree planted ten feet from the next, each house was solid, quiet, and tidy. The sameness of the architecture and expectation had its special oppressiveness. Cramped, cold and dark, the rows of sooty pebble-granite homes were to Orton a grey backdrop of impoverishment: set-pieces for a lifetime of making do. 'I remember as a kid feeling there was no escape,' says Leonie Barnett, Orton's youngest sister and the one member of his family with whom he remained friendly. 'Fayhurst Road where we all grew up hasn't changed. It's still as mucky as ever. I always thought, "This is it, mate. Either you swim or drown".'

Orton's plays dug angrily at this numbed acceptance. The epigraph to *The Good and Faithful Servant* (1964) is from the *Concise Oxford Dictionary*: 'Faith, n. Reliance, trust, *in*; belief founded on authority.' Like Buchanan, the play's central figure, who has given a lifetime and an amputated limb in loyal service to the company, Orton's parents had only wounds and paltry dividends to show for their faith in industry. Elsie Orton had lost a lung in an early battle with tuberculosis. After decades at the knitting machine, her eyesight failed badly. She was forced to leave, and became a char. Seeking financial security, William Orton had taken a job as a gardener for the Leicester Council in 1929 and lost a finger pruning the trees of a public park. He was not compensated. His security was as 'durable' as the toaster and alarm clock Buchanan receives on retirement from the firm. 'Now, you see, when I should be having a good life, I'm almost blind,' explains William Orton, retired, bewildered and alone. 'I worked hard for that pension. I had to give it to the blind to keep me.'

Orton's laughter was an enemy of work, not only interrupting

it but casting doubt on its seriousness. Orton took his revenge on
the devouring work routine which had robbed his family and the
society of so much of its humanity:

RAY. I don't work.
BUCHANAN. Not work!? (*He stares, open-mouthed.*) What do you
do then?
RAY. I enjoy myself.
BUCHANAN. That's a terrible thing to do. I'm bowled over by this,
I can tell you. It's my turn to be shocked now. You ought to have
a steady job.
EDITH. Two perhaps.

Before Orton found the right language to satirize the work
ethic, his adolescent diaries recorded the boredom of routine and
the banality of his surroundings. He called his early diaries, kept
between sixteen and eighteen, 'conversations with myself'. In his
private and often mis-spelled thoughts, the need to make money is
already at odds with his resentment at unstimulating toil:

9 JANUARY 1949
Very quiet day. Listened to Gilbert and Sullivan on the wireless.
Went to bed feeling ill at the thought of work tomorrow.
10 JANUARY
Work again. I felt so 'tired' when I got up. Fed up . . .
14 JANUARY
Thank god it's Friday again. I wish I belonged to one of the idle rich
and didn't have to work . . .
24 JANUARY
Work, how I hate it in the morning when Dad says, 'It's ten to
seven'.

With their neat gardens and peaceful tree-lined streets, the
Saffron Lane Estates kept the suburban fantasy of leisure and the
good life in the foreground. But Leicester's industrial landscape was
always in the background – as ugly and unheroic as the jobs the
workers held. From the front door of the Orton house, the barren
horizon loomed up over the maple trees. A clutter of electricity

pylons were strung like scarecrows against a skyline dominated by 'BRITISH MADE' emblazoned on a behemoth smokestack. Over the years, the canal two streets away from Fayhurst Road, where Orton liked to walk and swim, became fouled with industrial debris. Garages and houses push up to one side of the waterway; on the other, storage barns from the gas works swell up out of the marshes like ugly sores. 'Who ... conceived the idea of building a house in the midst of a rubbish dump?' Sloane asks the old father, Kemp, in *Entertaining Mr Sloane* (1964). Orton, who saw himself as the physical prototype for Sloane and whose father, like Kemp, was almost blind and was called 'Dadda', always felt the desolation outside the cosy home his mother tried to make. If 9 Fayhurst Road wasn't the model for the wasteland Orton examined in *Entertaining Mr Sloane*, it was symptomatic of the sad bargain so many Englishmen made with their society and the scraps of life they settled for. Orton couldn't stand it. 'I was sacked from all the jobs I had between sixteen and eighteen because I was never interested in any of them. I resented having to go to work in the morning and very often I didn't bother – I just looked in shop windows, or if it was a nice sunny morning I'd sit in the Town Hall Square and have an ice-cream.'[3] Orton put Leicester and family behind him at eighteen; but Leicester had left its mark. In his early writing, he dreamed of doing damage to authority and its smug indifference:

Words were more effective than actions; in the right hands verbs and nouns could create panic ... The blast of a long sentence was curiously local, and a lot of shorter sentences seemed better. And then there was the problem of gathering enough of the enemy together in order that they might listen. He started wondering where and how he could hit the enemy most. He started calculating and found some sentences were puny against large targets. Then perhaps a new type of sentence ... His figures showed that when a particularly dangerous collection of words exploded the shock waves were capable of killing centuries afterwards.

(*Head to Toe*, 1961)

The vigour of Leicester's indifference was stifling. The authorized history of the county even maintains proudly that Leicester is marked 'by the absence of any extreme or distinctive movements in politics, religion, or culture'.[4] Orton spent over half his life there. His plays wanted to rattle the underpinnings of society with a rage spawned by a city whose essence was in its motto: *Semper eadem* – Always The Same.

William Orton first met his wife in her favourite Leicester habitat: the pub. 'Elsie used to do a few turns – singing – in the pubs. All over Leicester, more or less. Very good mezzo-soprano, she was. She sang classic operas.' Three years later, in 1931, they were married. He was twenty-six. She was twenty-seven. They thought themselves lucky to be allocated the corner house at Fayhurst Road in 1935. Like everything else in their life, they'd had to wait for it. They were in lodgings when John Kingsley Orton was born on 1 January 1933. He was their first child. They had three more children at Fayhurst Road: Douglas (1937), Marilyn (1939) and Leonie (1944).

The house which the Ortons looked forward to occupying was never a happy home. Low-ceilinged and drab, the main room was the front room: a dingy square with two small sash windows looking out on the woodshed and neighbourhood laundry lines. Above the fireplace was the room's only picture – a print of Highland cattle. On the wooden sideboard were William Orton's mementoes from six years' duty in the medical corps in the Second World War: a Nazi dagger with the swastika sawn off and a beer stein in which Elsie kept flowers cut from William's private garden. Between the fireplace and the window was a piano – an incongruous extravagance in the spare, uncomfortable room. Elsie Orton had purchased it so that John, whom she favoured as the most gifted child, could learn to play. He didn't, and the only tune she could bang out on the keys was 'Don't Fence Me In'.

'Everybody seemed to be happy but us,' Leonie Barnett remembers. 'We always seemed to be bickering.' The house caged them.

The thin walls were covered with sombre flowered wallpaper that stank with the odour of fried food and damp. The kitchen was painted dark green; the hall was grey; and the front door was chocolate brown. The bleakness had its effect on Orton, whose acute asthma as a child kept him at home much more than the others. He painted his bedroom a glossy white and decorated it with the mysterious hieroglyphics of Pitman shorthand. 'Maybe we'd have been more of a family if we'd had a car and had money,' Leonie thinks now. But there was no privacy and no peace. The house was as threadbare as their lives. 'I had a hard life,' William says. 'It was just a means of existing.' His house embodied this sad, makeshift destiny.

Aspects of William Orton's frail, cowed presence reappear in many Orton characters: the myopic Kemp in *Entertaining Mr Sloane*; the flower-loving and woebegone husband, McLeavy, in *Loot*; the lost and crumpled commissionaire Buchanan in *The Good and Faithful Servant* who out of his uniform is described by Orton as 'smaller, shrunken and insignificant'. A country boy, William had tried his hand at the boot and shoe trade in Leicester. He was a 'puller-over', stretching the tip of the shoe over the sole while a machine tapped in the nails. It was piece-work, and William found it hard to compete with others. He was not a fighter. When he became a gardener for the city, he earned £2 10s. a week; and by the time he retired thirty-five years later, he was up to £14. It was a meagre sum; but he was happy in the outdoors. Each morning at seven, after he'd brought Elsie her tea and roused the children, he'd mount his old black bike and pedal fifteen miles to Stoneygate on the rich north side of Leicester. 'I had nicer flowers to plant.' On Sunday William Orton would often bike out to his greenhouse and light the heaters. There, he had his tea and his flowers and his quiet. He was a simple man; and the flowers could not talk back. 'Gardening kept you busy. You always looked forward to something coming up, you see. It was exciting to see if they came up and see how they were doing every year. I liked the area. It was the richest place in Leicester. There were a lot of trees. A lot of grass.

More space.' Sometimes William took his children with him. The boys were indifferent and went out of a sense of duty. But the girls loved it. They could ride the bikes left at the nearby university during the vacation. But if William let them share his world, he could not share theirs. 'Dad was always an old man,' Douglas Orton remembers. William never played with his children or bought them presents or even ate dinner with the family. He rarely went on holiday with them; and, in later years when he and Elsie took a holiday, she would take one of her friends along for company. From William the children inherited their angular, lean faces – the sharp beady eyes and fair complexion. But there was little else they would be able to acknowledge. A sense of anger at this absence sneaks into Orton's exaggeration of McLeavy's gardening obsession in *Loot*. Hal, McLeavy's bisexual son, has Orton's detached wit as well as his surface appearance. He renders the verdict on his father:

HAL. Do you know what his only comment was on my mother's death?
FAY. Something suitable, I'm sure.
HAL. He said he was glad she'd died at the right season for roses. He's been up half the night cataloguing the varieties on the crosses. You should've seen him when that harp arrived. Sniffing the petals, checking, arguing with the man who brought it. They almost came to blows over the pronunciation. If she'd played her cards right, my mother could've cited the Rose Growers' Annual as co-respondent.
FAY. The Vatican would never grant an annulment. Not unless he'd produced a hybrid.

Hal's attitude to McLeavy has the same aggressive disdain Orton held for his father. Even as an adolescent he bought birthday presents for Elsie but never anything for William. When Leonie telephoned him in 1966 to say that William had been hit by a car and had fractured his skull, Orton replied 'That won't make any difference to his brain'. Indifference had been a factor in the family equation from the beginning; and mockery was one way of filling the void. William had been at the centre of the problem. Unwilling and unable to control his family, he never earned its respect. Elsie rarely treated him like a husband. 'I'm mother and father to this family!' she'd scream. 'I've raised four kids on one lung!' No one, least of all William, could deny her claim. William was a stranger to his wife, his family and himself.

Elsie claimed later that she'd married William on the rebound. She confided the fact to her children and never stopped reminding her husband. 'I should've married him,' she'd say, reminiscing out loud about her first engagement. 'It was only pride. This fella's mother was an alcoholic. I thought he'd turn out the same way.' Elsie had such high expectations from life that almost everything was a let-down. Certainly William was. Her thin, handsome, passive husband was a will-o'-the-wisp she could never crush with her disappointment. The children were always within earshot of their parents' many one-sided brouhahas. They remember Elsie throwing William's money back at him and yelling 'I want more than this!' And when he'd protest that the gardening job gave him security when he retired, Elsie would counter 'I don't want the money *then*. I want it now!' They remember the taunting scenes when Elsie, taller and heavier than her eight-stone husband, ridiculed him for his size. 'You look like a mouse! You eat like a bloody mouse!'

Elsie was never satisfied with William; and the same theme was broadcast in many different stories. 'In all the years I was married to your father I had the chance to have affairs. But I never went off with another man. I was always true to *my* children.' The point was not lost on them: it was to the children, not William, that she was loyal. In retrospect, William agrees with his daughter Marilyn that what Elsie wanted was some six-footer to give her 'a bloody good hiding'. 'Then she'd have thought all the more of me, wouldn't she?' But William never gave her a 'backhander' or an argument. 'You ever lay your bloody hands on me, it's the last bloody thing you'll do,' Elsie crowed at William while he stared up from his newspaper. 'She wanted him to fight back,' Leonie says. 'So she could hit him.' But William never responded to her hectoring. He disappeared behind his *Leicester Mercury* or escaped into his garden or went down to the Saffron Lane Working Men's Club for a drink and a game of skittles. Besides gardening, skittles was William's only other pleasure. He was good at it. He played in club tournaments. Often after a competition he'd bring home a small silver-plate trophy inscribed with his name. It was the one sign of a victory in his life. But Elsie commandeered the trophies as egg cups. They were always stained with egg. After a while, they turned brown.

'Dad was everything John didn't want to be,' Douglas Orton says. 'You could push Dad around. He was domineered. If you said sit there, Dad would sit. He'd never tell John what to do. He could do whatever he wanted. He never showed any affection.' The emotional starvation took on the outrageous dimensions of one of Orton's plays. None of the children can remember their parents displaying any public affection. 'I never saw Mum and Dad kiss – not once, not in all my life,' Marilyn says. And until Elsie died and William started visiting his children's homes, they never kissed him. After Leonie was born, Elsie banished William to another room, giving William's incessant coughing as an excuse. Elsie slept in a double bed with her youngest daughter. 'I had four accidents,' she'd explain. 'A fifth would be a tragedy.' After 1945 William never again had sex with his wife. 'Mum hated sex,' Marilyn says. 'She told me she hated it. She said to me "How I ever got four children I don't know". She hated it. She meant it.' Orton's life and his laughter were hell-bent on making sexual connection. Kath in *Entertaining Mr Sloane*, Madge in *The Ruffian on the Stair*, Mrs Prentice in *What the Butler Saw* are in some way punished by their sad hunger:

MRS PRENTICE (*quietly*). I hardly ever have sexual intercourse.

PRENTICE. You were born with your legs apart. They'll send you to the grave in a Y-shaped coffin.

MRS PRENTICE (*with a brittle laugh*). My trouble stems from your inadequacy as a lover! . . .

PRENTICE. How dare you say that! Your book on the climax in the female is largely autobiographical. (*Pause. He stares.*) Or have you been masquerading as a sexually responsive woman?

MRS PRENTICE. My uterine contractions have been bogus for some time!

In the play world of *What the Butler Saw*, husband and wife make a sexual adjustment and are able to love again. But Orton's mother and father never did. Sex was dirty, and so was the body. 'I never saw her body,' Leonie says. 'I only saw her head, her hands and her legs.' Elsie's prudery was laughable. Like Kath in *Entertaining Mr Sloane*, who claims that 'Until I was fifteen I was more familiar with Africa than my own body', Elsie kept her children in the dark about sex. She never knew that John had been molested at the same cinema they attended each Monday after work and where she'd caution her children not to look at the couples kissing around them. Orton had more mischievous memories of those family entertainment outings:

Watched an old film on television called MY FAVOURITE BLONDE with Bob Hope. This had sentimental overtones for me. It was at the companion picture, MY FAVOURITE BRUNETTE (also with Bob Hope) sometime in the early forties that I was interfered with. A man took me into the lavatory of the Odeon and gave me a wank. I re-lived those happy moments as I sat watching the picture today. I remember coming down his mac. I must've been about fourteen.

(19 February 1967)

At the pub, Elsie had a vivacious come-on: 'How you fixed for a giddy barmaid?' Elsie kept to her own pub and her own friends. Away from William, she put on a jolly rambunctious face for the world with the same broad garishness that characterized her clothes. Still, she was shocked and disgusted by men who – not surprisingly – tried to pick her up. Once, when Marilyn was with her at the pub, a man approached and offered her a chocolate. 'Yes, please,' Elsie said, picking one from the tray. The man leaned over to her: 'Come outside and I'll let you have the whole box.' Elsie's face flushed. 'I wouldn't come outside with you for a box of Cadbury's Black Magic.'

The animality of sex offended the alabaster image Elsie had of herself and her children. She could not abide jokes about sex. And she didn't like language that admitted physical contact. 'I remember when I was courting a fellow,' Leonie recalls, 'and I said to Mum, "I'm gonna give him up". She says, "Why?" I says, "He's dead randy". Her eyes were like organ stops.' Elsie never discussed sex with her children. 'Feel your own way through life, you did,' Leonie says. 'Sex was dirty. It bloody was. She wouldn't have anything to do with it.' The taboo about the body was felt by Orton, whose adolescent diary switches to shorthand when describing anything to do with his body or sexual practice. In later years, when Leonie suggested that John was 'queer', Elsie sternly invoked her familiar censorship: 'Don't say that!' When Orton invited Elsie to see *Entertaining Mr Sloane* – a play which put so many of her pretensions bitterly on stage – he pretended to be out of town and sent Kenneth with her instead. Elsie cooed over the play to friends, but sidestepped the central issue of sex in her demure way by confessing 'it were awful in parts'.

Orton was always shocking his mother. When, as a teenager, he paraded downstairs swathed in a bathtowel and flexing new muscles from his body-building exercises, Elsie would shoo him back upstairs. 'Look at you – you're disgusting walking around like Sabu!' In 1955, after Douglas's wedding party, Orton sneaked a bridesmaid upstairs to his mother's bedroom. Elsie caught them in bed, and her caterwauling reached such a hysterical pitch that Leonie – then ten – started to cry out of fear for John. 'Get that whore out of my house!' Elsie shrieked. 'What do you think this is, a bleeding brothel!'

Elsie's preposterous propriety would always haunt Orton. A month before his death, he visited Kenneth Williams for tea and met Williams's mother, 'Louis'. He was astonished by their camaraderie. Williams traded stories with his mother, who had a delivery as salty as her son's. 'She was staring so rudely I very

nearly said, "Wait a minute, I'll get a basin for your eyes".'
Williams also remembers his mother saying, 'Posh? Spit in her
eye and it wouldn't choke her'. Orton loved the performance and
listened carefully. 'J.O. liked Louis very much,' Williams wrote
in his diary on 5 July 1967. ' "You come out with everything in
front of her. Very different from my mother. I could never talk
like that to her." '

Elsie's advice to her children was the same in theme, if not diction, as Mrs Vealfoy's advice to Raymond, the young hedonist in
The Good and Faithful Servant who puts his girl-friend in the family
way:

MRS VEALFOY. . . . There is no finer sight than two married people
making love.

The double meaning of Mrs Vealfoy's words escapes her. So it was
also with Elsie Orton, who never realized how clearly her children
saw beneath the web of words and memories she spun around herself
to disguise her false pride. Fantasy renovated every sad corner of
her life. The cheap pink Woolworth glass dish which she fussed
about and kept under lock and key in the sideboard was, she maintained, a Jacobean heirloom. The £40 beaver coat she paraded in
the middle of summer at the pub as a token of William's affection
after twenty-five years of marriage had been purchased by Elsie
herself on the correct assumption that William would not remember
their anniversary. 'She would never admit she was poor,' Douglas
recalls. Elsie envied the wealthy and dreamed of what she'd do with
the money if she won on the pools. 'She was going to buy us all a
house,' Marilyn recalls. 'She was going to buy her own house.
Send some money to "our John". She never mentioned Dad.'

Between them, she and William never earned more than £23 a
week; and for many years, while the children were growing up,
their income was much less. They had no phone, no car, no ap-
pliances, and, so Elsie thought, no life. 'She lived in cloud cuckoo-
land,' Douglas says. 'She wanted to live like a queen but she
couldn't afford it.' If there was a choice, Elsie would plump for the

best: Players instead of Woodbine, best ham instead of spam, opera instead of Gilbert and Sullivan. She was always in debt, but pretending to friends that the family was well off. She was for ever juggling her bills and dodging court actions, paying off her extravagances in five- and ten-shilling instalments. Creditors often came to the door collecting for food and clothes. 'John used to say, "Mum won't pay him this week, 'cause it's not his turn",' Douglas remembers. 'She hadn't got the money. She'd buy the things, and worry about paying later. But me Dad wasn't like that. He wouldn't have anything he couldn't pay for. She thought he was a skinflint; but he just hadn't got the cash.'

Elsie's desire to shine went as far as her dentures. She preserved her life-of-the-party smile not with conventional cleanser, but by keeping her teeth in bleach. Orton's comedy delighted in sending up Elsie's eccentric pretensions. 'My teeth,' says Kath in *Entertaining Mr Sloane*, 'since you mentioned the subject, Mr Sloane, are in the kitchen in Stergene. Usually I allow a good soak overnight. But what with one thing and another I forgot. Otherwise I would never be in such a state. (*Pause.*) I hate people who are careless with their dentures.' Kath, of course, loses her dentures in the play's tensest moment; and this 'carelessness' is taken still further in *Loot* when Hal, having dumped his dead mother out of her coffin, uses her teeth as castanets.

Elsie had always dreamed that her voice, not just her teeth, would be on stage. Elsie once considered a career in show business. She took singing lessons as a teenager, hoping to strengthen her lungs. 'If I'd had the money when I was a child,' she confided, 'I'd have been in Covent Garden today.' Elsie was liable to break into song anywhere, not hackneyed pub ballads (although she enjoyed belting these out) but arias from *Tosca*, *Madam Butterfly*, and *Rigoletto*. Her soprano voice could sometimes be heard trilling an aria on the local bus. 'She made a spectacle of herself,' Leonie says. 'I used to say "Stop it!" And she'd say, "Oh shut up, you! I'm enjoying myself!" I used to be that ashamed. But everybody loved it. It was only us kids that didn't.' Elsie loved a party, and her singing –

whether at the pub or on a coach outing – always made her the centre of it. Her children never brought dates home to meet the family because Elsie could not be trusted not to sing at them. 'Just For Awhile', 'You Are My Heart's Delight', 'It's Only A Shanty In Old Shanty Town' were the highlights of her repertoire. If the world hadn't treated her voice as special, at least she did. 'Vera Lynn was a club turn to her,' Leonie laughs. Often, when Elsie returned home sozzled after a singalong, she'd act high-falutin and swan outrageously around her living room. Nothing in the Orton life had the elegance, class, or promise which Elsie vainly tried to conjure. Her refusal to admit the ordinariness of her life had its corollary in an obsession with living up to the expectation of others. This hypocrisy was a major source of family unhappiness; and her children never forgot it. 'She wanted us to look nice but only so people would look at us and say "What lovely children",' Leonie remembers. 'She did everything for what other people thought. Not what we wanted, but what she wanted.' Orton's dialogue, which playwright John Mortimer called 'South Ruislip Mandarin',[5] revelled in this fatuous slavery to appearance. Orton's plots were a revenge on the normality to which his mother gave unstinting lip-service. At the end of *What the Butler Saw* after a fiesta of sexual perversity and with everyone stripped to their briefs and bras, Dr Rance reminds everyone, 'Let us put our clothes on and face the world'. Facing the world was all Elsie could do. She could never face herself.

For seventeen years, Orton tried to live up to her dream of him. His mother felt he was special, and he inherited her faith. He read books; and so it was deduced he was 'gifted'. He was also handsome and well-groomed. Elsie used to hold up John as a model to the rest of her brood. 'John was always the goody-goody,' Douglas explains. 'He could never be in trouble. He could never do anything wrong. I was the tearaway . . .' Elsie's ambitions were stalled, but her dreams of success were to live again in John. When John failed the eleven-plus because of recurring asthma attacks which kept him away from school for long periods of time, Elsie was stunned. She would not allow him to attend the secondary modern. Her children must have the best. No other family in the Saffron Lane Estates of 1,500 homes sent their child to private school. But Elsie enrolled John in Clark's College. She liked to drop the word 'college' at the pub (just as 'my son at RADA' and 'my son the playwright' succeeded each other as her boasts). Elsie also liked the stylishness of John's maroon Clark's College blazer and grey slacks, which set him apart. Sadly, she was paying for a private education without realizing that Clark's College was the wrong kind of school for her son, with a commercial rather than an academic curriculum. According to Orton's teacher at the college, which he attended between 1945 and 1947, 'John was semi-literate. He couldn't spell. He couldn't string a sentence together. He couldn't express himself. He used to start a sentence and then get all het up. He had no vocabulary. It was ridiculous sending him to Clark's College because he couldn't get the right kind of tuition. He was really the secondary modern type.' But the thought seems not to have daunted Elsie. She offered Douglas the same opportunity but he refused to attend such a 'la-di-da school'. Elsie had to pawn her wedding ring to pay the school fees. She told her cronies that she lost the ring while hanging the laundry in the garden. She never got it back.

'John, I look back on my life and wonder where I have slipped up,' Elsie wrote Orton in 1963 in one of her rare letters. 'I have always tried to be a good mother and shield all of you where as it got me, by the way don't think I feel sorry for myself I don't I'm getting passed it . . .' Elsie's memory of her accomplishments as a mother was as erratic as her spelling. Always quick to defend the family name, Elsie was often indifferent to the family. In Orton's adolescent diaries she makes infrequent appearances – none of them affectionate. She scouts jobs in the *Leicester Mercury* and sends Orton off to interviews. She is the censor from whom at seventeen Orton must hide the fact that he's smoked a cigarette. 'Mustn't let Mum know, though.' She is the worrying presence whose apprehension is as much a threat as an assurance of love. When Orton spits blood after an asthma attack, he ponders 'Don't know whether to tell Mum I spit up tonight. I don't want to worry her.' She is the drain on his carefully accumulated spending money. With some weariness, Orton notes how much money Elsie has asked to borrow:

I think dry rot must have set in on this holiday. Mum asked if she could borrow £2. Of course there was an argument, and Mum suddenly flung her coat on and said she was off home. So we went to Rhyl for the afternoon and of course when we came back Mum was there in a furious temper.

(7 September 1950)

Elsie always hoped that, after her son's literary success, he would give her an allowance and let her indulge herself. He didn't. Orton frowned on her extravagance. He hated the waste and the mediocrity that stimulated Elsie's consumer zeal. He was as dutiful a son as she was a mother. He brought her little presents when he arrived for his two-week visit each summer. He wrote Elsie letters, which she rarely answered. He even bailed her out of debt when she was in hospital and worried about her finances. But he made no provisions for his family in his will.

The ambivalence towards family which Orton would dramatize was also something his brother and sisters felt. 'Since my mother's death in 1966, I've never missed her, never wished her back,' Leonie says. A family that never received love had little to give. Orton never got on with his brother; neither sister liked the other; and the running battle between Elsie and William was the numbing backdrop of daily life. 'Nobody discussed anything with anybody,' Leonie remembers. 'We lived in our own little environments.' The family's mutual indifference was interrupted only by Elsie's sudden rages.

Although in company Elsie would talk posh and reprimand her children for using rude words, in private she swore like a soldier. Her most infamous curses were about money. When William turned over his odd-job money to her, Elsie accepted it with a ferocious 'It's neither arse-hole, nor water-cress!' And when Leonie gave Elsie the first £2 she'd ever earned at the hosiery factory, Elsie scowled. 'What am I supposed to do with this? Do wonders and shit miracles!'

Elsie's brutality and frustration were not only verbal. 'She was a cruel bitch,' Leonie says. Listening to this summary of his dead wife, William says, 'Yes, she was.' Very few of the children's memories of Elsie are benign. Once, when Marilyn refused to get dressed and Elsie was rushing to work, she grabbed her daughter by the hair and swung her around. Then, clutching the copper poker by the fireplace, she started to beat her. 'She got me in a corner with this stick and she just wouldn't stop hitting me. I had welts across my back. I thought I'd broken my thumb. I went to my teacher, and she sent me to the clinic. I told the nurse that me Mum hit me with a copper poker. She was horrified. When I told Mum what the nurse had said (I can remember this as clear as yesterday), she said, "Don't say that, Marilyn. You'll get me had up."'

Elsie could not abide her children laughing at her authority. Another time, in another fury, she knocked Marilyn unconscious against an iron mangle. Elsie thought she'd killed her. Leonie also got a taste of the violent side of Elsie's temper when she wouldn't eat her breakfast. Elsie shoved her head into the cereal bowl. 'It quite knocked me out,' Leonie says. The penalties for disobeying Elsie's orders were harsh, Leonie remembers. 'Marilyn and me used to go down to the gas works where they make coke fire fuel. When Mum didn't have money to buy coal, me and Marilyn used to take an old pram and get a bag of coke. I remember once I wouldn't go. "Right," she says. "You won't sit by the bloody fire". She made me sit in the bloody lav.'

Nobody felt close to the family, and Orton always put inverted commas round the word in his adolescent diary. William, who never kept a family photograph, admits 'There was a time I thought of leaving her. Now and again. I don't know why I didn't. I think it was the children.' He is equally blunt when asked if there were

times when the family got on well together. 'Yes,' he says. 'Several.'
Trying to squeeze some smidgeon of enjoyment from her leisure
time, Elsie often neglected her children. Sometimes they had to
wait outside her pub – the City Arms – and call for her to come
home. Elsie would stick her head out the front door: 'What do you
want?' 'We wanted to go home, we wanted to eat,' Leonie says.
'She never worried where we were. She let me stay out to midnight. When I was only sixteen I stayed out all night. When I was
six, I was miles away from home and she never cared where I was.'
Elsie never 'called in' her children around eight at night the way
the other mothers on the Saffron Lane Estates did. 'Deep down, I
really hated it,' Leonie says. 'I wanted to be called in, and looked
after like the others. I wanted my mother to get me into the bath
and get me into bed.'

When Orton met Halliwell in 1951, he found a surrogate brother
and formed the only family he would ever acknowledge. Halliwell
by then was a genuine orphan. His letter requesting scholarship support from RADA played on this theme: '. . . I am an orphan
with no relatives keen enough on my going on the stage to sponge
on . . .'[6] Symbolically, Orton felt himself an orphan too. He had
found neither support nor friends in his own family. At first he was
merely 'different'; later, with success, he was a kind of freak. 'John
must have been a throw-back,' Marilyn says. 'Where did it come
from? We're ordinary people doing our little bit. Doing ordinary
living, and earning ordinary wages.' Orton's resentment at the emotional wasteland of his family first expressed itself in adopting a
sexual bond which offended and denied the bourgeois sense of
'family', and a life style which mocked the sermons about work that
William and Elsie tried to give their children: 'You've got to graft
bloody hard for your money. And then when you've grafted, you
have your enjoyment . . .' Later, Orton's anger found its creative
form in comedy which made pleasure irresistible. Ray (*The Good
and Faithful Servant*), Sloane (*Entertaining Mr Sloane*), Wilson (*The
Ruffian on the Stairs*), Nick (*What the Butler Saw*) share two attri-
butes. They are young and have, so they say, no family. To have

lost the family or never to have known it are conditions which Orton presents without a tinge of sentiment – a laughable fact in his comic world which was a cruel fact in his life.

Orton's last glimpse of his family merely confirmed the vision of them he'd carried through life. When Elsie died on 24 December 1966 – slumped in a chair downstairs where she slept because of her bad heart – Douglas had lifted her on to her bed. According to Orton, William – recuperating at Leonie's home after a road accident – returned to the house to sleep with the corpse.

Orton's first reaction to the death was ambivalent. 'I'll have to send a telegram to find out details of my mother's funeral', he wrote in his diary.[7] 'I can't go home if there's nowhere to sleep. And I don't fancy spending the night in the house with the corpse. A little too near the Freudian bone for comfort.' The shift in the Orton family structure had all the familiar pathetic and farcical touches that Orton recreated in his plays:

28 DECEMBER

Leonie rang about six . . . She said that Dad had gone back home. Sleeps in my mother's bed downstairs with the corpse. After his accident he can't piss straight and floods the lavatory with it whenever he goes. She said, 'Well, I'm shocked by our Marilyn, you know.' I said, 'Why, what's she done.' Leonie said, 'Oh, you know, she behaves very ignorantly all around. And when I told her Mum was dead all she said was – "I'm not surprised". Well, you know, what kind of remark is that?' Dougie was upset. Remarkable how those without hearts when young suddenly develop them in later life . . .

I promised to go home tomorrow. Leonie and George will come around in the evening. As the corpse is downstairs in the main living room it means going out or watching television with death at one's elbow. My father, fumbling out of bed in the middle of the night, bumped into the coffin and almost had the corpse on the floor . . .

The Joe Orton who returned to bury his mother in December 1966 had changed dramatically from the John Orton who sixteen years before, almost to the day, was trying to coax himself into a model of conventional behaviour:

1 JANUARY 1950

During 1950, writing must be improved . . . Tennis must be taken up seriously this year not half-heartedly like in the past . . . Gramophone must be paid for this year and an effort made to save.

Orton's special courage as a comic writer was in facing and chronicling the intense and ambivalent emotions which he had learned to accept in himself. Elsie's funeral brought together all the complexities of his past and his present.

29 DECEMBER 1966

I arrived in Leicester at four thirty. I had a bit of quick sex in a derelict house with a labourer I picked up. He wore a navy blue coat with leather across the shoulders. He carried a sort of satchel. Some kind of roadmender, I thought. The house was large. Windy because the doors were off. We went into the hall. He took his pants down. He wouldn't let me fuck him. I put it between his legs. He sucked my cock after I'd come. He didn't come himself. It was pissing with rain when we left the house. Mud all over the place.

I got home at five-thirty. Nobody in the house. My father was across the road with friends. He can't see now. The accident has affected his walking. He trembles all the time . . . Later on George and Leonie came round. We went to see mum's body. It isn't at home as I'd supposed. It's laid out in a Chapel of Rest . . .

We all went to the Chapel of Rest. It's a room, bare, white-washed. Muted organ music from a speaker in the corner. The coffin lid propped up against the wall. It said 'Elsie Mary Orton aged 62 years'. Betty [Douglas's wife] said, 'They've got her age wrong, see. Your mum was 63. You should tell them about that. Put in a complaint.' I said, 'Why? It doesn't matter now.' 'Well,' said Betty, 'you want it done right, don't you. It's what you pay for' . . .

Mum quite unrecognisable without her glasses. And they scraped her hair back from her forehead. She looked fat, old and dead. They made up her face. When I asked about this the mortician said, 'Would you say it wasn't discreet then, sir?' I said, 'No, it seems all right to me.' 'We try to give a life-like impression,' he said. Which seems to be a contradiction in terms somehow. I've never seen a corpse before. How cold they are. I felt mum's hand. Like marble. One hand was pink, the other white.

Great argument as we left. The undertaker gave Marilyn a small parcel containing the nightgown mum was wearing when she died. Nobody wanted it. So the undertaker kept it. Not for himself. 'We pass it on to the old folks,' he said. 'Many are grateful, you know.'

Didn't sleep much. Awful bed. Damp. And cold. House without mum seems to have died.

30 DECEMBER

I got up at eight o'clock. I went downstairs to the kitchen. My father appeared in the doorway of the living room dressed only in a shirt. He looks thin and old. Hardly more than a skeleton. He weighs six stone four. I said, 'Hallo'. He peered blindly for a second and said, 'Hallo'. After a pause he said, 'Who are you?' 'Joe,' I said. He couldn't remember I'd come last night. Then he said, 'D'you know where my slippers are?' I said, 'What do you mean – where your slippers are?' He got down on his knees and began feeling around. 'I can't find my slippers,' he said. 'They're on your feet,' I said. And they were. He'd been wearing them all the time.

I made a cup of tea and shaved. Then I went out to try and buy some flowers. I had no intention of getting a wreath. Putting money in some ignorant florist's pocket. I couldn't get flowers. The shop said they didn't deliver until ten thirty. The funeral is at ten. So I didn't give mum any flowers. Actually when I read the dreadful, sickening wording on the other wreaths, 'To a dear Mum. At peace at last with little Tony' from Marilyn and Pete I was glad not to be involved.

When I got back home Leonie and George had arrived. Also Dougie and Betty. My father was in such a state that he had to be dressed. I took him to the bathroom and shaved him. At ten the undertaker arrived. 'What about the flowers?' he said. I said I'd no idea what to do with the flowers. 'Where's father's tribute?' he said. 'I think just father's tribute on the coffin.' He found my father's wreath and put it on the coffin. Then we all got into the cars. My aunt Lucy was upset because strict protocol wasn't observed. 'They're all walking wrong,' she said. 'They shouldn't be with husbands and wives. Just immediate circle should be in the first car.' Several women were at their garden gates as the cortege passed. I noticed two old women weeping on each other's shoulders.

At the chapel in the cemetery they held a brief burial service. They didn't carry the coffin into the chapel. They wheeled it in on a trolley. The vicar, very young and hearty, read the service in a droning voice. And then the coffin was wheeled out and to the graveside. It was a cold, bright morning. My mother's grave was a new one. Her last wish was to be buried with Tony, my nephew who was drowned aged six, eighteen months ago, but Pete and Marilyn refused to have the grave re-opened and so my mother's last wish was ignored...

The coffin was lowered. The vicar said his piece. The earth was sprinkled over the coffin. My father began to cry. And we walked back to the waiting cars. Immediately the mourners left the graveside a flock of old women descended on the grave, picking over the wreaths and shaking their heads.

We got back home at half-past ten. Sandwiches and tea had been prepared by a neighbour. The party got rather jolly later ... My father sat through the party looking very woebegone. The only person who seemed to be at a funeral. Mrs Riley, mum's lifelong friend, was crying quietly in a corner and drinking endless cups of tea. 'I don't expect I'll see you again,' she said as she left. 'Your mother was very dear to me. I shan't come up here now she's gone. Goodbye,' she said, kissing my cheek. 'I hope you have a happier life than your mum did.'

Leonie and I spent part of the afternoon throwing out cupboardsful of junk collected over the years: magazines, photographs, Christmas cards. I found a cup containing a pair of false teeth and threw it in the dustbin. Then I discovered they belonged to my father. I had to rescue them. I found my mother's teeth in a drawer. I kept them. To amaze the cast of LOOT ...

After I left Leonie, I picked up an Irishman. Pretty baggy. I wasn't going to bother but he had a place so I said 'O.K.' It was an empty house. Not derelict. Just unoccupied. He had a room on the ground floor of a large house. The place was damp, not lived in. A smell of dust. He didn't live there. He rented it for sex. There was a table covered in grime. Bits of furniture. A huge mantelpiece with broken glass ornaments on it. All dusty. There was a double bed with greyish sheets. A torn eiderdown. He pulled the curtain which seemed unnecessary because the windows were so dirty.

He had a white body. Not in good condition. Going to fat. Very good sex, though, surprisingly. The bed had springs which creaked. First time I've experienced that. He sucked my cock. Afterwards I fucked him. It was difficult to get in. He had a very tight arse. A Catholic upbringing, I expect . . .

2 JANUARY [back in London]

In the evening P. Willes rang . . . I told him about the funeral. And the frenzied way my family behave. He seemed shocked. But then he thinks my plays are fantasies. He suddenly caught a glimpse of the fact that I write the truth.

When Orton died, William heard the news not from the family, who were notified immediately by the police, but from television. Shut away in an old people's home, life was even more remote than in the park greenhouse. Now, existence was reduced to small memories and idle chat with old men and women who sat like corpses in the red straight-backed chairs of the Smoking Room. For a time, there was a woman with whom William could be seen holding hands. She had proposed both sex and marriage. But William was now unfit for either. He had never impressed himself on life ('I never seemed to get anywhere. I was always a failure'), and now he was fading slowly out of life with the tepid, brutal anonymity his son had chronicled so movingly in *The Good and Faithful Servant*. 'You have philosophy then?' asks Buchanan, who is about to be retired. 'Are you resigned to anything in particular?' Buchanan is talking to Edith, with whom he'll soon decide to spend his last days. 'No', Edith says. 'Life in general. Isn't that enough?' Orton never saw his father's new home; but its details – a traffic sign saying CAUTION: BLIND PEOPLE CROSSING, the aviary and goldfish ponds, the polished entrance hall with white canes for the blind crammed like golf clubs into a box – evoke just such a life of perpetual loss as Orton's laughter captured and tried to control. William, who died in January 1978, kept a photograph of 'his John' on the Formica bureau of his antiseptic room overlooking the car park. The picture was of John aged eighteen, taken just after he went to RADA: a suave smile contradicted by the boyish olive-smooth complexion and the shock of straight black hair curling like a comma across his unlined forehead. The photograph, the family agreed, made John look like a young Dirk Bogarde. William kept no other family picture near him. 'His John' flowered by some bewildering accident like none of the others, and then had been cut down in full bloom. It was typical of William's life and luck. He had loved his son but never connected with him. Even the plants he cared for never seemed to flourish. 'I didn't think I was a good gardener. It upset me. I didn't tell anybody. Always kept it to myself.' William wanted only one thing in life: a greenhouse. He never got it.

The colourful Pitman shorthand characters with which Orton decorated his bedroom walls were symptomatic of his desire to paint over the banality of Leicester life. Orton hankered for the extraordinary. The books he cherished were *Alice in Wonderland*, *Peter Pan*, *Bullfinch's Greek Mythology*; the roles he longed to play were Ariel and Puck. These characters appealed to his mischievous desire to change shape and turn invisibility into a lethal asset. 'Hope that I am allowed to let my imagination run riot', he confided to his diary in 1950,[8] contemplating a production of *The Tempest* in which he would play a mariner and a spirit. 'Have notion of putting red sequins on my eye lids and having carmine for eye shadow. This would give the impression – I hope – of eyes of flame – ah-la – Jabberwocky.'

When Orton discovered the theatre, he found a focus for his energy and an answer to his needs. 'I was never able to imagine myself as ordinary all my life,'[9] he said at the height of his success; but theatre was then the only thing that elevated life 'out of the ordinary'. Besides, it was a friendlier, better-educated community than his home, where Orton could invent possibilities for himself and indulge an imagination which was of no use in the workaday world and of no interest to his parents or teachers. 'He wasn't terribly bright, but he had ideas,' recalls Mrs C. A. Bish, who taught Orton at Clark's College. 'He came to me one day and said, "I'm very interested in the theatre and the only thing I want to do is go on the stage". I dismissed it.'

The only person not to dismiss Orton's hopes was Orton himself. At sixteen, his future seemed cast in the dreary routine of an office factotum. Theatre and the promise of productions were an antidote to his stalled life. His fantasy of theatrical success was as desperate and unfounded as the rest of his aspirations. Even before he had spoken his first three lines on the stage, he'd dedicated his life to it:

It's nearly 12 noon. I am writing this on paper at work. I know I am slacking but I don't feel like work. I am longing for dinner time to come because then the time whizzes by and it's soon 6-30. I will work really hard this afternoon and forget the theatre for a while at least. Last night sitting in the empty theatre watching the electricians flashing lights on and off, the empty stage waiting for rehearsal to begin, I suddenly knew that my ambition is and has always been to act and act. To be connected with the stage in some way, with the magic of the Theatre and everything it means. I know now I shall *always* want to act and I can no more sit in an office all my life than fly. I know this sounds sentimental and sloppy but it is all perfectly true.

(13 April 1949)

Orton's diaries are filled with peevish asides about the grinding tedium of work. 'This week has gone by like a century'; 'Nothing much happened as usual'; 'Nothing to do'; or – a familiar entry scrawled and underlined beside many days – 'QUIET DAY. WORSE LUCK'. Excitement was one commodity Leicester didn't manufacture. Orton had to create his own events. Even before he discovered amateur dramatics, he was resourceful at keeping busy. There were classical records, books, films and plays to devour and then comment on in the front of his diary (9 January 1950: '"Last of the Redskins". Story about war with redskins. Very poor film, came out before end'). In his anxiety to coax any response from the world, Orton kept up a constant correspondence: letters for job interviews, letters for pen pals, letters for body-building courses, including the Charles Atlas chest-expander. The prospect of a reply gave his life a sense of expectation:

> ... Came home at dinner time browned off. Mum said there was no letter from Bolton and B. I felt as though I'd like to lay down and die. Anyway, I had dinner and went into the hall and in the box was a letter. I had got the job, but I've got another interview tomorrow. Feel extremely happy tonight.
>
> (9 June 1949)

The 'urge' to join the Leicester Dramatic Society, the city's oldest and most prestigious amateur group, seized Orton on 13 January 1949. 'I have written the Manager asking him for a subscription. Will send the letter tomorrow. Query: Hope I don't forget.' Orton had joined the society before, two years earlier, but had let his membership lapse. The LDS boasted Richard Attenborough as its most famous alumnus, and it had the advantage of having the Little Theatre, the best-equipped amateur stage in Leicester. But, as Orton learned, it had its own self-perpetuating aristocracy which made it difficult for ambitious newcomers to get decent roles. Orton auditioned for *Richard III* on 1 March and waited impatiently to see if he'd been selected. On 19 March he had his answer:

> Feel thrilled to death. Had a TELEGRAM from the Little Theatre saying that rehearsal is tomorrow at 6.30. Boy oh boy! I'm in at last.

Immediately, the drab days were overshadowed by the aura of adventure theatre gave to his evenings:

> No need to say what tonight has been like. Wonderful. I play two very small parts, still I don't mind. I am Dorset, the son of some Queen (Elizabeth, I think) and a messenger. Am just a little worried as I have never had to speak Shakespeare before ...
>
> (20 March 1949)

Orton's nervousness about speaking Shakespeare was symptomatic of his uneasiness with language in general. 'He couldn't express himself,' Mrs Bish, his teacher, recalls. 'He'd get so far in talking with you and then, if you didn't understand immediately, he'd become impatient. He would close up, move away, go back into his world. I think he was afraid of being made fun of...' Orton had difficulty making people pay attention to his dreams, and the disregard maddened him. But the text of a play was a poetic blueprint for language which made it possible to master words and make people listen.

A boy without society's credentials, Orton struggled to build up his mind and body from their skimpy and undernourished beginnings. 'He read and copied styles,' Mrs Bish remembers. Like his books and his body building ('I shall be the most perfectly developed of modern playwrights if nothing else,' he wrote to Peggy Ramsay in 1966,[10] still doing his exercises), theatre was an extension of Orton's passion for self-improvement. Theatre consolidated Orton's fascinations – literature, music and make-believe – and made them legitimate labour. On stage, 'the magic of the Theatre and all that it means', as Orton put it then, was the magic of transformation in which the actor, isolated by light, costume and role, could lose himself and his past. In play, identities could be exchanged, time and destiny momentarily mastered. On stage Orton could be visible, the centre of attention instead of on society's periphery. Orton's identity was always fluid. 'I'm not committed in politics or sex or life,'[11] he said in 1964. This detachment was present even in adolescence; its mischievousness gave acting its special appeal. Bernard Widdowson, a close amateur-acting friend of those years, with whom Orton walked the streets of Leicester after rehearsals talking passionately about his stage dreams, recalls Orton's chameleon quality. 'The physical image of Orton always remained the same: he always looked terribly thin and cold. Winter or summer. He wore the same riding mac and green lovat corduroys. But this was the only thing about him that remained static. His ideas would change from day to day. You could never feel certain he'd be exactly the same.' Acting, with its demand for energy and disguise, suited Orton's mercurial personality.

At work, Orton found himself 'yearning for rehearsal' and on days when there was no theatre in his routine the whole amperage of his life seemed to sink, making him feel 'so low'. He could hardly contain himself at the prospect of an approaching rehearsal:

... I had a bath. Must look 'all right' for tomorrow's rehearsal. Have sorted out a nice box for my make-up box. Oh please god let me have another part before the season ends. Or I shall be so disappointed. Query: What *are* the numbers of the make-up I use. Silly of me but all I can remember is cleansing cream.

(26 March 1949)

Orton's moments on stage in *Richard III* were drastically reduced when 'the producer . . . explained very nicely that I was too young to play Dorset. The producer said that historically I was supposed to be 23. Well, I don't look or sound 23. So I am a messenger with one line to say and a soldier with nothing to say'. Even with these meagre roles, Orton luxuriated in fantasies of conquest. Sitting in the Little Theatre two weeks before the opening of *Richard III* in April, he was ravished by the thought of fame. 'Found myself thinking what I would say when asked to take part in a broadcast called "How I became an Actor". Probably start "I think I have always had a sort of yearning . . . etc, etc". Pulled myself together quickly.'[12] Orton stood careful guard over his emotions. His dreams were too brittle, his emotions too raw to withstand scrutiny. Around older people, he erected a persona of shy detachment and worked hard to keep envy and self-doubt from upsetting the surface.

Must check growing tendency to think
a) Nigel Pochin (he plays RIVERS, NORFOLK, and LARGEST MESSENGER) got his part through influence (his dad's assistant stage manager).
b) That because quite often I sit and read on my own (I hardly know anyone) people think how lonely I must be (which is ridiculous).

(3 April 1949)

Orton was too busy with plans for himself to be lonely. Adolescent self-consciousness dictated every gesture with a sense that the whole world would be watching. Two days before the opening, Orton locked himself in the bathroom and made up:

I did this partly because I wanted to see if I know how and partly because I don't want the greasepaint to have that 'never-used-before' look.

(10 April 1949)

Behind Orton's fussing about his appearance was a fear he wouldn't be noticed. After the photocall at the final dress rehearsal, he wrote: 'I am in two [photos]. Don't know whether I'll be seen.' But these worries were swept aside by the exciting anticipation of an audience.

When the first night arrived, Orton's only comment was 'felt a little nervous but not really'. He was resigned about the reviews. 'Quite good on the whole except for elephantine efforts of scene shifters. Of course I wasn't mentioned as I only had three lines.' By the end of the week, Orton was already complaining of 'a strange feeling of flatness'. There were only three more performances of *Richard III*; and, completely stagestruck, Orton was now overwhelmed by a new ambition:

Feel a mixture of feelings after ten days of speaking three lines a night and trying to look intelligent; but this is drowned by the fun I've got out of it. I shall be very sorry when it's over. Have heard that Derek Crouch who plays Clarence is at R.A.D.A. He once said he was 'a gentleman of leisure', but I thought he was a student or something. I do envy him. But thinking on it, he's older than me and must have been in the same position as me at 16. Am wondering if, if I saved at least 5 shillings a week I could go to R.A.D.A. in the remote future. Of course I have no idea what the fees are, etc. . . . In the course of conversation làst night I found that the fees for R.A.D.A. are 20 guineas per term. But I am determined to keep on saving . . .

(26 April 1949)

Sentiment was rare in the Orton family, but at the last performance Orton was overcome with feeling:

Feel an awful touch of nostalgia tonight when the costumes were all packed in their boxes and the dressing room was bare. When shall I be in another play at the Little Theatre?

(27 April 1949)

A year and a half later, the question would be answered by Orton himself in a letter of resignation to the Leicester Dramatic Society:

I have been a member for two years now and during that time you have presented 22 plays. In April 1949 I was asked to play a small part in *Richard III*. Since then I have heard nothing from the society ... I don't expect a part every month but 17 is more than I'm prepared to stand.[13]

Orton was not the hot acting property he hoped to be; and his bravado backfired. 'LDS acknowledged my letter with a very cold note', Orton confided to his diary on 13 September 1950. 'Not (as I hoped) with a part.' In the intervening months, however, Orton had not been idle. Following *Richard III* in 1949, he joined two other drama clubs, the Bats Players and the Vaughan Players, an amateur group associated with Vaughan College. 'At night I belonged to an amateur society – in fact I belonged to so many it got ridiculous – the rehearsals for the shows clashed,'[14] Orton said. His passion for the stage seemed to increase as his enthusiasm for girls decreased:

My opinion of women is going down. At present it is zero. Dot [Dorothy Crashley] never turned up at all [for a date to see *The Mikado*]. Am completely fed up with girls in general. Bought two sticks of greasepaint.

(2 April 1949)

On stage, Orton's vulnerable ego could be reinforced and protected. But socially he was, by his own admission, 'a bad loser though I try not to show it'. Theatre could be counted on to yield pleasure. Girls on the other hand, never seemed to pay him the right kind of attention. They confounded and often rejected him, a familiar adolescent obstacle which was made more daunting by the deep distrust of women Elsie Orton's volatile behaviour had bred in her son. 'I'm fed up with girls' was a phrase he wrote often in his 1949 diary, as they systematically intruded on his fantasy of perfection:

I'm really mad tonight. Penny said she would come to dancing school tonight and was to meet me outside the library. I turned up, but did she. NO she didn't, and I waited like a fool in the howling wind and pouring rain . . .

(9 February 1949)

This is really the last straw. D.L. and I went to the theatre and we saw Penny with Dickie B., George B and some other boy, 14 I think. Well, if she prefers their company to mine, she's welcome to it. I have finished with her completely.

(12 March 1949)

Speaking in 1964 about Eddie, the bisexual brother of Kath who also fancies Mr Sloane, Orton said 'He's quite potent or could be potent again but he just sort of got fed up messing around with women and all the things one has to put up with in a woman'.[15] This was Orton's attitude towards his own sexuality and heterosexual courtship. As an adolescent, Orton was as much a stranger to sexuality as Kath claims she was in *Entertaining Mr Sloane*.

The transformation of Orton's attitude towards women from ambivalence to anger is chronicled in *Head to Toe*:

They closed in: he heard their voices now only as myriad and interminable insects . . . when he was younger, a boy, a youth, he had loved the sight of female flesh and the sound of women's voices, of walking and sitting alone with them under trees. He never knew the danger. Then the pavement, the stones, became actual, savage, filled with, evocative of, the claws of birds, maddening, terrifying sounds. He was afraid.

With success and the social confidence it brought, Orton lost his angry edge, but not his ambivalence towards women. There were moments in adulthood when he found himself savouring fantasies of physical contact he'd long ago abandoned:

Went to the Windmill and because the beautiful German (or Danish) Vipsil wished to buy some souvenirs I walked her into the Casbah. How slow women walk. She talked all the way about how Islam women were 'Treated so bad, you know'. How she couldn't walk down the street without 'the bad things being said to me, you know'. And I thought what a beautiful cow and how right the Arabs were about women. I enjoyed the looks of envy as I walked along with her. In a shop a shopkeeper lifted a silver chain and offered it to her. 'Where does it go?' she said. He was just about to put it around her waist. He completely accepted the reason for my taking the waist-band from him, accepting also that she, whilst in my company, was my possession. And so, in fact, for a morning's walk around the town, I possessed the most beautiful and desirable girl in town. I was curiously excited by the fact.

(19 May 1967)

But the only conquests he made in 1949 were stage-managed. He lived in a daydream of theatrical success. Orton's public recollections of his early fascination with the stage miss the sense of urgency and obsession he invested in it. Time was measured by the hiatus between productions. As 1949 drew to a close, Orton assessed his 'career' sadly:

Nothing much has happened since I last wrote in this diary. I have played Tyltyl in the Vaughan Players Production of 'The Bluebird' from 12th–17th December. Also Robert in the Bats Production of 'Without the Prince'. Now I am back where I was last April. No player at nothing and no chance of being in one for at least a couple of months. Vaughan are doing 'Murder in the Cathedral' in February but I am not in it and don't think I shall be in any of the LDS productions. The Bats only do two productions a year and they did 'W.T.P.' in November and there will be a break of two months at least.

(24 December 1949)

Orton had made a particular splash in Maurice Maeterlinck's *The Blue Bird*. As the child who, with his sister, sets out on an odyssey to discover the blue bird of happiness, Orton had a substantial part. The boy, Tyltyl, is supposed to be ten. The combination of Orton's innocent vulnerability and playful imagination made him credible in the role. Previously he had read for another Vaughan College production and made a poor showing. 'I had a bit of a chest bout that night and the reading . . . didn't go down too well, in fact it was bloody awful.' But Tyltyl was a character he could immediately identify with and love. When Orton got the role he was 'overjoyed . . . I learned three acts all at once, but then cooled down a bit because I didn't know what scenes were going to be cut'. Orton brought to Tyltyl his own aura of wonder and will-power, which were right for the part. 'It's a play that calls for a boy who has visions and ideals, and that's what John gave it,' says Joanne Runswick, who directed Orton. 'Off stage he didn't laugh much, he was ever so serious. When he did laugh, he laughed in the play. He was living in a world of his own in the play. It was uncanny. He was always going on about how he was going to be a great actor. He was so tense about it – about becoming somebody. He spoke like a man of twenty. He lived in a fantasy world . . . I had the feeling there was something wrong. He seemed like a child who'd missed a lot of love. I used to want to draw him to me because he used to "go away" . . . always apart. He was so apart.' This quality of dissociation from events later would give Orton's stage writing its comic bite. The *Leicester Mercury* praised Orton for 'great confidence'; but enthusiasm and theatricality don't shine through the cast's picture in the paper. Orton sits forlornly in the front row, his hands self-consciously hiding his bony knees from the camera. He stares blankly into space, lost in thought.

Orton's acclaim in *The Blue Bird* made his dreams of being an actor more luscious. He had jumped from a three-line walk-on in his first play to 'star' billing in his second. His new-found talent seemed confirmed. The buzz of excitement and visible proof of his accomplishment from the audience had made him, according to Joanne Runswick, 'a bit cocky; he really thought a lot of himself by the end of the show'.

.   .   .   .   .   .

Orton had turned seventeen on New Year's Day 1950. The new decade, which was heralded in the papers as an era of abundance and progress, held no promise for him. 'I feel so fed up, fed up with girls, my work, and life in general. I'll be damn glad if I do have to go into the Army. At least, it'll be a change.' Orton had no theatrical productions on his horizon. He retreated into his theatrical daydreams. He mounted the programmes from his previous productions on his brightly painted walls. He designed a lighting plan for *Richard III*. To pass the time while he waited to hear about parts, Orton took up drawing. He designed 'marvellous sets' for *Blue Bird*, *The Palace of Happiness* and *Land of Memory*. The only theatrical area where Orton could see himself making progress was the dance floor. Grace, Charm, Poise – the entire tinsel production of would-be elegance that ballroom dancing staged – appealed to Orton long before he understood and satirized the sweet conformity of its fantasy. 'Our disability bonus was won by Mr Laurie Russel of Market Harborough', Erpingham's voice announces about the ballroom competition in *The Erpingham Camp*. 'Both Laurie's legs were certified "absolutely useless" by our Resident Medical Officer. Yet he performed the Twist and the Bossa Nova to the tune specified on the entrance form.' In his youth Orton knew the compulsion to look good. He was a high-stepper and proud of it. 'Can now dance the Quickstep, Waltz, Barn Dance, Military Twostep, and St Bernard's Waltz. Well, well, well.'

With RADA as a vague goal, Orton needed steady work. As a junior clerk earning £3 a week, he lived to please and had to please to live. He tried to refashion the dogsbody's terror of necessity into something suitably heroic when he surfaced in 1964 as the successful author of *Entertaining Mr Sloane*. 'When I'd go to the Labour Exchange to ask for work – a question of necessity – they always seemed to offer me a labouring job.'[16] Asthmatic and frail, Orton never held a labouring job in Leicester. But by February 1950 he was struggling tenaciously to keep the job he had. The trouble began on 27 January when Orton arrived at work groggy from a

Leicester Dramatic Society party the previous night. He reported happily to his diary 'I was pleased when someone said, "Well, if it isn't Johnny Orton" ... Was quite surprised how many people I knew.' But the office jolted him into his familiar status of marginal man:

Work today, oh how tired I felt. I didn't get in till 12.30 and I had to be up at 8. Felt dizzy all day and am sure some people thought I was drunk. (Hope they did.) Saw in my stamp book 'Leicester Mercury and reply' 5d. Do hope they are not advertising for a 'Junior Clerk' as I'm out if they are ...

(27 January 1950)

Orton searched the accounting department letter files the next day for a memo about the advertisement. He found nothing. Finally, sneaking a look at the secretary's notebook, he decoded her shorthand and discovered the order for the ad. Panicked, he devised a scheme to come to work early and intercept the mail: 'If it's alright and has nothing to do with me getting the sack, I shall take it out and repost it. If it encloses anything about me, it will be burnt.' Despite his 'morning vigils', Orton was fired at the weekend.

Out of work, Orton flung himself on the merry-go-round of job hunting. Although he wanted nothing to do with his parents' world, Orton's life – like theirs – was shaping up into one long forced march to the rhythm called by interviewers and employers. His days had a familiar, inevitable repetitiveness:

Lying in bed this morning half awake, Mum barges in with two letters. 1. Freers, Bauskell and Co., like the sound of this one and 2. British Railways – don't like this so much but I'll go see. FB's tomorrow at 11, so I can lounge about today doing nothing which is pleasant.

(13 February 1950)

Still without a job in late February, Orton wrote adamantly in his diary: 'Rehearsal the only thing I want to do'.[17]

All through the cold and dismal winter, Orton warmed himself on his hothouse dreams of the stage. In the last week of January, he was back at the task he longed to make his real work.

Playreading tonight. Three plays were read. No. 1 was 'Before You Cook Your Beef', a Spanish play in which I read Francisco, a very jealous husband. No. 2 'The Foeman' about border feuds in the 17th Century. I read Davie. And No. 3 in which I didn't read was 'The Sword is Double-Edged' about a Greek artist who calls upon the gods to bring life to his beautiful statue. This was very funny. Wish I could play this. But imagine to my surprise and joy when, upon picking characters Mr Atkinson said, 'I think we'll have this young man to play Davie.' I'm in a play – oh joy, oh joy. Must put all my thoughts of the Greek play out of my mind. I'm lying down in my bed now and am going to mark my part. Query: Did they wear kilts in the 17th Century?

The promise of a production consolidated Orton's attention. His life had immediate direction. 'I have a great passion for energy', Orton wrote that year. And theatre was exactly that: a scintillating exchange of energy. His diary is cluttered with rehearsals for *Foeman* and the sweet anticipation of parts from other playreadings. 'Glad when Sunday comes for the casting reading [Vaughan College Players' production of *Aria da Capo* and *The Golden Fisherman*]. Do hope I get in one or the other of the plays. But I am not desperate because I am in one already.' 'Desperate' was Orton's word for his need to perform. At the end of February, with a handful of rejection letters from local businesses, theatre gave him his only taste of success:

'Joy of joys' as I lay in leaden slumber this morning Mum's angel sweet voice?? floated through the air telling me there was a p.c. for me. Dressed hurriedly hoping all the time for details of a play and telling myself that it could only be from the library. Got down and it was from Vaughan. It said that a meeting to discuss the production of 'Aria da Capo' would be held on Friday. Rehearsals would be held on Tuesday, Wed., Frid. and Sun. . . .

(2 March 1950)

The sudden buzz of stage activity bolstered Orton's determination to make a life of theatre. In his eagerness, Orton took the advice of anyone who cared to give it. He was inventing himself, and every suggestion helped fill in the shadowy outline. The first indication of his seriousness is on 4 March 1950:

Long discussion with our insurance man last night about me taking up the stage. He advised me to get some elocution lessons, so I am going to. Then when I come out of the Army – I shall try and get into repertory.

Orton didn't act immediately on his career plan. But, in the month that followed, his rehearsals earned him enough praise to confirm his unabashed confidence in himself. Both *Aria da Capo* and *The Foeman* were entries in the National Festival of Community Drama. Orton took his playing seriously, and his enthusiasm was immediately applauded:

Rehearsal of *Aria da Capo*. We did the piece with the shepherds (Thyrsis and Corydon). Feel rather pleased with myself as the producer was obviously pleased with me. I couldn't say the same for the person who is playing Thyrsis. He is very wooden indeed.

(7 March 1950)

Orton was equally critical of *The Foeman*. To his annoyance, rehearsals never began on time and the atmosphere seemed to him 'unprofessional'. Orton didn't like the play. 'Must find some way of getting more life into an uninspiring part'.[18] Since he lived for his moments in front of an audience, Orton had to invent the kind of detail that made his precious performances count. His studiousness paid off. *The Foeman* won third place in the festival competition.

By 1 April the excitement of both productions was over. Life, Orton reported to his diary, 'is very flat indeed. For the next few weeks I know (until I am in another play) I shall keep looking at the calendar and thinking THIS TIME WEEKS AGO I WAS MAKING UP FOR *ARIA DA CAPO*, ETC.'[19]

Sunk into a chasm of inactivity, Orton made a stab at rectifying the situation. On 5 April he wrote to the Information Bureau about

RADA and two days later, on a whim, sent letters to two regional theatres. 'Wrote to the Birmingham Rep and Peterborough Players. Don't really know what I expect to get out of them. But you never know your luck.' Even a ripple of response was better than the present still water. In later years, the spark of Orton's malicious wit, the jokey outrageousness he tried to cram into every line, betrayed a similar restlessness: an imagination in isolation trying to keep itself amused. In 1950, Orton knew the boredom, but not the furious alienation which gave his style its belligerent extravagance. Not only did theatre allow Orton to invent and inhabit worlds more interesting than his surroundings, it transformed his sense of well-being. On 10 April, with his letters to professional theatres still unanswered, he was asked to play in *And No Birds Sing*. 'Oh boy, oh boy. I have a deliciously warm feeling inside me.' The next morning, despite a cold, he reported: 'Delicious feeling still with me'. After a month of fatiguing anticipation, things suddenly began to fall into place. No sooner did he have a new part than answers from the repertory companies arrived. 'Both advised me to get some training at RADA. Information Bureau sent me the names of some people to get in touch with regarding RADA.' A newspaper article by Laurence Olivier on 15 April fanned his hopes still higher:

He says there are scholarships one can win to the R.A.D.A. And for the exceptionally talented there are maintenance grants as well. Hope one of those elocution teachers I wrote to answers my letter. Failing this, I'll write R.A.D.A. itself. I know the address is Gower Street. But I must get an evening job somehow . . .

The brazenness of Orton's enterprise sometimes deluded him into equating the size of his ambition with his ability. When the Vaughan Players announced a casting reading for *The Tempest* he had written in his diary: 'In the letter it said, "largely a male cast but some singing, goddesses and attendant spirits and Miranda". Not a mention of Ariel. So perhaps they are having Ariel played (as it should be) by a male, if so I do hope I get the part'.[20] But two weeks later and the next reading, Orton's daydream took a pratfall. 'Not very profitable as far as I'm concerned because I didn't even read Ariel, so I can't possibly play it. I read Trimalchio quite a lot, although whether I've a chance of playing it, I don't know.' When Orton hadn't heard from the director a week later, he was scheming of other ways to get a part:

Am going to take my costumes for 'Aria' back [to Vaughan College] tonight. This is only an excuse to show myself at 'The Tempest' rehearsal as I am only hoping the producer will give me a part. Query: Is this a vain hope. Answer: 'Fraid so.

(28 April 1950)

The adult amateur players didn't have the same estimation of Orton's talent as he did. He got a part playing a lowly spirit. 'Of course I am very lucky to be in it at all, but after playing quite big parts for the Vaughan, it is rather a blow to one's pride to be lumped together with somebody who has about as much acting ability as a flea: namely – Widdowson, Burchell and quite a few *new* people'.[21] But in hot pursuit of transformation, Orton's energy hurried him past any temporary setbacks. If his role in *The Tempest* was unchallenging, the disappointment was balanced by the prospect of elocution lessons. Voice was the first signal of class distinction. Orton's East Midlands accent drawled vowel sounds, turning 'duck' into 'dook', and made a sloppy indistinct blur of aspirants that changed 'he has' to ''e 'az'. This pigeon-holed Orton into a class and a whole series of attendant expectations. Orton's upper lip protruded over the line of his mouth, which impeded clarity and gave his delivery a casual, slightly slack-jawed look. The sound he produced was monotonous, the inflection faltering. The effect, even to him, was unimpressive:

I found myself listening to my voice and my acting and thinking how awful I sounded.

(3 May 1950)

In later years, Orton often slipped into a working-class accent which, like his dark blue labourer's overcoat, added spice to his sexual capers. But in 1950 he wanted to lose every vestige of his past. His sudden awareness of serious limitations in his voice had been sparked by the elocution lessons he began in late April.

Orton chose a handsome lady who called herself 'Madame' Rothery to eradicate his Leicester accent. She came recommended by the Information Bureau and his former Clark's College teacher, Mrs Bish. 'I don't know why they called her "Madame",' Orton recalled in an interview in 1967. 'There was nothing Madamish about her at all. She was just an ordinary pompous middle-class lady.'[22] But at their first meeting, Orton's eyes were on his goal and not on her condescension:

> I went to see Madame Rothery at her house. We had a long talk about the scholarship, etc. She said that I could get a maintenance grant from the Education Committee to go to R.A.D.A. Then she said she would give me private lessons (fees 4 guineas per 10 lessons). I got £1 towards it and with my ten shillings spending money at the end of the week makes 30 shillings. But honestly don't know how I'm going to get the rest. I'm not going to ask Mum for anything at all because she can't afford it. Wrote a letter to the library about a job this evening.

The young man to whom Madame Rothery listened had not impressed her. 'He was just an ordinary, unsophisticated boy. I was quite staggered he wanted to go on the stage. His people were ordinary working-class people. There was no culture, no education. I felt sorry for him. Here's a boy that wants to do something. He's not got much talent, but I was out to help him.'

Whether Madame Rothery told Orton to his face that he had no talent (as she claimed) is unconfirmed in his diary. Perhaps an insult of that magnitude was too painful to include in those hopeful pages. His single-mindedness seems to have brushed aside her dismissive attitude while harbouring resentment about it. As Orton would tell it in later years, Madame Rothery left him with a painful impression of his own inadequacy:

> She didn't think much of me, just a yob, I could tell that. She offered coffee and I said yes, and she asked me did I take sugar and I

said yes; and she went away and came back with the coffee with sugar, but it wasn't sugar, it was saccharine in the bottom of the cup and so I thought, 'Oh yes, she's a right bitch', and she had these biscuits in a biscuit barrel, you know, these awful cheap biscuits. Oh, she didn't think much of me. She thought more of a pompous middle-class young man who was going to her because she thought he was going to be God's gift to the English stage. I was very glad to notice that he turned out to be a disaster. She had no taste.[23]

With success, Orton might let language get even for old wounds. But then, determined to make something of himself, he knuckled under to authority. Madame Rothery was the only architect of his hope. He needed to believe in her:

. . . Polished up my Ariel speech from 'The Tempest' and although the way Madame wants it isn't my way, it's coming on famously.

(17 May 1950)

The modesty of Orton's effort conflicts with his later memories of Madame Rothery's dismissal of his dreams: 'She'd always say "You'll have to try some other school like the Guildhall" and then she went even lower naming schools I don't think exist now.'[24] But his diary is only enthusiastic about Madame Rothery's suggestions:

Elocution lesson. Madame asked me if I would like to take the Guildhall exam or R.A.D.A. I plumped for R.A.D.A. Do hope I get it as it would show everybody that I can do something.

(21 September 1950)

Madame Rothery says I have improved considerably and would like to see me revise Ariel's speech (I did this for my very earliest elocution classes) to see if it has improved.

(23 June 1950)

The first tangible measure of improvement was a stage technical exam in mid-July. Orton was 'rehearsing like anything for it'.[25] He had chosen two pieces which indulged his appetite for fantasy and theatrical excess: a speech from J. M. Barrie's *Peter Pan* and one from A. A. Milne's *The Ivory Door*. He was uncharacteristically apprehensive. His fears were compounded when he watched another classmate rehearse her scenes from *Vanity Fair* and *Children in Uniform*. 'The reading really impressed me, if that is the competition I am up against, I don't think I shall go far.'[26] The exam tested not only Orton's ability, but the credibility of his dream:

Exam. Did feel scared. Felt just as if I was going to the dentist and was counting how many people had to go before me. Then came my turn. I told the girl in charge where to put the chair for *The Ivory Door* and then (with heart quaking) I went in and announced that I was doing a scene from *The Ivory Door* by A. A. Milne. The adjudicator said 'Thank you'. I did it without a blemish and went on with *Peter Pan*. Got through that. And imagine my surprise when the adjudicator said I'd got 70 marks out of 80. Wonderous.

(8 July 1950)

Orton inched closer to his goal:

Feel very elated as Madame Rothery suggested I should do my RADA entrance for January. Of course I've got a lot to do before that, but, oh boy, at last it's been mentioned. But before then I'm going to try for the Nottingham Festival of Music and Drama. Do hope that I get a chance to go on the stage.

(14 July 1950)

Orton won third place at the Nottingham Festival, teaming with another of Madame Rothery's pupils to do the Oberon–Titania quarrel scene from *A Midsummer Night's Dream*. They repeated the performance later in the year when Madame Rothery held an evening show to display her students not only to their parents but to the educational authorities. Emboldened by his success at Nottingham, Orton seized his opportunity.

I had a marvellous idea. I thought I'd play Oberon green, so I bought a lot of green distemper from the local shop. I'd no idea about stage make-up and put on a pair of bathing trunks and just covered myself from head to foot in green, including my hair, surprisingly I didn't get skin rash. Then, I got a green bedspread from my mother's and father's bed and wrapped that round me and appeared on stage in this fantastic outfit, the bedspread was covered with green distemper while the girl wore a conventional muslin ballet dress as Titania. Anyway, it was very successful because Madame introduced me afterwards to this man who was in charge of giving away grants. I had a long talk with him. He thought the performance was very interesting.[27]

The man also conveyed his enthusiasm to Mrs Orton. 'John is absolutely wasted in an office,' he told her. Elsie quickly countered: 'Well, I can't afford to send him anywhere.' The man explained about local grants. Later, the Leicester Educational Committee contributed a generous £310 a year to furthering Orton's education. It was the second acting grant ever awarded from Leicester.

Orton applied to RADA on 6 November 1950. Besides his stage technique exam, the only thing Orton could list under Special Distinctions or Examinations Passed was Pitman's shorthand 100 w.p.m. and typewriting 40 w.p.m. On his eighteenth birthday, Orton packed a small bag, took the train to London and did two auditions for RADA, one for entrance, the other for a scholarship. Once again, he brazened his way to attention. 'I did a piece from *Peter Pan* between Captain Hook and Smee, both at the same time, a kind of schizophrenic act.'[28] Like Hook, Orton felt himself handicapped; but he also had an innocence and sense of fun that fought against it. The Hook–Smee exchange contained the frenzy that always fired his imagination. 'It was quite alarming,' Orton recalled. 'It impressed the judges.'[29]

RADA accepted him. He went immediately to tell Madame Rothery. 'When I took the letter round to Madame she could hardly conceal her rage that I'd gotten in. She continued to be bitchy, because when I went to RADA I was supposed to have had eight lessons, actually I'd had seven, and she kept writing saying I hadn't paid her for the last lesson.'[30] Even now Madame Rothery disdains Orton's 'surprising' result: 'Fate was with us. It was just after the war and men were extremely scarce; so they would have taken practically anything that could stand up.'

Orton's success was dampened almost immediately by an appendicitis attack which made it impossible to begin RADA the next term. He would have to wait until summer. But no sooner had Orton come out of hospital than the prospect of attending RADA's summer session was jeopardized. The Army called Orton for his physical examination. A year before, Orton had welcomed the idea of a two-year National Service stint as a relief from the tedium of his job: 'Goodbye Fire Services, Army here I come!'[31] But now Orton plotted frantically. Leonie remembers: 'As the scabs from his appendix operation fell off the stitches, John was sticking them back on so the scar looked worse. He never smoked in his life, but he puffed cigarettes to try and bring on an asthma attack. When he went for the medical, he wanted it to seem as though he were dying.' The asthma, combined with his appendix and a fictitious hearing complaint, improvised on the spot in front of the Army doctor, convinced them that he was not military material. 'If the doctor could have seen me racing down the street after the exam,' Orton told his mother, 'he'd have fetched me back and passed me A-1.'

When Orton left Leicester for RADA, in May 1951 he closed the door on his past. Elsie cried for a few days after he'd gone. She confided to Leonie: 'I know I've lost him. I've lost my boy. He'll never, ever, come home again.' But Orton had never, ever, really been with the family. They loomed in his mind as vague and incidental intrusions, like extras in an epic. His absence was felt, but he felt no absence. 'Whenever John looked aloof, distant and off-hand it was in relation to his family,' Bernard Widdowson says. 'He used to dry up every time the family was mentioned.' Their long walks which wound their way along the High Street towards the Clock Tower and then to Victoria Park ended at the junction of the Saffron Lane Estates. 'Orton made it fairly obvious that this was as far as it went.'

Orton left a photograph of himself with the family; and Elsie quickly framed it and locked it in the china cabinet, where a few years later she enshrined his RADA diploma. The picture commemorated the new John Orton – composed, seasoned, too staunch and sleek to fail. The image fitted the pedestal on which Elsie placed him. The rest of the family carried with them warmer, happier images. Douglas remembers the fastidious John, the one his mother bragged was so well-kept and well-mannered that somebody had asked to adopt him. Douglas pictures him folding his clothes neatly on the bank of the canal before diving in. He sees him kneeling on the bank beside Leonie with a jam-jar and a net snaring fish he'd later try and keep alive in the bathroom tub. This is the 'Cut' Elsie shouted to the kids to keep away from and where Orton escaped for long walks. His brother throws their rust-red mongrel – Ronick – into the narrow, muddy canal to watch it swim. This was their childhood playground and, later, when Marilyn's six-year-old son drowned there, a landmark of the quiet harshness of their lives. Douglas laughs at the thought of John dressing him as a bear and making him parade in his living room Christmas pageant. John was always doing something 'strange', 'different', provoking this aloof family into gaiety.

Marilyn has memories of the weird mystery of John's 'lovely speech'. She remembers him on the bus coming home from Clark's College, his head bent over a book while the other boys giggle and joke around him. 'Nobody left an impression the way he did. You always wanted to live up to him after he'd left.' Leonie remembers Orton's dry laugh. How his head would jerk back, then the sudden flash of teeth, and finally he'd register his amusement with a sound as sharp and short as the clap of a hand. Leonie smiles at the memory of John filling her Christmas stocking. 'Whenever he bought you anything, it was good. He bought me *Alice in Wonderland*. It was a blue leather-bound.' She laughs at the recollected sight of John with her in tow stealing a copy of *Black Beauty* from the Bishop's Street Library where he spent so much of his time and where she almost gave him away. He read her Greek mythology and Oscar Wilde's *The Importance of Being Earnest*. She can still see John looking up from the play with an eyebrow arched in mock astonishment exclaiming in a fluting voice 'A handbag!'

Home was not where Orton's heart was. He had no sentimentality about family matters. When Marilyn's son died in 1965, he wrote her:

There's nothing I can write that will make any difference. I know how you must be feeling. Do understand that I would've come home if I'd known, and if there was anything I could've done . . . I haven't been told when the funeral is and I suppose it's over. I wouldn't send a wreath. I don't begrudge the money, but it seems a lot of show. Nothing can bring the kid back.

(31 March 1965)

Orton's aloofness was something the family understood and accepted. He wrote home frequently, but the family rarely answered. In 1962 Leonie started up a correspondence. 'He used to write me mother and me mother never used to write back. He kept writing and nobody answered.' Orton's yearly visits for a fortnight each summer were happy occasions, especially for Elsie. But they had the hurried, strained inadequacy of a conversation with a friend who was anxious to depart. When he was back with his family, Orton got up to his familiar pranks. He enjoyed turning off the television sound and laughing at the people on the screen who mouthed words like puppets on an invisible string. He took Elsie's women's magazines and got Leonie to read the questions on the problems page. Orton invented irreverent answers. He liked to outrage them with his loud clothes and brash claims. 'He reminded me of Cassius Clay,' Leonie says. 'He did actually say "I'm the greatest". So I says, "What about Shakespeare, then?" And John said, "I hope I never write first plays as bad as his . . ." '

Orton's excuse for cutting short his family holiday was always Kenneth. He declined every Christmas invitation because Kenneth would be alone. Elsie often suggested he return to live in Leicester. 'What's the attraction down there?' Orton smiled and said nothing. His first mentions of the mysterious 'Kenneth' were interpreted by

Elsie as another of her John's practical jokes. When Orton sent a picture of Halliwell, she was shocked by his baldness. 'What do you want to live with a bald man for?' Elsie asked him. Orton just laughed.

Kenneth Halliwell was Orton's emotional home, and that relationship began almost as soon as Orton found digs in London.

'Darling,' Orton wrote to Joyce Holmes, an aspiring Leicester actress on whom he had a crush, three weeks after RADA began, 'What do you think of "free love", I think it's cute. Some of the types in this place, seven-eighths of them look at you as if it's an insult to be a virgin (I'm still pure, but only just).' What Orton referred to as Joyce Holmes's 'virginal qualities' had appealed to him since he'd first met her at a Vaughan Players' rehearsal. Orton found her accessible, intelligent and irresistible. Bernard Widdowson, who often stood with Orton outside the second-floor window where she lived above her father's sweet-shop, says 'Orton had an almost unhealthy preoccupation with her. She'd gone, he mistakenly thought, to a convent school. That seemed to excite John more than anything'. They shared a love of theatre; and both had families that thought their interest 'daft'. Orton was swept up in the delight and excitement of the big city, and his gossip is filled with a timid lover's oblique affection. He wanted to encourage her to come to RADA. He'd already seen Alec Guinness in *Hamlet* and Orson Welles's *Macbeth*. 'He's supposed to have made it in 28 days, was quite surprised, thought he'd done it in two.' Orton's letter bubbles with gaiety. 'Wilfred Pickles and Mabel (Mabel Pickles sounds like something you have with cheese) came into the room last week as we were doing a queer class called movement, which consists of flopping about in the most obscure positions. The teacher, I am quite convinced, invented even more "obscure positions" just for Mr Pickles' benefit, they so damaged the bone structure of the class that six of them are in hospital and having their necks re-twisted and I have my left leg permanently round my right ear ... On Mondays, we have a sort of gym class. The teacher shows his legs and wears body make-up, he also makes obscene suggestions in a polite way. We have in the class something called "free running", not to be confused with "F.L." [Free Love].' Orton's tall talk tried to conceal his romantic interest, but it glowed through the bravado. 'I'm just longing to come home and see you, your company is so refreshing. I know you don't believe me, but then I'm always "misunderstood".' Orton asked for her photograph 'to keep the cats away' and signed off with 'Yours until I have a better offer'. The offer came soon enough.

Orton had acquired two room-mates: Lawrence Griffin and James Hilbern, an American acting student. They had basement digs at 31 Gower Street, two streets away from RADA. Orton quickly acquired a new style. He sent another photo of himself back to Leicester, a dramatically revised fantasy of the sophisticated actor John Orton. He was Dirk Bogarde in this one: white shirt opened 'naughtily' to the third button, tousled hair, mouth turned up in a tentative, new flirtatiousness. This was the first picture with a hint of sexuality. The family saw only the smiling, smooth face, not the naïve aspiring sex symbol. In July, during the summer vacation from RADA, Orton took part in the Vaughan Players' production of *Measure for Measure*, in which he was praised for his 'odious, fantastical Lucio'. He also kissed Joyce Holmes in the lighting booth, a curiously unsexual embrace that left her thinking 'He's just a boy'. By now Orton had found a lover more eager for his affection. His RADA diary tells the story in a style as teasing as his new photo. It would be the last entry before he became famous fifteen years later.

15 MAY 1951
Started at RADA O bliss!
16 MAY
Met Florentic G. A sister. You are she.
17 MAY
An actor's life for me.
18 MAY
Digs in Gower Street. Such fun.

19 MAY
Oh the larks.
Memo
Someone in the other class keeps looking at me.
20 MAY
Did nothing.
21 MAY
Mr Constable's special movement. Was eyed.
22 MAY
Florrie ate all the biscuits.
23 MAY
Florrie ate all the cheese.
24 MAY
Florrie ate all the eggs.
25 MAY
Met Ken and John at Charing Cross Road.
Memo
I don't quite understand Ken.
27 MAY
Did nothing.
28 MAY
Mr Constable's movement.
29 MAY
Florrie ate all the nuts.
30 MAY
Florrie ate all the bacon.
1 JUNE
Met Ken and John again. This time with Rex Butler.
2 JUNE
Flo rang Ken.
Memo
Am beginning to understand Ken.
3 JUNE
Did nothing.
4 JUNE
Mr Constable's movement. Well!
5 JUNE
Florrie ate all the cheese.

6 JUNE
Florrie ate all the cake.
7 JUNE
Fuck Florrie.
8 JUNE
Met Ken. He invites us to live with him.
9 JUNE
Went to the pictures.
Memo
I am puzzled.
10 JUNE
Did nothing.
11 JUNE
Must leave our digs.
12 JUNE
Ken offers to share flat again.
13 JUNE
I say No.
14 JUNE
Ken offers again.
15 JUNE
We accept because we must.
16 JUNE
Move into Ken's flat.
17 JUNE
Well!
18 JUNE
Well!!
19 JUNE
Well!!!
20 JUNE
The rest is silence.

3

UNNATURAL PRACTICES

> The solitary, in his own way a combatant, feels
> the need to populate his solitude with enemies,
> whether real or imagined.
>
> E. M. Cioran, *The Temptation to Exist*

> The citizens boo loudly, wave their banners.
> McTurk and Low turn and walk away. The gap
> between the citizens and the two boys widens.
>
> Joe Orton, stage direction in *Up Against It*

The English public first learned of Orton and Halliwell eleven years later in 1962. It was not exactly the debut they'd dreamt of. On 15 May the *Daily Mirror* devoted a banner headline to a story about a mischievous form of literary vandalism. Books from the Islington and Hampstead libraries were appearing on the shelves with photographs and book jackets humorously altered. The *Mirror* story was headed GORILLA IN THE ROSES, which referred to a monkey's head pasted in the middle of a rose on the cover of the *Collins Guide to Roses*. In Leicester the Orton family had skimmed the *Mirror* and all except William had gone to bed. He settled himself in front of the television. During the commercials, William picked up the paper again. He perused 'Gorilla in the Roses' expecting to find some gardening tips. When he read the small print, he rushed upstairs to tell Elsie. 'Our John's been nicked,' he announced. Elsie wouldn't believe it. She phoned the paper to confirm the story.

Orton, aged twenty-nine and described as a 'lens cleaner', had been arraigned with Kenneth Halliwell, aged thirty-five and a 'cleaner', at Old Street Magistrates' Court for stealing seventy-two library books and 'wilfully' (the word was carefully typed over 'unlawfully' in the court citation) damaging a number of books, which included the removal of 1,653 plates from art books. Total damage was estimated at £450. They had been sentenced to six months in jail.

The story was funny copy (reprinted by the *Reader's Digest* and featured in the other national English newspapers), but the scope of Orton's antics never got into print. The notorious 'gorilla' was a gibbon grimacing in wide-eyed terror. Its small pear-shaped head was in exact proportion to the rose stem, and the yellow petals curved snugly around its face like a bleached-blond bouffant. The juxtaposition was startling and disturbing. 'One of the greatest things at the trial, the greatest outrage, the one for which I think I was sent to prison, was that I had stuck a monkey's face in the middle of a rose,' Orton said years later. 'It was a very beautiful rose ... What I had done was held up as the depth of iniquity for which I should probably have been birched. They won't ever do that, so they just sent me to prison for six months.'[1]

Orton's jacket designs didn't stop at gardening books. In a critical study of the poet, a pot-bellied old man tattooed from head to toe and clothed only in a skimpy swim-suit stood stiffly beside the name JOHN BETJEMAN. The first volume of Emlyn Williams' collected plays had a curious repertoire of 'Knickers Must Fall', 'Up the Front', 'Up the Back', 'Olivia Prude', 'He Was Born Grey', 'Mr Winifred', and 'Fucked by Monty'. Instead of their photograph a biography of the Lunts had tacky Christmas figurines including a stuffed snowman, red and white reindeer, and two red and white does called Jill and Judy. In Alec Clunes's biography his face was replaced by a skull with a hole in the cranium. *Glok*, an American novel by Richard G. Stern, had its author as Hedda Hopper in one of her preposterous feathered *chapeaux*.

Orton remembered others. 'I did things like pasting a picture of a female nude over a book of etiquette, over the picture of the author who, I think, was Lady Lewisham. I did other things, very strange things. There was the business when I got the biography of Sir Bernard Spilsbury and there was an illustration, which said: "The remains discovered in the cellar at number 23 Rosedown Road". I pasted over the illustration, which was a very dreary one of a lot of earth, David's picture of Marat dead in his bath. It was in black and white. I left the original caption underneath. This picture of the corpse in the bath had quite an effect on people who opened the book.'[2] Orton's most successful paste-up illustration was of Dame Sybil Thorndike locked up in a cell as Nurse Edith Cavell. A man peeks surreptitiously through a window at her. But what he sees is Dame Sybil staring at the mammoth genitalia of a superimposed Greek torso. The caption reads: 'During the Second World War, I was working from dawn to dusk to serve the many thousands of sailors, soldiers, and airmen. American GI's came in shoals to my surgery and some had very peculiar orders for me.'

'I used to write false blurbs on the inside of Gollancz books,' Orton remembered. 'Because I discovered that Gollancz books had blank yellow flaps and I used to type false blurbs on the inside.' Halliwell told the police: 'I saw Orton typing on the covers of books. I read what he typed, and I considered it a criticism of what the books contained.'[3] The target for most of this mischief was Dorothy Sayers's Lord Peter Wimsey whodunits:

When little Betty Macdree says that she has been interfered with, her mother at first laughs [Orton wrote on the flap for *Clouds of Witness*]. It is only something that the kiddy had picked up off television. But when sorting through the laundry, Mrs Macdree discovers that a new pair of knickers are missing she thinks again. On being questioned, Betty bursts into tears. Mrs Macdree takes her to the police station and to everyone's surprise the little girl identifies P.C. Brenda Coolidge as her attacker. Brenda, a new recruit, denies the charge. A search is made of the Women's Police Barracks. What is found there is a seven inch phallus and a pair of knickers of the

kind used by Betty. All looks black for kindly P.C. Coolidge . . .
What can she do? This is one of the most enthralling stories ever
written by Miss Sayers.

It is the only one in which the murder weapon is concealed, not
for reasons of fear but for reasons of decency!

READ THIS BEHIND CLOSED DOORS. And have a
good shit while you are reading!

'My blurbs were mildly obscene,' Orton admitted. 'Even at the
trial they said they were only mildly obscene. When I put the
plastic covers back over the jackets you couldn't tell that the blurbs
weren't printed. I used to stand in corners after I'd smuggled the
doctored books back into the library and then watch the people
read them. It was very funny, very interesting.'[4]

Although Orton never admitted to it publicly – choosing to
emphasize his satire on pulp literature – he and Halliwell also jazzed
up many of the drab designs for the outstanding Arden editions of
Shakespeare with tactful collages from the art books they'd stolen.
Their cover for *Titus Andronicus* combines an opulent Renaissance
banquet in the foreground with two superimposed images of
Goya's *Saturn Devouring His Children* in the background. The visual
effect is shocking and strong. When tampering with Shakespeare,
they respectfully restored the name of the editor as well as the
title of the play on the cover. It was their disrespectful images that
scandalized the court. Birds' heads pasted over the faces of eminent
figures of Tudor history; monkeys adorning a book of exotic
caged birds; a cartoon cat's head featured as one of the schizoid
personalities in *Three Faces of Eve* – these typical grotesqueries as
well as the photographs of their collage murals in the bedsitter at
Noel Road led the prosecuting counsel to maintain to the magistrates: 'In some thirty years of experience I have never seen anything of this nature before.'[5] Most perturbing to the court was not
the abuse of private property but the care and intelligence with
which Orton and Halliwell tampered with the books. 'For some
reason which seems not to be clear,' the prosecuting counsel said,
'the two men had not only stolen the books but had caused the

most extraordinary damage to them.'[6] Orton and Halliwell never admitted their rationale for this prank to the court. The senior probation officer mentioned that 'in a sense both defendants were frustrated authors'.[7] Rejected by the literary world, they made a spectacle of published books and the public that evaded them. They turned the library into a little theatre where they watched people reacting to their productions. It was one way of getting into print and making their statement. There was sorrow in their anger, but also hilarity. In its ruthlessness, the caper displayed the solitary's groping to connect and the prankster's wish to turn the world into his playground. In later years, forgetting the debt he owed to the Leicester libraries, Orton used Good Taste as his explanation for defacing the books:

The thing that really put me in a rage about librarians was that I went to quite a big library in Islington and asked for Gibbon's *Decline and Fall of the Roman Empire*. They told me they hadn't got a copy of it. They could get it for me, but they hadn't one on their shelves. This didn't start it off, but it was symptomatic of the whole thing. I was enraged that there were so many rubbishy novels and rubbishy books. It reminded me of the Bible: 'Of the making of books, there is no end', because there isn't. Libraries might as well not exist; they've got endless shelves of rubbish and hardly any space for good books . . . You can obviously say when some things are rubbish and some things aren't. I can obviously say Gibbon isn't. He said a very funny thing about books: when the Arabs took Alexandria they used the contents of the library to provide fuel for the baths and Gibbon thought the books were doing more good being so used than they were being read . . .[8]

Halliwell smuggled the books in and out of the libraries in a service gas-mask case. Orton used a satchel. 'Ken would be with me on most occasions,' he told the police. 'I wouldn't know what he was doing, but when we got home, I'd show him what I'd stolen and he'd show me what he'd stolen.' When the police asked Orton why he'd done it, he replied: 'I wanted these books but haven't been able to afford them. That's why I took them.'[9] But, apart from the art books, most of the stolen titles were frivolous. The actual anarchic intention was spelled out in Orton and Halliwell's autobiographical novel *The Boy Hairdresser* (1960) when Donelly and Peterson confess to a female visitor to their room that they steal books:

'I think it's terrible,' she said.

'We're public benefactors in a way. We steal – the shops order more – the publishers are pleased – and everybody is happy. We finance literature. We are a sort of Maecenas.'

He kept his malice under control.

'You wouldn't even begin to understand the real reason why we do these things.'

'Do you understand yourself?'

She wandered around the room, touching things, wrinkling her nose in disapproval.

'Do you know what subreption is?' said Donelly.

'No.'

'To obtain something by misrepresentation. That is what our civilization does – it holds carrots in the air to make donkeys work. Do you know what it wants in exchange for a house, a car, a larger house, two cars, a television in every room?'

'No.'

'It wants our lives.'

Orton and Halliwell began stealing books in 1959. As they boasted in *The Boy Hairdresser*, they never expected to be caught. But the library had been quietly on the lookout for them for eighteen months. In January 1962 a branch librarian became suspicious of two men who always visited the library together and shared the same address. At the suggestion of the police, assistants from other library departments, who would not be recognized as staff, were posted as browsing readers at the time when Orton and Halliwell changed their books. According to an article in the *Library Association Record* about their prosecution, 'It was hoped that they would be caught red-handed illicitly replacing "doctored" books on the shelves. After several weeks of unproductive observation, we contrived to obtain a sample of typewritten matter done on a machine

belonging to one of the two men.'[10] The responsibility for out-
foxing Orton and Halliwell fell to the Islington Borough Council's
legal clerk, Sidney Porrett. 'I had to catch these two monkeys. I
didn't want the case. I had to get results,' says Porrett. 'I played
them a slightly dirty trick. I thought "OK, I'll let my ethics slip
a little bit". I wanted to get them aggravated. They were a couple
of darlings, make no mistake.' Porrett's letter was written in the
bureaucratic jargon which Orton and Halliwell hated.

15 Feb. 1962

Dear Sir,

Standard Vanguard – KYR. 450

The above numbered vehicle appears to be abandoned in Noel Road,
and I have been given to understand that you may be the owner
thereof. As you are aware, my council has recently been given power
to remove abandoned vehicles which obstruct the highway. But
before looking into the question of enforcing its remedies in the
matter, I give you the opportunity of taking the necessary steps to
cause the vehicle to be removed from the highway. I attach a notice
addressed to yourself in this matter.

Porrett's cagey letter flushed out an unexpected salvo from
Halliwell:

17 February 1962

Dear sir,

I should like to know who provided you with this mysterious
information?

Whoever they are, they must be a liar or a moron: probably both.

I have never possessed a car of any make whatsoever and never
wish to.

I can only presume that somebody is staging a leg-pull with you
or me or both.

I would suggest that in the future you obtain your information
from some more reliable source before pestering people with inexplicable letters.

Halliwell signed his letter 'Yours contemptuously'. But his type-
face matched the blurbs of the defaced books; and the police had

sufficient evidence to make an arrest. At 9 a.m. on 28 April 1962, Detective Sergeant Henry Hermitage and Detective Constable Gray knocked at Flat 4, 25 Noel Road. Halliwell opened the door. 'I said to him, "We are police officers and I have a warrant to search your flat as I have reason to believe you have a number of stolen library books". He said, "Oh dear".'[11]

'We think it was very naughty of you to send us that letter,' Orton told Porrett when he and Halliwell first stood before him. Porrett said to them: ' "I fetched myself down to your level. I'm quite happy to let you think I'm a fool, but I'm one step ahead of you all the time." It was just my psychological attempt to get on top of them. They realized they'd met somebody as cute as them. When I saw them standing there, I thought Orton was the over-grown schoolboy who was trying to draw attention to himself; Halliwell was the older, and, I would have said, the dangerous type. Deep-thinking. Surly. He couldn't look straight at you when he spoke. Both looked like a couple of silly boys lost.' Orton was never abused by the police, but he felt threatened. 'I wasn't actually beaten up,' he said. 'But they hovered around . . . I found that the best thing was to be as nice as possible and as utterly vulnerable as possible because it was no use standing on your rights once they've got you in their power.'[12] Privately, Orton contended that their severe sentence was 'because we were queers'.[13]

Orton did most of the talking about prison afterwards in public; but it was Halliwell, who then dominated the relationship, who spoke for them in court. They pleaded guilty to five counts of theft and malicious damage. Halliwell disputed the court's assessment of the damage of their prank. He also explained that, if each defendant were forced to pay £200 from their Post Office banking account the mortgage on their £2,000 flat would be jeopardized.

But the presiding magistrate – Harold Sturge – rebuked them sternly from the bench: 'What I am anxious to see is that the decision of this court should make it abundantly clear to those who may be clever enough to write criticisms of other people's books – public library books – or to deface them or ruin them in this way are made to understand very clearly that it is disastrous . . . I am most concerned about the malice shown by both of you in what you did – sheer malice towards fellow users of this library who, until these books are replaced, will be denied what they might have reasonably have expected to enjoy . . .'[14]

'Magistrate' would become a term of abuse in Orton's vocabulary – a word which epitomized everything quietly violent, sterile and inflexible in the English middle class. 'The kind of people that walk out of *Loot* in a rage are the kind of people that are magistrates,' he said years later. 'Now they can't do anything to me as the author of *Loot* but if I was up before them and I was the prisoner and they were the judge, they would be able to do something against me. I was exactly the same, though I hadn't written *Loot* and *Sloane*, and I was in the clutches of people who walked out of *Loot*. I mean, it was absolutely unforgivable. I'm not excusing myself, I'm just unrepentant.'[15] The trial festered in Orton's imagination. In *Loot* he dramatized the terror of being hamstrung by authority:

> *Door chimes.*
> FAY. Would you excuse me, Inspector?
> TRUSCOTT (*wiping his brow*). You're at liberty to answer your own doorbell, miss. That is how we tell whether or not we live in a free country.
> FAY *goes off left.*
> (*Standing over* HAL.) Where's the money?
> HAL. In church.
> TRUSCOTT *kicks* HAL *violently.* HAL *cries out in terror and pain.*
> TRUSCOTT. Don't lie to me!
> HAL. I'm not lying! It's in church!
> TRUSCOTT (*shouting, knocking* HAL *to the floor*). Under any other political system I'd have you on the floor in tears!
> HAL (*crying*). You've got me on the floor in tears.

Orton and Halliwell were taken first to Wormwood Scrubs and then sent to separate open prisons: Orton to H.M. Prison Eastchurch, Sheerness, Kent; Halliwell to H.M. Prison Ford Arundel,

Sussex. While at the Scrubs both men were interviewed by the resident psychiatrist. Halliwell told the truth; Orton did not. 'I didn't trust the psychiatrist because I knew anything I told him would be reported to the authorities.' Always a good actor, he charmed the psychiatrist. As Orton told it later, the psychiatrist confided to him 'I think your friend is homosexual'. 'You don't say,' Orton replied, his forehead wrinkling in amazement.

The moment was a rare flash of humour in an otherwise dismal situation. At the time, both Halliwell and Orton were mortified by their imprisonment. Orton would not allow his family to visit him; and Halliwell, writing to the caretakers of their building, the Cordens, confided, 'We have been utter fools and hope there will not be too much bad feeling about it when we return to Noel Road ... What a mess!'[16] Orton adapted to the situation more easily than Halliwell. 'I was locked in my cell for twenty-three hours a day. I used to have a half an hour's exercise in the morning and half an hour in the afternoon. Now this didn't worry me so much, but it worried a lot of other people. I used to read a lot. I didn't read the Bible which we were supposed to read. I read strange things like *Hatter's Castle*, the sort of thing I wouldn't normally dream of reading, cheap novels and capers ...'[17]

Halliwell was repentant; Orton was not. 'I'm afraid my tendency to get into hot water will never be entirely squashed', he wrote to the Cordens. 'However, I am treading very carefully here: I want to get out on September 14 – only forty-five more days.'[18] Characteristically, Halliwell was more tentative about the future. Disappointment had dogged his life too closely and too long for him to put complete faith in any expectation. 'Look forward to seeing you all for a more protracted period', he wrote to the Cordens. 'Though, of course, one never knows ... we are not quite out of the woods yet, though John may decide we are ...'[19] Both Halliwell and Orton tried to laugh away their incarceration. Their smiles were strained. 'Glad to hear of Miss Boynes' holiday', Orton wrote about the tenant below them at 25 Noel Road. 'I hope she had better weather than we're having here. I'm sorry I booked for so

long. I definitely shan't come again next year.'[20] Halliwell struck
the same jocular tone. 'As you will see from the address, John and
I are at present guests of her Majesty.'[21] To the Cordens, Halliwell
worried about the security of their flat ('Even convicts, I presume,
have their property under the protection of the law'), the electricity bills, the house provisions. Orton was not interested in the
minutiae of domestic details. Instead, his letters reveal a bumptious
energy, and anger at the manoeuvrings of the authorities which his
public statements about life in prison never admitted. When the
Borough Council tried to get money from Orton's and Halliwell's
savings accounts, Orton was up in arms. He wrote urgently to the
Cordens:

. . . This is, of course, the Islington Borough Council trying to pull
a fast one. Now I have NO intention of signing away any of my
money. I would be very surprised if Ken did either. You know he
thinks I'm a bit of an idiot. So will you write to him, tell him about
the letter . . . The thing to impress on Ken is I'm not signing anything! Of course I don't need to tell you not to let my bank book out
of your grasp. Guard it with your life. It's all the money I have in
the world . . .

I don't know how much you know. You may be completely in the
dark, but I'll try to do a little explaining. The Islington Borough
Council's lawyer wanted a fine, not a prison sentence. The magistrate
wisely and fairly, in my opinion, opted for a term of imprisonment.
The IBC threatened a Civil Case (they had their eyes on that money
acquired quite legally by Ken and myself. This new try-on is either
in lieu of a Civil Case or more likely an attempt to get the money
without the expense of having one. They know that once I get out
of here I shall withdraw my money. I hate to burden you with all
this, but I really feel so *angry*. Admittedly what I did is not to be
defended, but I'm paying for it here. They want me to come out of
prison literally penniless. Also they must imagine I'm a mental case
indeed if they think that kind of tactic is going to succeed with me.
Or Ken either, unless prison has altered him for the worse.

Anyway, once again, do write to him and let him know that I'm
too old, and after all this, too wise, to be caught that easily.

My mother said she read of the case in the *Daily Mirror*. Did you also? You must have read such a garbled account of it. I don't know what the *Daily Mirror* said. I would probably be extremely embarrassed if I did. I do hope it wasn't too sickening. I know what they make of the simplest case.

Once again, my apologies for not being amusing . . .[22]

Orton and Halliwell were scheduled for release on 14 September 1962. While still in prison, they received a summons to appear at the Clerkenwell County Court on 17 September. The Council had reduced the estimated damage of the books to £262; and they would have to pay it. Orton could hardly contain himself:

I had hoped to get out on the 14th and try to pick up the pieces and forget what had happened – however that is not now possible . . . Talk about the Hounds of Vengeance![23]

When Orton and Halliwell returned to their flat, it was stocked to order with their familiar and minimal necessities: half a dozen eggs, a pound of sugar, cheese, a large sliced loaf. Mrs Corden had even washed and pressed their sheets – symbolic, so she wrote, of the fresh start she hoped they would make. 'The future, if not rosy, at least will be bright.' (Mrs Corden decorated her language as absurdly as her flat. 'My vagina has come up the size of a football', she told Orton when he visited her in hospital after a spilt cup of tea had scalded her in the lap. 'The Matron of the hospital said to me that in all her years of medical experience she'd never seen anything like it. But I've no complaints. I've been given top-class penicillin.'[24])

At the court hearing, Orton and Halliwell agreed to pay £200 from their Post Office account immediately for damages. They went on the dole (and didn't come off the £3 a week allowance until 1964, when *Entertaining Mr Sloane* was an established commercial success). But Porrett wasn't finished with them. He had, as he says, 'another trick up his sleeve' to ensure that he got the remaining £62 in damages. He threatened them with a charging order which would give him power of sale over their mortgaged apartment to meet the unsettled debt. 'I wanted to let them know that I was still the governor in this matter. I was still that much on top.' From 1 January 1963, Orton and Halliwell agreed to pay £6 a month. 'They paid up like little darlings,' Porrett smiles. 'I left them financially pretty rocky.' In his final letter to Porrett on 4 December 1962, Halliwell hinted at a bureaucratic vindictiveness which Orton teased in later years when he'd pass Porrett in the street and offer him tickets to *Loot*:

I should like to point out that (as the employment situation looks at the moment) we shall be paying [the £6 a month] out of our National Assistance it will thus entail an element of real hardship.

For what was (surely?) a comparatively mild crime, we have thus:

a) lost our jobs and been thrown on the barest subsistence level of National Assistance.

b) done six months prison sentence.

c) paid practically all our pathetically small bank accounts.

Justice has certainly been done. Some people might think, perhaps, even a little bit *more* than justice.

Prison was more of a turning point in their life than either Orton or Halliwell at first admitted. Orton found a focus for his anger and a new detachment in his writing. For Halliwell, prison was more humiliating – a symbol of the larger pattern of defeat in his life. It made mockery of his dreams for himself, dreams which Orton had adopted in 1953. Within the year Halliwell would try to slit his wrists. Having once savoured the role of literary renegades, they now had bona fide criminal credentials. Their decade of disappointments had its consummation in their prison record. Failure was complete – they were now resolutely at the bottom rung of their society. Orton persevered because he expected nothing from life and was now strangely free of society's values. But Halliwell was stymied because, no matter how hard he tried, he could not forget how much he'd been led to expect and how dramatically these expectations had receded. As Donelly, Halliwell's surrogate in *The Boy Hairdresser*, taunted himself,

And so the gods distinction drew,
Good luck to art, a sod to you.

Charles Halliwell, Kenneth's father, was a man of few words and much responsibility. A chartered accountant, he was chief cashier at Cammell Laird and Co., one of Liverpool's biggest shipbuilding companies. His neat semi-detached house at 286 Heath Road, Bebington, was as tidy and sombre as he was. The furniture was heavy oak; the rooms were dark green. Kenneth Halliwell was brought up there; and when, at twenty-three, he took over the house, his next-door neighbours recall that he immediately painted the furniture and the walls bright colours. The bedroom became light pink; the dining room was papered with murals composed of art-book reproductions; the lawn was revamped to include a sunken garden. But no matter what hopeful veneer he gave to his house, there was no way of pasting over the past.

Halliwell had been a shy child. 'Kenneth tended to keep to himself. He was keen on dressing up and acting. He was a great reader,' remembers J. P. Howarth, who lodged with the Halliwells between Kenneth's seventh and eleventh year, 1933-7. 'Kenneth was very much a mother's boy. He tended to cling to his mother. If she came into the room, he'd come in with her and stay by her the whole time.' Daisy Halliwell was a stout, tall woman with a vibrant personality. 'She was a very cheerful and charming lady while Kenneth's father was a quiet, unassuming man with very little conversation. "I have to talk for both of us," she'd say when she was alive.' Daisy had wanted other children; but the Caesarean operation which brought Kenneth into the world on 23 June 1926 made it dangerous for her to have more. She pampered Kenneth and was ambitious for him. 'They talk of the silver cord between mother and son,' Mr Howarth says. 'Well, it would never have been severed between them.' It was broken off traumatically in September 1937, the month in which Kenneth started at the Wirral Grammar School. Daisy's gruesome, sudden death from a wasp sting was a profound shock to Halliwell and his father. 'Kenneth became very introspective and difficult to talk to,' Mr Howarth says. 'Obviously after his mother died, conversation between Halliwell and his father would have been very limited – just the essentials.' The next year

Halliwell ran away from home, the first of many dramatic exits. He left a rose and a note. Mr Howarth and Mr Halliwell found him sitting at a local restaurant where Kenneth and his father often had lunch together.

Halliwell's drastic measures could not earn his father's attention or love. His mother had pampered him, his father ignored him. They inhabited the same semi-detached house at Bebington in the Wirral, but they shared nothing. 'Mr Halliwell was a man I never saw smile,' Mr Howarth remembers. 'He had no warmth. He could never hold a conversation.' Typical of his habitual reticence, Mr Halliwell left no note for his son when he committed suicide. Halliwell could not love someone with whom he'd had only the meagrest relationship. When he discovered his father in the kitchen, Halliwell stepped over the body, turned off the oven and put on the kettle. After his morning tea and shave, he reported the suicide to the next-door neighbours.

'Kenneth never seemed young.' This is how Halliwell's neighbours, Mr and Mrs Noel Lacey, remember him. They watched him grow up, housed him briefly after his father's suicide and acted with him in amateur dramatic productions. Halliwell was often cast in older roles (he played Count Orsino in *Twelfth Night* at sixteen for the Carlton Players). He impressed people with his intelligence and precocity. He had been sobered by study and pain. He recast his sense of separation in a more heroic artistic mould. Halliwell excelled at school but stubbornly refused to continue his education at university. 'His classics master said that Kenneth was a born classical scholar,' says J. P. Howarth, who also taught at the Wirral Grammar School. 'And that he'd have no trouble getting into Oxford or Cambridge.' Halliwell was being groomed for the conventional English middle-class success; and he had the ability to achieve it.[25] Much was expected of him. His father wanted him to become a teacher; his mother had talked of her young son being a doctor. But Halliwell had decided on an acting career. To his father and relatives, who aspired to respectability, the idea was preposterous. But, convinced of his intellectual gift, Halliwell wanted to display it in a spectacular way. 'What wretched creatures we actors are', he observed, in his first play, *The Protagonist*, written in his early twenties about Edmund Kean. 'Our art has no existence until it is recognized. What was the use of my power when I could only display it before yokels? This is the end to which my being has been directed: the acclamation of the world and nothing less.' After leaving the Wirral Grammar School in 1943, Halliwell enrolled at the Liverpool Playhouse. He craved attention. His life had been touched early by grief, and he opted for glory to even the score. 'I have always challenged Fate,' Halliwell made Kean say in *The Protagonist*, 'I shall always challenge it.' Halliwell had a well-trained mind and an untutored heart. His fear of confronting the world was transformed into the heroic isolation of creative make-believe. He yearned for so much from life that only the imagination could satisfy the scope of his craving. Here, too, Kean spoke for him:

> I dreamed of a life of simplicity. But it was a sham. The only world for me is the world of make-believe. And to it I will return. Where else can I find anything that fulfils its promise? In my imagination only. In glorious make-believe.

Unlike Orton, who elbowed his way into minor parts, Halliwell was warmly welcomed into the Carlton Players. Male actors were at a premium in wartime. Between 1942, when he joined at the age of sixteen, and 1950, when he left for RADA, Halliwell would take prominent roles in twenty productions. He had been discovered by Roy Mothersole, a member of the theatre group, who had been teaching a class on verse drama at the Wirral Grammar School. Halliwell and another friend were the only two boys who showed talent. 'They were active homosexuals even then,' Mothersole recalls. 'They told me about the number of schoolboys they'd "had". Halliwell's friend was very handsome and blond. He was the extrovert. Halliwell was quiet. Even when he talked animatedly, he was detached and remote.' There was nothing effeminate in Halliwell's manner. When he talked, he craned his neck so that his head tilted back and his chin jutted out. It was a familiar posture and it gave him a haughty look. Halliwell spoke with authority (and, even then, could be bitchy), but he impressed the people around him as a gentle, mild person.

The Carlton Players rehearsed four nights a week; and when not performing, actors were put to use backstage. Halliwell was always around. He had found his calling and a real home. He helped build the Little Theatre, a three-hundred-seat house converted from an old church, which was to house the group after 1950. Halliwell fastened on to the leaders of the Carlton Players, Edna and Harold Rowson. They appreciated his intelligence and put it to use for the Carlton Players. 'Kenneth had a terrific sense of humour,' Mrs Rowson recalls. 'He always found the most unusual angles on his part. He had a terrific sense of the ridiculous. He was an exceptionally good actor by any standard. He used to get right into the heart of a character. He was wonderful to act with. He gave so much.'

Their faith was rewarded with loyalty. 'He was always very sympathetic if you were troubled or upset or if anything went wrong,' Mrs Rowson says. When she broke her foot during rehearsals of Road to Rome in 1943, Halliwell arrived at her home every night with his bicycle and wheeled her to the theatre and back. A conscientious objector to the war, Halliwell became a 'Bevan boy' in 1944, working in the coalmines at Wigan, Lancashire. He hated it. On his first day in the pits he adopted a Lancashire accent in an effort to be accepted by the miners. He could not drop the masquerade and was trapped in a permanent Lancashire performance. 'Kenneth came back once to see us while he was in the mines,' recalls Mrs Rowson. 'It had a terrible effect on him. He couldn't bear the darkness and the claustrophobia. He was suicidal.'

Halliwell ran away to Scotland, the first of a long list of retreats from his ideals. He had a hunger for victory but not the stamina for battle. He acted with the Perth Repertory Company for a few months, and then took a more permanent job with the Dundee Rep.

Halliwell returned to his home in Bebington in 1946. His hair had receded dramatically, giving him an austere, adult and jowly presence. The hardships of a wartime economy and the routine slog of repertory had given Halliwell an appetite for leisure and luxury. After his father died in 1949, he could afford to indulge himself. His father had left him £4,321. A man of independent means, he started to enjoy himself. He hired a housekeeper (he could never keep them long), dressed himself in expensive clothes, including a camel-hair overcoat with sash belt that he draped over his shoulders at rehearsal, and settled down to become a writer. 'He gave the impression he didn't need to work,' Mrs Rowson says. 'We felt this was a pity. If he hadn't had so much money and had to earn a living, he might have stuck at acting and made more of a success of his career. When he came home after the war, he said to us "I'm fed up with theatre. I'm getting down to writing." He was terribly dedicated.' (Occasionally, he would tell friends he was writing an article for *Reader's Digest* or that Heinemann's was interested in a novel. But nothing came of it, and none of his acquaintances saw the work.) The only writing he showed was *The Protagonist*. It was the first play ever written for the Carlton Players, but it was never put on. The play strained and sank under the ponderous weight of its pretensions.

On stage, Halliwell could connect with people where in life he kept his distance. 'There was something bottled up in Kenneth that prevented him from fully expressing himself like other people do. He would go so far and then the shutters would come down,' Mrs Rowson says. 'There was a barrier between Kenneth and the world, something you couldn't penetrate. A separation from people.' Theatre was the bridge not only to people but to emotions. As a stage character, Halliwell could 'lose himself'; and this unleashed powerful, disturbing passion that he kept otherwise well guarded. Halliwell defended himself against betrayals. Off stage he was 'retiring'; but on stage he was outgoing and capable of terrifying displays of aggression. In *Judgement Day*, a courtroom drama by Elmer Rice, Halliwell was cast as the lawyer for the prosecution, a role in which his suppressed anger had a field day. 'I played opposite him and I didn't have to act. He scared the living daylights out of me,' remembers Sylvia Sargeant. 'Halliwell had the ability to draw fear out of anyone.' The production was voted the best of the year (1950) by the local press, and Halliwell received special attention:

I doubt if Kenneth Halliwell has ever done better than he did in this fiery role as that of the prosecuting counsel. Here was a part that called for an actor who could dominate the stage. Here was an actor who could do it.

(*Birkenhead Adventurer*)

By 1950 Halliwell had had two other theatrical successes. He was amusing as Shipuchin in Chekhov's *The Anniversary* and terrifying as the sinister escaped criminal in Clemence Dane's *Granite*. Bolstered by his success, he shelved his literary aspirations and applied to RADA in mid-August 1950. He was hoping to win a scholarship for the autumn term. It was an impulsive decision, and Halliwell's application was far too late to be considered. He had to reapply for an audition in December. Halliwell did not need a scholarship; but he promoted the myth of himself as an impecunious orphan. 'If I am not good enough to win an outstanding scholarship with maintenance to live in London,' he wrote to RADA with a familiar hint of arrogance, 'I could not consider going to the Academy.'[26] What Halliwell wanted was some tangible confirmation of his talent from the most prestigious of English drama schools. Everyone who acted with Halliwell anticipated his success. He auditioned again in January, the same try-out at which Orton won a place. He did a scene from *Pygmalion*. But he did not impress the judges. The rejection flummoxed him. He wrote to RADA asking for explanations, a plaintive insecurity beneath his questioning. 'I wished to enter for the Scholarship test and then to be given as good a Scholarship as they thought me worth. Or did they not think me worth any scholarship of any degree?' And he went on to flap at the registrar: 'I should like to know whether my age is against me. Because if so, it will be little use my going in for it again in April when I will be three months older.'[27]

Halliwell 'discovered' an aunt in Clapton whose hospitality in London, he claimed, would allow him to apply for a scholarship without maintenance. (When he moved into London, Halliwell bought his flat at 161 West End Lane, West Hampstead.) By the April 1951 audition, Halliwell had dropped the pretension to a scholarship.

'Who Pays the Fee to RADA' asked the school questionnaire of its new students. 'Self' Halliwell had written on 15 May, the first day of term. His success was somewhat dampened in his eyes by his fee-paying status. But he still made his exit from Cheshire as dramatic and portentous as possible. Abandoning his first directing assignment, he left the Rowsons a note of resignation and farewell:

> I have been accepted at RADA, and I am going.
> I am terribly sorry for letting you down.
> I cannot tell it to your face.

Halliwell wrote to the Rowsons from London, and at first his letters from RADA were posted on the Green Room bulletin board and read by the company. He was the first and last of their eager group to reach RADA. In one letter he said 'I shall never return to that muddy little town beside the Mersey'. He kept his promise. Halliwell never saw the Rowsons or Bebington again.

RADA was not a happy time for Halliwell. His theatrical experience had been primarily with adults; now he found himself surrounded by less tolerant and more talented teenagers. 'Halliwell was an old man to us,' remembers June Clark Howarth, who acted opposite him in *Wild Decembers*. 'Most of the girls and boys were seventeen or eighteen. I thought Halliwell was much older than twenty-five. He looked easily between thirty and thirty-five. He was very bald and very dark; only one other actor in the school was bald. I suppose we were a little afraid of him.' Halliwell was victimized by his moods, which aggravated his reputation for ominousness, and his isolation. There was no warmth or simplicity in his personality. When one young actress, Diana Scougall, teased him before a rehearsal and pulled his tie, Halliwell slapped her. In an acting class, he shocked both the students and the teacher with the anger behind his improvisation. 'Halliwell acted a scene with an imaginary cat. He began by loving the cat. He was nice to the cat. A plaything,' recalls his teacher Mary Phillips. 'Then his expression changed, and he strangled it. Everyone was horrified. It was so unexpected. There was a laugh from him.' Halliwell's displays of anger were memorable. 'He would colour up,' says June Clark Howarth. 'You could see him grow gradually pink, working its way from his neck to the shiny part of his dome. All the muscles around his mouth would tighten. Then he'd go red. It would highlight his five o'clock shadow.' Students kept their distance.

Halliwell affected a sinister superiority. His suits were invariably grey or black pin-stripe, worn with black tie, black beret, and gabardine raincoat. The shaved head, the padded shoulders, and the lifts built into the black crepe soles of his shoes were calculated to make him look imposing. But Halliwell's personality was completely at odds with his presentation. 'He was perpetually wiping the palms of his hands with a handkerchief,' Margaret Whiting remembers. 'He was always sweating. Clammy hands. His handshake was weak, absolutely desperate. He never stood still when you spoke to him. Very nervous. Never looked you straight in the eye. Very unrelaxed. He did anything to make himself appear bigger.' The same deadly insecurity was in his conversation. He saw himself as a wit and a great actor. 'He gave the impression that he was better than anyone else at RADA,' says Lawrence Griffin, who moved with Orton into Halliwell's apartment in 1951. 'He used to criticize the other actors who got parts that he thought he could do better. Halliwell had the idea that he'd win the Bancroft Medal for the outstanding performer.' He didn't. Margaret Whiting (who acted opposite Halliwell in *The Brontes*) won the prize in Halliwell's and Orton's year. 'In *The Brontes* Halliwell was so self-conscious he could hardly bear to do mime,' Margaret Whiting says. 'He always surprised me with that. Ken, who thought he was such a wit, who sent up other people unmercifully at their expense, wouldn't come out of his extraordinary shell. When it came to being really inventive from within, to exposing himself, he just couldn't do it. After listening to his palaver, the incessant talk of ambition, ambition, ambition, when he got up to perform you were looking at a shy, very inhibited, self-conscious little man.' Halliwell was too defensive to 'give himself away'; his various postures only made his emotional impoverishment more blatant. 'His voice was dreadful,' Margaret Whiting says. 'The quality of his sound was terrible. It happens with a lot of actors. They get nasal strangulation. Tension. I remember in *The Brontes* Ken couldn't get his elbows away from his body. You see a lot of bad actors do this. They imprison themselves. He was terrified to let go.' Wrapped in his fantasy world, Halliwell dreamed of glory and talked for victory. But his tantrums were a signal of an undisciplined and uncreative imagination. 'You don't behave like that if you have any kind of ability,' Margaret Whiting says. 'If you've got ability, you're too busy working on it.'

Orton was not frightened or put off by Halliwell. He was also having a difficult adjustment to RADA. 'I completely lost my confidence and my virginity' was Orton's summary of his first term. 'I was lost. I didn't have a very good time because I found that in the very first term that I wasn't learning anything.'[28] A provincial boy whom his classmates saw as a 'lad', Orton was learning more about life and literature from his surly new adult acquaintance. They were a curious combination. 'Orton was the bubble,' June Clark Howarth recalls. 'Halliwell was the drag.'

The greatest impression Orton and Halliwell made at RADA was on each other. Neither had previously been able to sustain a close relationship. Both were disgruntled and lonely. Each filled an absence in the other's life. Halliwell found in Orton a surrogate brother, a companion who looked up to him, who needed him, who had faith in his intelligence and his aspirations. Orton was good company: a buoyant, inquisitive chatterbox who was also a good listener. Boyish and handsome, his features had aspects that matched with astonishing coincidence the idealized beauty Halliwell had imagined in Edmund Kean: 'he is pale, with untidy black hair, and large, smouldering black eyes'.

In Halliwell, Orton discovered someone who could be both father and friend: an authoritarian figure older and wiser in the ways of the world, who shared his interests and was prepared to engage in an unequal but enthusiastic dialogue. Each answered a crucial need in the other: Halliwell offered knowledge and stimulation, and Orton gave attention and good spirits. Orton came to understand the sibling overtones in their relationship. In the stage version of *The Ruffian on the Stair* (1967), Orton makes it explicit by having Wilson, the grieving friend, talk about his 'brother' in a very moving autobiographical fragment of dialogue:

MIKE. It's the Assistance Board . . . They say my circumstances have altered. I haven't any circumstances to alter. They should know that. I've filled in a form to the effect that I'm a derelict.

WILSON. Yes. My brother and me had the same trouble . . . We lived in Shepherd's Bush. We had a little room. And our life was made quite comfortable by the N.A.B. for almost a year. We had a lot of friends. All creeds and colours. But no circumstances at all. We were happy, though. We were young. I was seventeen. He was twenty-three. You can't do better for yourself than that, can you? (*He shrugs*). We were bosom friends. I've never told anyone that before. I hope I haven't shocked you.

MIKE. As close as that?

WILSON. We had separate beds – he was a stickler for convention, but that's as far as it went. We spent every night in each other's company. It was the reason we never got any work done . . .

Halliwell was seven years older than Orton. Despite the gap in sophistication and accomplishment, it was Orton, not Halliwell, who was chosen to perform in the public show at the Phoenix Theatre at the end of their two-year course. Halliwell – 'the stickler' – was well-intentioned, earnest, hard-working and wooden on stage. He had not stunned RADA; rather, he had been stunned by it. A sense of umbrage seeps through the right-mindedness of a letter to the registrar explaining why he will not attend the final fortnight of his RADA training:

> . . . As I am not in the public show, I intend to get on with the serious business of getting a job . . . I remain convinced that there is nothing further to be gained in the next ten days, and that I am therefore 'doing the right thing' . . .[29]

Halliwell's teachers at RADA were never convinced of his ability. Actors are technicians of the spirit; and from the beginning, Halliwell was inaccessible to himself. The RADA reports charted Halliwell's physical and imaginative limitations – characteristics of a personality that could never free itself from emotional impoverishment. Halliwell's voice was marked by monotony and heaviness. 'A good natural voice, plenty of power', said his voice coach in the first term. 'He must acquire more lightness of touch, variety of pace.' He could analyse a character but never successfully breathe life into it. 'Seems to be unconvinced that acting is the expression of emotions', observed one acting coach in Halliwell's last year. 'The result is that his approach is all mental – giving a tight, almost prim aspect to his work. I should like to see a more *generous* attitude of mind developing with this student in relation to his ideas of acting. A good student with a keen sense of wit – if not real humour. Must not be *afraid* of acting.' On graduation Halliwell received the Certificate of Merit, which was given to students who had passed the course but fell below the RADA standard as actors. In awarding Orton his Diploma, the first words of RADA's Principal, Sir Kenneth Barnes, were emphatic: 'He has talent.' From Orton's first term, his teachers reacted to him with enthusiasm. 'This boy has vitality and imagination'; 'His performance as the Ancient Trajanos was very attractive. A promising student'. The word 'promising', like the words 'imagination' and 'talent', was never used about Halliwell. Orton's boyish playfulness earned him the role of Feste in *Twelfth Night* in his first year. Orton had a clown's gift of impersonation. He was a good mimic. 'Good sense of character', wrote the director. 'But the work lacks strength. There is a sad note to your personality which must be held in check.' Orton's sense of isolation and his urgency to recoup his life from its barren beginnings would linger beneath the hilarity in all his plays. His teachers remarked on his diligence, describing him as 'extremely keen', 'very hard-working', 'quick to learn'. There was something unshaped, amorphous in his personality which was conveyed on stage. 'A fluid, flexible youth who might turn into anything.' Orton was inventive and uneven in his work, but, according to the director who worked with him when he played Richard in *Ah! Wilderness* in his fifth term, 'at all times interesting to watch – either in rehearsal or performance'. One other trait, mentioned in his last term at RADA, contrasted dramatically with Halliwell's reports: 'Can be very funny'.

Language, at first Orton's bogey, became his obsession, and finally his triumph. 'At present,' wrote an instructor in his last term at RADA, 'he has little knowledge or control of variety of speech – range of tone – timing . . . etc.' Part of the vindictive gusto of his comedy would be strutting his mastery over the mother tongue. At RADA, 'general tendency towards flatness and monotony' was the consistent complaint of his voice teachers. Orton's frustration took the form of mockery.

By the fifth term at RADA I'd got very cynical [he recalled in 1967]. I remember doing a diction test. It was the Buckingham speech from *Henry VIII*. Well, I thought it was silly being sincere about a thing like that, so I just did it on a purely technical basis, booming in a parody of the RADA manner. I won the diction test, and I got congratulated, all the teachers coming up to me and saying it was 'marvellous'. This was terrible because I knew it wasn't. It was a fool of a thing to do. I went on like this for the next term, doing absurd caricatures of the RADA voice and the RADA manner. This was of course before the new style at RADA, and I got into the public show. I played Bates in *Venus Observed*. Did absurd things. Wore absurd costumes which were quite wrong. I looked like a sort of gay girl out of a 1920 revue.[30]

Orton took his acting career more seriously than he recounted it in hindsight. Billing himself as John K. Orton, he went to the Ipswich Rep as an assistant stage manager immediately after graduating from RADA. Halliwell had to settle for a less reputable summer season in a resort town on the Welsh coast. He had taken the name Kenneth Marlowe. 'I am doing quite nicely here', he wrote to the RADA registrar from the Grand Theatre, Llandudno, explaining his absence from RADA's prize-giving. 'We only do 6 performances a week – at 8 p.m. And am this week playing the juvenile lead in "Quiet Wedding". But I shall not be staying here very long as the future list of plays to be done is quite beyond the pale. And at this stage in one's career the experience of acting in tolerably good plays is of primary importance.'[31] The idea of Halliwell in a juvenile lead as misguided as his visions of theatrical stardom. He would get no more stage work after the summer.

Orton's experience was also disheartening. 'Repertory is terrible', he said, recollecting his four months at Ipswich between April and July 1953. 'It so lacks ideas. Most people have bad ideas, but at least they're their own. The people in rep have just none at all.'[32]

'I did a lot of moaning'[33] is how Orton remembered his Ipswich experience. For an aspiring and impatient actor, the lot of the assistant stage manager was not a happy one. 'We spent most of our time trudging the streets of Ipswich looking for props,' recalls Rosalind Knight, who shared ASM chores with Orton and went on to an acting career. She remembers Orton as sallow, spotty, and sniffling from a perpetual cold. 'John wasn't very good at getting the props or doing the work. He never got cross. He was just lackadaisical.' In later years Orton quipped that the only thing the Ipswich Rep taught him 'was not to write in too much business about drinks or telephones in a play because it is so awfully hard on the assistant stage managers to have to fix all that sort of thing'.[34]

After each show, Orton would go back to his boarding house

with the stage manager, Jack Payne, and read Shakespeare into Payne's tape-recorder, a novelty in 1953. 'The particular parts that delighted Orton and which he never tired of repeating were Puck and Ariel. We also had great fun doing the Bottom scenes from *A Midsummer Night's Dream* in which we did all the voices between us, imitating the dreadful accents. Orton would roar with delight at the playbacks.' Orton spent a lot of his free time in long conversations with Payne. Orton's talk was frank and barbed. He made no attempt to hide his homosexuality but he was not camp. Payne, who was much older than Orton, was a great source of theatre lore and gossip. 'Orton would always urge me to tell him more – whether about the history, the technique, or the current theatrical scene,' Payne says. 'He was only twenty, but I was still impressed by his knowledge of subjects unusual for a boy his age. His knowledge of Greek gods and goddesses took me by surprise.' Orton was the youngest occupant of their boarding house; and the landlady fussed over him. Orton was always polite and well-mannered around her. She loved it and responded by overfeeding him. 'I remember once Joe couldn't finish his plate of food and scraped it under a bush in the garden. The landlady discovered the food next day and collared the four tenants for an explanation. Joe just grinned quirkishly. Nobody squealed.'

Too young and inadequate an actor to get major roles, Orton was also too ambitious and full of fun for the arid grind he discovered was the regimen of the rep actor. His contract at Ipswich was not renewed. 'I was bored,' he explained later. 'I left the theatre and got married.' Orton was never married except in his imagination. 'I was too young,' he told interviewers. 'We just drifted apart.'[35] He was twenty; and his 'bride' was now twenty-seven and totally bald.

Orton had originally moved into Kenneth Halliwell's apartment in West Hampstead with Lawrence Griffin and Maxwell Burten-Shaw, another RADA student from their class and a former ballet dancer. It was a comfortable arrangement and a great improvement

over Orton's previous cramped cold basement digs. Halliwell's
home reflected his age and his urbane image. To Orton, it was
impressive. Halliwell owned what most people in Orton's life had
had to borrow: his house, his books, his records. Instead of the
usual cooking ring, Halliwell had a kitchen set apart from the
living room by louvred doors. He knew about wines; and he cooked
for his flatmates, not the meat and mussel pudding which Orton
was used to, but continental dishes. Halliwell charged thirty shillings
a week, a pittance compared to the £2 10s. Orton had agreed to
pay the landlord of his first flat thinking it was the entire rent instead
of the price per man. Griffin and Burten-Shaw slept on sofas in the
living room; Orton shared Halliwell's double bed. 'In the beginning,' Lawrence Griffin recalls, 'most of the feeling came from
Halliwell to Orton, not from John to Ken. John just accepted it
because it was nice digs, a nice situation to be in. He must have
liked Kenneth Halliwell. He'd do anything Kenneth wanted him
to.' Burten-Shaw saw Halliwell as the dominant force. 'Ken was
the much stronger personality, very much *I* am and will be and
you will one day work for me. John had much more depth but was
uncertain of himself and prepared to be led.'

In Orton, Halliwell sensed a perfect companion. He used to
stroke Orton's sleek head in front of Griffin and call him 'my pussy-
cat'. Halliwell played the man of the world, and Orton was
impressed. Halliwell tried to mould Orton into the Ideal Friend.
'Halliwell was like a Svengali to John,' recalls Griffin. 'He took
John over. It was as if he were playing God. When they went
shopping, he'd suggest that John buy certain colourful clothes. He
showed John what to wear, what to read, where to go.' Halliwell
spent his money as well as his attention on Orton. Since Orton only
had his £300 grant for tuition and living allowance, Halliwell subsidized their frequent excursions to the theatre, concerts and movies.
(Anna Magnani, the flamboyant Italian actress, was one of their
favourites; and Halliwell claimed her as the major influence on his
acting.) But Halliwell's generosity was already matched by fits of intense moodiness. 'Orton put up with more than I would,' Lawrence

Griffin says. 'Halliwell would arrange things and everyone had to fit in with what he wanted. Even when we'd planned to go to the movies, if Kenneth decided to stay in, Orton would stay with him. He was very loyal to Kenneth.' Sometimes shouting matches flared up within earshot of the other flatmates. 'They'd argue because they weren't having sex. Kenneth wanted to, and John refused,' explains Griffin. 'Kenneth was a little sadistic with him. He could be cruel. He could laugh at other people's misfortune.' But Orton wasn't put off. Always the flirt, Orton was flattered by Halliwell's affection – he was the first person to pay him serious sexual attention. They became constant companions, each buoying up the other's fantasy of himself. 'They looked upon themselves as being very special,' remembers Lawrence Griffin. 'They had the idea they were going to be brilliant actors. Sometimes I used to feel the odd one out, they practically convinced me they were so good.' Halliwell was unsure of Orton and very possessive. At parties he gave in his flat and at the Rising Sun, Halliwell kept a careful eye on Orton and separated him from other men in whom he showed interest. Orton didn't bridle at this intrusion. 'Halliwell was useful. He provided a base Orton could go back to,' Lawrence Griffin says.

Writing, like most things at the beginning of their relationship, was Halliwell's idea. He was working on a novel when Orton moved in; and before long, Orton was seated at the living room table contributing to Halliwell's effort the only literary skill he possessed: his typing. But as Orton transcribed Halliwell's novel, he would make suggestions. Halliwell found them useful and incorporated them into his work. By including Orton in his literary ambitions, he was also binding him closer to his life. He was never threatened by the idea of a collaboration because there was never any doubt who was the writer. Halliwell was the man with the vocabulary, the tenacity, the sense of literary tradition. Orton had only his curiosity and enthusiasm. Following Halliwell's lead, Orton began to write material to perform at his RADA diction classes. 'I never wanted to be a writer, I always wanted to be an actor,' Orton recollected later. 'But then I found that I had a talent for writing.' His talent existed at first solely in the eyes of Kenneth Halliwell.

When their acting careers had sailed rapidly into still water, Orton and Halliwell fell back on writing. For a few months after Orton returned from Ipswich in 1953, he and Halliwell took refuge from their repertory disappointments in the idea that they would work in the West End. Halliwell organized auditions for them with H. M. Tennent Ltd, the producers who dominated London's commercial theatre and who, in 1969, would be co-producers of the posthumous production of Orton's *What the Butler Saw*. They organized a portfolio of photographs and found themselves an agent, whose homosexual connections Halliwell assured Orton were bound to get them work. But they got nowhere, and gradually their energy and their dreams shifted from the stage to the page.

They set about their collaboration with typical single-mindedness, Orton's coltish high spirits matching Halliwell's adamantine will. Orton's talent had never found its focus at RADA. 'Is inclined to give the impression of being casual about his work', Sir Kenneth Barnes concluded about Orton in his final RADA report. 'He is young, and I think he will realize how essential it is – having talent, to do his best to make it evident to others by careful application and whole-personality concentration.' Halliwell's partnership provided what Orton blatantly lacked: discipline. The business of reading and writing had a renegade appeal to two people so convinced that they were special. Orton had always hated the tedium and waste of the workaday world. Halliwell's intellectual prodding and financial support bolstered Orton's determination not to succumb to convention. 'Men and women who work in shops, factories and offices are prostitutes slaving for a super pimp', says the shrill anarchist Donelly in *The Boy Hairdresser*, demolishing Peterson's vague yearnings for a more respectable life. Like the mates in *Loot* and the brothers in *The Ruffian on the Stair*, Orton and Halliwell set out together with 'no prospects' and 'no circumstances'.

In order to save Halliwell's dwindling inheritance, they instituted an ascetic regime. They kept electricity to the minimum, choosing to rise with the first morning light and go to bed at dusk. They wrote in the morning. Their afternoons were spent reading and, when the weather was good, sunbathing. Sometimes they'd borrow large books from the library, like Gibbon or Lady Murasaki, and read to each other. They lived on £5 a week. Their routine was modified between 1957 and 1959 when they worked half of each year (earning £30 a week) at Cadbury's to buy a new flat. Orton loaded boxes of chocolates; Halliwell did clerical work. 'Went back for a fortnight's work at Cadbury's', Halliwell wrote to friends in 1959 from their new address in Noel Road, Islington. 'Could not stand it. Don't know how one stuck it before. I shall go to the Labour Exchange in due course and register for 'clerical work'. I hope they can't give me any, and then they will have to pay us dole and National Assistance; but I fear they can probably always find one a job of some kind.'[36]

Orton and Halliwell were drop-outs before the fall-out of Beat literature in the 1950s filtered down through English society, and made it modish. They questioned the culture's values but absorbed its literary traditions. It was a hermetic existence, at once a pleasure and a necessity. Neither their identities nor their literary style was strong enough to venture into a society that threatened and angered them. Their solitude was a barometer of their vulnerability and suspicion. It also became a consolation for literary failure. 'I don't know if you have any convictions about the way life is run: its inexorable rules and so on', Halliwell wrote to Charles Monteith, an editor at Faber and Faber, after the publishing house had rejected his novel *Priapus in the Shrubbery* (1959). 'Personally, I am convinced that "what you lose on the swings, you gain on the roundabouts" and vice versa. So it would, quite frankly, not be in the logic of things for John and I to have much success in any sphere. We live much too comfortably and pleasantly in our peculiar little way.'[37] Monteith had been interested in their writing since 1955, when they submitted *The Last Days of Sodom* to Faber. He had passed the manuscript on to Richard Brain, at Hamish Hamilton, who also found it interesting but too rarefied for publication. They arranged to meet Orton and Halliwell. 'They seemed as strange as their writing,' Richard Brain recalls. 'I quite soon got the impression that this was the oddest pair of people I'd met.' Halliwell wore a beret to the rendez-vous on 4 January 1956, at the Imperial Hotel in Russell Square. 'They more or less intimated that they were at a loss. This was the first time they'd met strangers by arrangement,' Charles Monteith remembers. 'I had a very clear impression at the first meeting that Kenneth was the one that did the writing. Kenneth was the talker. He liked to turn words around and savour them. Kenneth's talk, his appearance, his age *vis à vis* Orton certainly gave the impression that Kenneth was the literary figure. I thought that John was quite simply his young, pretty, and rather vivacious boyfriend. It took me some time to see that John was more than an acolyte of Halliwell's.'

Having befriended them, Monteith gave a party for Orton and Halliwell the next year. 'I realized that they had no friends whatsoever. The purpose of the party was to let them meet people who had influence in the literary world. It was a big party. They sat on the sofa the whole evening and didn't speak to anybody. Halliwell and Orton were hopeless socially. The party was a total flop.' Halliwell laid the blame for their social awkwardness on their solitary life. 'We are just no good at parties', he wrote to Monteith on 22 May 1957. 'Personally, if there are more than six people in a room I just feel confused. There are prices one must pay for leading a hermit's existence, however happy.' Throughout the letter, Halliwell had emphasized 'I', but signed it 'Believe us'. This was typical. 'They were two people with the same voice by then,' says Richard Brain. 'There was never any dissension or disagreement.' The hermetic life was a united front against an untenable world. Orton and Halliwell lived and spoke as one.

Orton began with a comic spirit, but no tools for communicating it. With Halliwell's encouragement, Orton began studying

Ronald Firbank's clowning classicism. Firbank, in Orton's estimation, 'was the only impressionist in the English novel'. After reading Evelyn Waugh's *Black Mischief* and finding it 'patchy', Orton wrote: 'Waugh isn't up to Firbank: the source'.[38] Firbank's convoluted rhythms and his characters' fluting voices hid murky passions beneath an elegant upper-class civility. (*Princess Zoubaroff*: 'Claude's such an extremist, you know. They say when he kissed the Pope's slipper, he went on to do considerably more'.) In Firbank's world, style becomes Fate. It was the manic manoeuvre of a solitary successfully killing time. Orton and Halliwell shared that solitude. Cut off from the world, they made a world of words. In maturity, Orton came to understand how the tempo of his life and his literary style were interrelated. 'I've got the ability to write the kind of dialogue because of the life I've led in the past', he told the BBC in 1964. 'I think that if you uprooted me and planted me in a different setting, a much more worldly setting, that I wouldn't be able to write as I do.'[39]

Orton saw his study of language as 'strategy'. Gombold, the pilgrim-hero of his allegorical fantasy *Head to Toe*, studies the destructive power of language so that lethal words can do battle with the enemy:

> Gombold bought a dictionary and began to study the construction of a sentence . . . He started calculating and found some sentences puny against large targets. Then perhaps a new type of sentence . . . He started to construct the perfect sentence . . . He studied the chemistry and behaviour of words, phrase design, the forging, casting and milling, the theories of paraphrase, the fusing and the aiming . . .

Like Gombold, Orton made lists of words, learning to spell them as well as to use them. He kept columns of neatly typed adverbs in a loose-leaf binder: 'oxymoronically', 'chrystalecently', 'allergically'. He free-associated with words: 'prize price prig priapus primitive prism privacy procreate procure promiscuous prison profane . . .' He experimented with funny sounds and word combinations in lists of imaginary book titles: Strange Pedicure, The

Painted Whip, Pigeon's Milk, Bugaboo, Zoomorphe, A Stag for Nanny, The Decapitated Pansy, A Cow Called Isis . . .

Orton composed pages of single sentences to build up his descriptive powers. 'Use any form of proposal you like', coos Fay, coaxing a marriage proposal out of the recently widowed McLeavy in *Loot*. 'Try to avoid abstract nouns.' Typing on the back of his first clumsy attempt at a novel, Orton struggled to make language vivid.

- Trees like twisted black arms against a red landscape.
- White oxen moved over the plain.
- On the tabletop stood a large anchor of peonies.
- A cypress rose blackly out of a mist of olives.

Gombold studies 'the propagation of idiom, the effect of adjectives and found pages on the penetrating power of faulty grammar'. So did Orton. His feeling for words and idiom came out of a desire to get to the meaning of them. His stage characters never listen to the implications of their idioms. 'I remember Joe recounting to me a lady who said to him "I speak as I find". And he answered, "What have you found?"' says Kenneth Williams. 'Another time someone said to him "*Loot* is unnecessarily filthy". Joe examined the phrase. "Isn't it funny?" he said. As though there was a *necessary* amount of filth.' In his comic distortions of language Orton at once celebrated and satirized the values and vernacular of the English.

The style isn't super-imposed [Orton maintained]. It's me. You can't write stylized comedy in inverted commas, because the style must ring of the man, and if you think in a certain way and you write true to yourself, which I hope I do, then you will get a style, a style will come out. You've only got to be sitting on a bus and you'll hear the most stylized lines . . . I don't like discrimination against style that some people have. Every serious writer has a style. I mean, Arnold Wesker has a style, but people don't normally think of him as a stylist, in the same way that they think of Wilde, Firbank or Sheridan. Style isn't camp or chi-chi. I write in a certain way because I can't express certain things in naturalistic terms. In the whole naturalistic movement of the '20's and '30's you can't ultimately have

anything except discussions of Mavis's new hat. You can't have
people. With the naturalistic style I couldn't make any comment
on the kind of policeman that Truscott is, or on the laws of the
Establishment. Oscar Wilde's style is much more earthy and colloquial
than most people notice. When we look at Lady Bracknell, she's
the most ordinary, common, direct woman; she's not an affected
woman at all. People are taken in by 'the glittering style'. It's not
glitter. Congreve is the same. It's real – a slice of life. It's just very
brilliantly written, perfectly believable. Nothing at all incredible.[40]

But long before Orton's intuition about language found its
expression in his own fluent comic style, he was analysing and
cataloguing the mannerisms of English speech. He made lists of
parts of speech which give English a formal and often comic sound:

> Are both, perhaps
> In the not
> not for not
> Thus, in you I
> not less than everything
> Towards the never
> Have has what
> I can only say how

He toyed with substituting new words in familiar metaphoric
constructions: 'the weakness of flesh', 'the damnation of heaven',
'the resolution of yet', 'the enchantment of never'. His notes show
him balancing words and trying to make new equations with
them: 'release from release', 'freedom from freedom', 'x without x'
'y without y'.

Orton's earliest writing was in crude imitation of Ronald Firbank.
He delighted in Firbank's zestful juggling of language. Firbank
could whip up words into a soufflé of sound ('Head archly bent, her
fine arms divined through darkling laces, the Duquessa stood,
clasping closely a week-old police dog in the ripple of her gown').
Orton's concoctions inevitably fell flat. One early untitled novel
(c. 1954) has a cast of typically swank Firbankean gargoyles including Helen Hagg, Lord Emission of Semen, Lady Cucumber, Lady

Melon, Olive de Pineapple. Helen Hagg has been unjustly accused of stealing her would-be mother-in-law's jewellery. But Olive de Pineapple is unmasked as the thief, paving the way for Helen's marriage into the aristocracy. 'What you say is preposterous!' said Olive de Pineapple, pressing her hands together and casting down her pale-coloured, treacherous eyes. 'You force yourself into my room and bully me because you think I am a woman alone.' In time, Orton would take Firbank's fluting mischievousness and bring it down to earth.

– I seek a porteress for a house of piety.
– His Hellenism once captivated me. But the *Attic* to him means nothing now but servants' bedrooms.
– Have you taken up transvestism? I'd no idea our marriage teetered on the brink of fashion.

Only the last joke is Orton's (*What the Butler Saw*), the others are from Firbank's only play, *The Princess Zoubaroff*. Orton's humour was more robust and gregarious than Firbank's rarefied fantasies. But he shared Firbank's obsessions and adapted many of his comic manoeuvres to a much more popular dramatic form.

Orton first absorbed these comic stances through Halliwell, who was also imitating Firbank. In collaboration with Halliwell, Orton's writing was smoother and more defined than in his solo efforts. Halliwell's name was typed above Orton's on the title pages of their novels; and Halliwell's sensibility dominated them. Their fiction explored certain ideas which Orton later elaborated successfully in his plays: a delight in sexual ambiguity, a questioning of the perverse in experience; an appetite for anarchy and farcical situations, send-ups of figures of authority, a fascination with innocents at large in a violent, corrupt world. In later years, Orton would refer to the early failed manuscripts for dramatic ideas. *The Ruffian on the Stair* was a rewrite of their novel *The Boy Hairdresser*. *Up Against It*, Orton's film script for the Beatles, combined a plot idea from their first novel, *The Silver Bucket* (1953), with Orton's last novel, *The Vision of Gombold Proval* (1961), which was published posthumously as *Head to Toe*.

By 1955 Orton and Halliwell were submitting their manuscripts for publication. The first was a science fiction spoof, *The Mechanical Womb*. 'The reductio ad absurdum of the bug-eyed monster science fiction,' wrote a reader for Faber and Faber, 'complete with mutants, ailing robots and a lot of nonsense kept whirling around by sheer bewildering speed but without any claim to coherence or design.' Charles Monteith confirmed the verdict. 'Rather good really', he scribbled on their submission letter. 'But not good enough.' In 1966 Orton reread the novel with the idea of reworking it into a radio play for the BBC. 'I'm afraid I can't let you read it', he wrote to the BBC producer. 'It just isn't up to standard. I did write it ten years ago. It would need an enormous amount of work, and in fact, all I'd use would be the title.'

Their second effort in 1955 was *The Last Days of Sodom*, a caper which had a purpose behind its playfulness. It was their most brazen comic assault on the relativity of moral values. The theme percolated all through their work. 'The values of society?' mocks Donelly in *The Boy Hairdresser*. 'What values? The things we take seriously will be laughed at in fifty years. Who doesn't laugh at nineteenth century attitudes and yet they imagined them to be the right ones.' In *Head to Toe*, Gombold, like Orton, finds a teacher, and 'study took the place of liberty: absorbed in acquiring knowledge, days, months and years passed in rapid and instructive course'. But when the teacher asks Gombold what is the abiding value, Gombold answers 'truth'. The teacher rebukes him: 'The rulers of whatever country you choose will designate as "true" that which is useful to them. Truth is relative, and always behind it stands some interest, furthering its own ends.'

In *The Last Days of Sodom*, Orton and Halliwell attempted to make a farce of social conventions. They told the story of Sodom, treating it as a modern western city. The novel recounted the lives led by male and female homosexuals before the city's destruction.

It began with Sodom in long shot from the window of a local psychiatrist:

> ... There were towers in brick the colour of rose, cathedrals moulded in gold and bronze. The sea lay like a shield. In the stillness, the voices of fishermen called to each other across the water ...

Abe Haranson sat back in the chair and surveyed his patient. 'What did you dream next,' he said.

'It was horrible, doctor, I was being chased by a –'

'Yes,' he probed.

The woman shuddered and hid her face. 'By a man. Oh what does it mean, Doctor, am I abnormal?'

The jokes turned the tables on manners and their morality. 'He's terribly nice. But I hear he goes to one of those loose bars where men dance with women.' The novel made its impression. 'Plainly there was a literary quality here,' remembers Richard Brain. 'The kind of jokes in the book were being told in the homosexual world of the early fifties. But the actual destruction of the city by fire and brimstone was a huge bit of purple patch writing. It was quite clear that from the point of view of subject matter – and to some extent of style – the novel wasn't good enough.' Charles Monteith had a similar reaction. 'I really am sorry to have to send back a manuscript which I enjoyed so much', he wrote to Orton and Halliwell. 'But I am afraid we are too dubious about its potential sales – it's such a *rarefied* joke – to accept it. Alas.'[41]

On 12 April 1956 Orton and Halliwell sent Faber and Faber *The Boy Hairdresser*, a satire in modern verse, which was quickly returned as an entertaining but uncommercial project. Undeterred, they continued to see Monteith and Brain. On 1 August Monteith took them to dinner with two other publishers. 'They were quite fun,' says Monteith. 'They did make the point that they hadn't eaten in a restaurant for years.' Three weeks later, Monteith and Brain understood their monastic existence when they visited Orton and Halliwell in West Hampstead. 'I never thought human beings could live this way. It was extraordinary,' Monteith says. 'The flat was in a state of considerable decay and disrepair. The bedroom in particular had been attacked by rising damp. Kenneth had turned the damp patches into an abstract painting by outlining each patch in a different-coloured broad stroke of paint. You felt like you were living inside an abstract painting of the New York School.' But the most memorable event of the evening was Halliwell's cuisine, which was as eccentric as the surroundings. 'We had a spartan and ghastly meal,' recalls Monteith. Halliwell served them a first course of rice with sardines and a second course of rice with golden syrup. 'On that occasion, John produced, I think, a very funny and penetrating piece of literary criticism,' says Monteith. 'I asked if they'd read Gibbon. To which John replied "What an old queen she is! Send up, send up, send up the whole time".' Orton's vitality was more apparent at this meal; and both Monteith and Brain came away convinced that it was 'Orton who provided a great deal of the striking comicality in their writing'.

However, it was Halliwell who still spoke for them when they resubmitted a revised version of *The Last Days of Sodom* on 22 May 1957.

Dear Charles,
Here we are again. It looks as if we will never give up.

With the spring, John's infectious enthusiasm drew me out of the T. E. Lawrence existence into which I had sunk during the winter. We gave in our notice at Cadbury's having saved enough money to live on until the autumn, and made a final gigantic attempt to *make* the Sodom novel publishable by sheer brute effort.

If it is no good this time, well that is the end of the line, and after trying it on a few more publishers, and perhaps trying one or two on the other side of the Atlantic, it must be consigned to the limbo of forgotten genius.

It has already been to Duckworths, and with their usual brilliant acumen they suggest turning it into a 'short story'! . . .

The revision was a dud. 'I'm afraid I thought – though I know you won't agree – that it isn't as good as the first version. It seemed to me to have lost some of its original subtlety', Monteith wrote.

'Now there's only one point – which is being made at rather too great length and rather too obviously.'[42] The rejection created a crisis in their collaboration. Six days later, Monteith received a diary novel, *Between Us Girls*; both the manuscript and the note appended to it were from John Orton.

Dear Charles,
We were sorry to learn you thought so little of the Sodom novel. However . . .

   Kenneth and I have decided that there is very little to be gained by our collaboration and so we have split (for the purpose of writing). Here, for your approval, is a novel by me alone.[43]

Susan Hope is the naïve, frivolous diarist of *Between Us Girls* ('Laddered my stockings, broke two of my nails, and had Dubonnet spilled over my Madge Chard hat. Life is simply sickening sometimes'). Like her name, Miss Hope is a dotty figure of faith, whose earnest and unreflective enthusiasm gloss the seediness of her world. She is 'in the theatre', but her stage is a strip club called the Rainier Revuebar. Ignorant of innuendo and experience, she walks po-faced through triumph and tragedy. Like so many of Orton's stage characters, Susan Hope never hears what she is really saying.
   Between Us Girls was an experiment in tone. Orton had abandoned Halliwell's baroque for a more direct, concrete and colloquial style. He was learning what he later allowed Gombold to articulate 'The blast of a long sentence was curiously local and a lot of shorter sentences were better'. Orton had always been a good mimic, and the first-person narrative – no matter how aimless it seemed in *Between Us Girls* – gave an energy and impact to his writing that Halliwell's strained third-person efforts lacked. Halliwell would continue writing in his strutting Firbankian mode, while Orton searched for new comic techniques. In 1959, when Halliwell submitted *Priapus in the Shrubbery* to Faber and Faber, his letter to Charles Monteith is as arch and insecure as his prose:

Dear Mr Monteith, sir,
I don't know whether you remember me, but about three years ago,

you were I hope, I think, interested in the Firbankian novel I was writing in collaboration with John Orton . . . I have been engaged in writing another novel, which will be finished in a few weeks time. I wondered whether you would be interested in seeing it on completion? I shall quite understand if you wouldn't . . . It is still somewhat Firbankian but has its feet more firmly on the ground. I am not writing any more in collaboration. John is writing a play . . .[44]

Halliwell signed his letter 'Yours humbly'. But humility in laughter is as unwelcome as modesty in a prostitute. Orton was never hamstrung by that problem. In *Between Us Girls* he had planned some irreverent surprises for Charles Monteith. The novel reworked the plot of *The Silver Bucket*. Susan Hope leaves the revuebar for what she thinks is a three-year contract at an exotic Mexican club. But the 'club' turns out to be a brothel ('Most of us had to wear too much or not enough. Senora Josefa dressed me in something which I am not going to mention'). Susan Hope escapes to L.A. and movie stardom. The entrepreneur who signs her up and owns the chain of bordellos is mischievously named Liz Monteith ('She was about as tall as a woman can be without having beans grow up her . . . The hall Miss Monteith led us into was quite bare like her voice, polished, anaemic, scraped and clean'). The novel, submitted on 2 June 1957 was returned on 5 June.

The trickster's function, as Karl Kerenyi says, is 'to add disorder to order, and so make a whole; within the fixed bounds of what's permitted, an experience of what is not permitted'.[45] *Between Us Girls* contains neither venomous satire nor scurrilous outrage. But in it the first tentative glimpse of Orton's trickster spirit – the mischief of the manipulated voice – begins to assert itself. The trickster is a protean figure, an outsider with the power to 'become' anyone. *Between Us Girls* was Orton's first exercise in literary ventriloquism: speaking and yet not seeming to speak. The ventriloquist's accomplishment is in 'throwing his voice', projecting sound as if independent of the body. The act was reminiscent of the mythic trickster who could crawl up his anus, detach his penis and carry it in a box, command one part of his body to fight another part. Orton's favourite literature was trickster tales: Greek mythology, children's fables. The protean mischief of the trickster – enemy of boundaries, spirit of disorder, agent of delight – was an important part of Orton's infantile fantasies of omnipotence. In *Head to Toe* Gombold crawled down the mouth of a giant and explored his massive body. He fought a war between the cleft in the giant's buttocks 'for the independence of the body's parts'. And in his plays Orton exhibits a trickster's glee in making a ghoulish, malicious spectacle of the human anatomy, taking the body to pieces and letting its parts have their own dramatic life. The eyeball of the deceased Mrs McLeavy rolls out of her coffin and under the bed in *Loot*; a severed hand is produced from a cake tin in *Funeral Games*. The trickster's rapacious hijinx are expressed most profoundly in *What the Butler Saw* when Sir Winston Churchill's 'parts' are almost produced from a box at the conclusion of the play:

> RANCE *looks inside the box.*
> RANCE (*with admiration*). How much more inspiring if, in those dark days, we'd seen what we see now. Instead we had to be content with a cigar – the symbol falling far short, as we all realize, of the object itself.
> GERALDINE *looks inside the box.*
> GERALDINE. But it is a cigar!
> RANCE. Ah, the illusions of youth!

Orton originally wanted Churchill's penis to be displayed. But the Lord Chamberlain would not allow it. 'It's only a statue,' Orton complained to his producer, Oscar Lewenstein, who predicted the cut on the grounds of libel. 'What am I saying about Churchill, though?' Lewenstein replied 'You're saying he had a big prick.' 'That isn't libel, surely,' Orton said. 'I wouldn't sue anybody for saying I had a big prick. No man would. In fact I might pay them to do that.'[46]

The trickster's emblem is the erect penis. Clowns, who embody the trickster's capricious and potent life force in their stage antics, often carried a vestigial phallus. The Elizabethan fool held a 'bauble' or 'plaything'. In contemporary comedy, the phallic anarchy is symbolized in Chaplin's cane, Harpo's horn, Groucho's cigar, Mr Hulot's umbrella.

Orton brought the clown's purest sexual impulse into dramatic literature. The phallus dominated his life and his laughter. 'Noticed somebody had got a large and impressive book called *The English Organ*', he wrote in his diary. 'It'd be nice to have the cover.'[47] Writing to a friend about the Arab–Israeli crisis while in Morocco, Orton said: 'All the silly queens out here can talk about is "this dreadful political situation". They've transferred their allegiance entirely from the circumcised penis to the secretary general of the United Nations. Fickle in their emotions.'[48] Even Gombold in *Head to Toe* swears an amazed and reverent oath to the awesome vista of the giant's gargantuan penis: 'A world of its own; beautiful and menacing. A vast erection of the earth. Gombold caught his breath as he muttered "Suspirum et decus puellarum et puerorum".'

Orton was in touch with his sexuality; and his plays chronicled sexual mischievousness. He is unique among modern playwrights in finding a way to convey in stage terms the trickster's seething and often hilarious sexual itch which the stage clown once incarnated. The phallus is sometimes mischievously invoked in the titles of his work: *Up Against It*, *Prick Up Your Ears*, *Until She Screams*. On the cover of Orton's scrapbook for *Entertaining Mr Sloane* he pasted the bulging blue-jeaned crotch of a muscular beach boy. But the real phallic power is always present in the teasing and unrelenting energy behind his laughter, which wants to 'goose' the audience, and take it for a tumble:

. . . Kenneth, who read the *Observer*, tells me of the latest way-out group in America – complete sexual licence. 'It's the only way to smash the wretched civilization,' I said, making a mental note to hot-up WHAT THE BUTLER SAW when I came to re-write. 'It's like the Albigensian heresy in the 11th Century,' Kenneth said. Looked up the article in the Encyclopedia Britannica. Most interesting. Yes. Sex is the only way to infuriate them. Much more fucking and they'll be screaming hysterics in next to no time.

(26 March 1967)

Orton's first full-fledged trickster accomplishment was the creation of Edna Welthorpe (Mrs) in 1958. Watchdog of public morals and notorious letter writer, Edna was conceived in the spirit of fun not literature. Her fatuous suburban tones foreshadow the essential Orton. Edna was a direct descendant of the fractious kill-joy Mrs Grundy, who was, as Oscar Wilde aptly observed, 'that amusing old lady who represents the only original form of humour that the middle classes of this country have been able to produce'.[49] Under Edna's *nom de plume* Orton carried his clowning into public life, spoofing Edna's idiocy and goading institutions into betraying their own. These pranks had a refreshing ease and brazenness which never found their way into Orton's early 'serious' writing.

2 November 1958

Dear Sir,

Your name has kindly been given to me in connection with the availability of the Heath Street Baptist Church Hall. If it is at all possible, I would like to begin rehearsals there during the next three weeks, and later to present for three performances, 'The Pansy', a play which pleads for greater tolerance on the subject of homosexuality.

It is with the utmost hesitance that I approach a minister upon so controversial a topic; but the attitude of enlightened Churchmen seems to have undergone a favourable revolution during the past decade. It is with this thought in mind that I decided to contact you.

I am told that you forbid dancing in your hall. This is a difficulty, as there is a certain amount of dancing in several scenes. However, if you too strongly object I could cut these as, at the request of certain members of the cast, I have already expurgated the scenes which were to have taken place in the Kilburn Branch Library in Cotleigh Road.

Trusting to have your reply in due course, I am,

Yours faithfully,

Edna Welthorpe (Mrs)

After a rude second letter to the minister produced only a note scolding her for her 'strictures', Orton declared Edna 'dead':

Dear Mr S—
I am writing on behalf of my late niece, Edna. . . . I have taken over from my niece the position of secretary to the Phallus Players, and I am anxious to know what we are to do with regard to the Hall.

Please let me say, sir, that I am not a party to the rude tone which Edna adopted when crossed. I feel that I must give a definite answer to the society, even though I myself do not altogether approve of the play . . . I did not want to put on this piece of near-pornography. I have the strongest opinions as to what should and should not be presented in a Church.

The letter coaxed out the minister's piety. 'I was shocked to learn that your niece had died', he wrote back. 'And I wish to say how sorry I am and would offer you my sincerest condolences on this unfortunate event. It is very sad to think that one's last contacts with anyone had been on the level that mine were with her, but you, if I may say so, have lifted the whole business on a higher level.'

Once invented, Edna busied herself with throwing spanners in a variety of works. She pestered the Home Shopping Service and then, when they replied, denied her existence. She requested seventy-eight tickets to the International Trade Fashion Fair, and rounded on the publicity department when they were not forthcoming. She badgered industry about their products:

30 April 1965

Dear Sir,
I recently purchased a tin of Morton's blackcurrant pie filling. It was delicious. Chock-full of rich fruit. Then wishing to try another variety, I came upon Smedley's Raspberry pie filling? There wasn't a raspberry in it. I was very disappointed after trying Morton's blackcurrant.

Please try to do better in the future. And what on earth is 'EDIBLE STARCH' and 'LOCUST BEAN GUM'? If that is what you put into your pie fillings I'm not surprised at the result.

I shan't try any more of your pie fillings until the fruit content is considerably higher. My stomach really turned at what I saw when I opened the tin.

The stage clown's appetite for vindictive triumph can be seen in his language for success: he 'kills the audience', 'lays them in the aisles', 'slaughters them', 'knocks them dead'. The 'Edna' persona was part of this lust for psychic annihilation, an attempt at comic domination in keeping with the closed-off, hermetic life which defended Orton and Halliwell against the world. With reproductions of great works of art layered like bricks up to the ceiling, their room became a 'wall of culture' between them and the mediocre world outside. Edna was an offensive weapon, a form of dissimulation in which Orton's personality remained invulnerable from society's judgement while sniping at it. Edna's tone was not just a practical joke; it was an exploration of an idiom and attitude of mind.

Edna's scolding voice often spoke out against Orton's own plays, adding vindictive insult to injury. 'Today's young playwrights take it upon themselves to flaunt their contempt for ordinary decent people', she wrote in the *Daily Telegraph* in 1964, fanning the scandal over *Entertaining Mr Sloane*. 'I hope that ordinary decent people will shortly strike *back*!'[50] Edna's unwitting violence amused Orton. The viciousness behind decency was a streak which Orton refined as his literary ability became more adroit. 'If you really wanted to spot the nasty equivalent of fascism in England you have to read the letters to the *Radio Times* and the *TV Times*', Orton said.[51] Part of Edna reflected this. But Orton relished the stupidity of her censoriousness. She wrote to Kenneth Williams 'taking up cudgels' with him over remarks which 'were quite uncalled for and tasteless in the extreme':

Especially offensive to me as a nursing mother was your attack on infants and their ways. My own baby, born recently, cried throughout the programme. Which I feel more than proves my point.[52]

Like her author, Edna's milieu and feeling for the *mot juste* improved with age. In a letter to the manager of the Ritz Hotel, Orton showed how clear a bead he had on Edna's sublime egotism. She shared with all his farce characters an elegant incomprehension of herself and the world through which she bulldozed:

Tuesday 14 February 1967

Dear Sir,

I'm writing to ask a question which, as a hotelier, I'm sure you'll be eager to answer. A month ago I visited the Ritz in company with Mrs Sally Warren – a tall grey-haired lady. During our brief stay at your hotel I lost a brown Morocco Handbag with the initials E.W. stamped on the flap. The contents of the bag weren't valuable – they consisted of a purse containing loose coins, a Boots folder with snapshots of members of my family and a pair of gloves made of some hairy material.

I wonder if you, or any of your staff, have come across my hand-bag? If you can give me any assistance in its recovery I'd be most grateful . . .

And may I take this opportunity of saying that, in my opinion, the Ritz is unbeatable. I was staggered by the splendour of it all.

Every comedian walks a tightrope between the sublime and the bestial; and his laughter marks this precarious balance. The trickster can be disgusting as well as delightful. Orton's impersonations also had a vulgar other side.

Postmaster: R. Ufick
North District Post Office

Dear Sir,

For some time now the pillar boxes in this area have had two holes in them. I am sorry to tell you that a great many of these have been put to improper use. The unpleasant fact is that the slot marked 'London' is being misused for the disposal of old French letters and other bric-à-brac, while the ones marked 'Other Places' is being wanked-off into . . . My object in writing is to ask you to make sure you post only 'normal' letters and that you insert these in the right slot. It may be that you have already taken care to do this: if so, I would like to thank you. If not, I can only ask you to keep your great cock out of our boxes.

In Morocco, Orton invented Uncle Whuppity, a lascivious schoolteacher. Whuppity was the creation of an imagination on holiday. Orton's wit was best when it was combative, and Whuppity was a character without a mission. Orton's scabrous and aimless monologues for the old pervert reflected this. Orton asked Kenneth Williams what he thought of Uncle Whuppity and was surprised at his lack of enthusiasm:

'Well, I simply loved Edna,' he said. 'But Uncle Whuppity is too rude for me.' 'Yes,' Kenneth Halliwell said when we got home, 'he can't take the other side of you.'

(5 July 1967)

Even as a successful playwright, Orton couldn't resist the idea of a romp for its own sake. 'If I've time on my hands at the end of the year,' he wrote in 1967, 'I'd like to amuse myself by writing a bit of rubbish under an assumed name: in the nature of a joke play.'[53] Orton's squandering of energy in pranks released a festive vulgarity which, when disciplined, found its way successfully into his plays. But when Orton indulged himself, his fun became frivolity, his outrage merely outrageousness. There was always a little boy in Orton – the Peter Pan part of him – that responded to Beatrix Potter and Daisy Ashford; who inflated prophylactics and dropped them into the caretaker's hollyhocks; who wrote obscene scenarios played against a backdrop of upper-class life. In *The Patient Dowager*, the butler has a radioactive cock, and the sex-starved dowager billows smoke from beneath her dress after masturbating with a newspaper ('I always told you the *Daily Sketch* was highly inflammable'). Orton wrote this pornographic sketch for Halliwell's amusement in 1960. The joke was to upstage elegance with obscenity. Orton and Halliwell acted the parts and taped them. Orton retitled the sketch *Until She Screams* when it was performed in Kenneth Tynan's erotic revue, *Oh! Calcutta!*:

As I think that this revue is doomed from the start I wasn't going to put myself out . . . Slightly altered some of the more deliberately pornographic element . . . Kenneth Tynan apparently said the revue was to be straight forward, and no phoney 'artistic' shit. Since the revue is called *Oh! Calcutta!*, it begins with an artistic title. Anyway, they can have the sketch. If they dare do it.

(24 February 1967)

'. . . I've never had anybody interfere with me since I was two', complains Lady Shane in the sketch. 'Except my old English sheepdog. And you occasionally.' There was a childish tameness in Orton's gross imaginings but also an energy which never got into his early writings. Pornography was the artless side of comedy's infantile fantasies. In Orton's sketch, style is on holiday; but the gloss of refinement imposed on unrefined sexual frustration is an essential characteristic of Orton's humour. Instead of dissecting a character with wit, pornography kicked muck on it. Orton enjoyed this irresponsible exercise. Mrs Dale was another target. Orton and Halliwell questioned her virtue in *The Boy Hairdresser*. 'I bet what she does in bed would shock her mother', says Donelly. 'These conformists give me a pain in the arse. They look down on so many things – and yet they have vices.'

Charles Monteith heard their version of *Mrs Dale's Diary* in 1959. Orton and Halliwell had recorded the show's signature tune and then faded it out for their own version of a typical day in Mrs Dale's life. Mrs Dale's chatty kitchen was transformed into the scene of an orgy in which she was the centrepiece. 'It was funny and very, very dirty,' Monteith says. 'Every possible aperture was used by everybody and every object. I believe a broom handle had been lost. And just as the broom handle was being produced from an unsuitable place, Dr Dale came in saying "Is there time for another cup of coffee?" '

Orton's pranks were also the by-products of an imagination struggling with hostility. Anger obsessed him. In *Untitled Play* (1959) he first made the intellectual connection between laughter and revenge, fantasizing about a purifying laughter with the power to devastate and renew. Under the motto 'Pox Vobiscum', Dr Petrie seeks converts to his faith in mockery. He finds them in Fred and Marge, a bored and aimless working-class couple who complain of the 'fatigue of living' and their empty routines. Madge assesses her friends as zombies: 'Nothing on their minds except the rates and no pleasures except the pools . . . They're not even alive, at least not what anyone who was alive would call alive. They're dead. But you can't go around telling people they're dead without annoying them, can you?' Dr Petrie does just that. An exhibition of his fulminating rage awakens 'the dead' and galvanizes them with a new sense of mission. Anger is dramatized as a source of life, a connection to society which short-circuits boredom. 'Is rage the prerogative of youth?' Dr Petrie asks. 'Must we cool with the years and die when our blood has chilled to the temperature of the society around us . . . No! We must hurt the feelings of our enemies, infuriate those we dislike, and never cease to delight in bringing the hornet's nest about our ears.'

Orton saw that laughter could break down the solid state of society. Behind Petrie's ranting is the comic's desire to reimagine the world. But *Untitled Play* was all talk and no destruction. Demolition was only an off-stage sound effect.

With each laugh or series of laughs the sound of falling masonry and cracking glass increases . . . The laughter grows more and more hysterical.

Orton had grasped the importance of panic to laughter, even if *Untitled Play*'s mishmash of borrowed styles showed he was still at a loss about how to construct it. But Orton had stumbled on to his theme: to let laughter be lethal and irresistible.

The fury in Orton's laughter was both a mask and an admission of dangerous feelings that were slow to come into focus. Orton began defacing library books about the time his writing became obsessed with laughter as revenge. *Untitled Play* had thrown a slack net around his anger, and Orton explored the idea of revenge more rigorously in *The Boy Hairdresser*, written with Halliwell between 1959 and 1960. For the first time Orton's name was typed above Halliwell's in this manuscript, which would be their last collaboration. They condensed the characteristics of their personalities and the suffocating detail of their isolation into realistic, solemn prose. 'We have always in the past, been unsure of what we have written', Halliwell wrote to Charles Monteith when they submitted the novel to Fabers on 20 June 1960. 'But this time we have written something both publishable and not lacking in brilliance. We have *tried*, successfully we hope, to write something much more realistic in style . . . We, of course, think its brilliance is unbelievable. But are we going round the bend?'

The Boy Hairdresser was their most serious, passionate book. Too ungainly and oblique to be brilliant, the book's importance was as a testament to their suffering. In Peterson and Donelly, Orton and Halliwell examined the tensions in their relationship. Looking at Peterson, Donelly thinks:

What a charmer he looks, with the light falling onto his hair: tough yet in a way weak: in need of protection . . . Peterson was as trapped as he was, and yet treated his cage as a playground, making the cage disappear, the bars melt.

Boredom is the enemy which shrinks and flattens Donelly's perception of the world. He can make no connections. Life is a barren parade of fragments. Actions and objections intrude on his solitude, and his mind records 'the lifeless progression of detail':

Lying in the warm water, he hummed a tune, flicked soap over himself and stared at his navel. The house creaked, there was a patter of plaster, the gurgling of a pipe. One day he would shoot himself, he was living already in the future.

Both Orton and Halliwell were obsessed with a sense of cultural suffocation, but Orton broke out through laughter. *What the Butler Saw* fulfilled the prophecy of *The Boy Hairdresser*'s fiction by turning a psychiatric clinic into a cage and then jauntily transcending it with a comic sleight of hand: a rope ladder is dropped from the skylight in a parody of the classical *deus ex machina*. Orton's comedy always returned to the nightmare of conflicting psychic forces. In *What the Butler Saw*, a wounded page-boy 'crawls, almost fainting' towards the psychiatrist and begs to be validated:

NICK. What about me, sir? I'm not mad.
RANCE (*with a smile*). You're not human.
NICK. I can't be an hallucination. (*He points to his bleeding shoulder.*) Look at this wound. That's real.
RANCE. It appears to be.
NICK. If the pain is real I must be real.
RANCE. I'd rather not get involved in metaphysical speculation.

Orton's laughter would triumph over his fears and afflictions. Halliwell had no such method of liberating anger. *The Boy Hairdresser* dramatized the frustration of the imprisoned will, and its negative but 'heroic' elevation into criminal revenge. Donelly, who 'had proved to himself the pointlessness of so many things, so many virtues, so many vices, without purpose, leading nowhere', has no link to life except Peterson. 'If Peterson were dead he could end it now', Donelly thinks at the beginning of the book. He and Peterson drift through the seedy back streets of London, glimpsed in coffee bars, pubs, porno bookshops. People float like voices through a numbed, undifferentiated landscape. Wandering is the condition of their rootless, disintegrating world. Donelly coaxes Peterson into living with him, and then into the frivolous subversions of their pranks:

They had been stealing for a year from bookshops. Peterson had a great enthusiasm for anarchy. The theft of toilet-rolls from public lavatories, pens from post-offices; the obscene telephone calls, the cards inserted in Praed Street windows giving the addresses of vicars' aunts and aldermen's widows . . .

Donelly sees something more menacing in these petty rebellions. 'They were rehearsals. One day he would show them.' Donelly dreams of having the last vengeful laugh on society. He plans to make a spectacle of his death:

When he went, he'd take others with him: five or six at least. Something for the Sunday papers to talk about . . . The idea staggered. Why not cure the population problem by even so small amount. It seemed as though he had cut himself free from everyone at that moment.

Despite its ferocious façade, revenge is an act of nostalgia: an attempt to force life back to an imagined earlier harmony. In its hatred, revenge registers a sense of loss and the yearning to put the moral universe in order. Donelly, echoing Orton's and Halliwell's familiar lament, longs for society's sullied slate to be wiped clean:

God knows the sooner the Bomb fell the better. And one day, with a finality beyond the axe, docks and fools parsley, brambles and thick primeval green will cover the cathode ray tubes and traffic signs. Only the mice and beetles in the semi-detached villas will know the perfection of those Mod Cons.

But Donelly, who hates life and musters every tattered scrap of nihilist jargon to prove it, can't kill himself. He finds his suicidal excuse when Peterson is knocked down by a car and killed. 'Suicide', Donelly thinks after Peterson's funeral, 'is an insult to the body'. It is a gesture that takes mockery to its extreme. Donelly hates himself as much as society for the pain. He wants to revenge it. Donelly starts to gun down people in the street, expecting to turn the gun on himself. But vengeance turns to farce. He loses consciousness, only to find himself waking up in a hospital.

'You did no harm to anyone but yourself', says his nurse, explaining that two of his fingers have been amputated. 'I've ruined my life, nurse', Donelly says, contemplating the charges of attempted murder that the police will make against him. Donelly wants to explain to the nurse the genesis of his rage. ('He wanted to shake her to the soul.') But words only diminish his profound sense of loss and dislocation. 'My mother was an ape. She couldn't give me the attention I needed. I never knew who my father was.' The nurse gives a bromidic reply. Donelly sees that his words are received as 'a harmless phrase'. As the nurse leans over to tuck in his blankets, Donelly grabs a vase of flowers and empties them on her head: the final unrepentant expression of his numbing frustration and isolation. 'I hope you feel ashamed of yourself', the nurse says. 'When I bring you lunch, I shall expect an apology.' The nurse locks Donelly in his room. He is still a prisoner. ('He closed his eyes and heard her turn the key.') The nurse's parting words demand capitulation to convention and manners. Mockery is always at odds with manners. To heal, mockery must break boundaries while manners must cling to established limits. Mockery is an act of no surrender. In the silence of his room, Donelly has a final elegiac vision of its heroism:

It was like this for the Incas, the Aztecs, the pure-blooded Polynesians, for the golden bearded kings of Atlas and the legionary upon the wall. For Genghis Khan and Savonarola too – though he may have thought it was different; for Alexander bringing fire by night to Persepolis.

They had ignorance and accepted custom in Alba Longa, Megiddo, and Ilion: they had chicken-hearts and sleek ideals upon those topless towers. Youth had been betrayed and tears shed for its loss too often and too long for anyone, anymore, to feel anything.

The endless spinning of the wheel; the perpetual closing of a circle.

God laughs and snaps his fingers . . . The only thing for a man is to imitate God and snap his fingers too.

In Orton's last novel, *Head to Toe* (1961), the pilgrim-hero, Gombold, prays: 'Cleanse my heart, give me the ability to rage correctly'.

As a spokesman for Orton's quandary, Gombold observes: 'But I want to get somewhere. I don't want to be lost in this wilderness forever'. *Head to Toe* sported with problems of sexual guilt, isolation and fulfilment which *The Boy Hairdresser* debated in its overwritten meditation on suicide and revenge. Gombold is lost in an alien terrain which turns out to be the body of a giant. Gombold's identity is under continual siege as he wanders through the body, which inevitably becomes a metaphor of the body politic. Gombold is always being captured by hostile forces and imprisoned, then escaping, only to be captured again. Gombold's sole refuge from this pattern of painful retreat and enforced powerlessness is his imagination. 'By use of images,' he thinks, 'it might be possible to extract from fantasy a kind of reality.' Gombold's journey is a fantasy in which Orton's images tease out of him the sexual and social confusions that fed his obsession with comic revenge.

Orton's compulsive promiscuity, the aggression in his humour, showed a need to confirm his maleness. In *Head to Toe*, this sexual uncertainty is given playful shape. Gombold at first finds himself in a territory peopled only by women. He is seduced by the Amazonian chief of police, Connie Hogg. Fearing her wrath and the threat of engulfment, Gombold does as he's told. He is ordered to be a woman:

> The clothes she produced for him to wear had a curiously unfamiliar feel . . . When he was dressed she watched as he minced before his image in the mirror.
> 'Promise me one thing,' she said standing over him, 'never wear Daddy's clothes.' Gombold was too busy trying on a frilly apron to listen; she shook him. 'Understand?'

Gombold breaks his promise and wears Connie's men's clothes. His identity is so fluid that clothes have the power to change it. 'Power resided in her clothes,' Gombold thinks. 'If he wore her clothes he would be powerful like her.' Farce laughs about the fragility of identity and makes a spectacle of its disintegration. Gombold was Orton's first attempt to explore what happens to human identity when the boundaries of the body become blurred. In his sexual confusion, Gombold admits: 'I have difficulty in distinguishing a man and a youth from a woman'. The confusion of man, woman and youth is always the driving force behind Orton's farces, the sexual turmoil in his own life that he works out in the equation of fun. *Head to Toe* never makes this psychic tug of war dramatic. But Gombold elucidates Orton's predicament, from which his plays finally extricated him. When Gombold is trapped in prison and sees no way out, he writes poems in the shape of darts and throws them out of his cell hoping they will bring about his escape. 'It was the kind of writing he had never done before, indeed, he was convinced it was a type no one had ever attempted in any language ... After a second or two the dart was returned. His heart sank. There seemed no one here either to appreciate his writing or engineer his escape.'

Orton's plays would be the darts that finally drew attention to him and freed him from his isolation. *Head to Toe*'s frantic playfulness was a search for the key to unlock the author's imagination.

Here for the first time Orton toyed with the farcical, trying to mingle violence and laughter. Farce is an act of literary aggression. On stage, Orton made visual the visceral battle between ecstasy and fear, reason and irrationality, that punished Gombold. *Head to Toe* made only crude flourishes in this comic direction. As a guerrilla assassin, Gombold dresses in drag and infiltrates a government cabinet meeting. The prime minister and the cabinet are women:

'All right, dears, calm down [says Lillian, the prime minister]. The International Field ... I've made a big decision. I'm going to the disarmament conference in a great flowing dress in white broderie anglaise with heavenly flounces ...'

Gombold – the victim turned victimizer – calmly assassinates the prime minister and escapes only to be confronted later by a series of 'unacceptable deaths'. Gombold, like so many of Orton's comic characters, illustrates that when life is preposterous, so is death. Even among the plant kingdom in this world the ability to inflict pain is the only defence against mankind. Gombold overhears a loganberry talking:

'Oh, I prayed a bit, I admit. You couldn't stop me. But it wasn't prayers that saved me.'

'What then?'
'It was my thorns . . .'

Gombold's adventures are the faltering first steps towards making a situation dramatize an idea rather than, as in *The Boy Hairdresser*, allowing ideas to swamp the situation. Gombold displays a slapstick comedian's resilience. He bounces back from every low blow society deals him. But the buffeting takes its toll. Pursued, trapped, betrayed, abused – Gombold becomes increasingly frustrated and angry. His discontent is internalized. He cries. He sweats. He 'has a sense of falling'. He sleeps. ('In the darkness he thought of rescue and dismissed each evolving plan. More and more impressed by a feeling of helplessness, he fell asleep once more. And dreamed . . .') Orton's anger seeps through his straight-faced portrayal of Gombold's innocent outrage. 'Can't we have a change of species?' Gombold begs his keeper when, as a prisoner of war, he finds himself on display in a zoo cage. The situation is intolerable. At the end of the journey, Gombold answers his own question about escape: 'to hope for any kind of relief is pointless'.

Orton allows Gombold one final gesture of revolt before he escapes. The anarchist wants to kick society's corpse, to register disgust at its structure. Gombold thinks: 'There was one thing he had to do, an awkward, unpleasant thing that perhaps had better have been left alone. But he wanted to do it and not just trust the indifferent flames to sweep the house away.' The house is the last emblem of opulence, waste and greed on the landscape. Orton dreamed of generating the intellectual heat to cauterize society, and Gombold acts this out when he pours petrol over the furniture and carpets of the house, lights a match and watches the flames gut it. Gombold climbs free of the giant's body, glancing over his shoulder at the house 'skeletal against the sky'. Nobody can save it. As Gombold had predicted of the apocalyptic last moment: 'there was nobody to see the end'.

On rereading *Head to Toe* for script ideas for the Beatles film in 1967, Orton was enthusiastic about it. 'It had always been my intention some day to rewrite it,' he wrote, referring to his decision to use part of it as an 'inspiration'. 'I found, to my surprise, that it was excellent. It had great faults as a novel, but as the basis for a film it was more than adequate.'[54] *Head to Toe* dreamed out loud about theatrical impact, and many of the novel's scenes were salvaged from discarded plays. The passion and concerns of his later plays were in the work; but his language was too private and his imagery too confused for ideas to be clearly communicated. Publishers immediately responded to these problems. The editor from MacGibbon and Kee, where Orton first sent the book, explained: 'The flight into fantasy is something I can't follow.' Orton then submitted the novel to Charles Monteith at Faber on 28 June 1961. The tone of Orton's letter anticipated rejection: 'I'm submitting this manuscript . . . in the hope that you'll find a certain amount of pleasure in reading it, and no guilt in refusing it'. Monteith refused it, explaining, 'Several degrees too odd'. The criticism was apt; but the imagery and anarchic energy of the writing came closer to Orton's later comic revenges than anything he'd previously done.

Head to Toe's metaphor was very close to Orton's life. Gombold had searched for the perfect destructive sentence. The design of his sentences was defective. They needed to be tested and their effectiveness improved:

Later he went into the city on his own to test another sentence: it was a failure. On the way back he saw an elderly woman in front of him. As she passed a group of children playing in the road, a small boy said something to her. The reaction was immediate. She turned bright pink; cracks appeared across her face, patches of skin flaked and chipped. She crumbled before his eyes. Gombold questioned the boy and found the sentence he had used was quite simple in construction.

Orton adopted Gombold's tactic and offended the public directly. The book-defacing was brash, simple, and often childishly rude. The library escapade set the stage for the literary impact that was lacking in Orton's fictions. Begun by Orton in August 1959, the project mushroomed obsessively with repeated literary rejection into a kind of art form by 1961. 'I was really occupying myself with these library books which I'd borrowed and also stolen, and then I used to go back with them a couple of times a day.'⁵⁵ The defaced books infiltrated the public and goaded it to respond. Orton was testing the destructive power of his laughter and watching for signs of shock. Gombold, the imaginary prisoner, presaged Orton's actual imprisonment in 1962.

The library prank was a misguided piece of theatre, but the work was very funny. The book jackets were concise, straightforward, irreverent and vulgar: everything that Orton's fiction was not. He had a strong visual sense, and the distortions of his cut-up images played off against language and made words more startling. By 1962 Orton had managed to attract the attention of the Royal Court and the BBC with *The Visit* (1961), a short play about a dying old man in a hospital ward and the chatter of his daughter and the nurses who surround him. The work had been praised and rejected by both institutions. The Royal Court found the writing 'excellent'; the BBC's verdict was 'excellent dialogue . . . the flaw is lack of dramatic shaping and dramatic impact'. Orton's book jackets had none of these artistic faults. The jackets were cunningly designed, and the prank carefully planned. Orton displayed in public what he still lacked on the page: a revenger's passion for plot.

As the famous playwright whose dramatic outrageousness had found its proper format, Orton enjoyed talking about prison and the defaced books. But he always sidestepped the question of the prank's success. Orton's statement to the police stressed the craft he'd put into the project. 'Over the last twelve months,' he told them on 28 April 1962, 'we started to cut pieces out of these books and make false book jackets. I tried to make them as effective as possible by making it look like part of the book.' Orton waited to see a reaction from the public, but got no satisfaction. 'He couldn't understand why the public wasn't getting stirred up,' Sidney Porrett remembers. The work did incite the public, but Orton couldn't gauge the reaction. When he understood the elaborate lengths to which Islington went to catch them, he realized just how disturbing the work had been. This pleased him.

Celebrity has a way of turning stigma into an asset, and Orton glossed his prison experience. 'Prison did not make me bitter, I enjoyed it very much', he told the *Daily Sketch,*[56] echoing the tone Kenneth Halliwell had taken with Sidney Porrett when, while still in prison, he'd ended a letter, 'Yours, having just had the best holiday of my life . . .' Orton swaggered to the *Evening Standard*: 'I didn't suffer or anything the way Oscar Wilde suffered from being in prison – but then Wilde was flabby and self-indulgent. There is this complete myth about writers being sensitive plants. They're not. It's a silly nineteenth-century idea, but I'm sure Aristophanes was not sensitive. I mean there's absolutely no reason why a writer shouldn't be as tough as a bricklayer.'[57]

Orton liked to think of himself as tough. And prison hardened him. Before prison, his anger displayed its wound and lost its aim. After prison, sentiment and self-pity were banished by a show of wit, and his laughter found its targets. 'I tried writing before I went into the nick . . . but it was no good', Orton told the *Leicester Mercury* in 1964. 'And it suddenly worked. Being in the nick brought detachment to my writing. I wasn't involved any more.'[58]

As Orton's rebellion came into focus, so did his style. Prison brought him 'the revelation of what really lies underneath our industrialized society'.[59] Laughter was the message sent back from his cultivated isolation. The boldness of Orton's distortions of reality, the brazenness of his macabre tone, demonstrated a new vivaciousness and innocent nihilism. After prison, Orton understood with his heart as well as his head that values do not exist and that the universe rolls on to no point or purpose. 'Before prison, I had been vaguely conscious of something rotten somewhere: prison crystallized this', Orton said. 'The old whore society really lifted up her skirts and the stench was pretty foul.'[60]

Orton had passed beyond suffering. His laughter and style slowly assumed the cool and penetrating directness of a survivor. His manic playfulness dramatized laughter as a temporary consolation for an existence in which there was no relief. It hid pain from the world, if not from himself. On the empty back page of Orton's clipping book for *Loot* he pasted an anonymous quotation almost as a parenthesis to the critics' near-unanimous praise:

I was not nearly so sure of myself as I should have liked, and this made me present a brassy face to the world and pretend to be more hard-boiled than I was . . . I developed a mocking, cynical way of treating events because it prevented them from being too painful . . .

4

MONSTROUS FUN

> When you can assume that your audience holds
> the same beliefs as you do, you can relax a little
> and use more normal means of talking to it.
> When you have to assume that it does not, then
> you have to make your vision apparent by shock –
> to the hard of hearing you shout and for the
> almost blind you draw large and startling figures.
>
> Flannery O'Connor, *Mystery and Manners*

The nations morals are like teeth: the more
decayed they are the more it hurts to touch them.

George Bernard Shaw, Introduction to
The Shewing-up of Blanco Posnet

Orton's professional breakthrough came in 1963 when the BBC
Third Programme accepted *The Boy Hairdresser*, later retitled *The
Ruffian on the Stair*. The BBC copyright form, dated 21 August,
lists Orton's payment as £65 for a forty-five-minute radio play.
Orton was another happy example of the BBC's institutional kiss
of life. In 1964, the year of its broadcast, there were 395 BBC
radio dramas, and Orton was among fifty-eight new writers.[1] The
BBC had introduced the work of John Arden, Robert Bolt, Willis
Hall, Henry Livings, John Mortimer, Bill Naughton, Alun Owen.
It had sustained Harold Pinter after his early stage failures. The
acceptance of Orton's play came within a month of marking a
decade of total literary failure.

The Ruffian on the Stair was the mirror image of *Entertaining Mr Sloane*, which Orton wrote between September and December of 1963. *The Ruffian on the Stair* dramatized the self-destructive bondage of people to their 'loved ones', and their inability to seize their freedom. The play's self-confessed revenger, Wilson, wants to engineer his own death out of grief for his brother's murder. Like Halliwell, Wilson has not the courage either to live or to die. His character displays the nihilistic, self-loathing aspect of anger that Sloane turns into a slick psychopathic style of survival.

With *The Ruffian on the Stair*, the BBC producers forced Orton to plot more carefully. He had to clarify his dramatic ideas and abandon his predilection for 'arty' dialogue which lost the line of action. Wilson intrudes on the shabby isolation of Mike and Joyce, a petty thief and a former prostitute who live together. While Mike is out, Wilson taunts and terrifies Joyce. Mike has run down Wilson's brother with his van, and Wilson goads Mike into killing him. 'The death', Orton wrote to his producer John Tydeman after the first of three rewrites, 'brings Mike and Joyce together for only a short time; she wants him to stay with her; after he calls the police she will be alone again. This time perhaps for ever.'[2] The theatrical preoccupations of Orton's later work are present but unfocused in *The Ruffian on the Stair* – a fact reflected in his inability to title or satisfactorily conclude the play. 'The title is difficult', Orton wrote to Tydeman. 'How about the Wrong Door? The Victims? Die with the Dying? I can't say I'm happy with any of them.'[3] Neither was the BBC, who asked for more work. On 6 December the BBC accepted the play, but not until 23 December (four days after *Entertaining Mr Sloane* was completed) did Orton furnish the right title. *The Ruffian on the Stair* was taken from a Victorian poem by W. E. Henley:

Madam Life's a piece in bloom,
    Death goes dogging everywhere:
She's the tenant of the room,
    He's the ruffian on the stair.

'It fits', Orton wrote to his producer, who thought it 'splendid'. 'And I don't think it's necessary to know the quotation for the title to be right.'[4] There were two versions of *The Ruffian on the Stair*: the radio version, based on the 1963 manuscript of *The Boy Hairdresser*, and the substantially revised stage version for the Royal Court's Sunday performance without decor (1966), later included in the double bill *Crimes of Passion* (1967). Between the drafting of these two scripts, Orton became a playwright.

'I FORBID the Royal Court to use the version of *The Ruffian on the Stair* printed in the BBC book of radio plays', Orton wrote to Peggy Ramsay in 1966 from Morocco, instructing her to 'burgle' his flat for a revised script. 'I absolutely won't have that version performed anywhere!!'[5] He had reworked the play for television, only to have it temporarily shelved by ITV as unfit for family viewing. 'It's much better, much funnier', Orton wrote to his agent. 'And altogether a more "Ortonish" play than the original the BBC published.' Orton had developed his own unique theatrical style; and the radio play, erected on the scaffold of Harold Pinter's plots for *The Room* and *The Birthday Party*, was embarrassingly derivative. Peggy Ramsay was told to locate the new version from the manuscript drawer underneath Orton's bed; the MS. was identified by a note in Orton's handwriting: 'Thanks for asking to read this. Sorry it had to be a carbon'. The note was to Harold Pinter. Orton could never quite get himself publicly to admit Pinter's influence. 'I suppose he influenced me', he told a BBC interviewer in 1964. 'I think there are other influences on my work far more important than Pinter, and of course you always have to remember that the things which influenced Pinter, which I believe are Hollywood movies in the forties, also influenced me.'[6]

Like Pinter, Orton wanted the seemingly artificial style of his plays to be seen as realistic. ('Had my hair cut at a new hairdressers in Knightsbridge', Orton wrote on 6 March 1967. 'It appears to be quite natural whilst in fact being incredibly artificial. Which is a philosophy I approve of.') And, as Orton's production notes to the

Royal Court imply, he also wanted to dissociate his mature style from Pinter's:

> . . . The play is clearly not written naturalistically, but it must be directed and acted with absolute *realism*. No 'stylization', no 'camp'. No attempt in fact to match the author's extravagance of dialogue with extravagance of direction. REALISTIC PLAYING AND DIRECTING.
>
> Every one of the characters must be real. None of them is ever consciously funny. Every line should be played with desperate seriousness and complete lack of any suggestion of humour. Only in this way can a mixture of comedy and menace be achieved. There must never, from the actors, be the least hint of send-up. The most ludicrous lines – those at the end of the play for instance about the police and the goldfish – must be played quite sincerely. Unless it's real it won't be funny. Everything the characters say is *true*. MIKE has murdered the boy's brother. JOYCE is an ex-call girl. WILSON has an incestuous relationship with his brother. WILSON does provoke MIKE into murdering him. The play mustn't be presented as an example of the now out-dated 'mystery' school – *vide* early Pinter. Everything is as clear as the most reactionary *Telegraph* reader could wish. There is a beginning, a middle and an end . . .
>
> The play must be directed without long significant pauses. Any pauses must be natural pauses. Pace, pace, pace, as well. Go for the strong and natural climaxes. Everything else should be simple.

Orton's note to the Royal Court is already suspicious of the aura of poetic self-consciousness that would infect Pinter's later work. Still, Pinter was the one living English playwright Orton respected. 'I've just finished filming a television play', Orton wrote to a friend in 1966 about *The Erpingham Camp*. 'Which caused a sensation (among the technicians, actors, extras and canteen assistants including H. Pinter, who likes it. He's a writer!).'[7] Orton was passionate about *The Homecoming*. 'Very brilliant play. The best he's written', he wrote to the same friend, drawing a comparison with *Entertaining Mr Sloane*. 'Sexual sharing takes place in that too. A girl though. Makes it more wholesome, I suppose.'[8] Orton saw himself as an influence on the play. '*The Homecoming* couldn't

have been written without *Sloane*', he said, remarking that his play
was on two years before Pinter's. 'And you know, in a way the
second act – although I admire it very much – isn't true. Harold,
I'm sure, would never share anyone sexually. I would. And so
Sloane springs from the way I think. *The Homecoming* doesn't
spring from the way Harold thinks.'[9]

'You're a bloody marvellous writer', Pinter wrote to Orton after
reading the rewrite of *The Ruffian on the Stair*, which he 'loved'.[10]
Pinter, who read a poem at Orton's funeral, found his work 'brilliant
and truly original. He has an instinctive grasp of construction'.[11]
And it was Pinter, who so dominated English theatre during
Orton's career, whom Orton began by imitating and ended by
parodying. 'My name is Caulfield. I've broken into your house',
says the detective intruder as he enters the room of the defrocked
priest McCorquodale in *Funeral Games*, thus lampooning Pinter's
high serious pronouncements about boundaries and 'the room'.[12]

Pinter invented images of entropy; Orton of action. In Pinter's
world, characters hide their needs and disguise the facts of their life.
As his note to the Royal Court shows, Orton was in stylistic
rebellion against this obfuscation. 'The whole trouble with Western
society today', Orton wrote in his diary, 'is the lack of anything
worth concealing.'[13] In Orton's world there is no uncertainty and
no secrets. Reality is outrageous enough without mystifying it.
People say what they mean; but the truth still does not help them.

'Melodrama', Eric Bentley writes, 'depends for its power on the
degree of fear it can arouse, farce on the degree of aggression.'[14]
Pinter's plays updated melodrama; and at first Orton stuck too
close to Pinter's formula for terror for his own aggressive comic
spirit to flourish. Like Wilson's revenge itself, the comic's murderous instinct is significantly still turned inward. Orton began
the radio play with Pinter's familiar smokescreen of pause and
patter as Joyce tries to coax some acknowledgement of her existence
out of Mike over breakfast:

JOYCE. Did you enjoy your breakfast?

MIKE. What?
JOYCE. Did you enjoy your breakfast? The egg was nice, wasn't it?
The eggs are perfect now that I have the timer. Have you noticed?
(*Pause.*) The marmalade was nice. Did it go down well?
MIKE. The egg was nice . . .

The scene is stolen from the opening of *The Birthday Party*.
Orton has changed the brand names, but little else:

MEG. I've got your cornflakes ready. (*She disappears and reappears.*)
Here's your cornflakes.
*He rises and takes the plate from her, sits at the table, props up the
paper and begins to eat. Meg enters by the kitchen door.*
Are they nice?
PETEY. Very nice.
MEG. I thought they'd be nice . . .

From *The Ruffian on the Stair*'s first beat, every theatrical move
seems to follow in Pinter's footsteps. Petey is hidden behind his
morning paper. Meg asks: 'Will you tell me if there's something
good?' Joyce's life is equally eventless, and Orton reworks Pinter's
line to prove it. Joyce cajoles Mike into taking a walk in the park.
'Go today', she says. 'It'll be something to tell me tonight.' Wilson,
himself a reversal of the typical Pinter intruder, occasionally hits a
note that foreshadows later Orton characters: 'The heart is situated
. . . just below the badge on my pullover. Don't miss, will you. I
don't want to be injured. I want to be dead.' But most of Orton's
choices stay close to Pinter's melodramatic plan. *The Ruffian on the
Stair* ends with the same unnerving rhetorical coda as *The Birthday
Party*. When Mike guns down Wilson in jealous rage, Joyce thinks
Wilson's death has brought them together:

JOYCE. This is a happy ending we're having.
Pause.
Isn't it?

The Ruffian on the Stair was broadcast in September 1964. By that
time, *Entertaining Mr Sloane* was a success; *The Good and Faithful
Servant* was completed, and *Loot*, subtitled 'a Farce', was under-
way. Orton's theatrical gusto was increasing as rapidly as his

reputation. The press dubbed him an *enfant terrible*, and Orton did his best to fit the image of literary hooligan. His first public statement was meant to shiver the timbers of his audience and make a case for *The Ruffian on the Stair* as farce. His special pleading says more about the insolence of Orton's emerging theatrical intentions than actual accomplishment:

If you weigh my play *The Ruffian on the Stair* in the balance of good taste you will find you have been short-measured . . .

Ten years ago this theme would have provided an addition to that moribund theatrical genre, Strong Drama. Since the mid-fifties, playwrights have forsaken the inshore fisheries for the ocean proper. Today it is farce.

In a world run by fools the writer can only chronicle the doings of fools or their victims. And because the world is a cruel and heartless place, he will be accused of cruelty and heartlessness. If he thinks that the world is not cruel and heartless but funny as well, he has given his critics an extra brickbat to fling and will be accused of not taking his subject seriously.

But laughter is a serious business and comedy a weapon more dangerous than tragedy. Which is why tyrants treat it with caution. The actual material of tragedy is equally viable as comedy – unless you happen to be writing in English, when the question of taste occurs. The English are the most tasteless nation on earth, which is why they set such store by it.[15]

Orton protested too much. Under the headline STRONG MEAT ON THE AIR, the *Observer* began by discussing taste, only to pass *The Ruffian on the Stair* with flying colours. 'Though not especially seamy,' the paper said, '[it] was wild, harsh, and terrifying, an exercise in fear that roared along like an early Graham Greene.'[16] The *Listener* pooh-poohed Orton's pronouncement in the *Radio Times* and flung an extra brickbat while proclaiming the play 'rather a hit – if you don't take it too seriously'.[17] Farce mixes wild fantasy with everyday reality; and it was clear in the extreme reactions to his play that Orton had not found the right comic chemistry for it. There was little aggression in his radio laughter;

and little laughter in the aggression. The sadness which once spoiled Orton's performing now muted the impact of his play. In the radio version, characters continually bleat their sense of loss and isolation. The day after Wilson's first threatening visit, Joyce hears another knock on her door. She contemplates praying. 'I'd try maybe a prayer. But the Virgin would turn a deaf ear to a Protestant . . . I can't be as alone as all that. Nobody ought to be. It's humiliating. (*Pause.*) God is so remote.' Orton would blue-pencil the excesses in Joyce's dialogue for the stage. A play must leave something for its audience to imagine; but Orton's explicitness robbed the first version of any genuine playfulness.

Gaiety must emerge from apparent seriousness; sadness from apparent gaiety. Orton hadn't learned this dramatic lesson in time for the radio version of *The Ruffian on the Stair*. There was no sprightliness in Wilson to play off against his morbid obsession. Self-pity sneaks into his character and diminishes him. His prose and his personality are lack-lustre. Wilson came across as weak – a whiner. 'I can see this is a failure like everything else', he says to Joyce when his staged seduction doesn't lure Mike upstairs to kill him. Orton had misjudged his main character and the play's offensiveness. The 'incestuous' relationship which Orton saw as shocking was too vague. The stage version reversed this. Orton's rewrite of Wilson has comic sparkle and innuendo:

I'm a Gents hairdresser. Qualified. My dad has a business. Just a couple of chairs. I've clipped some notable heads in my time. Mostly professional men. Though we had an amateur street musician in a few weeks ago. We gave him satisfaction, I believe.

Wilson now talks with a hint of swaggering egotism that ear-marks all Orton's stage characters. In an exchange about his brother's death, Orton also establishes Wilson's kinkier side.

WILSON. . . . He was a sportsman before his decease. He wore white shorts better than any man I've ever come in contact with. As a matter of fact, strictly off the record, I'm wearing a pair of his

white shorts at this moment. They're inconvenient ... because
... (*He blurts it out.*) – there's no fly. (*Pause.*) He wore them two days
before he was killed ...

'Orton never wrote another play with emotions of this kind',
says Peter Gill, who directed *The Ruffian on the Stair* in London.
'It's the only play where he tried to write about genuine homosexual emotions. It's really very powerful and very upsetting
because Orton hadn't completely found himself.' Wilson's brother
is his narcissistic ideal, his physical replica; 'I don't take after him.
Except in a physical sense', he says. Wilson proudly admits that they
'spent every night in each other's company'. He has magically
linked his identity to his brother's. With his brother's death, he
finds himself with no 'heroic' aura to protect him from his own
inadequacy and isolation.

WILSON. . . . He was the go-ahead type. His mentality was fully
   developed. He used to read a lot about expansion. His death put a
   stop to that ... I get a bit lost without him, I don't mind admitting.

'There is an atmosphere of total bleakness at that moment', says
Peter Gill. 'The landscape the actor is seeing is incredibly bleak.'
Success gave Orton a distance on his craft and his early life, and
Wilson's revenge became, in the stage rewrite, Orton's partial
revenge on his own past. He added his and Halliwell's biographical
detail to Wilson's – the bedsitter; the cosy life of 'no circumstances'
on the NAB; the twenty-four-hour companion. 'All our family
seem to be some kind of an idiot', Wilson says, in a bitter speech
that echoes Orton's feelings. 'If anybody so much as mentions the
British Legion to my dad he goes into a trance. On armistice day
he takes part in all the rituals. He eats poppies for a week before-
hand. I haven't seen him since the funeral. I expect he's in a home
by now.'

'The English art of compromise is the thing', Orton said. 'I see
plays as a piece of meat which buries the hook of what the author
has to say. Too many plays are just bare hooks that will never make
anyone put it in their mouth.'[18] The rewrite of *The Ruffian on the
Stair* exemplifies Orton's search for a compromise between his

sense of chaos and comedy. In the increasingly baroque rhythms with which he delivered his dark laughter, Orton evolved a balance between pleasure and pain, idealization and need. Language elevated Man above the animal, and also hid the 'beastliness' in Man from himself. Orton found the juxtaposition of intentions hilarious:

I read Genet's QUERELLE OF BREST. An interesting book, but unformed ... Undoubtedly Jean Genet is the most perfect example of an unconscious humourist at work since Marie Corelli. I find a sentence like: 'They (the homosexuals of Brest) are peace-loving, citizens of irreproachable outward appearance, even though, the long day through, they may perhaps suffer from a rather timid itch for a bit of cock' irresistibly funny. A combination of elegance and crudity is always ridiculous.

(23 January 1967)

Orton wanted hilarity and terror to co-exist as they do in farce. But in the radio version, with such earthbound characterization, he couldn't accomplish the farce momentum to elevate the everyday into the extraordinary. By contrast, the stage version knows where it's going and how to get there. Situations now speak for themselves. Orton tells his story *with* character and action; not *about* character and action. Like Wilson, Mike is reconstructed larger than life, his personality and language inflated by bolder and broader theatrical strokes. No longer the beleaguered layabout of the radio play, he is quickly established as a criminal, and his dapper self-confidence never admits the sadness in the situation. Joyce doesn't want Wilson inside her house. But Mike takes no notice of her fear and invites him in:

WILSON. I'm a Gents Hairdresser.
MIKE. You wouldn't happen to be dabbling with birth-control devices? That's no way for a Catholic to carry on.
WILSON. I don't handle that part of the trade. My old man does it. He has the free-thinking frame of mind. I can't approve, of course. It's the Latin temperament which has been the curse of our religion all along.
MIKE. The Pope is Italian.

WILSON. You have something there. I'd like to see a Liffey man on the throne of St Peter myself. I'd be proud to hear the Lateran ring with the full-throated blasphemies of our native land.

MIKE. What are you thinking of? The Vicar of Christ doesn't blaspheme.

WILSON. He would if he was Irish and drank Guinness.

The strut and swagger of their first exchange move Mike and Wilson confidently towards the grotesque. In their distortion lies Orton's special perception of human caprice: the timid animal asserting its feeble powers, roaring at a dangerous world to keep life at a safe distance.

'I suppose I'm a believer in Original Sin', Orton said. 'People are profoundly bad, but irresistibly funny.'[19] Style – or attempts at it – was a stage-managed redemption. The bow-wow idiom of Mike and Wilson demonstrates their heroic posturing while spoofing the weakness it tries to hide. Increasingly Orton's characters would bolster themselves with stylized speech, dramatizing in every exchange the vital lie of human character, man's necessary dishonesty in defending himself against an awesome reality. 'The morals of Nineveh were hardly so lax,' bellows Mike, in a grandiloquent curse which continues for a page and elevates Joyce's imagined adultery with Wilson to the size of Old Testament sins. Mike's revenger's 'aria' was meant as a parody of Jacobean tragedy. Language is staged as a convincing self-hypnotic gesture of triumphant control in a life that denies it. Orton's words require a delivery of great self-possession, but the situation always betrays the tone. In *The Ruffian on the Stair* all the characters worry about possessing others but are never in possession of themselves.

The repertoire of emotion Mike and Joyce encounter includes incest, murder, rage, fear, frenzy and loneliness; yet they deny it, demanding that a benign and dignified face be imposed on experience. Orton's savage laughter refuses both his characters and the audience the comfort of their heroic illusions while dramatizing why they are necessary. *The Ruffian on the Stair* makes a spectacle of this preposterous evasion, which was only a notion in the radio play. Wilson wants to be killed in the most heroic and authentic heterosexual circumstances. Just before he is shot, Wilson 'unbuttons his shirt, pins a badge on his shirt above the heart and unzips his fly'. When Mike bursts into the room, he fires two bullets; one shatters Joyce's goldfish bowl, the other hits Wilson in the chest. Wilson crumples to the floor, speaking his last words as 'blood spurts from his mouth':

JOYCE. He's fainted.
MIKE (*laying the gun aside*). He's dead.
JOYCE. But he can't be. You haven't killed him?
MIKE. Bring a sheet. Cover his body.
JOYCE. I've a bit of sacking somewhere.
MIKE. I said a sheet! Give him the best.
    He goes into the bedroom and drags a sheet from the bed which he puts over WILSON's *body.*

Mike and Joyce then invoke 'the best': their ideal sense of themselves – love, bravery, loyalty – to cover up their confusion:

JOYCE. What excuse was there to shoot him?
MIKE. He was misbehaving himself with my wife.
JOYCE. But I'm not your wife. And he wasn't.
MIKE. He called you Maddy.
JOYCE. Somebody must've told him about my past. You know what people are. (*Pause.*) Did you have anything to do with his brother's death?
MIKE. Yes.
JOYCE. This is what comes of having no regular job. (*Pause.*) Is the phone box working by the Nag's Head?
MIKE. Yes.
JOYCE. Go to the telephone box. Dial 999. I'll tell them I was assaulted.
MIKE (*horrified*). It'll be in the papers.
JOYCE. Well, perhaps not assaulted. Not completely. You came in just in time.
MIKE. You'll stick by me, Joycie?

JOYCE. Of course, dear. (*She kisses him.*) I love you.
  She sees the shattered goldfish bowl.
  Oh, look Michael! (*Bursting into tears.*) My goldfish!
  She picks up a fish.
MIKE. One of the bullets must've hit the bowl.
JOYCE. They're dead. Poor things. And I reared them so carefully.
  And while all this was going on they died.
  She sobs. MIKE *puts his arms round her, and leads her to the settee.*
  She sits.
MIKE. Sit down. I'll fetch the police. This has been a crime of passion.
  They'll understand. They have wives and goldfish of their own.
  JOYCE *is too heartbroken to answer. She buries her face in* MIKE'*s*
  shoulder. He holds her close.
                    Curtain.

The blunt and brutal comic ending was upsetting even to the
director. 'I felt my whole moral nature called into question', Peter
Gill says. This was the intention behind Orton's comedy. 'I remember quoting Joe a line from T. S. Eliot: "We must be forever
rebuilding the temple",' Kenneth Williams says. 'And Joe said
"That's it, exactly". It wasn't shock for its own sake he was after.
He wanted to force you to deliberately re-examine the structure – of
language, of manners, of morals, of institutions. His instinct was
always healthy.'

The serious aim of Orton's humour was misguidedly dubbed
'sick' by the press – a know-nothing phrase which overlooked the
moral anger and the generosity in Orton's comic performance.

What is a healthy play? Just name me one [Orton said in 1966].
Every good play expresses something of the time in which it was
written, and at the moment we're living in a very sick society. During
the '50's, when people were still concerned with changing the world
and finding useful political solutions, plays like Arnold Wesker's
Chicken Soup with Barley were quite representative. But today there
is a general sense of despair about politics because we know it can't
provide any real solutions. Still, I would never claim that I was a
pessimistic writer. I'm too amused by the way people carry on to
give in to despair.[20]

'Just before I wrote *Sloane*, there was a point at which I wavered, looking into the future and seeing nothing, when I thought – "I'm not going to be anything".'[21] Orton knew the terror of psychic death: impotent, invisible, unfulfilled. He had imagined himself dead in fiction; and, on TV, he even played dead as the corpse of Erpingham, the panjandrum of a holiday camp. There was a ghostly disruptive ambition to his humour, haunting the society with the power acquired from forays between seen and subterranean worlds. Wilson, like Orton, wants to win the power of the dead by imitating the dead. Wilson is the first of many Orton characters to seek triumph over a sense of trapped energy. Orton's stage laughter signals his freedom, but his characters never laugh. There is something ghostlike about them. They are mischievous and often malicious. They haunt and terrorize people: externalizations of Orton's own struggle for imaginative freedom.

Like his characters, Orton's life was filled with many tentative gestures of ghostlike mastery. 'John Orton' the failed novelist and acolyte of Kenneth Halliwell returned as 'Joe Orton' to distinguish himself from John Osborne in the public mind. Private failures were turned to public triumph. Wilson's friendship with his brother, like Halliwell's with Orton, had been a neurotic solution to life; his desperate remedy to put things 'right' was also Halliwell's constant threat to Orton. In working out the gloom of the past, Orton's laughter got even for the pain.[22] Orton haunted not only his past but the public. 'Edna Welthorpe' was a phantom delighting in her invisible power to provoke and confuse the community. Orton aspired to be the 'fly on the wall' – his term for his nameless adventuring through London. He knew that eavesdropping was essential to his craft, and he guarded his anonymity:

On the tube today I listened to a conversation about a 'lovely girl' called Rosalind. An elderly man leaned across to a woman and said, 'My last memory connected with her was when she was home from college and she took a job in a nursery.' The woman with him smiled and said, 'That's why they had such lovely bulbs in their beds.'

(1 March 1967)

. . . I heard a most fascinating conversation between an old man and a woman. 'What a thing, though,' the old woman said. 'You'd hardly credit it.' 'She's always made a fuss of the whole family, but never me,' the old man said. 'Does she have a fire when the young people come to see her?' 'Fire? She won't get people seeing her without warmth.' 'I know why she's doing it. Don't think I don't,' the old man said. 'My sister she said to me, "I wish I had your easy life". Now that upset me. I was upset by the way she phrased herself. "Don't talk to me like that," I said, "I've only got to get on the phone and ring a certain number," I said, "To have you stopped".' 'Yes,' the old woman said, 'and you can, can't you?' 'Were they always the same?' she said, 'when you was a child? Can you throw yourself back? How was they years ago?' 'The same,' the old man said. 'Wicked, isn't it,' the old woman said. 'Take care now,' she said as the old man left. He didn't say a word to her but got off the bus looking disgruntled.

(18 January 1967)

Even Orton's sexual encounters, as he recorded them in his diary, have an eerie anonymity. In every meeting, Orton is both present and absent, shadowing himself and his pick-ups: listening, judging, observing, absorbing the detail of each encounter but always outside the experience:

In a lavatory I met a middle-aged man with a cropped haircut. Not very attractive. He said he lived in a council flat. 'I'm waiting to go back to sea,' he said. We walked for about a hundred yards and he said, 'You don't want it stuck up your arse, do you?' I said I wasn't keen. 'And you're not going to suck me off, are you?' he said. 'No,' I said. 'You just want to shoot your gun,' he said, 'like me.' He turned around. 'We'd better go back,' he said. 'You can pick up a queer in that toilet. They've got cars. And houses. The best time is dinner time. They've got cars most of them. I've fucked their arses in their rooms,' he said, lighting a cigarette. 'I expect you have too.' We went into the lavatory. Only one man there. I stood next to him. The man with the cropped hair went away. The man I stood next to was a Greek-Cypriot. He wasn't very young. About thirty-five. Very stupid looking. 'Come to the park,' he said, in an ice-cream seller's accent, 'I'll shag you.' I thought it was a stupid idea. And when we got to the park it seemed as though I'd met a maniac. 'See over there,' he said. 'Two men. They shag. And over there,' he said, pointing to a clump of trees that were perhaps three feet away from a well-lighted pavement. 'Please let me shag you,' he said, 'I'll be quick.' 'But we're in the light!' I said. 'We can be seen.' 'Naw,' he said, 'nobody notice.' Up against a tree I dropped my trousers and he fucked me. He was quick. Afterwards he tossed me off. As we were walking away he said, 'I shag a boy last week. I pay him £2. You don't want money, do you?' 'No,' I said, 'I've plenty of money.' He laughed at this and said, 'Me too. I've plenty of money. Too many people shag here,' he said, ambling off across the dark ground. 'Maybe next time we shag in a room. Maybe next time you shag me as well.' I said that it would be a pleasure and left him.

(13 July 1967)

The detachment in *The Ruffian on the Stair*'s stage laughter matched Orton's personal style. It gave him a curious tranquillity in public. 'Joe's vision was bleak,' Peter Gill recalls, 'but he was very stable in a funny sort of way. He had no worries. He had none of the neurotic panic of someone like myself who always thinks he's going to get killed in a sexual situation. Joe had a ruthless self-sufficiency.' Peggy Ramsay was also impressed by Orton's 'lovely detachment': 'His detachment is what makes me feel he is better than practically every author we've looked after. I admired him for it more than anything else. It made him a consummate artist ... He wasn't prepared to sacrifice his ambition to life. The theatre is a mere reflection of life, dear; but it's life that's the important thing. The theatre throws it back, enhances it with a good play, makes life wonderful. Joe was never kidded that it was more than a reflection.'

When *Crimes of Passion* opened at the Royal Court in June 1967, Orton returned from Morocco nervous and exhausted. 'Took two of Kenneth's secret "suicide pills". Nembutal. Fell into a deep sleep.' At the last dress rehearsal on 5 June he found 'RUFFIAN very slow. ERPINGHAM rather good though impossibly ragged and needed a lot of rehearsing. Peggy unenthusiastic. Think it isn't going to be a success. Had dinner with Bill Gaskill, Peggy and

Oscar Lewenstein. "It's quite an amusing evening," Oscar said.
Felt annoyed. ERPINGHAM is the best (stage) play of mine performed so far. If only Arthur Lowe were playing Erpingham they'd
all be raving...' But Orton faced the opening night and the
reviews with equanimity:

The big day...Peter Gill spent most of the day tightening
ERPINGHAM especially scene changes in the blackouts. I had a cup of
tea with Joan who works in the box office. She's just confessed to her
husband that she's been having an affair with another man for eight
years...'I've been having a sort of minor breakdown,' she said,
'that's why I fainted a few weeks ago.' 'You're not going to get a
divorce,' I said. 'Oh no,' she said. 'You don't want to?' I asked. 'As
long as your husband doesn't mind why shouldn't you love two
people at once?' She said I was the only person she knew who had
taken this attitude. 'It's perfectly sensible,' I said. 'Why break up your
marriage, have a lover. Just carry on as before.' ...I got to the
Royal Court at 7. They were having difficulties with the programmes
– only a few had arrived. I went to my seat and sat down. Saw Sheila
Hancock sitting with Oscar. She smiled and blew a kiss. RUFFIAN
began. It seemed slow at first. It was the best performance this cast
has given of the play. The whole thing came over as a sad little play.
Spoke to Sheila at the interval. She adored the play. 'I liked the bits
about loneliness,' she said. 'Loneliness in the theatre is usually so
embarrassing.' ...The bell rang and we went back to the theatre for
ERPINGHAM CAMP – the main part of the evening. It went extremely
well. A great deal of enthusiasm from the audience. I was pleased that,
within the limits and bearing in mind the difficulty, it went so well.
I admired Peter's production. It had style. Too much enthusiasm
afterwards though. I feared that when so many 'pros' were raving
in the dressing room after. 'This should be transferred,' someone said
in a loud voice. 'We must wait until tomorrow for the verdict,' I
said. 'Oh fuck the critics,' Peter Gill said. 'They don't matter.' This
is bravado. Of course they matter. B. Gaskill seemed pleased and so
did Oscar. Everybody enthusiastic. Had a drink in the club of the
Court. I left early as I wanted a bit of sex. Took two valium tablets
and waited for the no. 19 bus in Sloane Square. Got off at Piccadilly.
Went to Holloway Road. Went to the Gents Lavatory. Nothing

much in there. A man of about 30. Then another man came in in his twenties. He began to suck the first man off. The first man dropped his trousers and offered me his arse. I said it was too dangerous. This was immediately confirmed when three men came in and stood inside the doorway. The man doing the sucking left. I rather fancied him so I followed. 'Who was that fellow?' he said in a little Irish accent. 'I don't know,' I said. 'Have you got a place?' I said. 'Yes, at Highbury,' he said. He took me back to his furnished room. I took off my shirt. 'You've a lovely body,' he said, running his hands over, 'and where did you get such a lovely tan?' 'I went to Torremolinos.' I chose this because it's quite a likely place for a working lad to go. The man dropped to his knees, undid my pants and pulled them down. I was going to get my cock out. Instead he nuzzled and sucked it through my underpants. After he'd done this for a bit I pulled him up and stuck my tongue down his throat and pulled him to the bed. He took his clothes off and I got on top of him. 'Oh you've got a grand cock,' he said stroking it. I realized how much of sex was missed in Morocco by not being able to talk the language. I lifted his legs in the air, spat on my hand, wiped my cock and got the end up his arse. 'Oh no,' he cried. 'No, no!' I stopped and then realized that this was part of his personal kink. I gripped him hard. 'I'm going to fuck you,' I said, 'keep quiet.' I pinned him to the bed with his legs up in the air and shoved my cock right up him. He gave a cry, 'Oh my God. Oh you're hurting me.' I began to fuck him. It was a very good fuck. 'Let me see,' he said. 'I want to see your cock going in and out.' I had to lift myself up so that he could see my cock. He stroked my balls as I fucked him and I left my prick in after I'd come. 'Oh I needed that,' he said. 'I needed a good fucking, you certainly know how to fuck.' He then wanted me to lie on my belly. 'Oh you've lovely muscles,' he said stroking my back. 'I'd love a threesome with you and some other chap,' he said as a final shot. I got dressed after washing my cock and kissed him goodnight and went home. I had to walk all the way back. Very tired. Outside a newsagent, I saw a placard announcing ISRAELIS KNOCK OUT ARABS. So I stole it. As a souvenir and a reminder that, whilst I was having a first night and fucking an Irishman (the second more satisfactory than the first) the third War would have been averted. Got in at 2 and slept until 7.30.

WEDNESDAY 7 JUNE

Went out at eight. Got all the papers. Read them. Not good reviews. All luke warm. Not a single review one could honestly say would do the box-office good. Rang Peggy. She's read the *Times*, the *Financial Times* was very cool, *The Guardian* had reverted to its original position on *Sloane*. *The Mirror* hostile 'Double bill that was almost a double bore'. Oh well I did have a good fuck last night. I got something out of my return to London. Had an interview at 10 with a woman from the *Evening News*. A telephone chat with some-one from the *Evening Standard* who had seen the plays at the dress rehearsal and liked them . . . Went to the Court. Very downcast at the lack of enthusiasm for the plays. I had an interview for *Town and Around* in which they asked, rather aggressively I thought, 'what the gimmick of having yourself drawn in the nude for the programme was'. I said, 'There are many people who might like a nude picture of me; I'm not unattractive you know.' They said they wouldn't be using the interview today, perhaps sometime next week, which in polite terms I suppose means never. I was asked to be on Late Night Line-Up with John Mortimer. We had to watch and discuss A FLEA IN HER EAR, the National Theatre production which was televised earlier in the evening. I hated it as much as I had done on seeing it in the theatre . . . It was directed and acted with great speed and no reality. I watched as I packed . . . A taxi called at 9.20, took me to the studio at Shepherd's Bush. In a special viewing room the play was still going on. I watched and all the time I wondered how the second night of CRIMES OF PASSION was going. Rang Peter. He said it was going v. well. Harold Pinter was in the front as well as all the weekly critics. Pinter, I'm sure, won't like the way ERPINGHAM is directed or acted. He liked the much more naturalistic way it was done on telly. Said goodbye to Peter. Said I was sorry it hadn't been better received. He said that someone had said that Harold Hobson liked the evening – don't entirely believe this. He was supposed to have liked LOOT but gave it a very small notice. No hope there I'm afraid. Did the Late Night Line-Up. Expressed my views on FLEA by saying that in Farce everything (the externals) must be believed. The actors were dressed as though they were period equivalent of Mick Jagger. Now it wouldn't be funny if Mick Jagger were caught in a brothel, but if Harold Wilson were caught in a brothel it would

be extremely funny ... After the programme I was taken to the air
terminal ... It was dawn by the time we took off ... Finally got in
to Tangier about tennish. Instead of a taxi I got the airport bus ... I
sat next to a blond beatnik type. He said he'd seen me before. 'Very
likely,' I said dryly, 'there was a quarter page picture of me in the
Sunday Times last week.' 'You're Joe Orton,' he said. It's the first
time I've been recognized ...

(7 June 1967)

Back at play in Tangier, Orton brought critics and life into perspective with a saving laugh. 'There have been a few "incidents" of
a political nature whilst I've been away', he wrote to Peter Gill. 'Yesterday I was out with some people, and in the street a boy made an
ambiguous gesture in my direction. "Was the boy spitting at me?"
I asked. "No," someone said, "he was blowing you a kiss." So
things are back to "normal" here. (Notice the "typical Orton use
of the ironic word!!".)'

'I'm an acquired taste,' Orton said in 1967. 'That's a double
entendre if there ever was one. The public will accept me. They've
already given me a licence, you see. What they'll do is say "Joe
Orton can do these things because he's a success". But I'm a success
because I've taken a hatchet to them and hacked my way in.'[23]
The Ruffian on the Stair, in retrospect a 'sad little play' to Orton,
was a flabby first jab at society. *Entertaining Mr Sloane* was the cor-
rosive successor to *The Ruffian on the Stair*, and Orton's first produced play. Acknowledgement of Orton's talent seemed to liberate
it. *Entertaining Mr Sloane* was a brazen fantasy of his new-found
freedom. The play had a buoyant, self-confident control of language and structure that none of Orton's previous writing could
muster. It stunned the British public and brought him immediate
international attention.

Orton had finished the final BBC rewrites for *The Ruffian on the
Stair* on 30 November; and on 19 December 1963 *Entertaining Mr
Sloane* was logged into the office of Margaret Ramsay. A former
opera singer and actress, who had clowned in pantomime as well

as sung at the Coliseum, Peggy Ramsay brought her special literary passions and eccentric energy to the English theatrical scene. Before becoming an agent, she had helped launch the Bristol Old Vic as literary adviser and publicist; read plays for Peter Daubeny; and managed the Kew Theatre, choosing and casting fifty-two plays in a year. ('We gave most of the current leading directors of the British theatre their first chance. And they haven't improved, dear.') In 1959, with a loan of £1,000, she set up her own theatrical agency, and her receptivity to new work soon earned her a reputation as imposing as her list of clients.[24] Orton had been steered to Peggy Ramsay by his BBC producer, John Tydeman, who sent her a copy of The Ruffian on the Stair, touting the play as 'fairly successful' and its author as a 'genuinely interesting and original writer'. Peggy Ramsay concurred. 'What struck me about Entertaining Mr Sloane was that it was luminous and spare, very spare and very sharp,' she recalls. 'What I didn't like about it was the convenience of the end. I didn't like the shape of the play. I didn't think it was a great play but I didn't hesitate when I read it. I read it in one night and the next morning [30 December] I wrote Joe a letter. I said: "I was very pleased to receive Entertaining Mr Sloane, which I think is extremely fresh and interesting. I'm not absolutely sure it will hold a whole evening, but I think it might." I asked him to come and see me. I knew nothing about him when he walked in. He had considerable confidence and charm. He didn't mind me speaking about his play in rather harsh generalities – that's one of the reasons I liked him so much. He smiled and said, "Yes, yes, I see". And then he added, "I'm glad you like my work. Next time I'll try and write you a better play". And I said: "Well, that would be gorgeous". As he was getting up to go, I asked him what he lived on while he was writing. "I'm living on National Assistance, £3 10 a week since I got out of jail." I couldn't believe it. I took his address, and he left. I rang Michael Codron. "I've just met a very promising writer, and he's living on £3 10 a week. Will you read his play immediately?" '

Michael Codron was then the artistic director of the New Arts

Theatre. He was a serious and savvy impresario who had been first to produce Pinter (*The Birthday Party*, 1958), Henry Livings (*Nil Carborundum*, 1962) and David Rudkin (*Afore Night Come*, 1962). 'I told Michael if he took the Arts for a year, he'd make his reputation and lose his money,' Peggy Ramsay recalls. Between 1962 and 1964, Codron certainly made his reputation, much of it by producing Ramsay clients: Livings, Rudkin, Saunders, Marcus, Wood, Mortimer. 'When I read *Sloane* I felt it was unique stuff,' Codron says. 'I really did. Totally fresh. Having produced *The Birthday Party*, I never thought of Joe as Pinteresque. I had a theatre to run, or rather it was running me. I had to put on a new play every four weeks. I made a quick decision.' The speed of the decision left even Peggy Ramsay incredulous. 'I don't quite know how it came about but we have sold your play to go on at the Arts March/April', she wrote to Orton on 20 January 1964. 'Michael Codron read it, loves it, Donald Albery says he will "come in" with Michael and they will present it together . . .'

'I have a strong hunch', Codron wrote to his investors about *Entertaining Mr Sloane*, 'that the new play I am doing (with Donald Albery) might turn out to have the most exciting commercial possibilities since *The Caretaker*.' The play generated a kind of enthusiasm from management that dazzled the Ramsay agency. 'It's very unusual for Managements to fall over themselves with eagerness to pay for an option on a play before the contract is signed', Peggy Ramsay wrote Orton on 5 February, herself investing £250 in the production unbeknown to Orton. 'But in this case it has happened. Wonders will never cease.' And wonders continued. The next month, the producers doubled Orton's advance to £100 (a sum that he never earned back in the Arts Theatre production, which was capitalized at £2,000).

'Only a society in deep despair about itself', wrote *The Times* in an editorial (1970), 'would accept the hostility to meaning of some of the artists in the '60's.'[25] By 1964 England was in a time of radical transition: from being top dog to becoming America's poodle; from a life built around the discipline of war-time scarcity to the ease of a new abundance; from thirteen years of Conservative rule to a Labour government. It was a time when the Lord Chamberlain still controlled the content of English theatre 'to prevent offence being given'. It was the era of the discotheque and the twist, when the English were beginning to move to new rhythms and adopt new styles. 'I saw no reason why childhood shouldn't last for ever,' Mary Quant told the press. 'I wanted everyone to retain the grace of a child and not to have to become stilted, confined, ugly beings. So I created clothes that worked and moved and allowed people to run, to jump, to leap, to retain their precious freedom.'[26] Even the Beatles, those 'lads' who mixed Cardin chic with Liverpool cheek, epitomized the daydream of abundance and eternal youthfulness. Their success was as exciting as their songs. By late 1963, even if Britannia no longer ruled the waves, the Beatles dominated the airwaves. At the centre of the New Boy Network of renegade energy and 'classless' attainment, their music and their popular saga gave British life the backbeat of promise.

Entertaining Mr Sloane caught the abrasive and expansive mood of the time. 'From what I remember they [his family] was respected', Sloane tells Kath. 'You know, H.P. debts. Bridge. A little light gardening. The usual activities of a cultured community.' Spoiling for a fight, the original script pulled back from its deep-seated anarchic intentions. 'The original ending', Orton said, 'was quite different and much more complex, and it was wrong. Many writers I think compromise themselves with over-subtle endings – Tennessee Williams is an obvious example. The new ending to *Mr Sloane* is very simple, but a natural outcome. This is how I always work: letting the situation emerge and develop gradually, without a preconceived plan – letting the characters take over.'[27]

The first version of *Entertaining Mr Sloane* ended abruptly with the murder of the father, a choice which didn't resolve the fascinating family relationships which revolve around him. The idea of sexual sharing was suggested to Orton by Peter Wood, who was

2. Orton at 16

3. Orton at RADA

4. Halliwell at 10 with family

1. Overleaf, Orton in 1967

5. Halliwell at 16

6. Wedding day, 1964 – George and Leonie Orton Barnett, Elsie and William Orton

7. William Orton, 1970

8. As Lucio (*right*) in *Measure for Measure*, 1951

9. As Tyltyl in *The Blue Bird*, 1949

10. As the bellboy in *Born Yesterday*, Ipswich Rep, 1953

Collins Guide to
ROSES

by BERTRAM PARK

DEREK STANFORD

JOHN BETJEMAN

Sybil Thorndike

An illustrated study of Dame Sybil's work, with a list of her appearances on stage & screen

Alec Clunes

An illustrated study of his work with a list of his appearances on stage & screen

15. 1966

16. 1962

The bedsitter 17. 1962

18. 1964

19. Halliwell, Morocco, 1967

20. With Halliwell, Morocco, 1967

21. Halliwell, Tangier, 1967

22. With Kenneth Williams and
Halliwell, Tangier, 1965

23. *The Ruffian on the Stair*, Royal Court, 1967

24. Orton (in cap) listens to Peter Gill discuss
sets for *Crimes of Passion*

25. The defrocked priest, McCorquodale (Bill Fraser), in *Funeral Games*

26. Mrs Vealfoy (Patricia Routledge) presents Buchanan (Donald Pleasance) with his retirement gift in *The Good and Faithful Servant*

27. Beryl Reid as Kath and
Malcolm McDowell as Sloane
in the Royal Court revival of
Entertaining Mr Sloane, 1975

28. Kenneth Cranham (*left*)
and Simon Ward with the
corpse in *Loot*, 1966

29. Halliwell's collage poster

30. Michael Bates (*right*), as Truscott, sifts the evidence. Sheila Ballantine (Fay) and Kenneth Cranham (Hal) look on as McLeavy (Gerry Duggan) explains the funeral fiasco in *Loot*, 1966

31. "Oh, this place is like a madhouse": Mrs Prentice and Nick, in Lindsay Anderson's revival of *What the Butler Saw*, Royal Court, 1975

32. Winston Churchill's missing part. (*Left to right*): Valentine Dyall (Dr Rance), Kevin Lloyd (Nick), Jane Carr (Geraldine Barclay), Brian Glover (Sergeant Match), Betty Marsden (Mrs Prentice), Michael Medwin (Dr Prentice)

33. Nick and Dr Prentice dispose of the drugged police sergeant

34. *Overleaf*, 1965

supposed to direct *Entertaining Mr Sloane* but was forced to withdraw because of other commitments. 'Originally the play had more echoes of Pinter in it,' explains Wood, who directed the first production of *The Birthday Party*. 'The play started very well but Joe became naturally fascinated with the actual dialogue shapes and the structure became dislocated. The killing of the father at the end didn't seem to me to be what the play was about. The play seemed to me to be about the interaction between Sloane and the brother and sister. It wasn't ironic or amoral enough.'

'I originally started with the Oedipus legend as a basis and threw it out halfway through', Orton told the BBC in 1964. 'It gave me the germ to start from. I got Eddie the brother and father relationship from *Oedipus at Colonus* – the old man won't speak to his son at all. There's no significance in the fact that I used the two Oedipuses at all, apart from the fact that it just gave me an idea and dramatists always need a plot. It doesn't really matter what you use as a plot on which to hang your dialogue and your ideas, but you must, I think, have a plot . . .'[28] The original ending was a vestige from reworking the Oedipus legend; the new ending brought the play much closer to Orton himself. Sloane was polymorphous and definitely perverse. 'I want a very young boy for Sloane', Orton wrote about casting suggestions for TV. 'Someone you'd like to fuck silly.'[29] Sloane was lethal and charming, a combination of magical black-leather meanness and boyish innocence – a sexy shadow of Orton's fantasy of himself. 'I saw him as small and stocky', Orton said, describing Sloane in his own proportions. Orton dreamed the prankster's dream of shattering taboos, and Sloane's shamelessness, which made taboos meaningless, was Orton's revenge on society. 'What many people have found difficult to understand about Sloane', Orton said, 'is the combination of innocence and amorality. The English always tend to equate innocence with ignorance, which is nonsense.'[30]

Sloane took his place among the theatrical rogues who characterized England in the sixties – Pinter's Mick (*The Caretaker*) and Lenny (*The Homecoming*); Osborne's Bill Maitland (*Inadmissible*

Evidence); David Halliwell's Malcolm (*Little Malcolm Against the Eunuchs*). Sloane's nonchalant anarchy was a radical contrast to the shabby genteel setting which was a familiar locale on the British stage. Sloane dramatized the psychopathic style that dominated the late sixties – that restless, ruthless, single-minded pursuit of satisfaction – transformed by drugs and rock music into myth.

'There aren't any big, brave causes left', hectored John Osborne's Jimmy Porter in *Look Back in Anger* (1956). 'In *Entertaining Mr Sloane*, Orton managed to write the first solid, well-managed commercial play which belonged, specifically and unmistakably, to the post-Osborne era', wrote John Russell Taylor in *The Second Wave*.[31] Where Osborne's theatre and his characters by 1964 were stale-mated by the impotent heroics of invective, Orton faced the loss of nerve in middle-class life and got beyond a sense of paralysis. Sloane's amorality was disillusion in action. *Entertaining Mr Sloane* made a myth of society's ugliness in order to expose it. Kath's house is in the middle of a rubbish dump; and everyone who enters it is tainted with a sense of waste. The characters live off the scraps of life, and their conversation consists of vernacular throw-aways. In a society without a heroic mission, surrounded literally by in-dustrial rubbish, Sloane becomes his own most valuable project. He is a model of narcissistic non-commitment. Orton wrote a letter about Sloane to his American director, Alan Schneider:

I don't know what you mean about the Eddie–Sloane relationship. Quite clear. Sloane knows Eddie wants him. He has absolutely no qualms about surrendering his body. None. He's done it many, many times. Sloane is no virgin. He's been in bed with men and women in the past. But he isn't going to give in until he has to. And while he can get away with . . . riding around in cars, just fucking Kath a couple of times a week, getting paid a good salary, why should he give up his trump card. Eddie, naturally, doesn't know how amoral Sloane is. He imagines that he has a virgin on his hands. He thinks he can get Sloane. Sure he can. But it may take a bit of time – cause Sloane is such a nice kid. Where's the problem? . . .

Orton described the plot: 'It's about a young man, eighteen or nineteen, who wants a room and comes into this house. He's met the woman of the house in a public library. He comes to the house and she shows him around the house. Then within about eight pages, I suppose five minutes of being in the house, she attempts to seduce him. A bit later on, she actually has the trousers off him, and then her brother appears, and we see that her brother also would like to have the trousers off him. As the play goes on, one finds that Sloane has murdered a man in the past who was going to take pornographic pictures of him, it was just accidental. The man happened to be the boss of the woman's father, and the old man knows that Sloane murdered his boss. Sloane finally murders the old man, which gives the woman and her brother the opportunity of blackmailing Sloane into bed with them.'[32] Orton's description emphasizes the characters' rapacious pragmatism.

'Sloane is dazed,' observes Dudley Sutton, who originated the part. 'This only comes out in the actual chemistry of performing the role.' Sloane, as Orton says, 'is the ambivalent figure', but all the characters share some aspect of his numbed survival. The play's imagery refracted the sense of threat and cultural death of the revolts of the late sixties. The rubbish dump makes the visual point that death surrounds Kath's house. The spectre of Dadda, the old man whom Orton conceived as 'tottering at the edge of the grave', brings the threat of death inside the house. The characters fend off this death by not admitting it. 'I'm going to die, Kath . . . I'm dying', says the Dadda (Kemp), panhandling for affection. Kath replies angrily: 'You've been at that ham haven't you . . .' And so it goes, each character negotiating his own violent truce with reality.

Sloane, uncommitted to anything but survival, adopts whatever identity suits the situation and serves his purpose. The shifts of his persona keep Sloane's freedom intact. 'Joe was a slippery bloke to talk to. A charmer. A manipulator,' remembers Patrick Dromgoole, who directed the original production of *Entertaining Mr Sloane*. 'He could put on any face. To that extent he was very much like

Sloane. He'd got the withdrawn, almost godly posture of the true Ironist who genuinely finds most things funny. He wasn't really with you. He'd fit his statements about life to his assessment of your character. The first thing he told me when we started working together on the play was that he was living with a "bird" and had to get back to her. He was very firm about it.' Orton could own up with disarming frankness to his tactics. Weighing the possibility of returning to London from Morocco for five days to see the last rehearsals and opening of *Crimes of Passion*, he confided to Peggy Ramsay, 'That gives me plenty of time to see, and if possible, charm everyone'.[33] Even Orton's jokes about himself hinted at his mercurial performance. 'The other day I visited a small village about 50 miles from Tangier', he wrote to Peter Gill. 'I went with a notorious one-eyed Welsh paederast. As we got out of the car, we were surrounded by boys. Several of them smiled at me and then spoke to the one-eyed paederast in French. "What did they say?" I asked, when we were away from the boys. "Oh," he said, "they wanted to know if you were English and did you do things!" I think that's my philosophy of life from now on: not to look English and not to look as though I do things.'[34]

Sloane's innocent appearance disguises his predatory instincts. He moulds himself into the expectations of others, transforming himself variously as son and lover to Kath; rude youngster and intruding lout to Kemp; and virginal, muscular Adonis to Eddie. He begins his changes as soon as he enters Kath's house. Sensing her need and the main chance, Sloane adapts with only a flicker of reluctance.

KATH. Poor boy. Alone in the world. Like me.
SLOANE. You're not alone.
KATH. I am. (*Pause.*) Almost alone. (*Pause.*) If I'd been allowed to keep my boy I'd not be. (*Pause.*) You're almost the same age as he would be. You've got the same refinement.
SLOANE (*slowly*). I need . . . understanding.
KATH. You do, don't you? Here let me take your coat. (*Helps him off with his coat.*) You've got a delicate skin. (*Touches his neck. His cheek.*)

He shudders a little. Pause.

KATH (*kisses his cheek*). Just a motherly kiss. A real mother's kiss. (*Silence. Lifts his arms and folds them about her.*) . . . You must treat me gently when I'm in one of my moods.

In Act 1, Orton emphasizes Sloane's role-playing by engineering the characters so that he is seen in bold relief with each of them. Sloane's initial passivity with Kath is replaced by tight-lipped aggression when he is left to chat with the feeble and squint-eyed Kemp. 'Entertain Mr Sloane now', Kath says to her father as she goes out. 'Give him the benefit of your experience. (*Pause.*) You want to learn manners. That's what you want.' Sloane tests Kemp, briefly trying on the posture of the courteous guest.

SLOANE. You don't resent my being in the house, do you?
KEMP. Not at all.
SLOANE. I thought you did. Just now.
KEMP. No.
SLOANE. This seems a nice place. Friendly atmosphere . . .

Sloane's ironies ricochet off the old man. This emboldens Sloane. His put-ons become more blatant and malicious as his judgement of Kemp's stupidity increases. In his mockery there is a glimmering of his own genuine scepticism. Kath's house: 'A perfect skyline you've got here. Lord Snowdon would give you something for a shot of that. Stunning it is. Stunning. Was this house a speculation?' Kemp's admission of a twenty-year silence with his son, Eddie, after catching him 'committing some kind of felony in the bedroom', having removed the lock from his door: 'There are fascinating possibilities in this situation. I'd get it down on paper if I were you.' Sloane's loathing of Kemp's puritan oafishness bubbles up at the old man's mention of his boss's death. 'Did he die for his country?' Sloane asks. And when the answer is an unsolved murder, Sloane's mockery goes over the top: 'A murderer not brought to justice. That's a sobering thought.' Sloane gradually realizes that the old man hunched in front of the electric logs toasting his crumpet on a fork is a witness to his crime. He asks a few nervous questions. Kemp grabs hold of Sloane's arm and yanks him down to eye level. 'I could still identify you', says Kemp, a death-dealer as well as a spectre of death. The sudden crack in Sloane's well-guarded identity scares him. Sloane's tone gives way to gruff abuse: 'Do lay off, Pop. You couldn't identify a herring on a plate!' Sloane calls him a 'superannuated old prat', a curse that earns him a jab in the leg with Kemp's toasting fork. Sloane turns the incident into a melodramatic production which sends Kath scurrying into action with antiseptic and bandages and gets Sloane's trousers quickly off him and the Dadda out of sight.

With Ed, Sloane adopts another course. Ed is visibly startled and pleased by Sloane's boyish good looks. His first words to Sloane pick up the idea of Sloane's being an orphan while making it very clear where his own enthusiasms lie.

ED. I . . . My sister was telling me about you being an orphan, Mr Sloane.

SLOANE (*smiling*). Oh, yes?

ED. Must be a rotten life for a kid. You look well on it though.

SLOANE. Yes.

ED. I could never get used to sleeping in cubicles. Was it a mixed home?

SLOANE. Just boys.

ED. Ideal . . . Well your childhood wasn't unhappy?

Ed presents himself as a hard-working businessman and a genial disciplinarian. ('I wouldn't want you to break your training', he tells Sloane. 'Drugs I abhor. You'll get to know all my habits.') He is already painting Sloane into his own 'strict' military fantasy of domination when he asks: 'You're interested in the army, eh? Soldiers, garrison towns, etc. Does that interest you?' Sloane answers yes, never demurring but also never admitting Ed's innuendoes. Sloane understands Ed's kink and whets his appetite by repeating the word 'orphanage' as he recounts his athletic ability:

SLOANE. We had a nice little gym at the orphanage. Put me in all the teams they did. Relays . . .

ED *looks interested.*

. . . soccer . . .

ED *nods.*

. . . pole vault, . . . long distance . . .

ED *opens his mouth.*

. . . 100 yards, discus, putting the shot.

ED *rubs his hands together.*

Yes, yes. I'm an all rounder. A great all rounder. In anything you
care to mention. Even in life.

Puffing cigarettes, stubbing them out as Sloane recounts his story,
Ed is 'burning' with excitement. Ed makes Sloane take an oath of
allegiance to keep his hands off his sister, Kath, but slyly angles it
against the entire gender. 'Women are like banks, boy, breaking
and entering is a serious business. Give me your word you're
not vaginalatrous?' Sloane, of course, gives his word without
hesitation, although minutes after Ed's exit he will be rolling on top
of Kath in the same room as the curtain comes down on Act 1.
Sloane's pledge produces the expected results. Ed promises security;
and Sloane plays the wide-eyed and grateful acolyte.

ED. I might let you be my chauffeur.

SLOANE. Would you?

ED. . . . We'll see . . . I could get a uniform. Boots, pants, a guaran-
teed 100 per cent no imitation jacket . . . an . . . er . . . a white
brushed nylon T-shirt . . . with a little leather cap. (*Laughs.*) Like
that?

SLOANE *nods. Silence.*

Ed is decking out Sloane in the paraphernalia of sexual fantasy,
building him into the ideal mate. Sloane, who can step into a new
set of clothes as easily as a new identity, adjusts instantaneously. He
has Ed firmly hooked. He will be Ed's 'little matey', 'the boy' in
contrast to Kath's 'baby'. Ed and Kath even haggle about sharing
these epithets for Sloane, verbal demarcations of their territorial
rights to his body.

ED [*to Sloane*]. That's a good boy.
    Pause.
KATH. Mr Sloane.
SLOANE. What?
KATH. Can *I* call you Boy?
SLOANE. I don't think you'd better.
KATH. Why not?
ED. I'm his employer, see. He knows you're only his landlady.
    SLOANE *smiles.*

In the first round of sexual combat which ends Act 1, the victory
belongs to Kath. From the moment she flounces into the living
room proclaiming to Sloane 'This is my lounge', Kath swoops and
flutters around him like a hawk disguised as a budgerigar. Like Ed,
Kath is not subtle about disguising her needs. The joke on all the
characters is that they think they're subtle. Kath's decorated vocabulary is as misguidedly elegant as the cheap bric-à-brac that clutters
the room. 'I married out of school', she confides to Sloane, obliquely
describing her first pregnancy. 'I surprised everyone by the sudden-
ness of it.' The pretension and precision of the line (Kath, of course,
surprised no one) consolidated a special kind of cultural impoverishment in the new abundance of post-war English life. Kath's
semi-literate badinage is peppered with the rhythms and phrases of
the mass media. Her language aspires to refinement; but the plush-
ness of her idiom, like her over-decorated parlour, only betrays
deeper emptiness. Sir Terence Rattigan, who provided England
with some of its most popular theatre in the forties and fifties,
heard in that line of Kath's the voice of the sixties. 'What Orton
had to say about England and society had never been said before.
The first thing it showed was a society diminished by telly-
technology. Everybody expresses themselves as if they were
brought up on television.'

With television, the public was capable of being touched by
everything and moved by nothing. Each newscast made the spectator an eye-witness to the pageant of human bestiality. Television
inundated the community with superficial messages, undigested

images, and a torrent of words. Orton's style was the first to embody this sensory overload, an eclectic brew of rhythms and idioms which captured and commented on the mutation of language.

The word Orton used to describe his distinctive literary style was 'collage' – the same amalgam and juxtaposition of borrowed imagery he'd practised for a decade with Halliwell on their walls. 'It does have a collage quality', Orton told the BBC in 1964, speaking of *Entertaining Mr Sloane*. 'Shakespeare and the Elizabethans did the same thing. I mean you have absolute realism and then you get high poetry, it's just language. I think you should use the language of your age and every bit of it. They always go on about poetic drama and they think you have to sort of go off in some high flown fantasy, but it isn't poetic drama, it's everything, it's the language in use at the time. I have to be very careful in the way that I write, not to let it become sort of a mannerism, it could very easily become a mannerism.'[35] Orton's language assimilated the input of the popular culture: advertising jargon (Kath: 'You ought to consult an oculist. See your oculist at once'); the stilted lusciousness of old B films (Kath: 'You have the air of lost wealth'); the bold-face shorthand of tabloid journalism (Ed: 'You're a constant source of amazement . . . a never ending tale of infamy').

Kath's language is funny, but there is panic and pathos in her craving. 'All the characters are basically likeable and should be sympathetically portrayed', Orton said. 'Much of the sympathy can be achieved through humour: the scene of Kath's seduction of Sloane is very funny and should also be very sexy. But sex doesn't just consist in undressing and wiggling as appropriate: sexiness can be just *there* without anyone moving a muscle . . . Humour should make the sex more real . . .' Kath's first attempt to establish a beach-head on Sloane's body comes while he's reclining, 'wounded' and trouserless, on the sofa.

KATH (*confidentially*). I've been doing my washing today and I
    haven't a stitch on . . . except my shoes . . . I'm in the rude under
    this dress. I tell you because you're bound to have noticed . . .

Orton made a spectacle of sexual appetite. Hunger and how people disguised it is what amused him. 'In Germany,' Orton wrote to Alan Schneider, 'Ed was the central pivot of the play. His stalking of the boy's arse was as funny and as wildly alarming as Kath's stalking of his cock. Unless this is so – you're in trouble.'[36]

Orton wanted to shock the audience out of their lethargy, and 'the only field still heavily unexplored is the sexual one'.[37] *Entertaining Mr Sloane* emerged six months after the Profumo scandal had reached its sad conclusion. 'In the late spring of 1963,' wrote Bernard Levin in his chronicle of Britain in the 1960s, *The Pendulum Years*, 'men and women all over Britain were telling, and others believing and embellishing and repeating, such stories as that nine High Court judges had been engaging in sexual orgies, that a member of the Cabinet had served dinner at a private party while naked except for a mask, a small lace apron and a card round his neck reading "If my services don't please you, whip me", that another member of the Cabinet had been discovered by police beneath a bush in Richmond Park where he and a prostitute had been engaging in oral genital sex . . .'[38]

In retrospect, the Profumo affair seems trivial. The over-reaction of the British public was a barometer of the society's nervousness about the future of its ruling establishment. Sexuality represented a threat to the old order. The Profumo case was one of the decade's watersheds. 'If, in the Sixties, the past was letting go of Britain, its grip was not to be prised loose without a struggle', wrote Bernard Levin. 'And the Profumo affair can therefore be seen as the last struggle of the old, false standards (. . . some would say the old, true standards) before a new attitude emerged.'

The mischievous wit of *Entertaining Mr Sloane* was directed against the hypocrisy and intolerance of the well-bred and 'right-thinking' middle class. Orton deflated the show of propriety in manners. Kath's 'refeened' gabble, like her actions, attempts to keep up appearances to hide her lust:

KATH. . . . Are you comfortable? Let me plump your cushion. (*Plumps a cushion behind his head. Laughs lightly.*) I really by rights should ask you to change places. This light is showing me up. (*Pause.*) I blame it on the manufacturers. They make garments so thin nowadays you'd think they intended to provoke a rape . . .

Ed too puts great store by his 'principles'. 'One thing I wanted to give you – my principles', he tells Sloane in a moment of crisis. 'Oh, I'm disillusioned. I feel I'm doing no good at all.' Principles create the feeling of being good; they are man's boundaries which prevent life from overwhelming him. The comic spirit is an enemy of boundaries. 'What I wanted to do in *Sloane* was break down all the sexual compartments that people have', Orton said. 'It didn't entirely succeed because it's very difficult to persuade directors and actors to do what you want. When *Sloane* was running for a while, it had got into compartments, so that Madge [Ryan] was the nympho, Peter [Vaughan] was the queer and Dudley [Sutton] was the psycho. Which wasn't what I intended at all, but people will put things into compartments. It's very bad in class, in sex, in everything.'[39] *Entertaining Mr Sloane* had a carnival effect. The world and its values were turned topsy-turvy.

Act 2 of *Entertaining Mr Sloane* fleshes out Orton's fantasy of festival liberty. Kath is pregnant. ('Kath has to be pretty fat, brother', Orton wrote to Schneider. 'A belly you could loaf on. Six months gone. And none of this shit I got from Madge in London. This is the pregnant Mother-Goddess in her lair!') Ed is passionately pressing Sloane into his service. Sloane is enjoying the favours of both.

In *Sloane* [Orton said in 1967] I wrote a man who was interested in having sex with boys. I wanted him played as if he was the most ordinary man in the world, and not as if the moment you wanted sex with boys, you had to put on earrings and scent. This is very bad, and I hope that now that homosexuality is allowed, people aren't going to continue doing the conventional portraits there have been in the past. I think that the portrait of the queer in Peter Shaffer's *Black Comedy* is very funny, but it's an awfully conventional portrait.

It's compartmentalization again. Audiences love it, of course, because they're safe. But one shouldn't pander to audiences.[40]

In 1964 homosexuality was neither safe nor accepted. At the time of the Wolfenden Report (1956), the maximum penalty for buggery was imprisonment for life. As late as 1963 there were still cases, like the one of a twenty-two-year-old labourer and a twenty-four-year-old US airman sentenced to three years' imprisonment for buggery and indecency, which bore out H. Montgomery Hyde's contention in his survey of homosexuality in Britain, *The Other Love*,[41] that 'throughout 1963 and 1964 homosexual offenders continued to be treated with considerable severity by the courts'.

On stage, the treatment of the homosexual was as violent and narrow-minded as the laws. In 1956 Terence Rattigan, explaining why he had transformed a homosexual incident to a heterosexual one as the basis for *Separate Tables*, said 'The Lord Chamberlain, our stage censor, bans any mention of that subject'. By the sixties the homosexual character had begun to appear sporadically on the British stage, dramatized primarily either as the limp-wristed queen, as a toned-down maiden aunt of pantomime high camp (*Beyond the Fringe*, *Black Comedy*, Charles Dyer's *Staircase*), or as the grave and often sentimental 'problem' (Shelagh Delaney's *A Taste of Honey*, Christopher Hampton's *When Did You Last See My Mother?*). The change in public attitude was 'from ignorance and terror to familiarity and contempt', as E. M. Forster wrote in the afterword to his posthumously published novel about homosexuality, *Maurice*. 'We had not realized that what the public really loathes in homosexuality is not the thing itself but having to think about it.'

Orton's laughter disarmed an audience of its stereotypes while defying it to face sexuality's complicated and uncompromising demands. 'Just as humour should make the sex more real, so too it should make Sloane's murder of Kemp more real', Orton said. 'Put a murder on the stage with a straight face, and it's just a whodunit and nobody takes it seriously. Make it funny and you make people think about it.'[42] The same was true of homosexuality.

In Eddie and Sloane, Orton aired the split in his own sexual nature, a struggle that the stage could resolve more elegantly than life. Act 2 raises the sexual stakes of the play as Eddie's fear of losing Sloane to women and the carefree life increases his demands on him.

Orton always emphasized that Eddie's sexuality is an act of rational choice. 'Only a man who's had experience with women can dislike them. The adorers of women tend to be *impotent*: the priests of the mother goddess were always eunuchs. But Ed's hatred isn't violent or vitriolic, he's had the sense simply to see the obvious alternative.'[43] Orton, who had no effeminate mannerisms, was quick to edit any signs of faggotry in the presentation of his characters. 'I don't like the ring on Eddie's finger', he noted for Alan Schneider. 'I don't think Eddie would wear a ring on his little finger. Queers have been doing that for years. Ed would know this and be self-conscious enough not to wear one.'

In *Entertaining Mr Sloane*, Orton's emotional ambivalence was translated into a contest between man, boy and woman – a crucial configuration in his life. 'Not a play about two women and a boy', Orton wrote to Alan Schneider. 'About a man, a woman, and a boy. Very, very important. Eddie is a great deal tougher than Sloane. Sloane is the ambiguous figure. Not Eddie.' Sloane, after trying to manipulate Ed and Kath, ends up, in Orton's words, 'the helpless victim of them both'.[44] *Entertaining Mr Sloane*, like *The Ruffian on the Stair*, acted out aspects of Orton's sexual dilemma and dummied up a destiny. Was he victim or survivor? The battle of possession by masculine and feminine forces is one of the themes worked out in this play: in *What the Butler Saw* confusion of genders would become the entire plot.

Entertaining Mr Sloane is the most blatantly autobiographical of Orton's major plays. It is the unhappy son's daydream of the perfect family in which he is never excluded and always needed. Kath and Ed talk of Sloane as 'boy', 'kiddie', 'baby', but they have no sexual connection to each other, only to him. Sloane had not only Orton's proportions, the same smooth skin, the same boyish look, but his survivor's pragmatism. His sleek black-leather outfit was Orton's style at the time. 'It was almost as if he'd come to read the gas meter,' remembers Peter Wood of his first meeting with Orton in 1964. 'He was wearing boots, shapeless trousers, a little leather cap. His whole appearance was in total contrast to his reading and frame of reference. Quite fantastic. Totally intriguing.' Orton knew the impression he made; and he gave Sloane a charmer's confidence in his fatal fascination. Likewise Kath is an amalgamation of many of Elsie Orton's mannerisms: the crooning of popular tunes; the obsessive neatness; pining out loud for a lost lover; the domineering indifference to the frail, almost unnoticed man about the house. Kath's connoisseur's appreciation of her trashy bric-à-brac ('This shepherdess is a lovely piece of chinawork. She comes up like new when I give her a wash') was typical of his mother's pretensions about her trinkets. Kath's longing for the best in life, her panicky search for pleasure were all part of the delusion and sadness Orton saw in his mother. 'That's my mum!' Leonie Orton Barnett laughed, watching Beryl Reid's brilliant interpretation of Kath in the 1975 Royal Court revival as she wrapped herself in a fancy négligé to seduce Sloane. 'That's her! It's like seeing a ghost. She was always overdressing. Once she got dressed in gold lamé and painted her shoes gold just to go to the pub. The paint cracked when she walked. There were gold flakes all the way to the City Arms.' Even the plot of *Entertaining Mr Sloane* was built around a family memory of Elsie Orton taking in a much-despised lodger. 'His name was Jim,' Leonie remembers. 'We hated him. He was a lorry driver. Everything were done for Jim, know what I mean? I don't think Mum had an affair with him but she pandered to this lodger. The house had to be so clean. It was Dad that said he had to go.'

In Act 2, it is the Dadda, like William Orton, who wants the lodger out. Kemp breaks his vow of silence with his son to confide that Sloane has been hot-rodding in Ed's car and has put his sister in the family way. He tells Ed that Sloane has been hitting him, a fact amusingly brushed aside by Ed when he confronts Sloane angrily with a list of his misdemeanours. Ed's lust is what stokes his disappointed rage.

ED. What a little whoreson you are, you little whoreson. You are a little whoreson and no mistake. I'm put out, boy. Choked.

Ed can't understand why Sloane gave in to Kath. 'I was worn out', Sloane lies. 'I was overwrought. Nervous. On edge.' Ed's rage has reached its climax, but Orton understands that anger is a heroic performance that must play itself out. Ed slips gradually from the role of wounded benefactor to tolerant saviour. His idealization of himself and the lecherous truth of his motive are caught by Orton's double-entendres. Embellishing Sloane's hazy picture of his 'confused' past, Ed suggests:

ED. Never went to church? Correct me if I'm wrong.
SLOANE. You got it, Ed. Know me better than I know myself.
ED. Your youth pleads for leniency and, by God, I'm going to give it. You're pure as the Lamb. Purer.

Sloane coaxes Ed into forgiveness, playing into his priestly fantasy by acting the penitent. 'Speak a few words of forgiveness', Sloane says. 'Pity me.' But it's Sloane who knows the right words to speak. He calls Ed 'pal', 'One of my mates' ('Am I?' Ed says, thrilled at the sound of the word. 'How refreshing to hear you say it'). Ed launches into a familiar riff. 'But do me a favour – avoid the birds in future. That's what's been your trouble.' Ed blames Kath; Sloane concurs. This scrap of allegiance is something to build on; and Ed offers an impassioned piece of advice:

ED. Why conform to the standards of the cowshed? (Pause.) It's a thing you grow out of. With me behind you, boy, you'll grow out of it.

The joke was on the censors as well as Ed. 'The funny thing about the Lord Chamberlain', Orton said, 'was that he cut all the hetero-sexual bits and kept in all the homosexual bits.'[45] The Lord Chamberlain disallowed Sloane's pinching of Kath's breasts and warned that any simulation of intercourse when she rolled on top of him at the end of Act 1 would be obscene. ('Must be a quick curtain to Act I', Orton wrote to Schneider in a preview note. 'Actually the Lord Chamberlain said there must be no attempt to simulate copulation. We'd be halfway to the kid's conception at the speed of last night's curtain.') Homosexual passion could not be so explicit; and the play benefited from the necessity to be oblique.

Just after Sloane and Ed have firmed up their new alliance, Sloane tries to smooth things over with Kemp on what Orton called Sloane's 'Messenger Speech'. It is Sloane's only explanatory outburst. The speech establishes Sloane's sexual ambivalence moments before he is forced to take sexual sides:

SLOANE. . . . It's like this see. One day I leave the Home . . . They'd found me a likeable permanent situation. Canteen facilities. Fortnight's paid holiday. Overtime? Time and a half after midnight. A staff dance each year. What more could one wish to devote one's life to? I certainly loved that place. The air round Twickenham was like wine . . . I thumbs a lift from a geyser who promises me a bed . . . All you could wish he was, a photographer. He shows me one or two experimental studies. An experience for the retina and no mistake. He wanted to photo me. For certain interesting features I had that he wanted the exclusive right of preserving. You know how it is. I didn't like to refuse . . . But then I got to thinking . . . And I gets up in the middle of the night looking for the film see . . . Well it appears that he gets the wrong idea. Runs in. Gives a shout. And the long and the short of it is I lose my head which is a thing I never ought to a done with the worry of them photos and all. And I hits him. I hits him . . .

Kemp isn't assuaged by Sloane's story. He threatens to tell the police. The terror and fury Sloane has described suddenly explode when he again feels himself cornered. Sloane knocks him behind the sofa. He kicks him. Orton relished the Grand Guignol horror of the scene, letting Kemp's head bob above the sofa as he struggles to his feet and then watching it sink slowly behind the sofa as he collapses. Sloane prods Kemp with his boot; 'Wakey, wakey', he says. 'Sloane doesn't immediately know what has happened', Orton reminded Schneider in a production note. 'It takes him a second or two to realize that the Old Man is ill. Let's see the change from anger during the beating up to sheer panic. I'm not getting the thought between the lines. He must think what has happened. And then the sheer panic of the end of the act is clear and right. If Sloane doesn't think, it's messy.' Orton rewrote the final image of the scene to emphasize that Sloane's decision about his sexuality is made for him by force of circumstance (as it was for Orton with Halliwell). 'SLOANE goes to the door,' Orton explained to Michael Codron in a letter accompanying his rewrite. 'Calls for ED, KATH tries to push her way into the room, SLOANE says "Not you," she asks what's happened, and SLOANE says, "Where's ED? I want ED." CURTAIN. A good situation – SLOANE rejecting her, calling for ED when he's in trouble, foreshadowing the end of the play. A good stage picture – the old man lying on the ground, SLOANE trying to keep KATH from entering the room.'[46]

The moment is the play's turning point, illuminating the irony of the title. Sloane, once entertained by Kath and Ed, will find himself their entertainment. Orton defended the Act 2 ending despite persuasive lobbying for change. ' "Take an old hack's advice," ' Sir Terence Rattigan recalled telling him. ' "Bring your second act curtain down when Kath says 'Dadda's dead' in the third act, instead of leaving the audience frozen by bringing the curtain down with Dadda apparently being kicked to death. You'll find them going out to their gins and tonics in a much happier frame of mind." But Joe wouldn't listen to me. I'm prepared to tell you that he'd probably have added three months to the run if he'd done it.'

'Let Mr Sloane regain his composure, Ed', Kath says, at the beginning of Act 3, carpet-sweeping her living room and eager to brush away the memory of family friction. The Dadda lies dead upstairs. The men know it. Kath, for the moment, does not. 'Sleeping off the excitement, is he?' she says. Kath is obsessed with sustaining a sense of order on the surface of life. She inflates every situation with her fantasy of perfection. 'I cooked a lovely egg yesterday', she twitters to Sloane. A life-and-death struggle is going on in her living room, and she seems anaesthetized to it. Orton dramatizes how much language contributes to her insensitivity. 'Did he insult you?' she asks Sloane about the Dadda. 'Was it a bad word? (*Pause.*) I don't expect you can tell me what it was. I'd blush.' By censoring language, Kath makes life 'safe'.

KATH. . . . How could you behave so bad. Accusing me of seducing you.

SLOANE. But you did!

KATH. That's neither here nor there. Using expressions like that. Making yourself cheap.

Kath doesn't want to appear 'cheap'. Truth, as she says, has nothing to do with it. Even when Kath discovers the Dadda's death, she can rationalize Sloane's violence: 'The Dadda was rude. He said a rude word about me.' And in her profound superficiality, Kath worries about her appearance at the Dadda's funeral: 'I shall never get in my black. I've put on weight since we buried mamma.'

Sloane, however, is no longer willing to play up to the other characters' fantasies about him. His panic makes him talk straight for the first time: nor will he allow the others their illusions. Ed is the first to feel the jolt of Sloane's matter-of-factness. Sloane suggests that they fake the evidence and tell the police that Dadda fell downstairs.

ED. . . . Now you ask me to help you evade Justice. Is that where my liberal principles have brought me?

SLOANE. You've no principles.

ED. No principles? Oh, you really have upset me now. Why am I interested in your welfare? Why did I give you a job? Why do thinking men everywhere show young boys the strait and narrow? Flash cheque-books when delinquency is mentioned? Support the Scout-movement? Principles, boy, bleeding principles. And don't you dare say otherwise or you'll land in serious trouble.

Sloane *is* in serious trouble. But it's typical of Ed's megalomania to defend the ideal of himself – his principles – against any assault while forgetting the murder upstairs. Ed's rhetoric, like Kath's clichés, becomes a verbal cocoon that protects him from accurately perceiving himself. Sloane cuts right through the pretence.

ED. . . . You must accept responsibility for your actions.
SLOANE (*sits beside* ED. *Lays hand on his knee*). I accept responsibility.
ED. Do you?
SLOANE. Fully.
ED. Good. Remove that hand, will you?

Sloane asserts himself. He has made his decision and declared his allegiance. He is equally abrupt and frank with Kath when Ed forces a showdown. Sloane is packing his bag. Kath is confused and protective. She's agreed to lie to the police about Dadda's death, telling herself that Sloane 'did it out of love for me'. She won't be disabused of her dignity by Ed's brutal catalogue of her limitations, and she can't comprehend why Sloane would want to leave.

KATH. What are you going to give him?
ED. The world.
KATH (*comes round the case, looks in*). The state of this case. Mr Sloane, dear, you can't even pack. See how he needs me in the smallest things . . .

'Must pause after Ed's "the world" ', Orton suggested. 'Kath has no reply to what Ed has said, she doesn't understand what he means, so, like any woman, she changes the subject rapidly to something else. Must see that for a fraction of a second she's baffled.'[47]

Orton contrives a double-barrelled demolition of Kath's fantasy. Ed parades her in front of a mirror and asks her to look at herself. 'What have you to offer?' he says. 'You're fat and the crows-feet under your eyes would make you an object of terror. Pack it in, I tell you. Sawdust up to the navel. You've nothing to lure any man.' Kath is devastated. 'Is that the truth', she asks Sloane weakly. 'More or less', he says. Ed tops the vicious spectacle of Kath's humiliation with one final rhetorical flourish: 'You showed him the gate of Hell every night. He abandoned Hope when he entered there.'

But Kath's revenge on Ed and Sloane is as delightful as it is cunning. She invokes morality. 'I won't practise a falsehood', she says, refusing to support their alibi. When the air has cleared, Kath spells out her demands:

KATH. I was never subtle, Mr Sloane . . . If you go with Eddie, I'll tell the police.
SLOANE. If I stay here he'll do the same.
ED. It's what's called a dilemma boy. You are on the horns of it.
    Silence.

Kath has foxed Sloane. There's a hint of triumph as she says 'You see how things are, Mr Sloane?' Stalemated, Sloane lashes out. He slaps her. Orton plays off the righteousness in their language against the violence of their actions. Sloane starts to throttle Kath with Ed mischievously incanting the kind of reactionary protest to Sloane's actions that Orton knew his audience would have to the play:

ED. Let her alone, boy . . .
    ED *lays a hand on* SLOANE'*s shoulder, tries to pull him away from* KATH. SLOANE *turns, shoves* ED *from him.*
SLOANE. Did you hear what I said? Keep out of it!
ED. Don't be violent. No violence at any cost. (SLOANE *gets* KATH *into a corner; struggles with her.*) What's this exhibition for? This is gratuitous violence. Give over, both of you!

The scene erupts, momentarily, into farce. By the end of the tussle, at the play's tensest moment, Kath is on her hands and knees groping for the false teeth Sloane has belted out of her mouth. But the hilarity never loses the serious purpose behind it. 'I'll still forgive and forget', says Kath, gumming the words as she searches for her dentures. Each character is a master at forgetting. In farce, the momentum of events has its own amnesiac quality, characters forgetting who and where they are as they scramble to set things right. Sloane helps Kath off the floor at her request. 'See, Ed,' she says, already erasing the ugliness from memory, 'he hasn't lost respect for me.'

Orton's finale takes the English art of compromise to its logical conclusion. Kath and Ed will share Sloane six months of the year, with certain exceptions – like the birth of Kath's baby – to be mutually agreed upon. 'It's all any reasonable child can expect', says Ed, the voice of conciliation, 'if the dad is present at the conception.' Orton spoofs the romantic conventions of the 'happy ending' with his own more realistic version:

SLOANE. Is it going to be O.K.?
ED. Well . . . perhaps.
SLOANE. I'll be grateful.
ED. Will you?
SLOANE. Eternally.
ED. Not eternally, boy. Just a few years.

'Well, it's been a pleasant morning', Ed says, concluding the arrangement. His exits with the play's last line. The word 'pleasant' is as sugary as the sweet Kath chews in contented silence on her sofa. The Dadda's death, Kath's battering, the rapacious stalking of Sloane and his bondage are all forgotten; the past is obliterated by pleasantries. Evil, to Orton, was indifference to suffering, a moral stupor which extended to the corrupting power of language. '*Entertaining Mr Sloane*', Orton said, 'is comedy in so far as the whole world and the whole human situation are comic and farcical.'[48]

Orton had learned to make an audience laugh to make it listen.

Orton gave Patrick Dromgoole an autographed copy of the published version of *Entertaining Mr Sloane*, inscribed with one of Kath's lines: 'I got over it though. You do, don't you.' Orton had never liked Dromgoole's direction or his style. The word 'Drom-goole' became an adjective of derision in his vocabulary. 'Lots of bearded "Dromgoole" types in the audience,' Orton wrote to Peggy Ramsay,[49] characterizing the middle-class audience at the Royal Court's notorious production of Edward Bond's *Saved*, which he thought a 'remarkably cissy play'. 'Dromgoole' evoked the hearty, liberal bourgeois synonymous with the name of his first director. But during rehearsals at the New Arts before its premiere, Orton was a model of tact. He sat quietly and intently behind Dromgoole in the eighth row making notes and adjust-ing his rewrites. Orton carried his papers in the same gasmask case Halliwell used to smuggle books. He dressed so casually that, in the first week, some of the stage-hands mistook him for crew. His unvarying outfit, National Assistance boots, high-cuffed blue jeans, white T-shirt and leather jacket, became a part of his personality. Halliwell often attended rehearsals with Orton, eccen-trically sporting a beret which he never removed. Once, early in the rehearsal period, Orton invoked Halliwell's opinion in an argument with Dromgoole and the director got furious. 'It got such an explosive reaction from me that he stopped,' Dromgoole remembers. 'I said "I don't give a fuck who you talked with about it, least of all that goddamn refugee from a second-hand-clothes shop." Halliwell was not allowed direct interference, but he'd try.' The situation was smoothed over but not forgotten. 'In doing *Entertaining Mr Sloane*,' Dromgoole says, 'I had the usual blind cer-tainty how to make it work. Inevitably with Orton as with others, this sets up conflicts. I don't think that they would have become in any way serious except for that little prick, Halliwell. Things ended up extremely uncomfortable.'

Entertaining Mr Sloane was dedicated to Halliwell; and in the presence of the director and the cast, Halliwell referred to it as 'our play'. Halliwell's words thrust him into the centre of the enterprise, but in the theatre he was kept on the periphery. The stage-hands dubbed him 'Mrs Orton'. If he had no say in the production, Halli-well could make his own scenes. 'He behaved very badly in the theatre,' Dromgoole says. 'I'd say to Joe "I want you to watch this scene" and Halliwell would say "Oh dear, I suppose it's going to take another half hour".' Dudley Sutton remembers Halliwell 'always in a terrific state of agitation and jealousy. At the Arts, the management wanted us to take a cut in wages. We had a company meeting. Halliwell was storming around outside wanting to know why he hadn't been asked to it.' Halliwell's insecurity and arrogance increased after the play's success. On the opening night of its West End run at Wyndham's Theatre, Dromgoole was with Robin Maugham and Sir Terence Rattigan as they tried to chat with Halliwell. 'Where do you go when you go out with Joe?' Rattigan asked politely. Halliwell answered: 'I don't go out with Joe Orton. I go in.'

'My main effort with Joe was trying to bring him down to something naturalistic,' explains Dromgoole. 'I recognized instantly that the value of Joe's comedy was that it went too far all the time. I didn't want to corrode that. But, for the sake of the audience, you need a feed for the comic, some safe place from which it can adventure. My influence on Joe was to bring him back from the fantastically exaggerated towards the reassuring. I directed each act [of *Entertaining Mr Sloane*] as a different play because the play seemed to me to be written in three different styles. The first act is naturalistic. The second goes into high comedy. And the third finished virtually as farce.'

While Dromgoole worried about how to present the play, Orton fussed about how to present Orton. A small biography was required for the Arts programme, and Orton drafted two versions. The first, written on 15 April, was sixteen lines of fact and flim-flam. In it, Orton maintained that he'd been 'married and divorced' and listed among his odd jobs 'helping in the making of sex hormones'. The posture of the joker prevailed. 'I was in prison for six months in 1962 for larceny (not really as grand as it seems).' He at least gave his correct age: thirty-one. Orton's second version, the one printed in the programme, was edited to eight lines of straightforward prose which only once hit a sardonic note: 'He has had various jobs and long periods of idleness'. As a second thought, Orton reduced his age to twenty-five, making him seem even more promising.

ORTON'S FIRST PLAY: the cut-out letters were pasted together by Orton on the inside of his scrapbook like a headline. Within a week, he would be glueing genuine headlines, with his name in bold face and his picture featured in quarter-page spreads: MR ORTON ARRIVES (*The People*); THEATRE'S NEW STAR SIGNS ON THE DOLE (*Daily Herald*). Beneath Orton's collage of his name was pasted the stub of his fourth-row opening night seat (E10) and a copy of the programme. On the back of the programme Orton taped the tepid *Evening News* review ('Murder With A Flippant Touch') over a North Thames Gas advertisement, leaving the first two lines of the ad as a playful epigraph to the critical waffle below it about Sloane's personality: 'Diplomacy, darling ... that's all it was ... I just let him ...' Orton's scrapbook exudes a sense of fun and naïve delight at his sudden celebrity. He enjoyed the hostility as much as the praise; bad reviews feature as prominently as raves. The most vitriolic attack on *Entertaining Mr Sloane* came predictably from the *Daily Telegraph*. 'Not for a long time have I disliked a play so much as I disliked Joe Orton's *Entertaining Mr Sloane*', W. A. Darlington began his review, adding 'I feel as if snakes had been writhing round my feet'.[40] To Orton, this was sweet comic revenge and he let Edna Welthorpe fan the flames in the *Telegraph* Letters to the Editor column:

As a playgoer of forty years may I sincerely agree with Peter Pinnell in his condemnation of *Entertaining Mr Sloane*.

I myself was nauseated by this endless parade of mental and physical perversion. And to be told that such a disgusting piece of filth now passes for humour.

Today's young playwrights take it upon themselves to flaunt their contempt for ordinary decent people. I hope that the ordinary decent people will shortly strike *back*!

A few weeks later, Orton was back in the *Telegraph* correspondence column, this time praising his play under the pseudonym of Donald H. Hartley:

I saw *Entertaining Mr Sloane* twice at the New Arts. I shall see it again at the Wyndhams.

God knows the theatre is dreary enough at the present time. Any oasis in the wasteland is welcome. And *Entertaining Mr Sloane* is not a mirage which disappears when the thirsty traveller approaches. The water is there, the exotic landscape is real. And if we find the customs of the country differ from our own – what else is foreign travel for?

There were other voices of disapproval and praise that were not Orton's. The *Financial Times* bemoaned 'a woeful lack of sophistication either in the way people act or in the way plays are constructed'. The *Daily Mail* found the play 'as mild and as tedious as soap flakes'. Sean O'Casey wrote: 'A play to make a man pull his trousers up.' But the grumbling didn't muffle the chorus of excited discovery. 'All good comes to him who stands and waits', wrote John Mortimer in the *Evening Standard*. 'And after what now seems a long time waiting round the moth-eaten wings of the commercial theatre something really quite good has come to me at last.' Alan Brien was even more outspoken in the *Sunday Telegraph*: 'Mr Orton is one of those rare dramatists who create their own world and their own idiom'. Orton was described variously as 'the Douanier Rousseau of the criminal suburbs' and 'the Grandma Moses of the rubbish dump' (*Sunday Telegraph*); his play was 'an unearthly marriage of Frank Norman and Muriel Spark' (*Evening Standard*), with 'flashes of wit which at their best can match Oscar Wilde' (*Observer*). But it was Harold Hobson's notice in *The Sunday Times* that took pride of place in his scrapbook:

I hope I shall not be misunderstood if I say that the English author of whom Joe Orton in *Entertaining Mr Sloane* reminds me most vividly is Jane Austen. Miss Austen had a keen eye for the absurdities of the fashionable fiction of her day; and so has Mr Orton. His

Entertaining Mr Sloane, all proportions kept, is the *Northanger Abbey* of our contemporary stage . . .

Entertaining Mr Sloane begins as a joke about moral horror; and as such a joke should it goes on to develop a horror of its own. It becomes a British counterpart of *Who's Afraid of Virginia Woolf?* and its third act does not succumb to the sentimentality that spoils Mr Albee's play. It is a vision of total evil and it is possible to perceive its merits without approving it. It might be a coterie success: a *Wrong Box*, a *South Wind*, a Beauvoir-Wences. I should not call it promising. It seems more like an end than a beginning.

'Hobson was the only critic who spotted what Sloane was,' Orton told Glenn Loney, an American friend and journalist. 'This was absolutely amazing. I wrote him a letter saying that I've always admired Jane Austen's juvenilia which she rewrote later in her life . . .'[51] When Loney sent Orton an article about his play, Orton replied: 'You sound . . . as if you aren't at all convinced that the *Golden Bough* and *Northanger Abbey* could furnish me with inspiration. I assure you that it is possible to draw poisoned water from the clearest of wells.'[52]

It was not the controversial claims of the author or the press but the unlikely enthusiasm of Sir Terence Rattigan that grabbed headlines for Orton and ensured the life of his play. Rattigan's first play, *First Episode*, had been produced when he was twenty-two, and by the age of twenty-five he was earning £25,000 a year in royalties. *French without Tears* (1936) and *While the Sun Shines* (1943) ran in the West End for over a thousand performances each. The name Rattigan became synonymous with the well-made play; and for two decades he provided the theatregoers on both sides of the Atlantic with such popular plays as *Love in Idleness* (1944), *The Winslow Boy* (1946), *The Deep Blue Sea* (1952), *Separate Tables* (1954). Orton's technical maturity – the extraordinary assurance in his manipulation of characters, his powers of dramatic organization – impressed Rattigan. 'I wouldn't have liked *Sloane* if I hadn't seen its classic construction,' Rattigan says. 'I saw the classical roots. The critics did not. They saw it as part of a movement. But Orton understood that a play, if it's any good, has to have its basis in structure. What was going to happen to Mr Sloane? It's no more than telling a story. And there's no theatre without story and never has been.' Rattigan escorted Vivien Leigh, a frequent star in his plays, to see the play in the first week of its run. 'I fell wildly in love with *Entertaining Mr Sloane*,' Rattigan says. 'Vivien saw it as a funny, rather camp play. I went much further than that. I saw style – a style, well, that could be compared with the Restoration comedies. I saw Congreve in it. I saw Wilde. To me, in some ways, it was better than Wilde because it had more bite. I was delighted by Orton's feeling for words. Albee and Coward have a certain kind of verbal felicity that usually isn't meant to express character. They are still in a naturalistic tradition of dialogue. Joe had something richer. Orton was way beyond a naturalistic tradition and yet you could read it as if it were perfectly naturalistic. Vivien said to me, "If you feel so strongly about the play, you ought to write to the author". I said all right if she'd write to Madge Ryan, whose performance she'd loved.' Orton was delighted with his first fan letter:

14 May 1964

Dear Joe Orton,

I don't think you've written a masterpiece – and you wouldn't want me to say that you had – but I do think you have written the most exciting and stimulating first play (is it?) that I've seen in thirty (odd) years' playgoing.

I think you *will* write a masterpiece before the decade is out – provided, always, that you don't try to. But your gift of dialogue is such that whatever you write will henceforth provide pleasure, not only to me, but to many hundreds of thousands of others.

Sincerest congratulations,

Terence Rattigan

P.S. But of course you will write that masterpiece.

P.P.S. And *this* one should give you a great success in the West End – whither, I trust, it is bound.

When Rattigan spoke to Donald Albery about his enthusiasm for the play, 'Albery wasn't sure he'd bring it in'. Notices were mixed, and although box-office receipts had risen from £250 for the first week to £439 for the third and last week at the Arts Theatre, the show had lost money. Rattigan ensured *Entertaining Mr Sloane*'s destination by investing £3,000 in a West End transfer. 'I told Donald I'd go half and half with him,' Rattigan recalls. 'I said: "I don't think we're going to make any money out of this, but this talent has to be nurtured. Quite nice notices. Four weeks. Then, that's it. There are so many plays like it. *Sloane* mustn't die at the Arts".' Orton appreciated but was embarrassed by Rattigan's generosity, the first of many writers' enthusiasms for his work which Orton couldn't repay with mutual admiration:

It never fails to amaze me how kind and generous people like Bill Naughton and Lord Willis are to me. I wouldn't have supposed it, judging from the things they write, that I'd appeal to them. I've never liked anything either of them have written. It's like Rattigan's eulogies: I can't return them with any degree of conviction. I'd like to think I'd be as nice to somebody if I admired their writing. But who could it be? 'God,' Kenneth Halliwell says.

(14 March 1967)

'Orton thought it very funny that I, of all people, should have thought his play so good,' Rattigan smiles, remembering their first meeting at the swank Ivy Restaurant, where Orton arrived in black leather without the required tie and ended being photographed with Rattigan's borrowed orange and yellow MCC tie draped around his neck. 'To my alarm, they plastered outside the Wyndham's Theatre that passage from my letter. People who came to see my plays were not likely to go and enjoy Joe's. In a way, I wasn't Orton's best sponsor. I'm a very unfashionable figure still, and I was then wildly unfashionable critically. My sponsorship rather put critics off, I think. They're not very quick at seeing something good straight off. It takes two or three plays before they realize. With Orton, it took perhaps a bit longer. When he died, they'd cottoned on to the fact that they'd lost possibly their best.'

On 29 June Orton became a West End playwright. His jubilation is recorded in his scrapbook, which suddenly explodes into a two-page collage to record the event. Surrounding the colourful letters that spell out MR SLOANE (inside the 'O' is pasted 'even the men will blush') were a series of fantastic headlines dominated by NEVER SO MUCH! SO QUICK! IN ITS 46TH CON-SECUTIVE YEAR. ALONE IN ITS GREATNESS. FIRST WEEK GROSS $ 128,450! IT HAD TO HAPPEN. Orton composed his own billboard, studding the page with adjectives – 'gorgeous', 'exciting', 'sensational', 'wow', 'London's most gayest', 'KING SIZE horrors!', 'kinky boots'. The only review interspersed between Orton's fantasy of triumph and the announcement of the transfer was Darlington's second try at coming to terms with the play. Under the headline

3 REPULSIVE
FOLK WELL
ACTED

Darlington, while still finding the characters 'shameless and repulsive in the extreme', added 'I have to pay the author's skill the compliment of admitting that I sat through it last night a second time on its transference to Wyndham's and was held throughout'. Orton's glee spilled over to other pages. The Wyndham's programme is framed by a series of cut-out comments: 'Audience reaction horrible – it laughed'; 'I'm broadminded – but this time you've gone too far'; 'This is a disturbing and terrible thing'. Three days after its opening in the West End, the scrapbook had more to boast. *Entertaining Mr Sloane* tied with Bill Naughton's *Alfie* in *Variety's* London Critics' Poll for the best new British play; and Orton came two votes behind Charles Wood (*Cockade*) for the most promising playwright of the year. All the news was good. After a decade of dreaming of breaking into print, the text of *Entertaining Mr Sloane* was to be published three times: as a book, in a Penguin *New English Dramatists* anthology, and as the August play of the month in *Plays and Players*. Orton, who had been surviving on three pounds a week until his first royalty cheque, found his weekly earnings as much as £239. The play was sold to Paris in August, and the next year to Spain, the United States, Israel, and Australia. It would also be made into a film and a television play. Orton had arrived in the style of his comedy – with a vengeance.

Orton made dangerous ideas popular. The fact that he mixed ideas and entertainment confused some critics who laboured under the false and infuriating notion that art and commerce are necessarily antagonists. Orton came up against this bias in the first extended piece of criticism about *Entertaining Mr Sloane*, by John Russell Taylor in his grudging discussion of the play in the introduction to Penguin's *New English Dramatists 8*: 'Living theatre needs the good commercial dramatist as much as the original artist.' Orton was furious at such critical stupidity. 'Are they different, then?' he wrote to Peggy Ramsay, quoting John Russell Taylor's distinction between commercial success and art and asking to have the play withdrawn from the volume. ' "Hamlet" was written by a commercial dramatist. So was "Volpone" and "The School for Scandal" and "The Importance of Being Earnest" and "The Cherry Orchard" and "Our Betters". Two ex-commercial successes of the last thirty years are about to be revived by our non-commercial theatre: "A Cuckoo in the Nest" and "Hay Fever". "Thark" is also mooted. I've no ambition to bolster up the commercial theatre, but if my plays go on the West End I don't expect this to be used as a sneer by people who judge artistic success by commercial failure. There is no intrinsic merit in a flop . . .'[53]

'There are good plays and bad plays,' Orton said. 'With *Sloane* – people were always saying "Oh it's just a commercial play". It infuriated me because it wasn't; there isn't such a thing. It was a good play or a bad play.'[54] Almost as soon as *Entertaining Mr Sloane* settled into its West End run, there were people eager to proclaim it a bad play. The public outcry was precipitated by Peter Cadbury, the chairman of Keith Prowse Ltd, London's largest ticket bureau, who, while announcing to his shareholders a £98,000 increase in ticket sales over 1963, took the opportunity to blast plays that were 'unsuitable and unacceptable to a large part of the public' and which 'reflect the lowest forms of human life . . .' In an editorial, 'Killing the Goose', on 22 August, *The Times* praised Mr Cadbury for 'rushing in where others who think as he does fear to tread', but disagreed with Cadbury's suggestion of stricter control over theatrical content. 'That', *The Times* said, 'would be worse than the disease he purports to have diagnosed.'

The advertisements took advantage of the furore. 'The persecution and assassination of ENTERTAINING MR SLOANE is still taking place ... WARNING: This play is not suitable for the narrow minded.' Orton relished the scandal which belied the comic truth of his play. The culture hid its violence behind a show of propriety. Orton's scrapbook is filled with cuttings from the outspoken and the outraged. Above them are bannered 'AUNT EDNA ROCKS WEST END', 'FILTHY TRADITIONS', 'VIOLENT ART'. West End impresario Emile Littler joined forces with Cadbury to denounce *Entertaining Mr Sloane* as 'absolutely filthy' and went still further by condemning the Royal Shakespeare Company's brilliant season of *Marat/Sade*, *Endgame*, *The Birthday Party* and *Afore Night Come* as a 'programme of dirt'. Littler's accusations were especially piquant to Orton, since Littler was currently producing (and had helped to write) *The Right Honourable Gentleman*, a play about Sir Charles Dilke and the sexual scandal that ruined his political career.

Orton had found the society's nerve. He was not the first English satirist but arguably the best playwright to engage in a war of attrition with the public, whose flagging robustness extended to its threadbare theatrical vocabulary about play, where 'vulgarity', 'sensation', and 'grotesque' were used as pejorative terms when, in fact, they were the essence of great comedy. *Entertaining Mr Sloane* defied critical categories. 'I don't think the four characters are "vile". Do you?' Orton wrote to Glenn Loney about the American critics' response to the Broadway production of *Entertaining Mr Sloane*. 'Has New York never heard of Total Theatre. That is what "Sloane" is. You accept it. Don't bother whether it's a comedy or a tragedy or a farce or a drama – it's all of those, and, perhaps, none ...'[55]

In his scrapbook Orton pasted a fragment which reflects his own attitude towards the violence which many found subversive: 'Great artists from Leonardo to Picasso have represented violence and have certainly done so believing they were denouncing cruelty'. Orton was against violence for its own sake. 'I hope that the violence in my plays is not of an inconsequential nature ... I'm always horrified by violence in some things, especially American films and novels ... I watched an American TV series called "The Invaders" and the violence in that seems to me totally gratuitous. I mean, it was necessary for the old man in *Sloane* to be beaten up on the purely pragmatic grounds of the plot, and I couldn't have had the play working otherwise. In the same way, to go back to the old cliché about Shakespeare, you can't have certain scenes in *King Lear* without having Gloucester's eyes put out ...'[56]

Orton thought of himself as a realist, not a cynic; and *Entertaining Mr Sloane* is more than an exploration of English hypocrisy and the cosy landscape of woollies, bickies, and garden gnomes. Orton made a deliberate spectacle of human animality and need to deny and transcend the body. Man's urge for self-aggrandizement and self-perpetuation, like any animal's, required killing: the need to impose – either literally or symbolically – a sense of suffering and death on others in order to ensure a sense of personal victory. In *Entertaining Mr Sloane*, the family live a lie and need the lie to sustain a sense of their well-being. The Dadda, with his knowledge of Sloane's murder and his determination to turn him in, threatens all the others' lives. His murder allows life to flow more plentifully to the others. In this sense he is a sacrificial victim, functioning along the ritual lines Orton claimed to have studied in *The Golden Bough*, where sacrifice encouraged a good harvest. Sloane, Kath, and Ed make a bargain which fortifies their magical sense of power over life and death. Everything is renewed; all failure is forgotten. Each sidesteps the threat of annihilation. Sloane wins his freedom and a guarantee of the good life. Ed and Kath, once terrified of abandonment, have multiplied their power and pleasure by sharing Sloane.

Ed's business acumen is validated ('Put it down to my skill at the conference table', he swaggers to Kath). And Kath, with Sloane's baby inside her, has symbolically defeated death and grown 'bigger' as the curtain comes down with her relaxing victoriously on the sofa.

Orton's comedy teased the society with its evil and tested what it held sacred. The youthfulness in his comedy inevitably forced a confrontation between generations. 'This confrontation between generations of depraved youth and age valiantly upholding decency and moral standards – is in one sense peculiarly modern', wrote Hilary Spurling, whose essays on Orton were among the most perceptive during his lifetime. 'But it is also an ancient dispute . . . If the public sometimes seems disproportionately excited – as it did with Orton or with Congreve, Wycherley, even Farquhar – it is because the outcry is directed . . . at the modish trappings (in Orton's case, vice, crime, ever more rarified brands of kinkiness) rather than the essential and more deeply offensive truthfulness which they conceal.'[57]

Orton's battles with the public were not always comic. He was fiercely threatened by institutions and the irrational control they wielded in the name of authority. 'Accept your condition without tears and without abusing those placed in authority', barks the inspecting psychiatrist, Dr Rance, in *What the Butler Saw*. In 1965 Orton went to the American Embassy to get a visa to attend the Broadway rehearsals of *Entertaining Mr Sloane* and found himself in a double bind as preposterous as any Dr Rance could invent. 'The Eagle on the American Embassy building in Grosvenor Square is made of black metal', he wrote. 'From a small distance it looks like a bat or a vulture about to sink upon its prey.' Orton wanted to stay in the United States six weeks; but his request was denied. It was not Joe Orton Playwright who stood before Embassy officials but Joe Orton Jailbird and Menace to Private Property. To contain his fury, Orton wrote down his negotiations with officialdom weeks before he finally won his case. His narrative was never published. But it showed Orton beset and suffocated by the very categories *Entertaining Mr Sloane* wanted to subvert:

. . . He hunched himself over my passport, my visa application form and my Memorandum of Conviction. His eyes darted from one to the other. Finally, he looked up, sat back, a bewildered expression on his face.

'What's all this about?' he said.

I didn't know how to answer. I said nothing. He sat up in his chair, stiff and upright. His eyes narrowed.

'Can you explain what this –' he pointed to the Memorandum, '– whole thing was about.'

'It was a joke.'

This wasn't true. The outrages against a middle-brow reading public were serious enough. They'd occupied my time and energies for close on five years before I was caught. They could never be justified. Or explained.

'A joke!' he screeched the word quietly. 'The – er – authorities don't seem to have regarded it as a joke.'

'No,' I said.

He sighed. 'I may as well tell you, Mr Orton, that your visa will be automatically refused. That is the law. Your actions, you see, resulted in the damaging of other people's property. And that counts as moral turpitude.' He paused to let the full weight of his words sink in. 'However, you can apply for a temporary waiver of ineligibility. In order to do this you must convince a consular officer that you are a deserving case. Do you wish to make an application?'

'Yes,' I said.

He fiddled with a drawer in his desk and produced a sheaf of papers, looked through them.

'I'm a policeman,' he said, 'and I must warn you that I have ways of checking your statements. If you make any false ones that will be another reason why we shouldn't issue a temporary waiver of ineligibility.'

'Yes,' I said. I'd been through this before. I knew that the thing to do was to be docile and polite. I didn't think he had the power to beat me up. But, you never know. 'I wouldn't make false statements,' I said . . .

'Are you a homosexual?' he asked, suddenly and rather surprisingly from the context.

'No,' I said.

He lapsed into silence ... 'Would you mind seeing a doctor?' he spat out the words as though to check any further revelations.

'Why?'

He spread his hands. 'You force me to be blunt. You may have a psychopathic personality. This –' (waving his hands to the papers on his desk) '– is a very, very disturbing case.'

'I don't mind seeing a doctor,' I said.

'Good. Now I want you to fill in this form.' He handed me a form. 'When do you want to go to New York City?'

'On the second of September. The director wants me to discuss the play with him before rehearsals begin.'

I dropped the name Alan Schneider, along with *Who's Afraid of Virginia Woolf?* I didn't think he'd heard of either. He certainly hadn't heard of *Entertaining Mr Sloane*. Just as well, I suppose.

'I can't have your waiver of ineligibility ready for the second of September,' he said. 'We'll try for the twentieth, shall we?'

'Yes,' I said.

'You go out there and fill in that form. I've a lot of paperwork to do.' . . .

I waited in the entrance hall. I spread the form out and studied it. It was worse than I'd expected. 'Name any clubs or organizations to which you have belonged since reaching the age of sixteen.' 'What is your itinerary?' 'Name the addresses of your residences since reaching the age of sixteen. With length of stay in each.' 'Have you ever travelled through a Communist country?' That was the easiest. I completed the form and waited.

Then the man at the first desk rang through and said I was ready. I went past the secretaries and found the man at his desk. He didn't say anything. I gave him the form.

'You've never belonged to any club. Never joined anything?'

'No,' I said.

He looked at me with fresh eyes, his tones were cold and dis-believing.

'Not even the Boy Scouts?' A pink flush appeared on his cheeks.

'No.'

He stood up and eased himself past me. 'Let's go talk to the doctor . . .'

. . . While I waited to see the doctor I studied the sheet of paper. It was a typewritten document with the arms of the United States on top:

It said:

'This office regrets to inform you that it is unable to issue you a visa because you have been found ineligible under the following section of the Immigration and Nationality Act, as amended: (Only the checked items apply to your case):'

There were two sections.

(i) 'Section 212 (a) (15) which prohibits the issuance of a visa to anyone likely to become a public charge.'

This wasn't checked.

(ii) 'Section 101 (a) (15) which prohibits the issuance of a temporary visitor's visa to applicants who fail to establish they are non-immigrants under the terms of the law.'

This wasn't checked.

The rest of the paper was blank. And then I saw a check. There was no explanation beside it, just the figures '212 (a) (9)' written in longhand. Nothing else.

. . . I went into a comfortably furnished room and shut the door. A tall, elderly man sprang to his feet. He said he was the doctor and asked me to sit down . . .

It escaped his notice, though not mine, that he sat on the couch while I sat at the desk.

'Now, young man,' he said in a quiet reassuring voice, 'tell me what "all this" is about.'

I went over the same ground . . . 'It was a joke,' I said. 'I don't do it any more.'

'It – um – uh,' he gave a little squeal of laughter, though not humorous, 'doesn't sound funny to me.'

'It was reported in the *Daily Mirror*,' I said. 'And *Reader's Digest*.'

I wasn't particularly proud of this. It was more something to say.

The doctor nodded, his eyes held a wary expression. 'It was in the press?'

'Yes.'

'Hmmm.' There was a silence. I could hear the women and children talking in the hall. Neither of us said a word, the doctor shook his head, his mind seemed to be concentrating on something that was worrying him. 'You got six months in an institution for this?' he said.

'Yes.'

'There must've been something else?' He leaned forward, his neck sticking from his shirt. 'Wha – What?'

'I used to write false blurbs,' I said. 'On the inside of the book jackets. The writing I did was exactly the same as the writing I do now. I used to type quite long pieces. Many people borrowed the book from the library on the strength of my blurbs. And returned them with complaints when the published story didn't live up to mine.' He wasn't listening. I stopped and began again. 'It was a more limited public than my present one. But the standard of writing was the same.'

A muffled groan escaped his lips. 'It's still going on?' He half rose from the couch. I thought he was about to call for help.

'No, no!' I shouted, anxious not to alarm him. 'I'm talking about my plays.'

'I don't know what they want me to do with this case,' he seemed desperate. 'Have you received any treatment?'

'Only in Brixton. I was on remand for medical and mental reports.'

'You saw a psychiatrist in prison?' He clutched at this straw.

'Yes.'

'How often?'

'Once. For about ten minutes.'

'What happened to you then?'

'I was sent back to the cells. I was in solitary confinement for twenty-three hours a day.'

He brushed aside a foreign country's attempts to rehabilitate me with a curt gesture and strode into the outer office.

'I want the report of the prison psychiatrist on this young man's case,' he said to the secretary. 'Will you see to that for me?'

'Yes,' she said.

'I'll see you again perhaps some other time then, young man,' said the doctor, re-entering the room. He couldn't conceal his relief. 'Good morning to you.'

After signing another form authorising them to check my records

I left the building. I couldn't hope to get to the United States on my own. I needed help. So I went to tell my agent what had happened. I caught a seventy-three bus. Behind me two women were discussing 'Dr Who and the Daleks'.

'Very far-fetched,' the first woman said. 'I like something you can believe in.'

'Yes,' said the second. After a long pause she said, 'You know where you are with human beings, don't you.'

When Orton finally arrived in New York, in September 1965, he was delighted by the city and his production. 'I find New York a very old fashioned city,' he wrote to Peggy Ramsay. 'It's like time-travelling back to the thirties. It has an old world charm.'[58] Orton explored Manhattan, sometimes with a young Cypriot waiter he'd picked up and with whom he was photographed grinning boyishly on top of the Empire State Building. At night, he was often in the company of his director. Alan Schneider was the high-roller of American avant-garde theatre and a notoriously spiky personality. His production of *Who's Afraid of Virginia Woolf?* was one of the major American successes of the sixties. With it, he became the most influential, if not always the most subtle, interpreter of the best of contemporary theatre. Schneider's productions introduced the American public to Edward Albee, Edward Bond, Harold Pinter, and Samuel Beckett. Orton was impressed by Schneider and respectful of the line of important writers to which his name was now added.

Orton had himself photographed under the behemoth signboard of the Lyceum Theater. Grinning in long shot and dwarfed by the towering billboards spelling out in gargantuan red letters the name of his play and his director, Orton, like his billing, was barely visible. 'Sheila [Hancock] is delicious. Oh, I wish London could see it,' Orton wrote to Peggy Ramsay, excitedly assessing the first Broadway previews. '. . . It's curious how Sloane changes. It was a terrifically German play in Germany. And now it had a smoothness which is oddly American. I know you'll shudder with horror when I say that it's slick here. But I mean it as a compliment. I mean

Virginia Woolf was too, I think. In a way, I suppose, the London production (gimcrack as it was) was typically English. Will the French one be French and the Israeli one Jewish. A play to suit all tastes perhaps.'[59] The only real worry Orton admitted to his agent was George Turner, the actor playing the Dadda. 'I don't like the old man,' Orton wrote to Peggy Ramsay. 'He's played as a spinsterish, malicious recluse. I was shocked at first. But, as it's so much geared to the whole production I can't ask for it to be changed. In fact it couldn't be changed because it's basic to Alan's production. However, it does worry me. But it achieves one thing – the old man is never a sympathetic character which means that no one will mind him being murdered.'[60] Schneider always had difficulty with the capriciousness of the murder; and by exaggerating the Dadda's ugliness the production somewhat sidestepped Sloane's amorality. It made the death 'rational'. In the same way, Schneider cut Sloane's recounting of his crime, 'The air round Twickenham was like wine...', because, according to Dudley Sutton, 'he couldn't elicit "excuses", meanings from me. My concern wasn't the meaning. My concern was the rhythm. That speech should be delivered like a machinegun.' Sutton objected to 'Actor's Studio fiddle-faddle' and saw Sloane as a 'survivor who's not analytic. As long as he's got a bed, books, the car, he can happily lay about the house and get well fed'. Sutton argued a lot with Schneider. 'I picked up this trick from Brendan Behan, an old drinking mate of mine,' Sutton explains. 'If you've got something to say and you want somebody to listen, you've got to attribute your idea to somebody else. Behan used to say "As Theophile Fuckin' Gautier once wrote" and then say what he wanted. I used to say to Schneider: "There's a very old expression in the Irish Theatre. 'Never mind the fuckin' acting let's get on with the fuckin' play' "'.'

Orton's only serious disagreement with Schneider was about staging the Dadda's murder. 'He wanted to bring the curtain down before the murder,' Orton wrote to Michael Codron. 'I said "NO!"' But Orton's buoyancy about Schneider's production still echoed through his letter to Codron:

. . . The first previews are over. Very well received on the whole. We had a packed house for Saturday night. Can't tell whether it will run, though. Better not be too optimistic. The usual comments in the intervals – 'Very weird', 'Well, *I'm* not impressed', and even 'This reminds me of "A Taste of Honey".' But the applause is genuine enough. The second act makes them stumble. Give you two guesses why. And some of them resent it being called a comedy. Alan and I have asked Slade Brown to take the 'comedy' off the bills . . .

Lee [Montague] is wonderful. Beautiful. Don't forget he's the author's casting. But Sheila is the pride of the faggots. They treat her like Judy Garland or Dietrich. Irritates me. But she's marvellous. I don't think she's better than Lee, just more camp. We've told her to tone down some of the camp. It's better when she's in control of it. But, all the same, she is terrific. Edward Albee saw it last night. He likes it very much. What more could you want. (An anonymous) silly old queen in the interval last night was shrieking, 'Marvellous, but of course, it won't run!'[61]

Entertaining Mr Sloane had two weeks of previews. At first, audiences were small; but word of mouth built quickly, so that the second week was sold out.

We've been having fabulous houses [Orton wrote to Halliwell]. Full almost every night. Last two nights it's poured with a tropical downpour just before the performance and angry patrons who hadn't booked have been turned away. I said it might be better if we didn't have the critics. Word of mouth is doing so well . . . Tennessee Williams has been to see it twice. And, so I'm told, is wild over it. Says it's the funniest play he's ever seen . . . June Havoc came last night. I met her at interval. With a blonde wig on (her not me). Peter Shaffer saw it the other night, said he didn't recognize the play from London. He said that over here he realized what a very brilliant play it was – talked about elegance and wit, etc. . . . And the only cuts I've allowed are minor . . . Just shows actually how much damage Dromgoole did. And (while I think of it) I've been wondering how much damage Wood did. But there I know you'll say I told you so.[62]

Orton expected the play to be more disturbing to an American audience than Schneider did. 'I'm not hopeful of success,' he wrote to Halliwell after the first week's previews, 'but then we never were, were we.'[63] He reported the audience's bitter resentment of Eddie.

Schneider won't face up to the extent of their resentment [Orton told Halliwell]. They laugh exaggeratedly with KATH and even SLOANE in order to assert their heterosexuality. Schneider will only go as far as saying that they're horrified of laughing with EDDIE in the first act. He says they don't know what EDDIE is. But I told him that they will when the reviews come out. But as EDDIE is being played right the audience are very worried that this attractive masculine man should be a power and a threat to them (they identify with KATH – Sheila gets rounds of applause on some of her lines – but it's only that they want to show their solidarity). Last night when she said 'It's murder' to SLOANE in the third act someone nearby said 'Atta girl!' – of course they imagine that that is the point where the action turns and the tide runs in her favour ending up with her winning. Imagine their disbelief when EDDIE wins! . . . People are loving or hating it . . .[64]

But by the end of the previews, Orton's studied detachment about the show had given way to excitement. 'Think of me on Tuesday night and, even more, about two o'clock Wednesday morning', he wrote to Halliwell. 'Such a pity if the critics do damn it. It really is good. Thanks to Alan.'[65]

The play opened on 12 October to a star-studded first-night audience. At curtain-time two of New York's then most influential daily critics – Walter Kerr and Richard Watts – were not in their seats. Schneider waited fifteen minutes. 'I'm saying to the PA "For Chrissake let's go up! Let's go up." He said, "We can't go up. We haven't got the *Tribune* or the *Post*".' At twenty minutes past curtain-time, Schneider walked down the aisle to explain the situation to Howard Taubman, then critic of the New York *Times* and by virtue of his paper the most important of daily reviewers. Taubman was nervous and glancing at his watch. But Schneider's gesture of politeness was a tactical error. No critic likes to think that another critic is more important than he, especially the critic of the New York *Times*, whose outrageous sense of importance is sustained by the equally outrageous hit/flop economic system in which American theatre seems doomed to continue. Theatre protocol forbids that any other critic be seated in front of the *Times* critic. Schneider approached Taubman unaware of this pecking order. After explaining to the *Times* that the *Tribune* and the *Post* were late and the reason for the delay, Taubman, unsmiling, replied: 'Am I my brother's keeper?' Finally, twenty-five minutes later (confirming the publicity wisecrack that the hardest thing about dealing with critics was to get them to go to the theatre) Kerr and Watts sauntered into the Lyceum and the show began. 'Never an auspicious way to begin,' Schneider says. 'Especially for a comedy.'

The reviews were blistering; and, typically, somewhat incoherent. 'I thought it was merely a smelly spectacle,' wrote John McClain, a writer who had been promoted from shipping news to drama critic in William Randolph Hearst's right-wing New York *Journal American*. 'We are right back at the Boston Tea Party, standing on the dock throwing homosexuals into the drink as fast as they are unloaded, and if this is their best play of any year they are in serious trouble . . .' The *World Telegram and Sun* claimed that the play 'had the sprightly charm of a medieval cesspool'. But the most damaging attack came from Howard Taubman. 'Whether it is in earnest or not,' he began, '*Entertaining Mr Sloane* is a singularly unattractive play. If it means to be drama it is forced and incredible. If it seeks to be comedy, it is too broad. If it aims to be caricature, it succeeds all too well . . .'

Schneider had driven Orton and Dudley Sutton to the loading dock at the back entrance of the New York *Times* to get an early edition of Taubman's review. Sutton sat in the car and read the notice out loud. Schneider was in tears; Orton was dazed. 'He walked around all night,' Schneider remembers. Orton left for London the next day. *Entertaining Mr Sloane*, with only a handful of positive reviews, closed after thirteen performances.

Taubman kept beating the play even after he'd helped kill it. In a Sunday *Times* essay after it had closed, Taubman indicted the play for the characters' lack of nobility, dramatizing in his smug and vicious moralizing the same lust to appear good that Orton dramatized on stage:

In itself *Entertaining Mr Sloane* is too insignificant to merit further belaboring ... Like so many other young playwrights Joe Orton is outraged by corruption and hypocrisy he finds all around him. He is prepared to cry out mercilessly that protestations of honor and virtue are an obscene sham ... Okay. A perfectly valid job for the playwright in any era. The Greeks did it superbly more than 2,000 years ago. William Shakespeare, Ben Jonson and friends in good Queen Bess's time relentlessly held up the mirror to nature ...

But how does Mr Orton go about it? Like so many of his modish tribe, he chooses, the easy, supercilious, repellent way. He uses characters so lost in honor and decency, so sunk in dirt and degradation, that his point is vitiated almost before he has begun ...

The handling of Kath is an object lesson in how to demean a play, with the director and performer guilty of complicity ... Such a performance might bring a smirk to the lips of a theatregoer of debased tastes. It might secretly delight those epicenes who look upon the public humiliation of women as grand sport. But it is repugnant to anyone who believes that even a foil in black comedy deserves something juster than nasty, vulgar patronizing ...[66]

'Thanks for Taubman's second front,' Orton wrote to Glenn Loney. 'I liked it better than the initial offensive. He's been forced to take the play seriously. When he says lines like "In itself E.M.S. is too insignificant to merit further belabouring" the Lady doth protest too much. I'm glad they hate it. And I agree whole heartedly with Judith Malina and Julian Beck. If critics adored one's work one would have to watch out ... I get a kick out of lines like "Ben Jonson and his friends in good Queen Bess's time". You see, there you have the reason why he can't understand the play. One of my characters would say a line like that – seriously, as seriously as Taubman says it. And *I* would think it was funny that the character says it ...'[67]

The week following Taubman's salvo in the Sunday *Times*, Schneider waded into the ruckus. 'What is it about the gnat of

"Mr Sloane" that strains him so profoundly?' Schneider asked. He pointed out that Taubman's overheated idiom – referring to Kath as 'a simpering idiot', 'an insult to a baboon' – had bubbled well beyond the bounds of reasoned debate. 'I shudder to think', he wrote, 'what Mr Taubman might say about the evils of two other somewhat more serious examples of this genre, *The Killing of Sister George* and John Osborne's *A Patriot for Me*.' Listing a number of impressive plays he'd, directed which had been maligned as 'meaningless aberrations on our chaste body theatric' – *Waiting for Godot, Who's Afraid of Virginia Woolf?, Endgame, Happy Days, The Dumb Waiter* – Schneider added 'While I am certain that neither Sloane's author nor its director has any illusions about the play's claim to eminence in this pantheon of depravity, I have not the slightest doubt of its ultimate vitality and durability in the history of contemporary drama, its relevance to our behavior and value patterns; as well as its dramatic virtues, relative say, to a much more praised recent British import "The Right Honorable Gentleman" which Mr Taubman recommends as an evening for adults – while reviling Sloane as fit only for degenerates and debased women haters.'

Schneider's reply to Taubman irritated Orton for under-rating his theatrical intentions:

I pasted the clipping very neatly into my cuttings book – which will eventually go to Boston University, USA for their 'Joe Orton Collection' (sic). Well, at least, they wanted a collection *before* the recent disgraceful goings on at West 45th Street [Orton wrote to Schneider's assistant who sent him the article – 'Mr Sloane's Director Talks Back'] – I thought Alan's letter to the *Times* good. On the whole. Though one or two passages brought out my paranoia. The one I'd like someone to explain is: 'I shudder to think what Mr Taubman might say about the evils of two other *somewhat more serious* examples of this genre, "The Killing of Sister George" and John Osborne's "A Patriot for Me".' End quote. Now – (as I roll up my sleeves) – I haven't seen A P. for Me. And I've no doubt at all that J.O. will have treated homosexuality in a 'serious' manner. But I have seen Sister George and it is a very, very little little piece about

Lesbians – or at least we're given to understand that it's about lesbians –
I couldn't find much evidence of any more lesbianic a relationship
than most women have with their mothers. So what does Alan mean?
(By the way – do read this letter in the spirit in which it's written,
not in a rage or anything like that. I find it difficult to smile in print.)
No, but seriously, Sister G. is light-weight . . . That's the way it's
being played. That is why it's having a success with the middle-brow,
middle-class audiences. It is not serious at all. Not nearly as serious as
Sloane. Which isn't 'serious' in the obvious sense, but 'serious' as a
piece of writing. I take my writing very, very seriously. It is the only
way to write . . .[68]

Orton signed his letter 'Joe – a serious writer'. *Entertaining Mr
Sloane* was the first fruit of a decade of hard work; but in public
he hid the seriousness and the pain of his search for a style. 'I'd
written several plays that were all more or less failures,' he told the
BBC in 1964, speaking as the West End's newest success. 'Even in
those, I could still write dialogue. A play isn't just writing dialogue,
it's something very strange. I don't know what it is. Maugham said
that being a playwright was nothing to be proud of because you
could be a moron and still be a playwright. It's just knack, like
walking on a high wire. You can be an absolute thick and walk
on a high wire. It's nothing to do with intellect or intelligence.
Just something that you have. If you've got the knack and the
ability to write dialogue, then there's no reason why you shouldn't
write a play.'[69]

Ultimately the literary fireworks of *Entertaining Mr Sloane*'s
naturalistic dialogue showed up the play's essential scenic tameness.
The piece did not use the stage with full playfulness – a fact Orton
recognized. 'The new full-length play [*Loot*]', Orton told the BBC,
'is, I think, an advance. But of course you can't tell until you've
written it. But I think it's an advance.'[70] In his subsequent plays,
Orton worked more boldly with theatrical artifice. In them, Orton's
dazzling capacity to manipulate words would be matched with an
equally startling talent for constructing hilarious stage images. *Entertaining Mr Sloane* toyed with farce but the cut and thrust of the

play's third act had a potential for mayhem that never made the transition from language to movement.

'I feel, looking back on everything now from a distance – six months and three thousand miles', Orton wrote in 1966 about the Broadway version of *Sloane*, 'that perhaps everything was too broad. But given a brilliant comic – viz: Sheila, in the lead, it's difficult to see how else it could've gone. I still stick to my statement – did I make it, I wonder? – that the New York production was better than London. If we'd had that production – plus Sheila – we'd've run a year in London. Of course the only place I've ever seen my play is still in Germany. Did I tell you that I'd been to Berlin where it was perhaps a shade better than Hamburg. There were thirty-eight curtain calls and every one deserved . . .'[71]

5

SCANDALOUS SURVIVAL

> One does not kill by anger but by laughter.
> Come, let us kill the Spirit of Gravity.
>
> Friedrich Nietzsche, *Thus Spake Zarathustra*

Killing is one of the forms of our wandering
mourning ...

Rainer Maria Rilke

The transition between *Entertaining Mr Sloane* and *Loot* was *The Good and Faithful Servant*, completed in June 1964 and produced on Rediffusion Television in April 1967. In this poignant and bitter one-act play, Buchanan – a commissionaire – is retiring after fifty years of service. Buchanan has lost an arm on the job. Like the company's gifts of a clock and a toaster, his body is on the verge of breakdown. When he visits a lady friend on the evening of his retirement, she's shocked at the sight of a whole man:

EDITH. Your arms! Where has the extra one come from?
BUCHANAN. It's false.
EDITH. Thank God for that. I like to know where I stand in relation
    to the number of limbs a man has.

Orton concentrates his irony on the slavish belief in industrial routine. At Buchanan's first get-together of ex-employees in the company's recreation centre, he talks to another old man – an exchange which maps the bleak horizon of their lives:

OLD MAN. I was almost mentioned in a well-known sporting periodical once.

BUCHANAN. I never got as far as that . . .

Later, Buchanan reminds the Old Man: 'I worked here. I was on the main entrance . . .' But Buchanan's life and his presence amount to nothing. 'Nobody knows me', he says to himself. 'They've never seen me before.' In the foreground, the shrewish director of activities, Mrs Vealfoy, claps her hands and forces them into recreation: 'We're going to run through all the songs with "Happy" in them . . .' Buchanan registers his gradual disenchantment by finally smashing his retirement gifts with a hammer. At the finale, as his new wife, Edith, chats to him about a holiday, Buchanan sits silently in bed, tearfully aware of his wasted life. He dies as she gossips about a forthcoming company dance, concluding: 'we have so much to be thankful for'.

Despite the seething disgust in *The Good and Faithful Servant* the blast of its irony was muted by the naturalistic format. Melodrama has a comforting predictability and is too tame for comic devastation. A survivor, Orton was compelled to exhibit his mastery of the dead world that *The Good and Faithful Servant* documented in a style as extreme as his success. The threat of anonymity, the suffocating memory of his upbringing and literary failures were symbolic deaths from which Orton now drew power for life. With success, he now embarked on a play whose manic laughter registered the weirdness of his scandalous survival.

Loot is about scandalous survivors: Fay, the predatory nurse with designs on McLeavy's money; Hal and Dennis, lovers and robbers; and the psychopathic detective Truscott pursuing his omnipotent fantasies first in crime-solving and then in larceny. 'I fancy myself as a ghoul', Hal says in a line cut from the first draft of *Loot*, after tipping his mother's corpse out of her coffin to bury stolen money. The joke defines a strange and indifferent universe, literally 'touching the dead' and showing death as capricious as life.

Written between June and October 1964, *Loot* was originally titled *Funeral Games* and subtitled 'a Farce'. 'If you don't like *Funeral Games* as a title, do you like Comedy of Horrors better,' Orton wrote Michael Codron on 15 October, the day before he delivered the play to his producer. '. . . It has a nice play on Chamber of Horrors and Comedy of Errors. Or is it too high for the public? . . . I prefer *Funeral Games* myself.' *Loot*, the genial title Kenneth Halliwell pinned to the play, had a whiff of a thirties whodunit which was apt for the plot but not for the lacerating moral spirit or the humour.

In farce, Orton could marry terror and elation in his highly stylized theatrical idiom. Violating social and familial pieties, farce's pandemonium created the panic Orton wanted in laughter. In tragedy, character is fate; in farce, where characterization is minimized and action emphasized, mischief is fate. Orton understood the kinship between tragedy and farce and made the most of it in *Loot*. '*Sloane* took a comedic view of things, *Loot* takes a farcical view of things normally treated as tragic', Orton said in his first public statement about the play. 'Farce is higher than comedy in that it is very close to tragedy. You've only got to play some of Shakespeare's tragedies plain and they are nearly farcical. All gradations of theatre between tragedy and farce – light comedy, drama – are a load of rubbish.'[1]

Orton's classic view of farce was not the traditional English equivalent of Parisian boulevard farce: the crude bedroom capering of the Whitehall farces or the frothy, well-plotted Ben Travers Aldwych escapades. In the hands of contemporary practitioners, farce had dwindled to a bourgeois fun machine. *Loot* returned farce to its age-old scope and ferocity, adapting the genre to Orton's own free-wheeling outspokenness.

I am a great admirer of Ben Travers [Orton said, discussing farce in *Plays and Players*[2]]. But the boundaries he set to present day farce are really too narrow. As I understand it, farce originally was very close to tragedy, and differed only in the *treatment* of its themes – themes like rape, bastardy, prostitution. But you can't have a farce about rape any longer. French farce got as far as adultery, but by Ben

Travers's time it was only *suspected* adultery, which turned out to have been innocuous after all. A lot of farces today are still based on the preconceptions of a century ago, particularly the preconceptions about sex. But we must now accept that, for instance, people *do* have sexual relations outside marriage: a thirties farce is acceptable because it is distanced by its period, but a modern farce which merely nurses the old, outworn assumptions is cushioning people against reality. And this, of course, is just what the commercial theatre usually does. In theory there is no subject which could *not* be treated farcically – just as the Greeks were prepared to treat any subject farcically. But in practice farce has become very restricted indeed ... My feeling is that the dramatist must have the right to change formal gear at any time. There's supposed to be a healthy shock, for instance, at those moments in *Loot* when an audience suddenly *stops* laughing. So if *Loot* is played as no more than farcical, it won't work.

The Good and Faithful Servant took aim at corporate paternalism. *Loot* was a more ferocious attack on this faith in authority. Mischievously, Orton raised the issue of faith directly in Inspector Truscott's final exit speech in the first draft. It was part of the formula of detective fiction which *Loot* parodied. That formula, as W. H. Auden brilliantly observed, requires 'an innocence which is discovered to contain guilt; then a suspicion of being the guilty one; and finally a real innocence from which the guilty other has been expelled, a cure effected, not by me or my neighbours, but by the miraculous intervention of a genius from outside who removes the guilt by giving knowledge of guilt'.[3] Truscott of the Yard, of course, inverts every expectation of the detective, and through him Orton sends up the daydream of a return to innocence. In the original the guilty remain free, having bribed Truscott into silence. True to detective form, Truscott pauses with a suitcase of stolen money in hand to pronounce the prerequisite hymn to moral harmony:

TRUSCOTT. ... Goodwill has been established where there was none before; our lives have been enriched; we have taken a positive attitude and affirmed something. I don't want to bring religion into this, but . . . I do think it proves, in a roundabout way, the abiding validity of the ethical system upon which this country is founded.

In *Loot* Orton's laughter found new strength by tilting against death, the Church, the English police and the idea of English justice. 'One *must* shake the audience out of its expectations', he said. 'They need not so much shocking, as *surprising* out of their rut.'⁴

Orton pushed laughter until it exposed tabooed areas behind public attitudes. The words 'sick' and 'filth' which so often were levelled at Orton's work contain a fear of infection. The taboo's aim is prohibition of 'infection', an inhibition of thought which demands conformity but provides no insight. 'Whenever one dares not question any further or when it does not occur to one to do so, one is dealing with a taboo.'⁵ The taboo represents society against the individual; and Orton's laughter was the revenge of the individual against a smothering consensus. Between the extremes of McLeavy's beleaguered passivity and Inspector Truscott's megalomania, *Loot* dramatizes the dangers of taboos that keep knowledge at a low level. 'I ignore stories which bring officialdom into disrepute', explains McLeavy, who assumes much to his cost that to overlook chaos is to create order. Where McLeavy is the quintessential victim ruled by taboos, Truscott is a bully who exploits the taboos about English justice for his own power. In his interrogation, Truscott continually places others in the childlike position of being forbidden to answer questions, the same role into which those who obey taboos are put by society. When McLeavy is arrested he finally protests about Truscott's abuse of power and asks to see a higher authority. Truscott treats him like a schoolboy: 'You can see whoever you like, providing you convince me first you're justified in seeing them.'

Sporting with a corpse and a coffin is chilling business, but Orton used it to tap a reservoir of deep and unexplored public feeling. In acting out his own oedipal resentments, he systematically examined the irrational associations that surrounded the ritual of death. 'If you're absolutely practical – and I hope I am – a coffin is only a box', Orton said, responding to the charge of offensiveness for staging *Loot*'s hijinx around a coffin. 'One calls it a coffin and once you've called it a coffin it immediately has all sorts of associations.'[6] *Loot* poses questions about the attitudes surrounding the taboo and then shocks its audience with the detachment of its practical solutions. 'As for the taboo ingredients of *Loot*,' Orton explained sensibly, 'I have a great reverence for death, but no particular feeling for the little dust of a corpse. And the family is strongly Roman Catholic for the traditional farcical reason that they must be respectable and believable – and there are no equivalent outward trappings in a Protestant household to establish the air of religious respectability.'[7]

Orton's previous plays delighted in exposing sexual prudery. *Loot* went a step further, unmasking the most profound twentieth-century prudery: death. The detective story was the prototype of the thriller/horror saga which found its most popular expression in the sixties fad for psychopathic slaughter, typified by the James Bond adventures. The deaths which people paid to see and which entertained them on TV were violent, spectacular, and gruesomely attractive. This phenomenon, which Geoffrey Gorer aptly dubbed 'the pornography of death',[8] paid no attention to authentic grief and mourning. The cosmetic idea of death succeeded at the box office and catered to the social prudery. Natural death replaced sex as society's unmentionable, and entertainment avoided it.

Loot revelled in the 'impropriety of natural death'. The play centres around a corpse which is stripped naked and then stashed in a cupboard. The Lord Chamberlain, whose job then was 'to prevent public offence being given', found this exceedingly offensive:

I am desired by the Lord Chamberlain [wrote the Comptroller to the producers on 31 December 1964] to inform you that he will only consider granting a licence for the above-named play if certain scenes are rewritten so that:
1. The corpse is obviously a dummy.

2. The corpse remains fully clothed throughout the play and is not undressed, even behind a screen, at any time; and the accompanying dialogue is adjusted accordingly.

3. The false eye business is removed.

'Anything is legal with a corpse', argues McLeavy, a statement to which Truscott and, evidently, the Lord Chamberlain took exception as defenders of 'the rights of the dead'. The Lord Chamberlain's instructions were an irony fit for the play's debate: the viscera of the dead were protected by authority while the work of a living writer was being eviscerated. This same refusal to admit death was crucial to the play's joke about the embalmer's art. Mrs McLeavy has been, as Fay says, 'scientifically preserved'. She is 'Good for centuries', Hal reminds Dennis, who's worried about the body juices rotting the cash in the coffin. Hal is implored by Fay to take a last look at his mother: 'You'll never see her again'. Hal is quick to notice the absurdity of the remark. There is hardly anything left of his mother in the corpse.

In the ritual of burial, the dead are staged as if they are alive. Mrs McLeavy not only 'looks as if she might speak'; dressed in her WVS uniform, she looks as if she might walk too. So Orton tests the prudery about clothing the dead by having the corpse undressed. 'Bury her naked? My own mum?' says Hal, combing his hair in the mirror during this crisis of conscience. 'It's a Freudian nightmare.' Mrs McLeavy is dressed to meet her Maker; by stripping her, the dream is defiled. Mrs McLeavy would never greet her husband, let alone God, in the raw. The body is 'corrupted', old, ugly and shameful; something, even in death, to be denied. While they denude the corpse, Hal dreams of building a temple to the living flesh in a three-star brothel:

HAL. . . . I'd advertise 'By Appointment'. Like jam . . . I'd have a French bird, a Dutch bird, a Belgian bird, an Italian bird –

FAY *hands a pair of false teeth across the screen.*

– and a bird that spoke fluent Spanish and performed the dances of

her native country to perfection. (*He clicks the teeth like castanets.*)
I'd call it the Consummatum Est. And it'd be the most famous house
of ill-fame in the whole of England.

At the finale, when Truscott discovers the body and asks McLeavy
if his wife wanted to be buried in the nude, mention of the word
'nude' sends the old man into a fury. He asks Truscott to leave the
house: 'I can't allow you to insult the memory of my late wife.'
McLeavy's sentimentality invests dead matter with human feeling.
When he first hears of the funeral parlour being robbed, he asks:
'Human remains weren't outraged?' In the original version, Orton
spelled out the detachment in Dennis's reply: 'Nothing human
was touched.' By mingling the diabolic and the delightful, Orton
shows up the unwitting irrationality of 'normal' behaviour. When
McLeavy discovers his son's crime, he's scandalized. Hal reminds
him of his own peculiar behaviour: 'You had her filleted without a qualm. Who could have affection for a half-empty woman?'
McLeavy groans in anguish, a despair which is always hilariously
self-referring:

HAL. You've lost nothing. You began the day with a dead wife
You end it with a dead wife.
MCLEAVY. Oh, wicked, wicked. (*Wildly.*) These hairs – (*Points.*) –
they're grey. You made them so. I'd be a redhead today had you
been an accountant.
TRUSCOTT (*removing his pipe from his mouth*). We really can't accept
such unlikely explanations for the colour of your hair, sir . . .

Orton makes a spectacle of laughter's satanic superiority ('God
is a gentleman. He prefers blondes'). Hal, initially, hides
the corpse in the wardrobe. He is forced to unlock the door
by Fay, who soon turns the discovery to her own financial advantage and gets a percentage of the loot. In the original, the corpse
fell out of the wardrobe at Fay's feet. Disallowed by the Lord
Chamberlain, Orton conjured in the minds of his audience a much
more offensive stage picture.

HAL *gives her the key. She opens the wardrobe, looks in, closes the* *door and screams.*

FAY. This is unforgivable. I shall speak to your father.

(*Pause.*)

She's standing on her head.

Mrs McLeavy is meant to be 'at rest'; not – as she grotesquely appears – at play. To Orton, once life had left the body, the corpse was an irrelevance. The image made the point which Hal underlined in the original by disputing his father's sanctimonious dismay: 'The position of the body in space can't affect you.'

'This is a house of mourning', Fay reminds Hal, insisting on ritual protocol as he shouts down the hall for his father to stop ogling the wreath from the Friends of Bingo. In the confusion of events, Mr McLeavy, who begins the day planning 'to keep her [his wife's] memory green' by planting a rose garden that 'will put Paradise to shame', has completely forgotten the sacredness of her memory by the end of it. Having held his tongue, flabbergasted, at the news that Mrs McLeavy changed her will and left all her money to Fay, he can't contain himself when Fay claims that in her dying breath Mrs McLeavy accused her husband of murder. 'Complete extinction has done nothing to silence her slanderous tongue', he says, having spent most of the play hiding a lifetime's residual anger behind platitudes. For all the pretence to decorum, Mrs McLeavy is never mourned.

'Grief is a delicate emotion', Fay says in one blue-pencilled line. 'Any kind of physical activity dispels it.' Laughter engineers a detachment from grief and anxiety; and Orton's play dramatizes this. 'Your sense of detachment is terrifying, lad', Truscott tells Hal. 'Most people would at least flinch upon seeing their mother's eyes and teeth handed around like nuts at Christmas.' *Loot* mocked life for its meaninglessness: a fact to which Orton was as resigned in life as in art. After Elsie Orton's funeral, Orton brought back a set of her well-polished false teeth to London and presented them to the cast of *Loot*:

I'd taken my mother's false teeth down to the theatre. I said to Kenneth Cranham [who played Hal], 'Here, I thought you'd like the originals'. He said, 'What'. 'Teeth,' I said. 'Whose?' he said. 'My mum's,' I said. He looked very sick. 'You see,' I said. 'It's obvious that you're not thinking of the events of the play in terms of reality if a thing affects you like that.' Simon Ward [who played Dennis] shook like jelly when I gave them to him . . .

(4 January 1967)

'On the subject of writing, Mr Orton feels that too many writers for the theatre become obsessed with dialogue', *The Stage* reported in 1966[9] after *Loot* was successfully moored in the West End. ' "A plot gives you something to fall back upon and gives rise to lines itself!" ' Orton was speaking from eighteen months' painful experience. A good proportion of the brilliant epigrams and exchanges of the final text were scrambled into the hodgepodge of the original. But the script Orton submitted to Michael Codron in October 1964 was all wild talk and tame action.

In the original, Fay dominates the machinations; and Truscott, the sleuth whom Irving Wardle in *The Times* a decade later would call 'as great a comic character as the English stage has produced since the war', had only eight lines in the first act. Orton had not fully explored his characters; and there was not sufficient leeway for comic complication. Dennis, for instance, has no real relation with or passion for Fay in the original. Without need, there is no laughter. He doesn't compete for Fay's affection as he does in the final version, where, by acquiring the loot, he can make himself a more attractive proposition to her than McLeavy. The pace of farce is hell-bent; and, however preposterous, the structure must dramatize necessity. The question of McLeavy's fate and Fay's avaricious designs on him, which keep an audience guessing throughout the final version of the play, are settled straightforwardly in Act 1 of the first draft. Fay tells McLeavy she is going to marry him: 'This is what I'm offering you. The chance to be pointed out as the contented husband of a practising Christian.' Jokes spelled out the greed which *Loot* would later let the actors play rather than

say (Fay: '. . . If hearts and souls are one, bank accounts must follow. That's logic'). McLeavy, having been manoeuvred to his knees
for a proposal of marriage in Act 1, the finale merely wraps up an
inevitable conclusion. In the first draft, McLeavy suggests a trade-
off with Dennis, but since there is no preparation for a switch in
the plot, the last-minute idea rings false. McLeavy's comic come-
uppance is to marry a self-confessed murderess and agonize when
and how he will become Fay's victim number eight: 'Does Heaven
reserve no crumb of comfort for the off-white of soul', he says in
the penultimate laugh of the first-draft finale. 'It's a punishment fit
for Judas.' Orton had galvanized the situation brilliantly by the
final draft. McLeavy is caught in a web of terrifying complications.
After he has lied to Truscott about the whereabouts of the stolen
money to protect his son, Hal double-crosses his father. He suggests
to Truscott that he'd be happy to testify against his father. So,
instead of threatening to frame McLeavy to protect his larceny as
Truscott does in the first version, Orton now lets Truscott actually
arrest him without explanation:

MCLEAVY. I'm innocent. (*A little unsure of himself, the beginnings of
panic.*) Doesn't that mean anything to you?
TRUSCOTT. You know the drill, Meadows. Empty his pockets and
book him.

   MCLEAVY *is dragged away by* MEADOWS.

MCLEAVY. I'm innocent! I'm innocent! (*At the door, pause, a last wail.*)
Oh, what a terrible thing to happen to a man who's been kissed by
the Pope.

   MEADOWS *goes off with* MCLEAVY.

Orton is now coordinating the word and the stage picture: the
result is astonishment.

'Joe Orton tells me the play is finished and I shall have it in my
hot sticky hands at the end of the week,' Codron wrote to Kenneth
Williams on 12 October 1964. It was Williams whom Orton had in
mind for Truscott, the play's best invention but also its biggest
problem. Codron, who had produced Williams in three revues
and one play, engineered a meeting between the two men while

Orton was in the middle of writing *Loot*. 'At the time, Kenneth was balancing the actor/cabaret-turn personas,' Codron says. 'He wasn't committed to not being a serious actor. Joe fell completely under his spell.'

Williams was surprising to meet – a complicated, touching man who bore no apparent relation to the haughty buffoon of the *Carry On* films or the whining camp voice from *Round the Horne* or *Beyond our Ken*. His actual speech was clipped, animated and vivid; but in recounting his stories his voice slipped easily into the wide range of delicious postures that had made him one of England's most popular comedians, sprouting plummy and pinched vowels as it swooped from posh to dead common. Williams made the act of speaking funny. There was something dangerous in the unpredictable gusto of his conversation. He spared no one – not even himself – in making a comic point. This approach was not the only thing Williams shared with Orton. Williams's own baroque powers of conversation had the same shape and satiric intention in the delivery that *Loot* was developing in its dialogue. Orton and Williams were immediately sympatico. 'At the end of the meeting,' Codron recalls, 'Joe said "I'm writing something at the moment. I'll write it for you".'

Orton and Williams were a good audience for each other. 'We did get on very well. He was a great *activator*. He had tremendous energy,' Williams says. 'At the end of our meeting Joe told me I'd influenced him. "Having met you I want to make this detective more like you."' Orton had never seen Williams on stage and didn't know his very special theatrical abilities. But the first draft of *Loot* bore the imprint of their meeting. 'He did suddenly get fired with the idea of writing a zonking great part for me,' Williams says. 'Instead of finishing his play and starting something else with me in mind, he dovetailed the two. As a result, Fay, the nurse, who begins as the prime mover of the plot and should go on being the prime mover, ceases to be. She almost becomes an appendage. I remember during the production Geraldine McEwan, who played Fay, said to me, "This character's extraordinary. She's a resolute

woman who comes into this household determined to run everything; and should – according to the logic of the first act – succeed
in doing so. But she doesn't. She begins marvellously and then
peters out." I never had the courage to say what I felt to be the
truth of the situation. I did really feel that Joe had overbalanced the
original intention.'

'When the play arrived, I could not see Truscott and Ken at all,'
Codron recalls. 'It needed a lugubriousness and dopiness. Ken is a
bright person. I thought the play was good and could be made
better; but I thought this is obviously not Ken's play. Ken must
turn it down. But he didn't.' Whatever his supposed qualms,
Codron was very excited about getting Williams to sign for the
play. A week after receiving the script, he was writing to Williams
to inform him that Peter Wood had been asked to direct what was
now to be called *Loot* and requesting in 'sweet reasonableness' for
Williams 'to stay in the play for the length of a normal pregnancy
as you yourself said very perceptively I thought . . .'

As originally conceived, Truscott was more a literary lampoon
than a satire on English justice. Orton intended both; but the
nature of Williams's outrageousness lent itself to broad parody and
Orton steered the role that way:

TRUSCOTT. . . . You have before you a man who is quite a personage
   in his way – Truscott of the Yard. (*He takes out his pipe and begins
   to fill it slowly, in silence.*) Have you never heard of Truscott? The
   man who tracked down the limbless girl killer? Or was that
   sensation before your time?
HAL. Who would kill a limbless girl?
TRUSCOTT. She was the killer.
HAL. How did she do it if she was limbless?
TRUSCOTT. That is a question I'm not prepared to answer to anyone
   outside the profession . . .

The detective, as Auden points out, 'must be either the official
representative of the ethical or the exceptional individual who is in
a state of grace'.[10] The appealing fantasy behind detective fiction
is the restoration of a state of innocence. Orton reversed these

expectations. Truscott is a representative of a corrupt society in which psychopathic ruthlessness substitutes for a 'state of grace'. Truscott's genius is for illogic, not logic. Unlike Sherlock Holmes with his passion for the answer or Inspector French of Scotland Yard with his devotion to duty, Truscott's only pure motive is his commitment to his legend.

Loot was rushed into production more on the impetus of Orton's reputation than on the accomplishment of his script. By December Codron had collected an all-star cast, including Duncan Macrae, Geraldine McEwan, Ian McShane and Williams, and planned a six-week tour before returning to London for a West End run. Peter Wood, who had originally given Orton the ending to *Entertaining Mr Sloane* and had been slated to direct it, was signed to direct *Loot*. Wood, however, was commuting between London and New York, directing Ibsen's *The Master Builder* at the National and Jean Kerr's situation comedy *Poor Richard* on Broadway.

While *Loot* was hurt by the absence of a director to help reshape it before rehearsals began in January 1965, Orton found inspiration for his rewrites in the character of Detective Sergeant Harold Challenor, whose outrageous crime-fighting methods captured more headlines than criminals. Challenor was the subject of the first police inquiry into their own ranks under the 1964 Police Act. 'Orton was obsessed with Challenor,' Williams remembers. 'He never stopped reading the reports and giggling uncontrollably. He said "This man's mad".' The conclusion was shared by a psychiatrist giving evidence at the inquiry who found the London detective 'quite mad indeed'.

A former male nurse, with the thick neck, cropped hair and ridged eyebrows of a prize-fighter, Challenor had been commended seventeen times for his work on the Metropolitan Police, but his concern for law and order had turned into a mania which led him to plant evidence on law-abiding citizens. He turned every situation into a spectacle of his own heroism and omnipotence. Once, according to his wife, he 'walked home seventeen miles through a storm and his clothes had dried on him. His feet were bleeding. He said he'd done it to keep fit.' Challenor also told her: 'If anyone tells you I am going to have a nervous breakdown, you are not to take notice'.[11]

The *Times* headlines implied method in Challenor's madness:

SGT CHALLENOR WORKED 102 HOURS IN ONE WEEK
Inquiry Told of Wartime Bravery
NOVEL CRIME FIGHTING METHODS SUCCEED

But the story that emerged was much more unsavoury. Challenor had picked out a demonstrator protesting at the Greek royal visit in 1963 and arrested him saying 'You're fucking nicked, my old beauty.' On the way to the police station, riding in the police van, the demonstrator told the inquiry, 'Challenor was leaping about. A girl's voice shouted, "Will you give us a lift?" And Challenor leaned out and shouted "Yes! Round the bleeding chops!" ' Later, according to the demonstrator, he'd been beaten seven times on his way to the 'charge room'. Challenor produced a brick from his desk, saying 'We have got to stop them throwing bricks at royalty.' He showed it to the demonstrator. 'There you are, my old beauty,' he said. 'For carrying an offensive weapon, you can get two years.' Another Challenor victim, whose conviction and sentence of seven years' imprisonment for demanding money with menaces and possessing an offensive weapon was finally quashed, testified that Challenor had planted an iron bar on him in his cell and fabricated the charge. He testified that Challenor, looming large in his dark blue raincoat, came into the cell saying 'Hello my little darling, hello my little darling. I don't want you. I want your pals.' When no names were forthcoming, Challenor threw down the iron bar. The prisoner refused to pick it up. Challenor threatened him with it and then punched him in the face.[12]

In February 1965 Challenor was finally suspended from the police force. 'I think it's very unhealthy for a society to love the police the way the English do', Orton said. 'When you have that kind of affection for authority, you begin to have the makings of a police state. I think wariness of the police is a much healthier attitude.'¹³ As a homosexual, Orton had been entrapped by police, so he told friends; and, once in custody, had been propositioned by them. This gave another dimension of anger to *Loot*'s satire. 'Obviously you've got to have police; they're a necessary evil', Orton said. 'I've no objection to them tracking down murderers and bank robbers, clearly you can't have people behaving in a completely anarchic way. I believe, though, that they interfere far too much with private morals – whether people are having it off in the backs of cars or smoking marijuana, or doing the interesting little things that one does . . .'¹⁴

In the final version of *Loot* Orton appended an epigram from George Bernard Shaw's *Misalliance*. 'Anarchism', says Lord Summerhays, 'is a game at which the Police can beat you . . .' Challenor was living confirmation of Orton's fantasy. Gradually Truscott assumed Challenor's salient characteristics. 'You're fucking nicked, my old beauty' was grafted verbatim into Truscott's dialogue as he nabs McLeavy. Truscott continues: 'You've found to your cost that the standards of the British police force are as high as ever.'

Initially Truscott lacked Challenor's psychopathic unpredictability which makes him dangerous and disturbing as well as funny. In the original version of *Loot* violence is ludicrous violence; and pain is generalized so that its implications are easily dismissed. The terrifying frivolity of the characters veers in the first draft towards silliness. Truscott's transformation from buffoon to bully was slow to evolve. In the first of many revised endings, Truscott sends Dennis, Hal and Fay to jail and keeps the money for himself, wheeling it off stage in a pram which holds a gramophone playing *Land of Hope and Glory*: 'Your guilt shall be purged. Society has weighed you in her balance and found that she has been short measured. To Judgement! To Retribution! To Justice!' The extravagant ending tried to unite Orton's comic statement with his star's persona. Kenneth Williams was the scapegoat for *Loot*'s literary inadequacies; the burden of the play's success or failure fell on his bony shoulders. Williams, like Duncan Macrae, who played McLeavy, was a celebrated theatrical exotic cast in a role that demanded a veneer of normality. Williams's stage presence was alert, glittering, hungry to please, tinged unmistakably by hysteria. Truscott, however, was unnerving because he vacillated between the articulate and the oafish. 'My wife is a woman,' he says, in a joke stolen from Wycherley's *The Country Wife*. Nothing about a Kenneth Williams performance was believably dim or menacing. Physically, he was slim; emotionally, despite the comic caterwauling, he was vulnerable. No amount of rewriting could disguise his personality or mobilize these qualities to serve the sinister side of the character. Williams sensed this from the beginning of rehearsal. His diaries recount his mounting anxiety as Truscott (and *Loot*) underwent literary surgery.

6 JAN 65. With Joe. We discussed LOOT. He said he wanted to add another character as an assistant to Truscott [Meadows] and try to find a third act ending. So, we're back at the old trial and error game with three weeks left to rehearse – no definite script. This play has been around since last October and now this sort of activity! I spoke against change unless it was something that altered the structure and it was concrete. I objected to a character being added . . .

21 JAN. My relationship with Wood is getting very strained. Today, when he asked me to alter dialogue I'd already learned once more – I refused. I dislike doing this as I'm well aware that defiance of authority is a bad example to the cast. There are occasions on which he forces one into rebellion simply because what he's doing is wasteful and futile. Again and again he makes the point about logic and reasonableness whereas the level on which this play will succeed is not that at all. The cast still don't know the lines well enough to use them. We are still mainly preoccupied with business, geography. There's a curious tiredness creeping in, too – despite the fact that there's no real hard work. Just loads of talk.

26 JAN. No one seems to get a real improvement on the scenes nor is the dialogue really flowing. It breaks and dries. Left at 6 – totally

depressed. Moreover, I'm now worried about the play – it seems a random collection of bits with no sense of wholeness.

28 JAN. I can't see any sense of construction in the piece, perhaps it's just a lack of an audience. Perhaps – oh this is the worst period of all – waiting to see if the thing will be able to fly . . .

The play is a disaster [Orton wrote to Halliwell from Cambridge after the opening]. There were hardly any laughs for Truscott. The audience seems to take the most extraordinary lines with dead seriousness. Can't you ring me? It's all so dreadful. I've already had two rows of nerve-wracking proportions. I've said to Wood that I'm not a commercial writer and perhaps he understands now why it's impossible that I should ever be a 'National humorist'.[15]

Still, Orton put on a brave public face. 'I think *Loot* should be a success',[16] he rashly told the press in the first week of try-outs at Cambridge, where the show had sold out. But in his scrapbook Orton had pasted a cartoon of a scowling bear with arms akimbo and a large welt on his head. DO YOU FEEL LIKE A BEAR WITH A SORE HEAD, the caption asked. For Orton, the answer was 'Yes'. The Cambridge reviews weren't bad, they were disastrous. 'A particularly nauseating article', began the *Cambridge Review*, '. . . an evening of very British rubbish.' The *Cambridge News* reported that the 'audience laughed more at the actors' skills than at the script and some of them found it difficult to laugh much at all'. Two weeks later the same Cambridge critic put not too fine a point on his reaction to *Loot*: 'a very bad play – shapeless and without style, inexcusably vulgar and even boring'. 'Horrendous' was Codron's one-word professional assessment of *Loot*'s debut. 'Kenneth, having decided he couldn't be himself, was playing Truscott like Himmler. He decided to disguise himself like a little gestapo in this extraordinary mackintosh. Nothing happened.' Orton's lines, the critics observed, were amusing from moment to moment; but they didn't seem to lead anywhere.

The problem was not only in the play's structure but in the entire production concept which groped for a style to deal with such a new and dangerous game. 'I made the mistake of thinking *Loot* far too much of a Restoration or early-eighteenth-century play in modern times,' Wood says. 'I tried to do the play with a kind of cod formality as if it were *Way of the World* or something. Joe quite liked the idea; or at least he never made any objection to it. It was a mistake not to have plumped for absolute realism. I was kind of afraid of the play. There was something about the body of the late Mrs McLeavy which could disassociate the audience. I tried to find a style which would allow the body to be thrown about and be totally accepted.'

'Unless *Loot* is directed and acted perfectly seriously the play will fail. As it failed in its original touring version', Orton wrote in his notes for the American production in 1967. 'A director who imagines that the only object is to get a laugh is not for me.'[17] In 1965, with his reputation on the line and a successful West End director stressing the artifice and the jokes, Orton kept his peace and paid the consequences. Every directorial device deflected attention from the macabre reality of the events and the characters. Desmond Heeley's set was a startling and streamlined art nouveau edifice painted wedding-cake white, which vied at every moment with the dialogue for the audience's attention. Like spectres, the actors stalked about this glossy environment dressed in black. 'We did it in black and white as a sort of Pop Art set,' Wood explains. 'I was thinking of things like Tom and Jerry cartoons where, no matter how hard they hit the cat over the head, it remains funny because the essential violence has been stylized to the point where it's essentially acceptable.' Wood's first reaction to the barrage of hostility that greeted the play was to increase *Loot*'s formality. At one point, Wood introduced a metronome which ticked away behind the footlights. 'What's that for?' Williams demanded, angry at being made still more like a puppet than a person. 'Wood said "This play is essentially stylistic. I wanted the dialogue delivered in a stylistic fashion".' At Cambridge the performances were turned out to the audience rather than towards each other. The effect was to make *Loot* more like a cabaret than a farce ensemble.

The panic of finding a style and an audience response sent each performer scurrying into his special successful mannerisms. The actors had been dissatisfied and confused in rehearsals; and Cambridge gave credence to their fears.

'*Loot* is a serious play', Orton stressed in his production note for the Americans. '. . . Ideally, it should be nearer *The Homecoming* than *I Love Lucy*. Don't think I'm a snob about *I Love Lucy*. I've watched it often. I think it's very funny. But it is purely aimed at making an audience laugh. And that isn't the prime aim of *Loot* . . . It's most important to get the subtext of the play right. The play shouldn't be one long giggle – there should be depths. It can never work as rival to *Barefoot In the Park*.'[18] In the beginning, this distinction was not clear in Orton's mind. Instead of the curtain coming up on a house of mourning where laughter becomes unsettling in such a ritualized context, the audience met Truscott pushing a pram with a gramophone as he reconnoitred with his police sidekick, Meadows, for a little burlesque cross-talk about their mission. Both were dressed as tramps. 'Were you issued a barrel organ,' Truscott asks, in a joke whose silliness tells an audience not to take him too seriously. Meadows says no and asks 'I wonder, sir, if I should change my boots. These are regulation issue and as such are well-known to suspected persons.' Having established their motive for the audience (and killed any surprise for Truscott's entrance into the McLeavy household) they set to work with Truscott's gramophone playing *Abide With Me* as the semi-detached housefront is rolled out revealing McLeavy sitting beside the coffin. The end of Act 1, which in the final version has the horrific and hilarious image of Truscott puzzling with his magnifying-glass over Mrs McLeavy's false eye, had at Cambridge a burlesque and completely conciliatory tone. Orton's anger at the abuse of police authority was reduced to a sight gag. As Mrs McLeavy is carted off for burial, Truscott is seen outside the house climbing the drainpipe. Meadows enters and approaches. 'As Meadows draws near to Truscott,' the stage direction read, 'he salutes smartly. Truscott returns the salute, clinging with one hand to the drainpipe.'

'I do my best work rewriting', Orton said in 1967. *Loot* was proof of this boast. 'What I usually do is cut because I find cutting is the real thing. An awful lot of plays could be made so much more brilliant by cutting only there isn't anything to cut. If you haven't got a story and a plot, you can't cut.'[19] After the Cambridge fiasco, it was clear that *Loot* needed more plot, sharper dialogue and a new production concept. Wood began to strip away the show's formality and to attack the play naturalistically. Orton was sent back to London to rewrite. 'The burden of my song to Joe was this – the play needs to reach in action the same anarchic conclusions of the dialogue,' Wood says. 'I wanted the whole play to rebound on an innocent person. Originally, it didn't.' On 9 February Codron and Wood presented the cast with the first pages of Orton's staggering series of rewrites. The original play was eighty-nine pages; and before the end of their six-week engagement, the actors would learn and insert in their scripts 133 pages of new rewritten material. Kenneth Williams, who from the outset disagreed with Wood's correct instinct about the need for logical complication in the farce, was livid:

Codron and Wood arrive [Williams wrote in his diary]. They brought with them the rewrites. I thought they were lousy and said so. At least see the show as it stands now that we've gained a bit of confidence and say that you want changes . . . So, the rewrites apparently are essential, and we start all over again. I think there's going to be an endless round ahead of putting patches on a leaking hulk that will never be right because of a basic flaw: the play begins about FAY and her story is never developed beyond Act I . . . After the show, went to see Noel Willman and Peggy Ramsay. He said I was at my best in the play when I appeared to be emotionally involved. This is a good clue to what I've been missing. (The Challenor bit – 'I'll have you, you young bugger, etc. . . .') Every time you get that kind of involvement in the performance – the whole play works.

The cast began a schizophrenic regime of rehearsing the rewritten play in the afternoon while performing the beleaguered original version at night. 'It was the most painful period of my life,' Kenneth Williams says. 'I felt again and again as an actor that we simply weren't gaining the audience's confidence. We never did establish the confidence for the simple reason that we were in a terrible quandary ourselves wondering which version was the right one. We were tentative, which is death for Orton. You must take the stage with enormous conviction and panache.' But panic had set in amongst the cast, as Williams's diary reports about the two days following Orton's first batch of rewrites:

10 FEB. Unconfident performance. One laugh for loss of another ... And it had the effect of taking away the character of Truscott. Before – with two interrogations – I had a chance of establishing the character. Now, with both of them split – I have completely lost it. Script in rags. Cast is utterly demoralized. I shouldn't have set foot near this rotten mess.

11 FEB. ... Wood talks to the cast about the evil of negative thinking. That's a lot of help! ... Laurence Olivier came round and said, 'You haven't got a play here, that's your trouble ...'

Williams wasn't the only one worried about Orton's rewrites. Peggy Ramsay, who'd seen the play at Cambridge and Brighton, wrote to Michael Codron on 10 February to lodge a protest, while admitting that the Brighton performance 'was very much slicker and more professional ... this play is already better than *Sloane* at any time ...' Wood's attempts to tighten the plot's logic led inevitably to the sacrifice of mischief for motivation. *Loot*, Peggy Ramsay thought, was 'beginning, very slightly, to lose Joe's personal and unique voice'.

The reviews were not getting better either. DAMP SQUIB FOR WEST END SPONGE was *Cherwell*'s headline when the company reached Oxford. TOO MANY FLAT LINES IN THIS MACABRE FARCE bannered the *North Berkshire Herald* above its review. 'As a farce, *Loot* isn't strong enough', wrote the critic from *Isis*. 'The climaxes misfire and the jokes – if so they are – are mistimed ...' While Williams was sceptical about the rewrites which came into the script almost daily, he shared the company's admiration for the stamina and calibre of Orton's work under pressure. 'Joe admired Wilde for the great pains he took with his work. He used to quote me Wilde's dictum: "Talent is the infinite capacity for taking pains". He took pains. Polish. Reconstruct. Give you another edition. Another page. Every word polished painstakingly until the whole structure *glitters*. His application, his industry, and his *consistent* diligence – astonished me in that period of three editions of the play. I know he was in circumstances which are awful for a creative writer. The pressure of commercial theatre – box office, deadlines, 'these actors have got to say this tonight but you've got to write another thing for them tomorrow'. In other words, his creation, his baby – and my God he was vulnerable about his baby – was being twisted, mangled, and mutilated. That is exactly what happened. When you saw the pages torn out, rehinged, and another set of rewrites put in. When you saw this boy's flow continually damaged by outsiders – all of whom were getting him in hotel bedrooms with that portable typewriter. The boy trying to cope with them, trying to meet the demands of either the censor or, in Manchester, the Watch Committee, or in this case, Peter Wood, who kept saying "This plot is not sufficiently credible to hold water, so that before the police arrive somebody's got to come in ... etc." You used to see Joe – eyes like slits, sitting in the stalls. By the third week, he'd got that weak thing, that awful weak giddiness when the pressure's been too much. You start to laugh. That awful laugh at no joke. That laugh that comes from nothing ...'

At Oxford, the hysteria mounted to breaking point.

Everyone on the verge of a nervous breakdown [Orton wrote wearily to Halliwell, enclosing a damning review from the *Oxford Mail* which he felt was justified]. Kenneth Williams disastrous – just all his old performances from *Beyond Our Ken*. And then he wonders why he isn't getting laughs. 'Ow many 'usbands 'ave you 'ad? (ugh!) ... We've now a rebellious company on our hands plus a temperamental star ... I wouldn't have believed when I wrote the

play that it could be so difficult . . . I try to keep very very calm . . .
Do try and hang on doing something if you get too fed up without
me. I'll get back as soon as humanly possible. I'm not just gallivanting
about down here. It's the most depressing few weeks I've ever lived
through.[20]

After a playful tussle with Ian McShane, Orton ended up bruised
with a black eye and embarrassed. The cast, as frazzled by the
rewrites as Orton, started to display their exhausted frustration.
Williams was angry at everybody; Duncan Macrae was coming
off stage muttering to himself; and even the equable Geraldine
McEwan, who told the press 'I can only work when I'm happy',[21]
finally cracked:

16 FEB. I [Kenneth Williams] said in front of the company and Wood
that the rewrites were all a mistake and our only chance was to go
back to what we started with. P. Wood said no. So on we go to
utter failure. Morale so low that people are getting either apathetic
or hysterical. I rang Codron and asked him to come down as quickly
as possible. He refused saying P. Wood asked him not to come down
and a load of crap about 'I must obey my director (we'd already had
P. Wood saying I must obey my manager)'. Utterly spurious of
course. He thinks I'm exaggerating and all is alright. Geraldine came
off shouting: 'I CAN'T GO ON WITH THIS ANYMORE!
I CAN'T GO ON'. And crying. I obviously can't come into
London with material like this.

18 FEB. Show went like suet pudding. Playing this stuff is like trying
to catch bath water in your hand. It keeps slipping through your
fingers. Geraldine now shaking and ill. Tonight at the hotel, David
Battley (Meadows) started crying uncontrollably and left the room.

22 FEB. We died in the second half and never got them back again.
An inquest afterwards with P. Wood, Joe Orton, and Codron. Poor
Joe just looked beaten into the ground; and Wood did go on at him.
'You've got to write more. More rewrites.' The boy's got nothing
more to write.

Last night was appalling [Orton wrote to Halliwell, in desperation
over Geraldine McEwan's hysterics]. She had to be taken home and

given sedation. The stage manager has collapsed with some form of food poisoning. Wood is now saying 'Perhaps we ought to take it off and bring it back much later and not risk the big commercial stakes. Bring it back at the Royal Court. It's coterie entertainment, and perhaps it shouldn't be forced on a public like this one.' I keep up a constant moan about 'I'm not a commercial playwright. I never said I was.' Last night he took McShane and me out to dinner and I suddenly found myself being subjected to a lot of psychological chat – 'Of course the trouble with you is that you can't communicate. It's your great fault as a person and as a writer.' Etc. . . . Wood says that a line like 'With your intimate knowledge of rare drugs' is private humour. Not funny with a wide audience. I don't agree. He said John Whiting always condemned that kind of humour. So I said, 'Well he never wrote a fucking decent play in his life. And *The Devils* has longueurs compared to which *Loot*'s are brilliant highspots.' I said to Ian afterwards that 'Wood wants something I have and resents that I have it.' I don't at the moment know what it is . . . Everybody here is behaving like the most ridiculous caricatures of Hollywood theatricals . . .[22]

Loot was still wordy, still too clumsily plotted; but under Wood's guidance, Orton had achieved a lot in the month of rehearsing. A farce structure, with its twists of plot and reversal of expectation, had been imposed on the material. Orton's original first act, which rambled to thirty pages of character exposition, had been successfully telescoped to fifteen. Dennis now lusted after Fay; and the triangle took on erotic complication. Fay, once the front runner in the farce, fell back to third lead behind Truscott and McLeavy, opening up new possibilities for action. Having reconceived Fay's role, Orton always emphasized to producers this shift in the play's balance. 'She must be kept in her place', he wrote about the American production. '(Always a difficult thing for the Americans to do with their women) . . . But she isn't to be allowed to swamp the play. It isn't a play about Fay . . . She should ideally be under thirty. I want the erotic idea behind a girl in her late twenties and boys in their teens. She isn't a mother substitute. None of your Tennessee Williams drag queens.'[23] The rewrites emphasized the erotic idea; and the triangle allowed Orton to have fun with the stereotypes of 'the homosexual', which was always part of the play's intended mischief. In the early versions, Orton pushed the sexual point too bluntly. He had Hal, panicked by the sight of the law, urging Dennis: 'Go on, act normal'. To which Dennis replies: 'What's that?' But the trio's sexual involvement made comment unnecessary. 'I don't want there to be anything queer or camp or odd about the relationship of Hal and Dennis,' Orton wrote in the US production note. 'Americans see homosexuality in terms of fag and drag. This isn't my vision of the universal brotherhood. They must be perfectly ordinary boys who happen to be fucking each other. Nothing could be more natural. I won't have the Great American Queen brought into it.' The *ménage à trois* gave *Loot* new areas of innuendo and stage business:

DENNIS. We've never involved a woman in anything unsavoury before.

> *He takes the lid off the coffin.* FAY *piles money into his arms.* HAL *does the same.*

(*To* FAY.) Half of this money is mine. Will you marry me?

HAL. We're splitting the money three ways now, baby. You'll have thirty-four thousand.

DENNIS (*to* FAY). Is that enough?

FAY. You've a slight lead on Mr McLeavy at the moment.

> *She kisses him.* DENNIS *trembles and drops the money back into the coffin.*

HAL (*angry*). Hurry up! What's the matter with you?

DENNIS. My hands are trembling. It's excitement at the prospect of getting engaged.

HAL. You're too easily aroused. That's your trouble.

Orton was learning to write action, and his jokes were becoming more economic and specific in service of the play's momentum. The rewrites show him struggling to reveal character through gesture. He'd already found some marvellous routines to indicate Truscott's disturbing megalomania. 'I conduct my cases under an assumed voice and I am a master of disguise', Truscott boasts to

Hal, doffing his trilby. 'You see – a complete transformation.' The detective pastiche was no longer tentative and generalized, but precise and subtle. Orton puckishly allowed Truscott to judge Fay's confession of murder in the way critics would assess Orton's own symbolic slaughter: 'Your style is simple and direct. It's a theme which less skilfully handled could've given offence.' Truscott no sooner meets Fay than he exposes her as the murderer of her first husband. 'My methods of deduction can be learned by anyone with a keen eye and a quick brain', he says. 'When I shook your hand I felt a roughness on one of your wedding rings. A roughness I associate with powder burns and salt. When found on a wedding ring only one solution is possible . . .' This not only sent up the detective's unerring 'logic', but built a much richer sense of Fay's past. It also enacted the wit of an epigram buried in *Loot*'s repartee: 'The process by which the police arrive at the solution of a mystery is, in itself, a mystery.'

'The nearer we got to London,' Orton said of *Loot*, 'the better it went. It's a London play.'[24] Orton's work was good; but the show, lumbered with the beautiful but ill-conceived set, was still not good enough. Orton became embattled and belligerent over the production. The strain caught up with him. A misunderstood remark of 'no comment' by Peggy Ramsay after seeing the play at Golders Green produced a furious letter from Orton which spelled out his view of the play and his future if it failed:

What have you got to be upset about? [he wrote to Peggy Ramsay on 28 February]. *Loot* is in far better shape than when we sold it to Michael. I wanted to write a farce. The nearer I come to it the unhappier you are. I have not turned 'an interesting failure' into a second-rate farce; I've turned a failed farce into a successful farce. There are a dozen writers who can turn out interesting failures. Phoney intellectuals think there's a merit in it. *Eh?* is what used to be called a mess not a farce.

I know that my authentic voice is better than anyone else. It is vulgar and offensive in the extreme to middle-class susceptibilities.

I've already told Michael that I'm doing nothing else to the play until I get an assurance that we're going to the West End. If *Loot* folds through no fault of its own, I'll wash my hands of writing. Don't imagine that failure will stimulate me. It never has done yet.

That you hated SLOANE I can forgive. Dromgoole's production, plus the acting, left a lot to be desired. But if you dislike *Loot* as well, perhaps it is the essential me as a writer you dislike. And we both of us better think seriously of parting company.

Despite the threats, Orton continued with rewrites and Peggy Ramsay. But the pressure mounted. At Bournemouth in the first week of March, Codron's more conservative co-producer, Donald Albery, took exception to the direction of some of Orton's pungent rewrites. Albery was not the only one who was not amused. BOURNEMOUTH OLD LADIES SHOCKED, headlined *The Times* on 3 March, with a story about the exodus of two dozen, who stormed out of the massive Pavilion Theatre on the opening night in protest at 'dialogue which uses the word brothel and which satirizes sex, patriotism, death and the law'. Orton referred to this segment of the audience as 'The Bump and Trot Brigade' – a phrase referring to the thump of the seats as the spectators made for the exit. Orton liked to wander through the foyer in the interval and would retail overheard fragments of conversation to the actors after the show. 'Well, my dear, I was at the Thompsons' only yesterday at their barbecue and they warned me it was filth. And like a fool I rejected their advice,' Williams recalls Orton telling him. It became their sport. 'In the hotel I heard people discussing *Loot*,' Williams says. 'One woman said to the man "It was a good job you didn't come. The play was disgusting, absolutely filthy." "What was it about?" "Oh – it's about Jesus, do you see . . . being a queer." There was no reference to Jesus being homosexual, not one reference. People did say the most extraordinary things. Presumably they must have come away very angry.'

They were angrier in Manchester, where police were stationed in the wings after the Watch Committee disallowed Truscott's query about Dennis's illegitimate children:

TRUSCOTT. . . . Where does he engender these unwanted children? There are no open spaces. The police patrol regularly. It should be next to impossible to commit the smallest act of indecency, let alone beget a child. Where does he do it?

HAL. On crowded dance floors during the rhumba.

Confident about the play's improvements, Codron promised Peggy Ramsay 'we shall not regard sneeringly what the Manchester papers say about *Loot* . . .'[25] There was no way to overlook the message in their reception: OH, NOT AGAIN KEN . . . PLEASE (*Sun*); DAZZLING AT TIMES BUT EASY TO FORGET (*Daily Mail*); EXPERIMENT IN FUN FAILS TO AMUSE (*Telegraph*). Only the *Manchester Evening News* went to the other extreme, calling *Loot* 'the funniest thing to have hit Manchester since "Beyond the Fringe" '. The round of rewriting continued. 'Manchester was terribly depressing,' Wood remembers. 'Nobody laughed. Joe and I would get together in his hotel room and work through the morning and then insert the lines in the afternoon,' Wood says. But after the Manchester notices, desperation set in. 'I took Joe Orton to supper,' Williams noted in his diary on 11 March. 'The boy admitted he was punch drunk with rewrites.'

Suddenly people began manoeuvring for safety in case of disaster. Codron wrote to Orton on 12 March asking for a guarantee of right of first refusal on his next play. 'I feel strongly that if I do manage to get a West End theatre for *Loot*, with or without the help of Donald Albery, and despite all the jeremiahs advising me not to bring it in, I shall be inevitably risking more capital than has been spent so far,' Codron said. Dissension also erupted between Codron and Wood over the director's apparent absence from a Manchester performance. 'I said to the cast "Oh well, I'm going off to watch the Hallé Orchestra", because Joe's rewrites were in the second half,' Wood explains. 'It was a joke. What I did was go upstairs and sit in the circle. There I sat through the first half roaring with laughter because nobody else was. I came backstage afterwards and Joe was very pleased. "Well," he said, "there's one person in

Manchester for whom the play is a masterpiece." I never dared say it was me.' But after the performance, Wood took Kenneth Williams and Geraldine McEwan to dinner and, according to Codron, 'at this meal, allegedly asked both the stars to support him in his pleas to me for the production not to be brought to London'.

'Wimbledon.' Williams noted in his diary on 15 March. 'Codron told us there was no theatre. The Phoenix would rather be dark than have us.' Wimbledon was *Loot*'s last stop before the West End, and the Phoenix's refusal was the production's final humiliation. The theatre was the white elephant of Emile Littler's empire which even Codron had to admit 'nobody wanted to play'. Codron cast about for other theatres and other directors. Patrick Dromgoole was asked to doctor the production but demurred. *Loot* wheezed to a flat and inevitable end. 'Geraldine confided to me in the dressing room that she will not come into town with it', Williams wrote on 19 March. The next day, the production's last, Williams wrote:

Wood turned up for the matinee after ignoring us for a week! 'I come to matinees. I can't stand the last performance . . .' The second house was very good. Went off very well indeed and a good reception. Michael Codron met the cast afterwards. If the company were keen, he could put it in the Lyric Hammersmith. But the company all said no. So the play died tonight after 56 performances of about three editions.

Loot was a dead horse, but it continued to be flogged. Two days after the show closed, the London *Evening News* ran a vicious, ranting article. 'Personally I thought it was one of the most revolting things I had ever seen', wrote a reporter who was not a drama critic; '. . . the management pasted over the bills at Wimbledon: "This show is unsuitable for children" . . . It would have been better if Michael Codron had displayed some new ones: "THIS PLAY IS UNSUITABLE".' The notice was the final nail in *Loot*'s coffin. The play became a legendary failure. 'It was an appalling flop,' Williams says. 'A great . . . big . . . flop.' Orton's reputation and his energy had been seriously diminished. 'After

Loot folded on tour,' Orton said, understating his upset, 'there was a long period when I didn't do anything at all.'[26]

'I hardly dare mention *Loot*. Is anything happening?' Orton wrote to Peggy Ramsay on 29 June 1965, from Morocco, where he was taking the first extended holiday of his life, proudly catching and curing the clap in his two-and-a-half-month stay. 'I know I'm greedy. Most writers with a play going on Broadway and a director of Alan's [Schneider's] calibre producing would be content for the time being. But I do have a feeling that poor *Loot* is being left out in the cold – moan, moan, isn't it from me. P. Wood said I'd greet him at midnight or 6 in the morning with a moan.'

Away from London, Orton's sense of urgency about *Loot* and the weight of its failure were lightened by the benevolence of sunshine and new sensations. 'I'm feeling fine', he pronounced to Peggy Ramsay. 'So tired though. I need two cups of very black coffee in the morning just to wake me up. Much more relaxing than Bournemouth.'

In England, *Loot* was stalled; and in America, after the disastrous reception on Broadway of *Entertaining Mr Sloane*, the prospects for relaunching *Loot* were stone cold. For the rest of 1965 Orton busied himself with a television play, his version of *The Bacchae*, a fun palace revolution set in a holiday camp and called *The Erpingham Camp*. Orton had first explored the notion as a film treatment for Lindsay Anderson and developed it as a Brechtian epic, complete (in early drafts) with illustrative banners such as SCENE 5: AN EXAMPLE OF THE ACTIVE LIFE OF THE CHURCH. ERPINGHAM PREPARES HIMSELF TO MEET THE PEOPLE. THEOLOGY DISCUSSED. THE PADRE PROVES THAT CHRISTIANITY IS ESSENTIAL TO GOOD HEALTH. Orton submitted the play on 24 October 1965, still planning, as he wrote to a friend, 'to spend the winter writing a stage play'.[27] But his worries about the fate of *Loot* and the March shooting schedule for *The Erpingham Camp* prevented him from getting down to work.

In January 1966 Oscar Lewenstein bravely picked up the option on *Loot*. 'I'm at the present on tenterhooks over *Loot*', Orton wrote to Glenn Loney in March. 'I had a meeting with Oscar Lewenstein and we put the first wheels in motion. We're flying high among the stars at the moment. We'll be down to earth again soon.'[28]

Orton had made plans to leave for his three-month holiday in Morocco on 12 April, the day after *Loot* was to open in the Century Theatre's production at the University Theatre in Manchester under the direction of Braham Murray. 'If I go away on the twelfth, with the fate of the play still undecided – I'm staying away', Orton wrote to Peggy Ramsay on 12 March, telling her to warn his producers. Orton's hectoring couldn't hurry Lewenstein and White into a production. They were interested in watching how the play did in Manchester. Murray, who as an Oxford *Wunderkind* had directed *Hang Down Your Head and Die* on the West End, had pestered Peggy Ramsay all autumn, and with no one else committed to the play by the beginning of 1966 she had let him have it. 'I honestly don't know whether he can be entrusted with it', she had written to Orton. 'We can't make any second mistake in the production of this play and we must be QUITE sure.'[29] Murray was no mistake. His production would be *Loot*'s new lease of life.

Murray understood the passion between *Loot* and Orton: 'That final image of *Loot* with Fay flanked by the two fellahs saying "Let's keep up appearances" – that was what Joe was about. He was trying to work out this central relationship of men to women. It was terribly Marlowe. Men in a mess. Truscott is the old conscience, the old morality; that conscience is dead in our time. It lingers and has become corrupt. Joe knew that the whole sexual thing was going to have to be redefined. He knew that in the violence and sex, especially in the sorts of relationship which had been regarded as being wrong and perverted, there was an immense power to be harnessed for good. In order to liberate the positive side of all those drives, you had to explore the deepest resources of your own nature. He knew that if he could go right into it and face it all himself, then he would climb into the light.' Orton worked with Murray on the revisions. Orton's experience in television with *The Erpingham Camp* gave him more faith in a naturalistic attack on the *Loot* rewrites. 'I'm very pleased with *The Erpingham Camp*', Orton wrote to Glenn Loney after the shooting. 'It's been directed and acted absolutely *real*. With astonishing results. H. Pinter says it's like *The Battleship Potemkin*. I won't go as far as this, but it's very good...'[30] In the *Loot* revisions, Orton built up the reality of the relationships and the horror. 'Joe's main objection to Peter Wood's version', Murray says, 'was that it overlooked the black side of the play. There was no horror. Wood made sure that a coffin didn't look like a coffin.'

Murray opted for a naturalistic environment. 'The style of the set ... the tone ... is right,' Orton wrote to Michael White,[31] who joined forces with Lewenstein as co-producer. Orton cut 621 lines from Wood's version, compressing the action and allowing the characters to react more immediately to each others' demands rather than be sidetracked by their own verbal felicity. And for the Manchester production Orton made Truscott's interrogation of Hal more specific and alarming. Instead of simply 'standing over Hal', when Truscott says 'Under any other political system I'd have you on the floor in tears!' Orton gave brutal impact to the line by adding 'shouting, knocking Hal to the floor'. Orton now wanted Truscott 'beating, knocking and punching him. Hal screams with pain'. After McLeavy is dragged off to jail, Orton intensified the predatory evil of his characters in short, quick strokes:

DENNIS. What will you charge him with, Inspector?
TRUSCOTT. Oh, anything will do.
FAY. Can an accidental death be arranged?
TRUSCOTT. Anything can be arranged in prison.
HAL. Except pregnancy.

Orton gave Fay a sly, curt coda to resolve the plot point. 'We'll bury your father with your mother', she says. 'That will be nice for him, won't it?' Fay's consideration coats the poisonous truth that McLeavy is as good as dead.

Loot was now finding the right balance between fun and pain, frivolity and fury. 'I'd like to get married. It's the only thing I haven't tried', Dennis tells Hal. In the Wood version of *Loot*, Hal's reply has no comic reverberation: 'Put her out of your mind, baby, and concentrate on the job at hand'. In Manchester, the line was recast to ricochet off the idea of Dennis's heterosexual fling. Hal says: 'I don't like your living for kicks, baby. Put these neurotic ideas out of your mind and concentrate on the problems of everyday life'. Instead of Hal dishing Fay with a lack-lustre 'She's not your sort. She's religious', Orton made the revised line dance: 'She's three parts Papal nuncio'.

But it was McLeavy who benefited most from the confidence of Orton's rewrites. McLeavy's credulous worry about human remains being desecrated and his bewilderment ('It's going to take me a long time to believe she's dead. She was such an active sort of person') were added in Manchester. Orton also underlined McLeavy's faith in authority. 'I hope he finds what he's looking for', McLeavy now said to Fay about Truscott. 'I like to be of assistance to authority.' With a clear understanding of how he wanted his play to rebound on McLeavy, Orton showed him kowtowing to law and order even as it oppressed him. His deference to the police also gave Truscott energy for new outrageousness:

TRUSCOTT. . . . I'm going to have this place turned upside down.

MCLEAVY. Oh. dear, what a nuisance. And in a house of mourning, too . . .

TRUSCOTT. There's no cause for alarm. It's a mere formality. You're quite safe. (*He smiles. To* MCLEAVY.) There's no one more touchy than your hardened criminal. (*He puts his pipe away.*) I'll be back in ten minutes. And then, I'm afraid, a lot of damage will be done to your property. You'll be paying repair bills for months to come. One unfortunate suspect recently had the roof taken off his house.

MCLEAVY. Isn't there anything I can do to prevent this appalling assault upon my privacy?

TRUSCOTT. Well, sir, if you can suggest a possible hiding-place for
   the money?

   MCLEAVY *hangs his head.*

MCLEAVY (*almost in a whisper*). I can't, Inspector.

TRUSCOTT. Very well. You must take the consequences of ignorance.

Murray managed to get the Lord Chamberlain to reinstate most
of the cuts imposed on the touring version. But when the play
reopened in Manchester, the police were in the stalls just in case.
To Orton's delight, *Loot* got a hearty welcome from the *Daily
Telegraph*, which, besides finding it 'very funny' and 'the plotting
as fast and frivolous as Feydeau's', commented that 'it seems a pity
that Joe Orton's *Loot* was withdrawn during its preliminary tour'.[32]
With a surge of renewed hope for his play, Orton dashed off last-
minute casting suggestions to Michael White before leaving for
Morocco. 'The way it's played at Manchester does leave me wide
open to accusations of a "message" ending. Quite wrong . . . Fay.
The way it's being played at Manchester – as a real woman, a real
nurse, is right . . . It is the third part in the play. I don't want any
of these "monsters". I want a real woman. Not a man in drag. And
this is about the most difficult thing to achieve in the West End
Theatre. So please Vivien Merchant or the girl in Manchester . . .
The boys in Manchester are poor . . . clean as a whistle sexually . . .
One can't imagine them having each other or Fay or anyone
. . . The director. This is up to you. I'm not good on directors. Get
somebody straightforward if possible. Somebody who'll know his
onions. I'm dead against anyone too arty. I think it's a good 75%
casting. Depending on what you think after you've seen Manchester I wouldn't violently object to Braham Murray. But then,
on directors, I'm a blank . . .'[33]

Orton's buoyant conviction about the prospects of *Loot*'s revival
evaporated almost as soon as he'd settled into his apartment on the
Rue de Menchamps in Tangier. Instead of bringing news of production plans, Peggy Ramsay's letters brought more exasperation.
'I'm certainly *not* rewriting *Loot*', he wrote to her on 8 May after
the *Evening News* had printed a squib about Orton being in Tangier

to rewrite his play. 'Didn't they read the Manchester notice in *The Daily Telegraph* ... Has anything at all happened with regard to that ill-fated play during the last month? I forget it for long periods of time here and then suddenly remember it and want to ring you.' Orton was eager for every scrap of news about *Loot*'s progress. The Royal Court, with William Gaskill taking over artistic control from George Devine, had shown renewed interest; and now it was rumoured that the National were nibbling. 'If the National want *Loot*,' Orton wrote to Peggy Ramsay on 12 May, 'move Heaven and Earth to see they do it. I'm tired of the dallyings of the commercial theatre. I'd be delighted to let them have it on any terms. As long as everybody stops *talking* and puts it on!!' Orton enclosed a scowling photograph of himself 'merely to indicate my state of mind when I remember that another six months option is running out and that *still* nothing appears to be being done about the play which so many people one hears are interested in (foul, foul grammar, but I'm doped to the eyes) ...' In a postscript, he pleaded 'Has any progress been made at all?'

Peggy Ramsay counselled Orton not to panic, assuring him that '*Loot* will go on some way or another'. But by June the news from London had gone from bad to worse. 'You say you hope I'm not frantic about the play and that if we have to wait a month or three months it would be worth it for a good production. I absolutely agree', Orton wrote Peggy Ramsay on 10 June. 'But November – the latest date to be mentioned is six months off. Oscar by then will have had an option for nearly a year! It will be *two* years since I wrote it. Even so I wouldn't be worried if it was put on this year. I'm starting to really panic at the idea of delaying it any longer than November. It must go on *this year*!!! ... I've just been reading *The Times* crit of "A Bond Honoured" and it seems to me that the kind of thing I ushered in in "Sloane" and do in "Loot" is provoking a lot of hostile press. Which is why *Loot* must *must* go on within the next six months. Or we'll run the risk of having them jeering "old hat" when it does appear out of sheer spleen.' In her reply, Peggy Ramsay reported the devastating news that the Royal Court, who had been stringing Orton along, enthusiastic about his work in general but ambivalent about *Loot*, would probably drop the play.

The news sent Orton into a fury. ' "When sorrows come they come not single spies, but in battalions" (Shakes.). I felt like Richard III receiving the messengers', Orton wrote to Peggy Ramsay on 18 June, in a zestful, vitriolic attack on the English theatre scene:

I think it's disgusting with so much utter shit put on in both the commercial and subsidized theatres that a play like *Loot* should have this difficulty. I'd understand it after Wimbledon, but not after a really pretty average Rep production which succeeded in attracting such a glowing notice in *The Telegraph* . . .

I'm sick, sick, sick of the theatre . . .

I think you'd better warn Oscar that if the *Loot* option runs out in January with no sign of the play being put on I shan't renew the option. I shall throw the play on the fire. And I shan't write a third stage play. I shall earn my living on TV.

I'm really quite capable of carrying out this, I've always admired Congreve who, after the absolute failure of *Way of the World* just stopped writing. And Rimbaud who turned his back on the literary world after writing a few volumes of poems.

Of course, I know you're doing your best. All the foregoing isn't including you. As they say 'I've every confidence in your abilities'. Certainly at the moment it's 'JOE CONTRA MUNDEM'.

Orton was so angry, he forgot to sign the letter, but added a typical postscript: 'A millionaire out here has gone dotty about me. He keeps smacking my arse and groping my cock and saying "You're an attractive little bugger". So perhaps I shall be able to give up writing after all!!!'

Back in London by mid-July, Orton's angry threats to Lewenstein had mellowed into regret. 'Could we meet perhaps and talk some more about *Loot*', he wrote to Lewenstein. 'It's getting a very old baby, isn't it? I'm about to write a new T.V. play [*Funeral Games*]. I don't want to be stuck in that medium for ever and ever.'[34] Orton didn't have to wait long for a London production. On 19 August *The Times* announced that *Loot* would reopen at the Jeanetta Cochrane Theatre under the direction of Charles Marowitz.

'It was a sort of Off-West End theatre,' explains Marowitz, who had set up a London extension of the Edinburgh Traverse Theatre at the Cochrane. 'This meant the play could be tried out in a London setting for only about £2,000; and Lewenstein and White could give *Loot* a London production without risking much capital.' Marowitz was an energetic and abrasive American expatriate who had settled in England in 1958 and hammered out a name for himself as a drama critic and experimental director. He was smart, tireless and equipped with a hustler's nose for publicity. He enjoyed controversy and took a New York street-kid's delight in making enemies of the Establishment. His literary instincts were excellent, although many felt them more secure than his directing talent. But if London had an avant-garde in the mid-sixties a large part of it resided then, as it does now, in him. Marowitz was committed to the new: not only to mounting the best of European and American theatre but to developing and exploring experimental performing techniques. *Loot* had the potential for both West End and avant-garde success. Marowitz saw in Orton another feather in his cap as Big Chief of the English fringe. But, whatever his ambitions, Marowitz had a clear and correct understanding of Orton's literary uniqueness. 'Orton, like Wilde, was a master of artificial diction,' he wrote in the New York *Times*, 'and, unlike Wilde, a master craftsman as well.'

As Marowitz tells it, he found *Loot* very funny, overwritten, and asked to work from the original script: 'The interesting thing is that our production was very much like the original script that had been departed from in the Wood production.' In fact, Orton, always suspicious of directorial tampering and now sure of his text, never showed Marowitz the shabby original version, which bore only a faint resemblance to the final *Loot*. He gave Marowitz instead a retyped copy of the Manchester script. 'Any Orton script is like a monkey wrench immersed in suds', Marowitz wrote in *Confessions of a Counterfeit Critic*.[35] 'In order to reach the hard metal underneath, you have to wash away quite a lot of lather.' This half-truth reflects the limitation of Marowitz's production. Marowitz and Orton had different ideas of just how plausible *Loot*'s action should be. 'Joe's idea of *Loot*'s plausibility was straighter and more serious than mine. He'd sometimes talk about the play in Chekhovian terms. It's not a serious play in Chekhovian terms. To Joe, it was in places. He was always saying to me: "We must make this absolutely truthful as it would happen in life". It was a very peculiar argument because in principle I agreed that *Loot* had to be played straight, realistic; but it couldn't be as it happens in life because nothing in that play happens as it happens in life. You've got to get the style of the play and make that style truthful.'

Marowitz believed in the laughter but not in the comic truth of Orton's tale. '*Loot* had all the prolixity of a splendid liar improvising a massive falsehood,' he said. But Orton insisted on the truthfulness of his metaphor ('Most people think it's a fantasy,' he said, receiving the *Evening Standard* award for *Loot*, 'but Scotland Yard know it's true'). He laughed at Marowitz's disbelief of his view of humanity:

I went to the Criterion . . . Marowitz was there. I told him of the man who'd written to Penthouse Magazine. 'He said he'd decided to see whether spanking wouldn't improve his marriage,' I said. 'And he'd talked it over with his wife. He said, "We'd decided that I would spank her should occasion arise, but that there must be a genuine occasion. Next day she came to me with a gleam in her eye holding up one of my best shirts which she'd scorched while ironing." So,' I said to Marowitz, 'he belted her. And, apparently the sex was marvellous. And now they do it all the time. Only it comes expensive on shirts.' 'What a morbid mind this character has,' Marowitz said, addressing everybody present. 'What about the other one,' Kenneth Cranham [who played Hal] said, 'Where she takes his thin pyjamas down and whips him savagely on the bare buttocks.' 'Oh yes,' I said to Marowitz, 'only he found that it hurt him. And now he wants to stop. Only his wife has developed a taste for it. And she won't let

him fuck her without first having her have his bottom spanked.'
Marowitz snickered to himself and said I'd made it all up.

(5 January 1967)

Marowitz became a figure of fun to Orton and the cast. 'Just a
line to let you know I'm having a total experience (as Charles M
might say) . . .', Orton wrote in a postcard to the inimitable Michael
Bates, who brought a new dimension of square-jawed oafishness
and terror to Truscott. Knowing Marowitz's reputation for experiment, Bates had insisted on a clause in his contract that he would not
improvise ('I'm not wasting my rehearsal time trying to be a chair
or a wastepaper basket'). Bates's Truscott was marvellous. 'He was
just a brainless idiot,' he explains. 'I borrowed quite a lot from the
sergeant majors I knew in the Army – the bellowing and frozen
smiles. But I had great respect for them . . .' Upright, religious,
patriotic, Bates was the antithesis to Orton in his private life; but
as a great farce actor, he was sympathetic to Orton's theatrical
instincts. 'Joe's ideas were often better than the director's. He felt
Loot should be very real. He would have liked the play more real.
He was right. If you've got something extraordinary, you've got to
make it believable. He was very practical, and I liked him a great
deal.'

What seemed extraordinary to the cast when they began rehearsals was not Orton's madness but Marowitz's method. 'The
first day we rehearsed,' Simon Ward says, 'Charles took Kenneth
Cranham and me aside. He sent everybody else out of the room. He
sat on one side of the table, and we sat on the other. Marowitz said:
"What do you think these boys do together?" I thought to myself: I don't believe it. This is nonsense. "I don't know, Charles.
I don't think there's any buggery," I said. "I think it's probably
mutual masturbation," Ken Cranham said. Marowitz said: "I think
that's right. Now who do you think initiates?" Kenneth and I were
kicking each other under the table. We couldn't believe this was
happening. "Which one of you is the active and which one of you
is the passive?" Marowitz asked. "Oh, I probably initiate," Kenneth said, who played Hal. Marowitz said: "Right. That's how

we're gonna play it. Dennis doesn't do anything." When we came
to do it, the first thing Dennis says to Hal is an active command –
"Lock the door!". It's absolutely the other way around! Marowitz
put us into this emotional straitjacket. He wanted the relationship
to be clear-cut: one of them a doer, the other a receiver. He couldn't
even accept that, like life, people aren't one thing or another. God,
his stupidity! He thought Hal's entrance wasn't funny enough and
because Hal has a line that indicates he reads comics, Marowitz at
first had Hal coming on in a Batman costume! In general, Charles
never really understood the joke of the play. He didn't understand
the lines. I didn't think he could move people around the stage;
and when I read the notices of the play, I didn't believe it was the
same one I was in.'

Orton had asked Lewenstein for a 'straightforward' director; and
Marowitz was head-on. Orton wanted success, so kept out of
Marowitz's way, although sometimes his guarded face betrayed
itself. 'Joe had a muscle in his forehead which would throb when
something was getting at him,' Marowitz remembers. 'It was a
kind of clenching in the forehead that was very visible, as if a hand
was on his skull and squeezing it tight. It was a signal . . .' Orton
kept his critical opinions about the production to himself before
the opening; but after *Loot*'s success, he spoke his mind about
Marowitz, even when suggesting that he mount the play in New
York:

> . . . God knows I'm not a fan of his. I think a lot of the direction in
> *Loot* is atrocious. But on the principle of Better the Devil you know
> than the Devil you don't, I'd think about it. With a stronger cast his
> direction wouldn't stick out so much. And it is a success in London!!
> Remember that.[36]

Marowitz and Orton had streamlined and restructured the
Manchester script to good effect. 'Joe has a tendency to tell a joke,
and then follow it up with another joke which only illustrates the
joke he's told. He's got a proliferating sense of humour. You've
got to cut the reverberating jokes which are a ripple and stick to the

gem which is the wave.' With Marowitz, Orton found two large
comic bits of business which clinched the play in a way Orton had
never before been able to manage.

It was Orton's prankster's notion to have Mrs McLeavy's glass
eye drop out of the corpse on to the floor and for Truscott literally
to stumble over it. But how to deliver the ghoulish surprise? In the
original, when Hal and Fay pick up the corpse, the stage direction
coyly indicates 'something falls from it and rolls away'. When Fay
asks what it was, Hal says 'Nothing'. His chagrin is kept to himself,
and so is the joke. Later, after Truscott picks the eye up and pockets
it, he produces it at the end of the second act:

TRUSCOTT. . . . Could you explain to me what this object is?
MCLEAVY (*looking*). It's a marble.
TRUSCOTT. No, sir. Not a marble. (*He regards* MCLEAVY *calmly*.) It
  looks suspiciously to me like an eye.
MCLEAVY. An eye.
TRUSCOTT. Yes. (*Pause*.) The question that I want answered is, to
  whom does it legally belong.
  MCLEAVY *looks dumbfounded*.
                        Curtain

In later rewrites, Orton merely embellished the joke, but never
found a way of properly orchestrating it into the mayhem. 'I'm
not sure it's an eye,' McLeavy offers in the Manchester script, 'I
think it's a marble that has been trod on.' To which Truscott
replies: 'It's an eye, sir. The make is clearly marked: J. & S. Frazer,
Eyemakers to the Profession'. The jokes were getting better; but
theatrically the situation was still static. Orton's growth as a craftsman can be measured in how within a year this information was
vividly recast for Marowitz's production. The eye's disappearance
becomes farce business, a shared anxiety for actors and audience
which is captured in word and gesture:

HAL. Something dropped out? We couldn't find it?
FAY. Yes.

HAL. I know what it was.

FAY. What?

HAL. One of her eyes!

> *They drop to their knees. They search.* TRUSCOTT *enters. They stand.*

Orton had put panic into his prank and set up the joke for a much larger pay-off. It comes unexpectedly at the end of the first act after Truscott's belligerent interrogation of Dennis, who claims Truscott is not from the Metropolitan Water Board but a policeman who kicked him when he was remanded on suspicion of bank robbery: Truscott grabs Dennis by the collar and shakes him: 'If I ever hear you accuse the police of using violence on a prisoner in custody again, I'll take you down to the station and beat the eyes out of your head'.

No sooner is Dennis out of the room than Truscott gradually discovers what the audience clearly knows already is an eye out of Mrs McLeavy's head. While the transposition of Truscott and Dennis's exchange had been made in Manchester, Marowitz cut away swaths of dialogue to leave as the last moment Truscott's elaborate and masterful double-take of the eye. 'At rehearsals of *Loot*, Orton took the greatest interest in the black devices: the corpse, the coffin, the dead woman's clothes, the glass eye', Marowitz wrote later in the New York *Times*. 'He was childishly delighted with the protracted business that had been devised with the glass eye at the end of the first act.'[37] Marowitz and Michael Bates worked out an elaborate pantomime, Bates provided the stage eye from a tiger his father had shot in India. It was a hilarious come-uppance. The rest of the cast watched from the wings as Bates, squinting above his brush moustache, caught sight of something on the ground, casually felt the buttons of his coat, then his fly, then picked it up, sniffed it, put it to his ear and rattled it, then took his magnifying-glass from his pocket and blinking first as if to get it in focus stared hard at the object, giving 'a brief exclamation of horror and surprise' as the curtain came down on Act 1.

. . . . . .

'Near the end,' wrote the *Daily Telegraph* critic in the Manchester review of *Loot*, 'Mr Orton seems to waver as if he were losing confidence.' The observation was accurate. The script huffed and puffed to its finish. Orton couldn't spring the final trap on McLeavy with the ease the satire required. Too often *Loot*'s sport with the law turned into loquacity:

FAY. You must prove me guilty. That is the law.
TRUSCOTT. You know nothing of the law. I know nothing of the law. That makes us equal in the sight of the law.
FAY. I'm innocent till I'm proved guilty. This is a free country. The law is impartial.
TRUSCOTT. Who's been filling your head with that rubbish? The law isn't impartial. Don't think for a minute it is.

Orton, at Marowitz's insistence, cut the last two sentences, eliminating the hint of lecture and maximizing the laughter. Truscott's avenging spirit was now fully drawn and focused in Marowitz's production. Whatever judgement Orton made on justice had to be conveyed in the action. Truscott is seen to be as criminal as the thieves, so it was no longer necessary for Hal to observe as he did originally: 'The successful villains have the stars of a half-dozen decorations on their breasts. The unsuccessful ones rob banks.' In earlier drafts, Orton's voice kept stepping out of character to make a point. Now he trusted his metaphor to speak his meaning. One vestige of the early scripts which Orton kept until the London production was Truscott's *bon mot* about justice: 'Justice is a whore so old that she uses her sword to prevent the masses getting near enough to sniff her skirts.' Too much of a mouthful, the idea was translated into action by the final draft. At the finale McLeavy finds himself handcuffed on a trumped-up charge and stymied by Truscott's fast-talk:

MCLEAVY. You can't do this. I've always been a law-abiding citizen. The police are for the protection of ordinary people.
TRUSCOTT. I don't know where you pick up these slogans, sir. You must read them on the hoardings.

MCLEAVY. I want to see someone in authority.
TRUSCOTT. I am in authority. You can see me.

McLeavy starts to panic and ends up being dragged off stage
screaming: 'I'm innocent! I'm innocent! Oh, what a terrible thing
to happen to a man who's been kissed by the Pope'. Originally,
Orton had McLeavy exiting with a ludicrous curse: 'You'll be
sorry you were born. I'm asking the Fathers to bring Bell, Book
and Candle. You'll probably disappear in a puff of smoke.' So
McLeavy ends not as a bellicose figure of fun, but as a beleaguered
Irishman who is the victim of his own ignorance. Before the
London version, the best reversal Orton could spring on McLeavy
was to have him collapse into a chair in exhausted frustration after
Truscott's routine about authority, only to have Truscott slap
handcuffs on him for 'trying to escape'. But the stage picture was
too small, the moment too static for the moral outrage the ending
demanded. As Orton finally wrote it for Marowitz, McLeavy's
disintegration and his struggle to assert his innocence raised the
scene to something large, active and memorable.

Once the play was put on the right theatrical track, it coasted
smoothly, delightfully, to its conclusion. In Manchester, *Loot* had
sixty-one lines of exposition after McLeavy was carted away. By
the time *Loot* reached London, Orton had brusquely accounted for
McLeavy's future in prison; established Truscott's police locker as
the safest place to stash the stolen money; and worked out the final
living arrangements of the other three in twenty-one lines. It was a
bravura bit of plotting.

In the course of rewriting the play, Orton had tried every
theatrical combination to end it. Each ending limited the play's
meaning instead of opening it up. Now, finally in control of farce
method, Orton played on farce's obsession with shattering appearances at the finale. The unmasked once again adopt their personas
to go into the world.

HAL (*pause, to* DENNIS). You can kip here, baby. Plenty of room
now. Bring your bags over tonight.
    FAY *looks up*.

FAY (*sharply*). When Dennis and I are married we'd have to move out.

HAL. Why?

FAY. People would talk. We must keep up appearances.

She returns to her prayers, her lips move silently. DENNIS *and* HAL *at either side of the coffin.*

Curtain

Loot opened at the Jeanetta Cochrane Theatre on 27 September 1966. It was a sluggish production with a drab set in which, as Orton wrote, 'a lot of the lines are muffed' as a result of 'having inexperienced actors in the parts. In general the tone of the London production is O K ... If we replaced Fay, McLeavy and (possibly) Dennis by more experienced actors (not necessarily better – just more experienced in comedy) the play would be a lot better.'[38] Orton's dazzling writing, however, triumphed over every limitation. By the end of the week, Orton saw *Loot* described by Alan Brien in the *Sunday Telegraph* as 'the most genuinely quick-witted, pungent and sprightly entertainment by a new young British playwright for a decade'. It was clear that *Loot*, as Ronald Bryden wrote in the *Observer*, 'established Orton's niche in English drama'. Bryden proceeded to dub Orton the 'Oscar Wilde of Welfare State gentility'. Orton also found himself compared with Ben Jonson, George Bernard Shaw and Lewis Carroll. He didn't demur at such comparisons. He took a stunned delight in his reviews and shared the critics' enthusiasm for his play and his talent. 'I have a lot of vices,' he told the *Evening Standard*,[34] 'but false modesty is not one of them. The best thing about *Loot* is the quality of the writing.'[39]

The battle for his play had been won. 'Rare, darling?' Peggy Ramsay says of *Loot*'s rebirth in the West End. 'It's almost impossible.' On 1 November *Loot* transferred to the Criterion Theatre, 'with huge success', according to the *Guardian*. Orton now had a telephone, a television, and a rack full of long-playing records; but otherwise the trappings of his life with Halliwell didn't change with *Loot*'s sudden acclaim. What did change was Orton's confidence. *Loot*'s reception set Orton's imagination racing and emboldened his sense of fun. By December, he had managed to finish the first half of *What the Butler Saw*, his last full-length play. He'd also begun his diary, an indication of the new eventfulness of his life and his confidence in his future.

Loot struggled at the box office. Orton and Halliwell made frequent excursions to the 'Cri.', with Halliwell affecting a walking stick with a silver knob and Orton anxiously checking the house receipts:

Went to the Criterion tonight. Gloom, gloom. The takings have dropped by about 300 pounds. We clearly aren't going to have a long run. About another month and we'll be off. This may be because there are no names in the cast. Much of the play's lack of success must be put down to the theme and the undoubted fact that the general public are, where plays are concerned, ignorant shits.

(18 February 1967)

Orton enjoyed the sparky backstage banter; and even Halliwell made friends with the cast and enjoyed some of the residual glory of *Loot*'s success. The camaraderie was new to both of them. The actors played up to Orton's sense of humour; and he recorded many of their stories in his diary: Simon Ward's mysterious letters and phone calls from an illiterate Scotsman who wanted to produce him in James Baldwin's homosexual novel, *Giovanni's Room*, and said to him over the phone 'Of course, laddie, we'll have extensive rehearsals. In depth'; Sheila Ballantine's overheard conversation between women in a bus: 'One woman said, "There's a lot of blue about lately". After a pause the other woman said, "Yes. And there's a lot of green about too". There was another pause and the first woman said, "And there's a lot of red. Have you noticed?"' Orton also had a lot to recount to the cast about the ludicrous spin-offs of success. There was the film producer who'd asked him to script the life of Alfie Hinds, the infamous ex-convict who escaped from jail to prove his innocence. ' "Your attitude to authority in *Loot* is exactly Alfie Hinds'. You see," he said, "in a way it's similar to *Loot* – an ordinary man fighting the might of the law. And winning." "Except that in *Loot* he doesn't win," I said. "Ah well," the producer said, looking a bit put out, "we couldn't expect you to write *Loot* all over again." '

But there were also more substantial things for Orton to celebrate with the cast: the publication of the play, the proposed option on *Loot* by David Merrick for Broadway and its production in a dozen countries within the year; and, most important, the selection of *Loot* as the winner of the *Evening Standard* Award for the Best Play of 1966. Where nothing seemed to go right for Wood's production, nothing seemed to go wrong for Marowitz's. Orton was in a weird, thrilling, slightly unnerving state of grace whose magic even his producer couldn't resist mocking:

I walked to Duke Street and called on Michael White. He had the original of the caricature of the cast in *Loot* on his wall. He said, 'I was going to give it to you'. I said, 'But, of course, you're too mean'. He said, 'Yes. And, in any case, you're too spoilt as it is'. We talked of the play. He showed me a review in *Queen Magazine* that I hadn't seen. The takings went up again last night. Good news which brought smiles to everybody's face . . .

(5 January 1967)

Orton had known since December that he was the winner of the *Evening Standard* prize. Its public announcement on 11 January 1967 came none too soon for *Loot*'s flagging box office. ('Perhaps', Orton wrote to Peggy Ramsay, 'you ought to arrange for me to appear nude at the Victoria Palace to give the show a boost.')[40] On the morning of the award ceremony, Orton rang Michael White, who told him 'This week was a disaster. If the award doesn't bring some people in we're sunk.'

The first edition of the *Evening Standard* came out at 10.30 a.m. Its banner front-page headline announced: SCANDAL! BUT LOOT HAS IT. 'There was no runner up', Orton wrote in his diary, thrilled with the 'splendid' headline. 'It was four to one. Penelope Mortimer thought *Loot* simply nasty. The four men overruled her, though.' The editorial, under the headline 'Glowing Theatre', praised the vitality of the contemporary English stage ('probably not since the Elizabethans has it displayed so much richness, colour, depth and imagination'). It was an important day for Orton, not only the culmination of *Loot*'s tortuous history but public acknowledgement of Orton's hard-won literary skill. He tried to work on *What the Butler Saw*, but found it 'too difficult to concentrate'. He was taking Peggy Ramsay to the luncheon ceremony. He set off for her office at noon, dressed for his moment of vindictive triumph in Halliwell's striped suit, a gaudy wide flowered tie, and a high-collared striped shirt.

I arrived at Peggy's office. There were three letters for me ... One was from the editor of PLAYS AND PLAYERS telling me that the critics, in their annual poll, had voted LOOT the best play of 1966. So I've got a bonus.

Peggy and I decided to walk to Bury Street to Quaglino's where the luncheon was held ... When we arrived at Quaglino's Sheila Ballantine was just going in. We greeted each other in a conspiratorial whisper. It was so grand inside. I left my coat and Peggy and I appeared at the top of a staircase. The Toastmaster, in a sort of hunting pink coat, asked our names. We gave them and he boomed them out over the crowd below. It was like a thirties film of *Lady Windermere's Fan*.

Quite crowded. Bill Gaskill came up. Very bright-eyed. 'Loved *Loot*,' he said. 'I'm so glad,' I said. 'It's always nice to convert somebody.' Spoke to Oscar for a while. Peggy saying how brave he was to have taken up an option. True in a way, I suppose. Though she has a convenient lapse of memory about the period (ten days before rehearsals were due to begin) when Oscar, dissatisfied with the casting, asked me if I wanted to cancel the production. 'If we cancel,' I said, 'when will we remount it?' 'I can't guarantee when we'll do that,' Oscar said. This is the play's last chance, I thought. If it comes to grief now plus the original tour, the dubiety as to *Loot* will harden into certainty. Everyone will be sure that the play is no good. 'It must go on,' I said. 'With this cast. I must let the London critics see the play. After that I'll shut up about *Loot* and write another play.' All this, naturally, wasn't mentioned, or even thought of, probably, except by me ...

The lunch was announced. On the board it said 'Mr and Mrs

Orton'. Peggy laughed. 'I'll be your wife for the afternoon,' she said. All I could think of was how embarrassing if, as I'd originally planned, I'd taken Kenneth.

In the doorway of the dining room I spotted Michael Codron. Dark-suited and a little po-faced. Though as this is natural with him I thought it was nature not the occasion. 'Congratulations Joe,' he said. 'You can imagine what I must be feeling.' 'No, I can't,' I said. 'I haven't got that strong an imagination.' All done with a merry sort of twinkle, but it had the effect of a knee in the groin . . .

After the coffee the Toastmaster announced that the meal had ended. Rather surprisingly I thought. The lights for the television cameras came on. And the business of speeches began. And then, after Frank Marcus had made a long speech about me ['I'm giving you the award on behalf of the Metropolitan Water Board, the Metropolitan Police and the Church of Rome,' he said. '. . . Don't let them make you respectable'], I went up on the platform. I was nervous. Drinking the wine hadn't helped much. I didn't say much. I said, as near as I can remember, 'In the early days we used to give complimentary tickets to various organizations. We sent a few to Scotland Yard. And the police loved the play so much that they rang up asking for more tickets. Everyone else thinks the play is a fantasy. Of course the police know that it's true.' And then I said that I hoped to get another award in about two years. Robert Morley, later on, said that it was no good having one. You had to have two for bookends.

A lot of funny speeches. One wonderful one from Frankie Howerd. Only I can't remember what it was now . . .

And then the Toastmaster said that was all. The lights were switched out and people started going home. It was over.

I was on the front of the *Evening Standard* receiving the award. I'm very happy. Pleased though that I've almost finished the first draft of *What the Butler Saw*. It'd be difficult to have to begin a play from scratch . . .

Orton brought the statuette back to Noel Road. He and Halliwell invited a few people from the building to watch the ceremony on television. Mr and Mrs Corden, from the basement flat, who had served as models for characters in other plays, were there. So was Miss Boynes, the old lady who lived beneath them, for whom

Orton fetched the Sunday papers. These people were Orton's ad hoc family – a strange, sad group he gathered around him to bask in the afterglow of his triumph:

We had a sandwich or two. I showed Mrs Corden the menu for lunch. 'How lovely,' she said. 'It looks like a skilled printing job to me. But, of course, the actual luncheon isn't as good as Mr Corden's firm's annual get-together dinner. It was at the Savoy. And we had a sweet which was like straw. I have never, in the whole of my life, tasted anything so scruptious. That is the only word to describe it. Scrumptious,' she said, saying the word twice and hoping that nobody would notice she'd made a mistake the first time.

Miss Boynes said, 'I had a bite yesterday. From a businessman,' she said. She was talking about her flat. 'Only he told the agent he wasn't prepared to pay more than £3,000 for it. Cheek!' Kenneth and I exchanged looks. I'd been thinking of offering her £2,500 . . .

Mr Corden, after examining the award statuette, suddenly said, 'Under the green baize bottom is a bolt which bolts the actual object to the marble plinth. If you were to strip the baize away you'd see the workmanship beneath.' Like turning round the Rokeby Venus to see how the frame was made.

Excerpts from *Loot* were to be shown on *Accolade*. During the rehearsals the previous week Orton had worried in his diary: 'There seems to be a sinister suggestion that *Staircase* is having more time than we are . . . I don't trust the television company not to slant the programme to give the impression that *Staircase* is at least equal with *Loot*.'[41] Orton's instinctive paranoia was accurate:

The programme called Accolade was a disappointment. The excerpt from *Loot* was good. The set seemed to have more style on film than in reality. The performances were excellent. Then we had a long excerpt from *Staircase*. For no good reason. It wasn't a runner up. As had been suggested (by inference) in the TV Times. The real blow fell when, after excerpts from Finney's new film, 'Two for the Road' and a long piece from 'Little Malcolm and His Struggle Against the Eunuchs', we came to the luncheon. But, by this time, the programme was over. When Frank Marcus announced me as award winner the sound was off. I appeared briefly with the sound still off and the captions and credits coming over my face. Then the sound came on for the other winners. The whole had the effect of the man with the bladder hitting the Emperor on the head as he rode in triumph. Just to take him down a peg and remind him that he wasn't a god ... Went to bed very disgruntled.

(11 January 1967)

Whatever the momentary blow to Orton's ego, its balm came quickly at the box office. Four days after the *Evening Standard* award, Michael White's business manager, Mark Linford, pulled Orton aside. 'Joe, come and see something,' he said. 'It's what you've been waiting for.' No botched spectacle of the playwright's triumph was as important or thrilling as this:

The stalls were packed. He took me upstairs to the circle. The circle was packed. And in the gallery they were standing. 'I hope it builds from this,' I said. 'It mustn't be just tonight. It must go on. We're not out of the wood yet.' 'We've not lost a single customer since the award,' Mark said. 'No one has complained since Wednesday. Now they've been told they can enjoy it they do.'

(15 January 1967)

Orton, who felt *Loot* was a young person's play, gave orders to the box office to refund money to any elderly couple who were outraged by it. He had other ways of dealing with younger irate customers. One man wrote to the management after leaving *Loot* in the interval: 'As Christians, we were naturally dismayed to see the Roman Catholic Church abused, but even were I not a Christian I should have been ashamed to take my mother and sister to hear the accompanying filth. I am in consequence writing to the Lord Chamberlain, suggesting that the play should be reviewed yet again, and at the least severely edited.' The letter was passed to Orton. Edna Welthorpe replied on 14 April 1967:

Please let me say at once that I am conscious of a great feeling of uneasiness at writing to you. I must write, however to tell you that you are not alone in disliking the play LOOT. I myself consider it to be the most loathsome play on in London at the present moment.

'Bestial' is how I described it to an acquaintance the other day. When I tell you that in the second act (which you had the good fortune to miss), there was a discussion upon the raping of children with Mars bars with other filthy details of a sexual and psychopathic nature I'm sure you'll pardon my writing.

Please, please, as a fellow Christian, let me applaud your design in writing to the Lord Chamberlain. I myself have written several letters to the papers (none alas published) and am trying to contact my M.P. at the moment. I took an elderly aunt of mine to see the play recently and really I had to go round to the manager afterwards and demand an apology. This truly horrible play shouldn't contaminate our streets.

It was most wrong of me to write to you, I'm sure. Your letter was passed to me for filing. I do hope you will respect my confidence in this. It has received the most respectful attention here. Naturally, I cannot express any opinion but my own. And that you have fully.

I am trying, in a solo capacity, to arrange a meeting with the Lord Chamberlain to protest against plays in general and this travesty of the free society LOOT in particular. I wonder if you'd like to be included in our mission?

Edna was never in higher spirits. She was stirring up trouble in public as well as in private. When the novelist David Benedictus objected to *Loot* winning the *Plays and Players* Award, Edna thrashed *Loot* in the magazine, calling it 'a piece of indecent tom-foolery' and continuing:

. . . Drama should be uplifting. The plays of Joe Orton have a most unpleasant effect on me. I was plunged into the dumps for weeks after seeing his *Entertaining Mr Sloane*. I saw *Loot* with my young niece; we both fled from the theatre in horror and amazement well before the end. I could see no humour in it . . .

These plays do nothing but harm to our image abroad, presenting us as slaves of sensation and unnatural practice. Mr Benedictus does well to point out the inadequacies of our present honours system!

But above Edna's letter was one by Donald H. Hartley, Orton's other pseudonym, praising his work and calling Benedictus's credentials into question: 'Really, if every pip-squeak circus pony were to give awards for the Horse of the Year, goodness knows where we should be!'

Loot's success didn't need Edna to generate publicity. Both Orton and Loot received an incredible boost when, after intensive competitive bidding, news of Loot's film sale for a reported £100,000 to Bernard Delfont and Arthur Lewis hit the newspapers on 1 March. According to The Times, 'it was one of the highest amounts ever paid for a straight play'. 'Absolutely ridiculous', Orton wrote in his diary about the figure. 'I suppose they've added the amount I'd get if the play ran for two years on Broadway.'[42] In his home town, the Leicester Mercury ran Orton's picture under the headline: EX-PRISONER SELLS PLAY FOR £100,000. 'It's better than carting around great loads of brick or sweeping up the cutting room floor of some Leicester factory,'[43] Orton bitterly told the Mercury reporter, not denying the rumoured sales figure.

Orton was now 'a name' – someone to be reckoned with. The avidity of the film producers was an indication of his new power. Orton learned about the movie sale when he and Halliwell visited Peggy Ramsay at her apartment to watch his guest appearance on Call My Bluff, Orton's first celebrity outing, where, along with Eva Gabor, Kenneth Williams and Maxine Audley on the quiz show, he came across – he thought – like 'a young Robert Mitchum'.[44] Orton had expected to spend the evening with Peggy Ramsay; instead he was greeted by Oscar Lewenstein and Arthur Lewis, who had just shelled out option money for the film rights of Loot:

This afternoon he [Arthur Lewis] rang Peggy and asked if he could buy the option. Peggy said that if he came round with a cheque for £20,000 he could have it. He rushed around. Oscar then said to Peggy, 'See what happens if you ask for 25'. So she did. He signed a cheque for £18,000 with another £7,000 when the contract is signed. When the man had gone . . . Oscar said, 'Only this afternoon I was saying to Michael White "I expect about £5,000 is all we'll get for LOOT now".' Remarkable the man must be. Especially as LOOT is quite unsuitable for filming.

Loot was a dismal failure on the screen; and on Broadway, as Orton also predicted, it flopped after twenty-three performances. 'I *curse* Michael White from the bottom of my pitiless soul for getting some sucker to agree to an on-Broadway production,' he wrote to Peggy Ramsay on 30 May, after the David Merrick negotiations had fallen through and Harold Orenstein had been found. 'It will flop in a fortnight. I was looking forward to The Establishment or Cherry Lane. White suddenly is energetic at the time when his usual lethargy would've been most welcome. Still, it's Kismet (Ah, the exotic east is in my blood!). We can but trust in the will of Allah and insist that we take Michael Bates and Kenneth Cranham to Broadway.' But Orton dismissed *Loot*'s certain Broadway failure with the insouciance of a man secure in his own success. 'Who cares what the Americans do – as long as they pay plenty of cash they can play *Loot* in the middle of Time Square', he wrote in his diary. 'Reputations are made in London, only money is made in New York.'

Loot brought Orton's craft to its maturity. Confident, independent and now successful, Orton was growing free of the fear that weighed down his early prose and forced it to revel in all that was dark, inferior and culpable in others. He was no longer oppressed in the same way by guilt and inferiority; and his plays, which were projections of these fears, took on an expansive good humour. There was a hint of forgiveness in his high spirits. Even Orton's handwriting changed from its cramped, adolescent jaggedness to an open, fluid, authoritative hand. The ten months between October 1966, when *Loot* made its London debut, and August 1967, when he died, would be Orton's most fecund literary period. He wrote his ghoulish capriccio about the Church and Christian charity, *Funeral Games*; a film script, *Up Against It*; the major revisions on *Ruffian* and *Erpingham Camp*, published, as they were produced, under the title *Crimes of Passion*; and his farce masterpiece, *What the Butler Saw*. Almost his entire œuvre was either written or rewritten in the comic voice he'd acquired through *Loot*. Orton's was a unique voice whose echoes invoked the descriptive comparisons to Wilde and Firbank; but it was indubitably his own.

In theatrical terms, Orton's comic voice made new dramatic demands on the contemporary actor, special demands that turned the act of speaking itself into a startling contest. The actor's competition with Orton's language (whose quality of wit seems always to be above the class of his characters) became part of the play's tension and fun. 'There's a performing technique to Orton,' Kenneth Williams says. 'You've got to breathe. If you're going to say lines like "The Vatican would never grant an annulment. Not unless he'd produced a hybrid" you've got to gather it up, otherwise it's lost. If you're going to stop in the middle, the whole impact is destroyed. This is in the tradition of classic English comic writing. It goes for Wilde, the same construction, the same intake of breath. It occurs also in Coward. Shaw uses the construction again and again. In *Saint Joan*, the Inquisitor says: "It's not enough to be simple. It's not enough even to be what simple people call good. The simplicity of a darkened mind is no better than the simplicity of a beast . . ." The accumulated momentum is deadly, going right to its conclusion. He is speaking to a simple country girl, but he replies in language of total authority. The same is true of Orton. It could be Truscott, or Erpingham, or Rance in *What the Butler Saw*. Orton's dialogue has impact; and to get the full thrilling clout of it, the dialogue *must flow*.'

The liberties Orton took with language and plot were built on a disciplined vision which his productions had yet to match. 'It suggests', Ronald Bryden concluded in his review of *Loot*, 'that the British theatre will need to find an Orton style, as it has done for Pinter, Wilde and Coward.'[45]

6

THE FREAKS' ROLL-CALL

> To be able to recognize the freak, you have to
> have some conception of the whole man ...
>
> Flannery O'Connor, *Mystery and Manners*

'How can you avoid tormenting men if one has decided to make
them gods?'[1] Orton copied Camus's question into his notebook
and used farce to torment the godlike vanity of his characters:

ERPINGHAM. I shall confiscate your luggage. What is your chalet
number?

DR RANCE. My brief is infinite. I'd have sway over a rabbit hutch if
the inmates were mentally disturbed.

TRUSCOTT. How dare you involve me in a situation for which no
memo has been issued.

Each character has his kingdom – whether holiday camp, psychiatric ward or police squad. Each is a freak of power and propriety.
The elegance of Orton's comic syntax aspires to perfection while the
characters who speak it are unashamedly imperfect. They speak a
language of reason but live a life of chaos. 'People think I write
fantasy, but I don't', Orton said. 'Some things may be distorted in
the way painters distort and alter things, but they're realistic
figures.'[2] The distortion captures the lopsided spirituality of an
unbelieving age which, by making man its ultimate concern, has
twisted and isolated him.

Farce, as Eric Bentley writes, 'is the theatre of the surrealist
body'.[3] Farce glories in fracturing from and sporting with man's
obsession with unity. Orton extends farce beyond the bedroom.

The chaos of confused identities and the riot of bodies galvanized by human need expose the flimsiness of reason with which man creates his patchwork of coherence. 'I've learned to accept the irrational in every day life,' quips McCorquodale in *Funeral Games*. Behind the carapace of normality, human beings are driven by unreasoning desires and defences which can turn them from the respectable to the rampaging. Orton wrote this into his plays. He also found it in his life:

When I left the theatre I took the Piccadilly line to Holloway Road and popped into a little pissoir – just four pissers. It was dark because somebody had taken the bulb away. There were three figures pissing. I had a piss and, as my eyes became used to the gloom, I saw that only one of the figures was worth having – a labouring type, big, with cropped hair and, as far as I could see, wearing jeans and a dark coat. Another man entered and the man next to the labourer moved away, not out of the place altogether, but back against the wall. The new man had a pee and left the place and, before the man against the wall could return to his place, I nipped in there sharpish and stood next to the labourer. I put my hand down and felt his cock, he immediately started to play with mine. The youngish man with fair hair, standing back against the wall, went into the vacant place. I unbuttoned the top of my jeans and unloosened my belt in order to allow the labourer free rein with my balls. The man next to me began to feel my bum. At this point a fifth man entered. Nobody moved. It was dark. Just a little light spilled into the place from the street, not enough to see immediately. The man next to me moved back to allow the fifth man to piss. But the fifth man very quickly flashed his cock and the man next to me returned to my side, lifting up my coat, and shoving his hand down the back of my trousers. The fifth man kept puffing on a cigarette and, by the glowing end, watching. A sixth man came into the pissoir. As it was so dark nobody bothered to move. After an interval (during which the fifth man watched me feel the labourer, the labourer stroked my cock and the man beside me pulled my jeans down even further) I noticed that the sixth man was kneeling down beside the youngish man with fair hair and sucking his cock. A seventh man came in, but by now nobody cared. The number of people in the place was so large that detection was impossible. And anyway as soon became apparent when the seventh man stuck his head down on a level with my fly, he wanted a cock in his mouth too. For some moments nothing happened. Then the eighth man, bearded and stocky, came in. He pushed the sixth man roughly away from the fair-haired man and quickly sucked the fair-haired man off. The man beside me had pulled my jeans down over my buttocks and was trying to push his prick between my legs. The fair-haired man, having been sucked off, hastily left the place. The bearded man came over and nudged away the seventh man from me, and, opening wide my fly, began sucking like a maniac. The labourer, getting very excited by my feeling his cock with both hands, suddenly glued his mouth to mine. The little pissoir under the bridge had become the scene of a frenzied saturnalia. No more than two feet away the citizens of Holloway moved about their ordinary business. I came, squirting come into the bearded man's mouth and quickly pulled up my jeans. As I was about to leave I heard the bearded man hissing quietly, 'I suck people off! Who wants his cock sucked?' When I left the labourer was shoving his cock into the man's mouth to keep him quiet. I caught the bus home.

(4 March 1967)

'You can't be a rationalist in an irrational world. It isn't rational', Orton wrote in *What the Butler Saw*. Orton tested reason more elegantly in his plays than in his life. 'I'm a great believer in the absolute logic of *Alice in Wonderland*', he said in the programme of *Loot*. 'It's the kind of logic I put into my plays.' Orton studied Feydeau, who went so far as to number his characters and their position on the stage as he made up the ground plan for his comedies. When Oscar Lewenstein spotted an inconsistency in *What the Butler Saw*, Orton patched it up reminding him 'The mathematical precision of the play is unimpaired'. Orton boasted about *Loot*'s logic: after all the ability to deploy it had been hard-won.

Funeral Games was the transitional play between *Loot* and *What the Butler Saw* in which Orton tried to solidify the stylistic advances of language and logic in *Loot*. Written in five drafts between July and mid-November 1966, *Funeral Games* dealt with charity as part of an ITV series on 'The Seven Deadly Virtues'. There was a new tone and texture to the play's laughter. 'In the garden of her detached ranch-type dwelling the vision of the Lord came upon me', Pringle explains, extolling the Lady of the Wand ('A woman of great humility and private fortune') and explaining the decision to seek revenge on his wife, Tessa, for her suspected adultery:

I was swept up and the springs of my heart were opened. I made a vow. Taking my cue from Holy Writ. 'My wife must be punished.' The words I spoke weren't rejected or pooh-poohed. I was hoisted high on the shoulders of two priestly personalities. (*Tears roll down his cheeks.*) The Lady of the Wand shook out the glorious strands of her golden hair. There were loud hosannas. Palm branches. I was girt in white. The grounds of that Surrey mansion were ablaze with the ecumenical spirit until the small hours. My commandment was repeated like a catechism: 'Thou shalt not suffer an adultress to live.'

The cadences of Pringle's speech swell his sense of control and bolster the illusion of reason. Bitterness has vanished from Orton's laughter, to be replaced by a buoyant sense of philosophical detachment. Tessa, who has befriended the ancient and ailing defrocked priest McCorquodale, holds up one of his watercolours. 'It was my intention to represent – in a symbolic form – the Christian Church', McCorquodale explains. Tessa scrutinizes the painting: 'A bird of prey carrying an olive branch. You've put the matter in a nutshell.'

The freak, repellent in life, is made compelling in *Funeral Games* by laughter which matches the caprice of nature with the caprice of language whose purpose is to lure the characters away from panic. Orton magnifies the monstrousness of his characters and their baroque prose. 'Take my dying curse. You diabolic crumb from the table of the damned!' McCorquodale shouts at Pringle, slapping him in the face for committing adultery with Mrs McCorquodale (Val) and forcing McCorquodale to murder her. Pringle retorts:

'I'll teach you to strike a man of admitted charity.' The men of God try to throttle each other.

Pringle is a religious charlatan. 'Sit down', he commands Caulfield, the man he hires to snoop on Tessa. 'Or kneel if you'd prefer. I want you to behave naturally.' Pringle's sect is called 'The Brotherhood' ('We've a house of contemplation, in the Arcade. Pay us a visit . . . We hang about on street corners'). A self-styled god, Pringle is also The Word: 'Copies of my brochure *Blessings Abound* are still available. It'd be wise to purchase one. It gives the background to my teaching.' The grotesque is a picture of the incredible which works a mischievous balance between ugliness and beauty, denial and affirmation. Orton's delight and disgust with his characters is built into their outrageousness, allowing him to startle his audience with the unforeseen. McCorquodale, who has buried his wife in the cellar under a ton of smokeless fuel, confesses his crime within minutes of meeting Caulfield:

CAULFIELD. You're a murderer?
MCCORQUODALE. These 'with it' expressions aren't familiar to me.
CAULFIELD. Wasn't it a happy marriage?
MCCORQUODALE. We bickered occasionally over the nature of God.
   Nothing more serious.

In *Funeral Games* Orton tried to rev up his plotting to create the sharp, brief juxtapositions which the grotesque requires. In Scene 4, Pringle is hell-bent on revenge. Caulfield reasons with him: 'You can't kill your wife. What about the sixth commandment?' Pringle replies 'If she can break the seventh, I can break the sixth.' He pulls out a gun and, invoking the humble and the meek's thirst for blood, goes off firing it. In the next scene Pringle confronts Tessa ('You'll soon be burning in some low, hot nook of Satan!'). Tessa, whose visits to McCorquodale are an act of charity, can't believe Pringle has murder on his mind. 'You must be mistaken', she tells Caulfield. 'We celebrate our wooden wedding in a fortnight.' But Pringle means business and is about to shoot Tessa through the heart when Caulfield crowns him with a bottle. Sobered ('You're still alive? I've broken my vow. I'm unworthy of the name of Christian'), Pringle is advised by Caulfield to forgive his wife:

PRINGLE. I won't tolerate forgiveness. It's a thing of the past.
CAULFIELD. Love thy neighbour.
PRINGLE. The man who said that was crucified by his.

In a few brief exchanges they reach a compromise which gives the plot another sharp turn. Instead of murdering his wife, Pringle will just say he's killed her. Tessa agrees to stay with McCorquodale as his 'wife'. 'This'll be worth a million in publicity. Make a bit of a splash in the weekend Press', Pringle says, already imagining the headlines in the Brotherhood's newspaper and savouring his righteous glory. ' "Vengeance Is Mine", says "No Nonsense Parson." These human interest stories can increase a congregation a thousandfold.' Having ruthlessly negotiated the 'death' pact, Pringle exits with a blessing: 'Trust in the Lord. We shall meet in the glory of the Infinite Morning'.

But in Part Two reports of the 'murder' turn Pringle into a star. Gifts are lavished on him – a ring 'From a fervent admirer of Western Civilization'; a silver-backed clothes-brush from a woman journalist who 'wanted the privilege of kissing hands that'd taken human life'. Orton's outrageousness is the theatrical equivalent of a shout – startling the English public with an idea it ordinarily won't accept: man's appetite for blood. In the morning mail, Pringle receives a letter from a reporter accusing him of *not* having murdered his wife. Pringle contemplates legal action for defamation of character. 'For saying you're innocent?' says Caulfield. 'You'd never get away with it. There must be hundreds of innocent people in the country.' Caulfield, who knows he can find a dead body in McCorquodale's cellar, is sent in search of 'proof'. 'You don't need a complete body', he tells Pringle. 'An arm would do. (*Pause.*) Or a head.'

The 'surrealist body' – the illusion of the torso freed from rational content or expectation by the momentum of farce – now becomes part of the fun of *Funeral Games*. Unaware of the corpse, Tessa prepares tea for Caulfield and McCorquodale as Caulfield emerges from the cellar, his hands and face 'smeared with coaldust'. The refined and the atrocious are juxtaposed. As Tessa puts the cake for tea on a doily, Caulfield is laying down a meat cleaver, carrying 'a human hand, severed above the wrist, wrapped in sacking'. Caulfield grumbles to McCorquodale: 'I couldn't get her head off. It must be glued on.' McCorquodale replies: 'She was always a headstrong woman.' The grotesque is the violent extreme of farce's capriciousness; and Orton instinctively pursues the genre's cruelty and gloats over the anarchy of his imagery:

TESSA (*to* CAULFIELD, *over her shoulder*). Do you want to wash your hands before tea?
CAULFIELD. Yes.
  TESSA *picks up a teapot and goes out.*
  CAULFIELD *goes to the sink. He washes the hand and his own.*

Caulfield hides the hand in Tessa's cake tin while they have tea. Orton's dialogue draws out the comedy of the hand, and its final horrific discovery. During the meal, Tessa notices Val's watch on Caulfield's wrist and becomes suspicious when Caulfield explains that he found it, 'In the street'. Val, Orton implies, was once Tessa's lover, and Tessa takes the watch with the intention of going to the police. 'Val had a lot of friends in the Police', Tessa says. 'She used to sing songs in praise of Authority at her concerts.' As Tessa clears away the dishes, she and Caulfield are suddenly at loggerheads over the cake tin. He is adamant; she is indignant:

CAULFIELD. Don't open that tin.
TESSA. Why not?
CAULFIELD. I bought a plastic hand from a novelty shop. I put it into your cake tin.
  TESSA *turns from wrapping up the cake.*
TESSA. That was very silly of you. Neville down the road is in trouble of that sort. His little playmate had a convulsion. Her mother is putting it into the papers. (*She lifts the tin.*) I'm glad you had the sense to tell me.
  She takes off the lid and looks in. She gives a shriek of horror.

(*Gasping with fright.*) It's real. (*Trembling.*) I can spot plastic fingers a mile off.

The grotesque sidesteps every normal response, allowing a variety of moods and emotions to exist at the same moment. Tessa demands to know Val's whereabouts:

MCCORQUODALE. She was taken up to Heaven. In a fiery chariot. Driven by an angel.
TESSA. What nonsense. Valerie would never accept a lift from a stranger . . .

In the next line the frivolous suddenly glimpses the pathetic. Tessa goes into the cellar 'to gauge the full extent' of McCorquodale's crimes. He knows what she'll find and has no choice but to tie her up:

MCCORQUODALE (*pause, weary*). In the closet you'll find a rope . . . I bought it a month ago. I intended hanging myself.
CAULFIELD. What stopped you?
MCCORQUODALE. The weather turned nice.

The logic in *Funeral Games* is more tortuous than in *Loot*. Tessa knows of Val's murder; but if she reports the crime, her 'murder' will be exposed as a fraud. Caulfield now suggests that Pringle should actually kill Tessa in order to break the impasse:

PRINGLE. I've already killed her once. I couldn't do it again. I'd be a murderer.
CAULFIELD. You are a murderer. In the eyes of the world. I'm only asking you to live up to your public image.
PRINGLE. That's a terrible thing to ask a man to do.
CAULFIELD (*pause*). Unless you kill your wife she'll accuse you of not being her murderer.

'Truth must win', Tessa proclaims, cutting herself free of her fetters with a dagger McCorquodale once used for 'circumcising the Faithful'. 'Otherwise life is impossible.' She is about to set off for the police when she discovers Caulfield and Pringle at the threshold of McCorquodale's room. McCorquodale recognizes

Pringle as his arch enemy, the 'ecclesiastical poltroon' who seduced Valerie and banished him from the religious order. He vows revenge: 'I'll see every soul in Christendom knows that the blood on your hands is a fraud.' They attack one another, the mayhem being aggravated by their reasoning. McCorquodale wants Tessa alive because she is proof of Pringle's innocence. Pringle wants Tessa dead because her existence belies his image as a holy murderer. Tessa tries to call McCorquodale off:

TESSA. You mustn't cause trouble. I shall deny that I'm alive.
MCCORQUODALE. I'll kill you, then.
    He grabs her, and holds the sword to her breast.
TESSA. You can't destroy me. I'm the evidence.
PRINGLE. You can't expose his guilt without establishing my innocence.

With the characters hamstrung by their logic, Orton again twists the situation:

    CAULFIELD *takes the gun from* PRINGLE's *coat and fires.* TESSA,
    PRINGLE *and* MCCORQUODALE *scatter. Pause.*
TESSA (*running behind sofa*). Who's he after?
PRINGLE. You.
    CAULFIELD *fires again.* PRINGLE *disappears.*
    TESSA *throws the meat cleaver at* CAULFIELD. *It crashes among the medicine bottles and drops down beside* MCCORQUODALE.

Caulfield finally catches Tessa, shoves a gun against her head and pulls the trigger. The chamber is empty. Crying in relief, Tessa exclaims: 'Somebody is going to pay for Val's death.' But justice in Orton's monstrous world is never done. Once Pringle's seduction of Val is made public, Tessa realizes she's been twice betrayed. 'Stealing my husband and concealing the fact that she had one of her own. It's scandalous behaviour.' Truth, justice and Val are immediately forgotten. 'She tempted the Lord', Tessa explains, referring to Pringle. 'It would be blasphemous to raise a hand in her defence.' The ending fizzles out, with Orton unable to bring off in imagery the dizzying confusions and final resolution that, a few months later in *What the Butler Saw*, he would accomplish with such aplomb. McCorquodale is reinstated into the Brotherhood and given the title of Bishop Bonnyface. Tessa remains with the new Bishop. Caulfield asks to be 'Taken on to God's payroll' and threatens blackmail. 'We're Children of Light. Not criminals', Pringle rebukes him before putting Caulfield on the 'priestly path'. 'Tangle with the Prince of Peace and you'll find a knife in your back.' Pringle too gets his happy ending, claiming Val as his adulterous wife and proudly taking credit for her murder as the police cart him off to jail.

Orton's freaks make a mockery of Christianity, but his comedy is Christ-haunted. 'Christ!' McCorquodale prays, in a line too solemn to survive Orton's blue pencil. 'Let me die tonight. Don't tease me. I've laughed long enough. I'm out of breath and tears roll down my cheeks.' Laughter becomes Orton's search-and-destroy mission. 'I've screeched at Heaven and received no reply,' McCorquodale says in one draft. 'If only I could find someone who'd been kissed or kicked by God. I wouldn't feel so bad. But, and you can quote me, I've seen neither hide nor hair of anything supernatural in a lifetime spent behind some of the best altars in the country.' Like the gargoyles on a Gothic cathedral, Orton used the grotesque to summon the totality of life, a living hell as well as an intimation of heaven. 'God is as likely to be found among the tripes as in the heart', he wrote in his notes. 'He created both after all.' Orton's outrageousness always challenged the moral whoopee about man's goodness and teased the public into accepting a much more complex view of human nature. 'Orton understood that his irreligiousness was entirely religious,' Kenneth Williams says.

'I think the Christian religion is a terrible mistake,' Orton said. 'In the beginning at the time of the Roman Empire, it had meaning because Christians were probably rebels against a dreary, boring Establishment.'[4] The Church had long been the Establishment; and to Orton faith was now frozen in cliché-ridden postures and threadbare ceremonies. Pringle explains the Brotherhood's Christmas: 'We call that the Festival of the Renewal of the Spirit ... We have a cot with a baby in it outside the church. I dare say you're surprised by the unusualness of the conception?' In life, Orton found Christmas 'a hateful time'. The tepid celebrations depressed him. 'Drunken people behaving in a foolish way', he wrote after a trip to the West End on 23 December 1966. 'Singing and shouting. What for I'd like to know. They've nothing to celebrate.' Material impoverishment was as disturbing as the spectacle of spiritual impoverishment:

Kenneth said when he went out he saw an old woman in Marks and Spencer's. She was very poor. And she'd bought herself a packet of jam tarts and half a chicken. Obviously she could afford nothing else. How awful to be trying to celebrate when you're old and lonely. I wish there was something to be done. We're not taking any notice of Christmas.

(24 December 1966)

But religious hypocrisy fascinated Orton too much to pass over Christmas Day without comment. He saw power and public manipulation where others saw piety. 'Usual messages from the heads of the establishment', he noted. 'The Queen from Windsor, The Pope from Rome: Pilate and Caiaphas celebrating the birth of Christ.'

'Let us go to prison', Pringle says at the finale of *Funeral Games* as Orton lampoons the faith of the faithless in resurrection. 'Some angel will release us from our place of confinement.' Orton himself was no longer the prisoner of his environment. He was no longer confined to the blinkered anonymity of a bedsitter existence. John Orton had become Joe Orton, a new man whose transformation even Orton's family accepted with amazed respect. 'Note how I started this letter', his sister Leonie wrote to him early in 1967, 'with your new name.'[5] Finally in control of his life and his talent, Orton had turned the threats of his past into promise. In the last year Orton's laughter took on a special richness that signalled his new sense of freedom. At the end of *What the Butler Saw*, the characters climbed out of the chaos, up a rope ladder into the blazing light. In private Orton was less ironic about the change of direction in his own life. 'I'm going up, up, up,' he wrote to Glenn Loney.[6]

In sixteen weeks between December 1966 and April 1967, Orton's career took a miraculous leap forward. *Loot* won the *Evening Standard* award, was slated for Broadway and sold for filming; *Entertaining Mr Sloane*, after being scuttled by ITV, was rescheduled for production; *The Good and Faithful Servant* went into rehearsal with Donald Pleasance; *What the Butler Saw* was through its first draft; *The Erpingham Camp* was revised for the *Crimes of Passion* double-bill at the Royal Court and, most unexpectedly, Orton had been contacted by the Beatles about writing the screenplay for their next film. Nothing, not even his mother's death on 26 December, seemed to impair Orton's fecundity. The plots of old, failed novels (some of them partly Halliwell's invention) were being recycled by Orton into new commercial products. He was free to be himself; and he had found a way of making that self acceptable to the world. He was throwing off the dead weight of his past while Halliwell was increasingly lumbered by his. Halliwell could only watch the small miracle of Orton's success and his transformation with seething envy and fear. *His* manuscripts gathered dust in the drawer; *his* mother's death was a fact from which he'd never really recovered. As Orton gallivanted around London seeing agents, producers, reporters, Halliwell stayed at home, his suffering excluding him from life and simultaneously draining it from him. He could never forgive Orton his happiness; and failure seemed life's corroboration of his worthlessness. Halliwell was suddenly Orton's answering service – and, when Orton required it, his sounding board. He found himself oppressed by the very subjects Orton mined for his laughter – sexuality, isolation, pride, rage, control. Once, hallucinating on hashish, Orton saw himself as a little boy being beaten by a teacher, and the teacher was Halliwell. Every nagging demand, every petty contradiction, conveyed the anger and unhappiness Halliwell tried hard to bridle. Orton began to look upon him as successful graduates often view an old tutor, with an affectionate nostalgia tinged with disdain.

Halliwell struggled to establish something for himself in the midst of Orton's windfall. In early January 1967 Orton and Halliwell carried five of Halliwell's collages to Anno Domini, an antique store then on the King's Road, whose proprietor, having seen Halliwell's screen at Peggy Ramsay's apartment, was interested in selling his work. To Orton, who was eager for Halliwell to find some outlet for his talent and an interest outside their relationship, it was an exercise at once hopeful and desperate:

The shop smelt of damp. It had natural coloured hessian on the walls. Freddie Bartman got up when we entered. He was youngish, middle-aged man with glasses. 'What have we here,' he said, with a certain eagerness as Kenneth placed the first of the pictures against the wall. It was a macabre Venus made of bits of fingers and mouths on a background that looked like a crumbling tube station wall. 'Well!' said Freddie, looking impressed. 'You've certainly got something here.' The next picture seemed to be of eggs bursting over a suburban landscape. A negress, cut from a book of African art, lifted up her hands and screamed. Freddie examined it and went on to the three I had brought: a hideous youth sitting in the foreground with a nightmare scene going on behind, a cadaverous monk and a wraith-like nun standing either side of a small picture which was captioned 'Rosencrantz was Jesus CHRIST?' and lastly, a bull made of human hair leaping around in a sandpit and charging three human eyes. Freddie turned the pictures around and said, 'I think they'd have to be dolled up a bit. Don't you?' He looked beadily around for confirmation. 'I think they ought to be mounted nicely. Don't you?' 'They should be framed,' I said. 'Oh yes,' he said. 'They'd want nicely framing.' . . . 'Let me show you my intentions,' Freddie said, leading the way to the cellar.

'I'd put them in this room,' he showed us into an underground cavern. 'I'd take those mirrors down,' he'd led us into another room, musty and evil-smelling. 'I'd make a show of it for you.' . . . 'You want a nice framer,' I heard him saying to Kenneth. 'I'll look out for one. Let you know. And what are you thinking of asking for them?' Kenneth looked vague. 'Let's leave that till they're framed and

ready,' I said, emerging from the lavatory. 'Right you are,' said
Freddie. 'We'll leave it to fate then, shall we?' He promised to ring
Kenneth with the name of a picture framer. Kenneth said he'd have
fifteen framed to start with. 'Just to start with,' Freddie cackled to
himself. 'After all,' he said, 'we don't know whether they're going to
bite, do we?'

(6 January 1967)

Every tentative step Halliwell made in the world was shadowed
by the heavy knowledge of the sudden discrepancy in their situations. Orton was big-time; and Halliwell's efforts were woefully
small-time. Where Orton's plays were accessible and well-
publicized, Halliwell's collages would be shunted into the basement
of an undistinguished shop. While Orton's work found enthusiastic
backers, Halliwell had to invest his own money in mounting his
'productions'. Orton, who had found a public, understood the
horror of public indifference and feared it for Halliwell. 'Whether
anybody will come is the problem,' Orton wrote on 13 February,
when he and Halliwell delivered the framed pictures to Anno
Domini. By the end of March, Halliwell's pictures were finally on
display. But, fearing prosecution, Bartman refused to hang two of
them. 'The two pictures are a nude Venus and a picture called
COSY COUPLES – several sections of young men cut from physical
culture magazines juxtaposed with large flowers and distant views
of houses', Orton wrote. 'Freddie B. is a nervous twit. Like all the
middle-classes. Too nervous to live. He was even timid of using
Kenneth's poster which makes use of Steinberg drawings. "As
though," Kenneth said, with some truth, "anybody will go and
see the pictures stuck away at the wrong end of the King's Road." '[7]
Not many people did see the exhibition, which became for Halliwell
yet another sour memory in a lifetime of bitterness.

There was no good news in Halliwell's life; and for Orton there
seemed to be very little bad. On 12 January, the day after Orton's
triumph at the *Evening Standard* awards had been spoiled by the
television programme about it, Orton was contacted by Walter
Shenson (who had produced *A Hard Day's Night* and *Help*) to

rewrite a new Beatles script. Shenson wanted to send Orton the script with a view to working on it. In one telephone call, Orton was being offered the keys to Celebrity City. 'I was very impressed by this, but I put on a nonchalant manner,' Orton said. ' "Well, I'm frightfully up to my eyes in it at the moment," I said. "I'm writing my third play." "I'd certainly love to have you take a look at this draft," he said. "I've discussed it with the boys. I mean I mentioned your name to them. They didn't react too much, I must say. But I think I can persuade them to have you." By this time I was feeling foolish and not at all nonchalant. "Yes," I said. "Please send the script over and I'll read it." '

Orton read the Beatles script and the first draft of *What the Butler Saw* on the same day. 'Pleased, but still a lot of work to be done,'[8] was Orton's verdict on his new farce. His usual procedure was to put away a play for a few months to get new ideas and objectivity about the work. The Beatles script would be a relaxing change of pace, and fit neatly into his timetable for *What the Butler Saw*. Inevitably a screenplay for the Beatles was a challenge too alluring to decline:

Liked the idea. Basically it is that there aren't four young men. Just four aspects of one man. Sounds very dreary, but as I thought about it I realised what wonderful opportunities it would give me. The end in the present script is the girl advancing on the four to accept a proposal of marriage from one of them (which, the script coyly says, we shall never know). Already have the idea that the end should be a church with four bridegrooms and one bride. THE HOMECOMING in fact, but alibied in such a way that no one would object. Lots of opportunities for sexual ambiguities – a woman's bedroom, at night, her husband outside, and four men inside. I also would like to incorporate a lot of material from the first novel Kenneth and I ever wrote called *The Silver Bucket*. In it a young girl is expelled from her native village for an unnamed offence. Already see how it could be one boy expelled from some great industrial metropolis accompanied by a ceremony of mammoth proportions. Could be funny. As long as I wasn't expected to write a naturalistic script . . . Basically the Beatles are getting fed up with the Dick

Lester type of direction. They want dialogue to speak. Also they're tired of actors like Leo McKern stealing scenes. Difficult this as I don't think any of the Beatles can act in any accepted sense. As Marilyn Monroe couldn't.

(15 January 1967)

Orton met Shenson for lunch the next day. ('I gave away a few of my ideas. Enough to whet his appetite . . . Over lunch he said that one of the ideas for a new Beatles film was THE THREE MUSKETEERS. "Oh, no," I said. "That's been done to death." "Bridget Bardot wanted to play Lady de-Winter," he said. "She's been done to death as well," I said. "Oh, heh, heh, heh, boy!" he said. "You certainly are quick." ') By the end of the day, Orton had a title for his original script, *Up Against It*, and had written the first two pages. 'Miss Drumgoole and Father Brodie have come to life as interesting characters. Which should delight the Beatles', he wrote. 'I'm not bothering to write characters for them. I shall just do all my box of tricks – SLOANE and HAL on them. After all if I repeat myself in this film it doesn't matter. Nobody who sees the film will have seen SLOANE or LOOT.' The next morning Shenson was on the phone to Orton saying that the Beatles' manager, Brian Epstein, was 'delighted' he'd do the film. Orton felt the first seductive strokes of the movie rub-down, the slap and tickle of famous names and big paydays:

'You'll be hearing either from Brian or Paul McCartney. So don't be surprised if a Beatle rings you up.' 'What an experience,' I said. 'I shall feel as nervous as I would if St Michael, or God was on the line.' 'Oh, there's not any need to be worried, Joe,' Shenson said. 'I can say, from my heart, that the boys are very respectful of talent. I mean, most respectful of anyone they feel has talent. I can really say that, Joe.'

(17 January 1967)

Movies are a dubious adventure for most writers, because they regard their work as part of the culture's permanent intellectual diet and end up being treated like flavour of the month. Orton was fascinated by power and the large public. An inveterate tease, he fancied the challenge. Orton's instinct was to woo the Beatles coyly. After waiting a week for The Call, it finally came at dinner-time on 23 January.

Epstein's adviser rang while I was eating a meal of mashed potatoes, tinned salmon and beetroot [Orton noted]. He asked if I could 'meet the boys' on Wednesday. Said I'd ring him back tomorrow to con-firm. [Orton arrived promptly the next day at Epstein's office to be faced with the screenwriter's first debilitating hazard: waiting.] After about five minutes or so a youngish man with a hair-style which was way out in 1958, short, college-boy, came up and said, '. . . I'm Brian Epstein's personal assistant' [Orton wrote]. It crossed my mind to wonder why the English have never got around to finding a per-fectly respectable word for 'boy-friend'. 'I'm afraid there's been a most awful mix-up. And all the boys' appointments have been put back an hour and a half.' I was a bit chilly in my manner after that. 'Do you want me to come back at six?' I said. 'Well, no. Couldn't we make another appointment?' 'What guarantee is there that you won't break that?' I said. 'I think you better find yourself a different writer.' This said with indifferent success, though the effect was startling. He asked me to wait a minute and went away to return with Brian Epstein himself. Somehow I'd expected something like Michael Codron. I'd imagined Epstein to be florid, Jewish, dark-haired and overbearing. Instead I was face to face with a mousey-haired, slight young man. Washed-out in a way. He had a suburban accent. I went into his office. 'Could you meet Paul and me for dinner tonight?' he said. 'We do want to have the pleasure of talking to you.' 'I've a theatre engagement tonight,' I replied, by now sulky and unhelpful. 'Could I send the car to fetch you after the show?' I didn't much relish this flim-flammery, left almost tripping over the carpet and crashing into the secretary who gave a squeal of surprise as I hurtled past her. This I never mention when re-telling the story. I always end on a note of hurt dignity.

Orton's first glimpse of the Beatles' world caught the same ludicrous contradiction in these cultural supermen: playing rebel and living posh.

Arrived in Belgravia at ten minutes to eight . . . I found Chapel Street easily. I didn't want to get there too early so I walked around for a while and came back through a nearby mews. When I got back to the house it was nearly eight o'clock. I rang the bell and an old man entered. He seemed surprised to see me. 'Is this Brian Epstein's house?' I said. 'Yes, sir,' he said, and led the way to the hall. I suddenly realised that the man was the butler. I've never seen one before . . . He took me into a room and said in a loud voice 'Mr Orton'. Everybody looked up and stood to their feet. I was introduced to one or two people. And Paul McCartney. He was just as the photographs. Only he'd grown a moustache. His hair was shorter too. He was playing the latest Beatles record 'Penny Lane'. I liked it very much. Then he played the other side – Strawberry something. I didn't like this as much. We talked intermittently. Before we went out to dinner we'd agreed to throw out the idea of setting the film in the thirties. We went down to dinner. The trusted old retainer – looking too much like a butler to be good casting – busied himself in the corner. 'The only thing I get from the theatre,' Paul M. said, 'is a sore arse.' He said LOOT was the only play he hadn't wanted to leave before the end. 'I'd've liked a bit more,' he said. We talked of the theatre. I said that compared with the pop-scene the theatre was square. 'The theatre started going downhill when Queen Victoria knighted Henry Irving,' I said. 'Too fucking respectable.' We talked of drugs, of mushrooms which give hallucinations – like L.S.D. 'The drug not the money,' I said. We talked of tattoos. And after one or two veiled references, marijuana. I said I'd smoked it in Morocco. The atmosphere relaxed a little. Dinner ended and we went upstairs again. We watched a programme on TV it had phrases in it like 'the in crowd' and 'swinging London'. There was a little scratch- ing at the door. I thought it was the old retainer, but someone got up to open the door and about five very young and pretty boys trooped in. I rather hoped this was the evening's entertainment. It wasn't, though. It was a pop group called The Easybeats. I'd seen them on TV. I liked them very much then . . . A French photographer arrived . . . He'd taken a set of new photographs of The Beatles. They wanted one to use on the record sleeve. Excellent photograph. The four Beatles look different in their moustaches. Like anarchists in

the early years of the century. After a while we went downstairs.
The Easybeats were still there. I talked to the leading Easybeat.
Feeling slightly like an Edwardian masher with a Gaiety girl.
And then I came over tired and decided to go home. I had a last
word with Paul M. 'Well,' I said, 'I'd like to do the film. There's
only one thing we've got to fix up.' 'You mean the bread?' 'Yes.'
We smiled and parted. I got a cab home. Told Kenneth all about it.
Then he got up to make a cup of tea. And we talked a little more.
And went to sleep.

(24 January 1967)

Orton looked upon *Up Against It* as a lark. His instruction to
Peggy Ramsay the next day reflected his insouciance:

'We should ask 15,000 pounds,' I said, 'and then if they beat us down,
remember no lower than 10,000. After all whether I do it or not is a
matter of indifference to me.' Peggy agreed. She said she'd ask 15 and
try to get 12 and a percentage. 'If they won't pay us 10 they can fuck
themselves,' I said. 'Of course, darling,' Peggy said.

(25 January 1967)

While the contract was being negotiated (£5,000 for the first
draft with the right to buy the script back if it were unacceptable
to the Beatles), Orton blithely continued writing. He had rummaged
through discarded manuscripts and found that *Head to Toe* gave
him the bare bones of action which he could beef up with his new
epigrammatic style. 'Might have been designed with the Beatles in
mind', he wrote after rereading the novel, pleased to discover
amidst the comic peregrinations and convoluted prose four male
characters embroiled in political assassination, guerrilla warfare,
and transvestite capering. 'In any case,' he concluded on 29 January,
'I shall enjoy writing the film.'

Orton didn't waste time. By 11 February, when he was sum-
moned to Shenson's palatial apartment for one final pep talk before
the contract was signed, the first draft of the script was almost completed. Shenson, sitting behind a cigar in a room that up to 1917

was part of the Russian Embassy, 'was most concerned to impress me that "the boys" shouldn't be made to do anything in the film that would reflect badly on them', Orton wrote, getting his first dose of the screenwriter's second debilitating hazard: the commercial compromise. 'You see,' he said, 'the kids will all imitate whatever the boys do.' I hadn't the heart to tell him that the boys, in my script, have been caught in-flagrante, become involved in dubious political activity, dressed as women, committed murder, been put in prison and committed adultery. And the script isn't finished yet. I thought it best to say nothing of my plans for the Beatles until he had a chance of reading the script. We parted at five o'clock amicably. With the contract, according to him, as good as signed. And, on my part, the film almost written.'

Orton's plans for the Beatles were more dangerous and murky than the Beatles' plans for themselves. 'We were the first working-class heroes in England to ever get anywhere without changing their accents', John Lennon explained in 1972 during a post-mortem on the Beatles in the *National Observer*. 'Changing the life style and the appearance of youth throughout the world didn't just happen – we set out to do it; we knew what we were doing.' Orton's laughter, as he half-suspected, would turn out to be too hard-edged and wild for the Beatles' image. Orton used the Beatles to deliver a barrage of startling comic ideas at odds with their benign personas. The two main characters in *Up Against It*, Ian McTurk and Christopher Low, are run out of town for their purported outrages against the living (McTurk's adultery) and the dead (Low's blowing up the town's Memorial to the Fallen). Orton's dialogue conjures up the wicked and faithless world McTurk and Low encounter, where there are no 'basic human values'.

LOW. I'm hungry and thirsty. I need help.
MRS O'SCULLAN. I'm not interested in your private life.

COATES. . . . If you're rich it doesn't matter whether you disgust

people or not. In fact I'll go as far as to say that the poor prefer the
rich to be disgusting.

THE MAYOR. Like most men in positions of trust I was engaged in
illegal activities . . .

The script teases the cosy, lustless screen rendering of romance.
'Anything worth doing is worth doing in public', McTurk observes. In their outrageousness, the characters are always comment-
ing on the absurdity of the courtly romantic setting. 'I must go',
Rowena says to McTurk, shafting him yet again in the last minutes
of the film. 'Love seems out of place in a garden in the moonlight.'
McTurk finds solace in the arms of a second woman who has
unsuccessfully pursued him throughout the film. 'My heart is
broken', he tells Patricia Drumgoole, about to propose marriage as
Orton lampoons the romantic equation of suffering with satisfaction.
'But everything else is in working order.' After their adventures,
the characters are more pragmatic about life. The marriage takes
place, a happy ending in which romantic propaganda is puckishly
inverted so the bride can have three bridegrooms. 'Just the happy
quartet', coos the photographer snapping the new marriage of
Love, Money and Lust on the steps of the church. The third husband
is a rebel leader who sees marriage as a radical act. 'Getting married
and having children is the most rebellious thing a man can do,' says
Jack Ramsay. 'It shows a disregard for the conventional bourgeois status-quo and a fine, careless anarchic sense of the absurd.'
Marriage, which institutionalizes the sexual scarcity romance
promotes, gives way in the film's final image to a vision of sexual
abundance:

> Int. Hotel bedroom. Morning. The sun streams into the room. Miss
> Drumgoole is in bed with Ramsay, McTurk and Low.
>
> MISS DRUMGOOLE. It's like a wonderful dream! I hope we have a
> happy married life!
>
> The young men kiss her. There is a struggle. Miss Drumgoole squeals
> with delight and disappears under the coverlet with her husbands.
>
> The End

'Oscar Lewenstein read *Up Against It* and liked it very much,' Orton wrote on 25 February, a day after he'd handed in his first draft. 'He thought it had a poetic quality. This is because I used all the romantic clichés – moonlight, roses, unrequited love and the Cinderella figure of the poor girl who loves him and is finally rewarded by his love in the last reel. O.L. said he liked least the scenes in the Albert Hall (with the shooting of the woman Prime Minister Lillian Corbett). This clearly because of the parody of the Kennedy assassination he doesn't think that Epstein, the Beatles or W. Shenson will opt for it.'

It was panic not poetry that the script emphasized. Orton also parodied the Sydney Street Siege. A mêlée erupts after McTurk, Low and Ramsay – enlisted as urban guerrillas – refuse to allow the Archbishop of Canterbury, who leads a procession of Lillian Corbett's mourners, into the cathedral. The Archbishop turns out to be a woman. 'I'm Princess of the Church', she says. 'Let me pass. I've some hard praying to do.' Upheaval is elevated to anarchist apocalypse in Orton's battle scene where McTurk, Low and Ramsay run their ambulance into an enemy truck and start a chain reaction of destruction from which no one emerges victorious.

Amid flames, explosions and wreckage, 'men with stretchers rescue the by now shocked, injured and well-nigh senseless McTurk, Ramsay and Low.' They are 'placed on stretchers and wrapped in blankets with the other victims of various disasters'. The dead and injured are reloaded into a larger fleet of ambulances; once again the ambulances are destroyed and 'hundreds of men with stretchers attempt to put the injured, the dying, the sick, unhappy army of victims into some sort of shape'. Nothing can diminish the panorama of suffering. Every heroic gesture turns into fiasco. Orton even produces the final abyss from which no one escapes:

... Shots are fired and the stretcher bearers collapse as badly injured as their patients. More stretcher bearers pick up the stretcher bearers. They're hit in their turn and collapse. The victims and the helpers struggle together in the mud of the battlefield. An army of ambulances moves away from the camp ... At this point, with a loud roar, the earth caves in and the ambulances, full of suffering humanity, crash into the hole which has opened up in the treacherous subsoil.

Havoc is Orton's metaphor for history: a tableau of viciousness in which to be saved from one disaster is only to be eligible for still greater violence and danger. Low, McTurk and Ramsay take their life into their own hands. 'Seeing what has happened before they decline to be helped and fight off the stretcher bearers.' The victims become victimizers in a struggle to cling to life and remain intact. A priest appears at this spectacle of carnage:

Shouts and screams from the injured. Blood pouring from bleeding wounds. On the edge of a gaping hole amid the carnage. Onto the scene steps Father Brodie, holding high the cross upon which our Lord died, accompanied by nuns and choir boys singing a hymn to the glory of immortal god.

The immensity of the contradiction floors the rebels. Low, 'struck dumb, kneels'. McTurk, overcome by despair, 'bursts into tears and sits sobbing'. Ramsay 'shrieks with maniacal laughter and begins to leap about in a kind of glee'. Orton chose the latter course. His grotesque laughter rejected the impotence of despair.

'I've just got McTurk in prison', Orton wrote on 6 February, when his hero's right to appeal had been refused on grounds of height. 'And, realize, of course, the whole script is about schizophrenia.' Like Orton, the characters teeter between optimism and disenchantment; rebellion and acceptance; male and female roles. 'Back! Back to the women. Our only hope!' pleads one character, grabbing the steering wheel of the car as McTurk and Low try to change from the all-female government troops to the male rebels. The driver replies: 'No! The men! We must go on!' Originally the split personality was crudely staged by having McTurk divided into four players who answer to the same name. But in his rewrite for Oscar Lewenstein, Orton wrote separate characters: McTurk, the nihilist; Low, the activist; and Jack Ramsay, the outrageous renegade whose tactics are 'the smear, the lie, and in extreme cases, the truth'. The characters inhabit a weird, dissociated landscape with its special menacing sense of insecurity. (The film's production plans called for a 'Max Ernst modernity' in which 'some sets have false perspectives and colour is used as a weapon'.⁹)

Up Against It flaunted Orton's new vitality, transforming the murderous into the marvellous. But Halliwell couldn't turn dread into delight. He was increasingly petrified by the awful fears that Orton remade into public pleasure. Kenneth Williams remembers dropping in on Orton and Halliwell in mid-February and finding only Halliwell at home. 'I was depressed. When I got to the flat, Halliwell answered the door. He hadn't got his toupée on and this great boiled egg came to the door, and said in a prissy voice "Yes." And I said "Hello." "Joe isn't here," Halliwell said. I said "Well, I'll come and see you." Halliwell answered "But Joe's not here, you don't want to see me." (Halliwell's terrible inferiority always came to the surface. He always believed he was only wanted because of Joe.) "Nonsense," I said. "I'd love to see you. And I can smell something cooking." "Oh, it's a bit of haddock I'm cooking for him," Halliwell said. "Oh, I love haddock," I said and walked in. "Well, there's only enough for two," he said. "Nonsense," I said. "Split the two bits in half and put an egg on top. We'll all have it!" I sensed Halliwell's inwardness and his desire not to talk, but I made him talk. I told him "It's rubbish, you answering the door like that. I like you very much." ' Halliwell had lived with self-loathing too long to believe anyone could like him.

Halliwell's identity was under such siege that every encounter was a potential danger. The slightest abrasion could send him into a fury. At the end of February, with *Up Against It* completed, Orton and Halliwell planned a holiday in Libya, for which they needed visas. Even here, Halliwell was forced to struggle for validation:

Kenneth and I made a trip to South Kensington to apply for visas to Libya. The man at the Consular section looked at my application and said, 'One pound please'. I gave him a pound and he asked me to call back on Monday. When Kenneth gave in his form and his passport, the man looked at him oddly and said, 'Will you call tomorrow morning?' . . . We went away. Kenneth making a great fuss. 'I always knew we shouldn't try to go to a country with visas! I don't intend going where I'm not wanted! . . .'

(23 February 1967)

Halliwell's instinct was always to retreat, rejecting the source of pain before it could reject him. Orton disarmed the world; but Halliwell's fear antagonized it. The threat of being invalidated on any level was so great to Halliwell that Orton had to telephone the Libyan Embassy for him the following day. 'Kenneth . . . is in such a rage that it isn't possible to get him to do anything', Orton reported to his diary. 'He has to go and see the consul tomorrow. "I can't get the photographs changed in time," Kenneth said. "It's just impossible." "Wait and see if that's what they want. They may just wish to check that you're not your own brother," I said.'[10] But the question of identity was no laughing matter to Halliwell. Any situation which rekindled his fears of 'being nobody' was always terrifying. Halliwell went to the Embassy 'very unwilling and with a long face'; he returned 'wreathed in smiles'.[11] The Embassy had only wanted to assure themselves that Halliwell, whose passport listed his job as 'free-lance writer', would write nothing about Libya. The Embassy's inefficiency over their visas filled him with a familiar foreboding:

'I had a dream last night,' Kenneth said, in a mournful voice, 'that we went to get our tickets and the plane was full.' 'I wonder you don't start chewing laurel leaves like the Delphic oracle,' I said.

(26 February 1967)

Halliwell and Orton left for Libya on 2 March. The preceding week had been especially exciting for Orton, and Halliwell longed for Orton's exclusive company away from the punishing glitter of his success. Peggy Ramsay and Oscar Lewenstein had read *Up Against It* and been fulsome in their praise. Lewenstein, who as a director of Woodfall Productions had been associated with *Tom Jones*, *A Taste of Honey*, *The Loneliness of the Long Distance Runner* and many other high-quality productions in the short-lived British cinema renaissance, thought *Up Against It* 'probably the best first draft of a screenplay I have ever read'.[12] Two days before their departure *Loot* was sold for filming, and the newspapers were ballyhooing the price the day Orton and Halliwell left the country. 'Joe Orton slipped out of the country to make a temporary home in a simple, second-class hotel in Libya', the *Evening News* reported. 'He is there not as a refugee from the £100,000 which Bernard Delfont and Arthur Lewis have paid for the screen rights to "Loot", but to work on an original film script . . .' A legend was being concocted around Orton. But Halliwell was never mentioned, never photographed, never seen. Orton's publicity exacerbated Halliwell's own terror of invisibility; and the one person whose presence had given Halliwell's life cohesion was fast becoming unreal to him. Halliwell, who sought so many 'magical' solutions to his problems, looked on their holiday as an important rapprochement. What was undertaken in hope ended in fiasco: the beginning of their end.

. . . At London Airport, K.H. came over rather stuffy, looking at the main entrance hall, crowded with people, he said, 'What extraordinary people to be at London Airport at this time in the morning'. When we went into the departure lounge he said, with relief, 'I see we've a better lot of people in here. Those out there were only visitors. They really shouldn't allow that kind of riff-raff in the Airport at all.' When I pointed out that his remarks were pretty amazing considering the circumstances, he said, 'I don't want a lot of people about in the airport I'm leaving from. It's spoiling everything'. He then went to the duty free tobacconist's and bought a hundred Sobranie cigarettes. He sat next to a Pakistani and his wife and opened the cigarette carton. A customs official appeared at his side, 'Excuse me, sir,' he said. 'Did you buy those cigarettes here?' Kenneth said he did. 'Then you're not supposed to break the seal, sir. You are infringing the regulations. I must ask you not to smoke them or they'll be confiscated.' Kenneth looked furious and embarrassed. 'Dreadful petty officials,' he muttered as the man went away. 'There's absolutely no need for all that kind of thing.' 'I told you to leave them sealed,' I said. 'If you'd allowed me to put them in your satchel like I suggested none of this would've happened,' Kenneth said very crossly. The flight was then called and we boarded the plane . . .

Idris Airport is very beautiful. For an airport. It is set among gardens and pepper trees. The main airport building is big and cool. Kenneth Halliwell says it's an aeroplane hangar left over from the war. He may be right. Outside the main building was a group of stuffy, tight-arsed English and American businessmen. 'I've never been here before,' I said to one of them. 'Can you give me the name of a good hotel?' He looked at me in a pondering sort of way. I expected him to turn on his heel and walk away. At last he said, 'Haven't you made a reservation?' 'No,' I said. 'Well, you may find it rather difficult to get into a hotel.' This brought me up sharp. I caught a glimpse of Kenneth's face looking as though he'd been pole-axed. 'Is it difficult, then?' I said. 'Yes,' the man said. 'Try the Libya Palace. And if you can't get in there I'd go to the Delmahari.' He shuffled away, uneasy; as though not wishing to be associated with such people. I called a taxi and told them to take us to the Libya Palace. The fare was four pounds.

The Libya Palace hotel is modern. It has a dim interior. A desk clerk came forward, though it took him seven or eight minutes to do so. 'I'd like two single rooms,' I said. 'Have you made a reservation,' he said, looking me up and down. 'No,' I said. 'We have no room.' He didn't say anything else and turned abruptly to a businessman and his dowdy wife who'd just arrived. I went outside and called another taxi. 'The Delmahari Hotel,' I said. 'Ask how much it's going to cost, for Christ's sake!' Kenneth said. 'What's the use?' I said. 'We've got to get there. There's no other way of doing it.' Kenneth, tight-lipped and angry, said, 'I'm not staying here. You know that, don't you? I can tell already that it's dreadful. It's everything I feared.' The Delmahari Hotel was perhaps one hundred yards away. The taxi cost ten shillings.

The Delmahari was full. 'Take him to the ship,' the desk clerk said to the taxi driver. We were led away from the hotel and back to the taxi. 'A ship!' Kenneth gave a cry of alarm. 'We'll find ourselves in Saudi Arabia branded as slaves.' 'Ship very good hotel,' the taxi-driver said. 'Hot and cold in all rooms.' He drove at a rapid rate onto a quay, stopped with a jerk, flung open the doors of the taxi and welcomed us to the T.S.S. 'CARINA' billed (on the side of the ship) as Libya's 'only floating hotel'. We paid the taxi driver and climbed the companionway.

The 'Carina' was a second or third class ex-German cruise ship. It was moored to a wharf. The town was around the ship in a half-circle. Inside the ship we found our way to the reception desk. I asked for two single rooms. 'We have no single rooms,' the manager said (he was fat, Greek or Levantine, he had dark glasses and kept them on always, even at night). 'We have only double room.' 'How much?' I said. 'Eightpound ten,' he said. 'For two?' He gave a smile and a shrug, 'I'm sorry, for one.' 'Eight pounds ten a week?' I said. 'A night.' 'I'll take a double room,' I said. The manager called a young boy to attention. The boy was fair-haired and plain in a pretty uniform. 'Take the gentlemen to 112,' he said. The boy, who didn't understand, or even care, what the manager said immediately disappeared down a stairway. We waited for ten minutes until he returned ... The page boy had parked Kenneth and I outside a cabin and left us after discovering that the cabin was already let. It took another half-hour as the manager, the page and the steward, separately and together, opened the door with a pass-key and stared in at two suitcases on the floor. After a long while they went away and left us alone in a tiny corridor outside a door marked, in fading, scratchy paint 'Herren'. 'Oh my God!' Kenneth said, rounding upon me savagely, 'look what a mess you've got us into now! Dumped on a ship in the middle of some wretched Fascist state! I'm going to faint!' I found myself saying, 'Pull yourself together! There's no need to behave badly.' 'I warned you what it would be like. No travel agency does Libya.' 'I'm not surprised,' Kenneth said. 'This is probably a brothel!' Even this would've been interesting but, as though to prove him wrong, a plum-faced matron was seen shepherding three young children down the corridor to the loo. 'This way, sir,' the manager said at my elbow, 'there's been a mistake.' Behind me Kenneth said, 'What's going to happen if they're full here? We shall be sleeping in the open.' 'Don't be ridiculous,' I said. 'I shall go to the British Consul.' 'He's probably an arab!' Kenneth said. 'That'll land us in a worse mess than ever.'

The fat manager opened the door of cabin 115 (also outside a door marked 'Herren') and showed us what we were getting for £8.10 a night . . . It was a cabin with two bunks, both already made up for the night, the sheets were spotless, the blanket obviously freshly laundered. The whole area of the cabin would've been a generous linen cupboard. 'The room also includes a shower,' said the manager rather proudly attempting to fling open the door of the shower and finding that it needed a little effort to do so. The shower was in the lavatory and so, as I later discovered, it wasn't possible to use the lavatory after a shower because the shower saturated the lavatory pan and reduced the toilet paper to a pulp. The manager went away leaving us alone.

'We could stay at the Hilton for this price!' Kenneth screamed with rage. 'I'd rather not discuss it,' I said. 'We must make the best of it.'

'We must get a plane to Malta tomorrow,' Kenneth said. 'It's bound to be horrible and English, but anything is better than the robot slaves of Esso and Shell' . . .

We strolled along an embankment into the city. Cars roared past . . . A few depressed and aged Libyans were seen at intervals under trees. It was altogether like a balmy night in Hull or Birkenhead . . . We walked back to the ship.

On board the evening was just beginning. Large numbers of English, American and German middle-class men and women (all the women seemed to be the same dyed blonde hag) were laughing in loud raucous tones. A few middle-class Libyans were strolling about. 'Wog bourgeoisie is even worse than the home product,' I said, rather wishing Kenneth was in a better mood to appreciate the remark. 'Shut up!' Kenneth said, pushing crossly past a gaggle of excited young women. 'I'm in no mood to appreciate your remarks.' We went to our cabin. I took a shower, Kenneth took his clothes off and then discovered that the curtains didn't fit properly over the windows. The window gave onto the deck and anyone strolling by could see right into the cabin. Whilst I was having a shower Kenneth discovered that it wasn't possible to open the windows more than an inch and that the ship had central heating. We were being suffocated in our cabin. 'Go and have a shower,' I said. 'It's supposed to be good for the nerves.' 'Fuck the shower!' Kenneth said. He hung a bath towel over the window to hide us from the world. 'I must have a drink of water,' he said. He then filled a glass of water from the washbasin and put an Alka Seltzer tablet into it, though as I pointed out Alka Seltzer wasn't sold as a protective against typhoid. 'It makes the water taste better, though,' Kenneth said. We both sat on our bunks sipping Alka Seltzer and listening to the bumping from the upper deck and the shrieking, laughing people pushing into the lavatories just outside our paper-thin door. 'Sleep will be impossible tonight,' Kenneth said. 'We might snatch an hour or two,' I said. 'What've they all come here for, I wonder?' The answer wasn't long in coming for a band, in the 'ballroom' just down the corridor suddenly struck up 'South of the Border' and the dancing began.

Until half-past two the next morning the band played a selection of dance tunes from the early forties. 'Put the Blame on Mame, Boys', 'Begin the Beguine', 'You'd Be So Nice To Come Home To', and 'Maria Illena'. 'It's as though they're still fighting the desert war,' I said. 'I wouldn't be surprised if Rommel suddenly appeared on deck.' I dropped off into a kind of delirium at two o'clock and woke up to hear an American woman saying, 'I'm going to the little girls', a lot of laughter and a man's voice saying, 'Me for the little boys' more laughter. More hysterical conversation from drunken gay oilmen and their drunken gay wives. Almost everything they said seemed to be in inverted commas. At the end of a hush which fell upon the ship at three o'clock, a steward knocked on the cabin next door and said, 'Your five o'clock call sir.' Kenneth and I engaged in desultory conversation until seven when we got up and dressed. We went to breakfast at eight ... We went to the travel agency at nine. We enquired if there was a plane to London. There was ... With a feeling of relief I booked two seats. The travel agent looked at our tickets. 'You came only yesterday?' he said, in surprise. 'Yes,' Kenneth said. 'The hotels are full.' The man nodded. 'The hotels are always full,' he said ...

At 2.30 we left the ship. At 3.30 we were at Idris airport. At 4.30 we waited to board the plane ...

On the way home, in the airport bus, I sat in front of a black lower-middle-class Noel Coward. He was with his fiancée and kept up a constant stream of dated badinage interspersed with outmoded forms of Imperialist thought like 'I fight with my hands', 'To use a knife is cowardly', 'I never swear in front of women', 'I always wear a tie at functions', and even 'The R.A.F. is the finest body of men in the world'. This mixed with the kind of facetious chatter that would be howled down in the fourth form. 'The depressing thing about a lot of coloured people,' Kenneth said, 'is their pathetic imitation of everything that is bad in the white races.' 'Did you hear his remarks on Communism?' I said, suddenly remembering a stretch of dialogue I'd forgotten. 'He said, "We should shoot the bastards. They are ruining the economic trade of the world".' 'What was he like?' Kenneth said. 'Oh, about thirty-five, bespectacled,' I said. 'I thought he was about seventeen,' Kenneth said. The taxi drew up at the flat and we both stumbled out – home again after a day trip to Tripoli.

(1–2 March 1967)

'I didn't see a cock the whole time – except my own and that glimpsed only briefly in a cracked mirror', Orton wrote to Kenneth Williams immediately on their return.[13] To Halliwell there was nothing funny about the trip. It was one more dismal disappointment, which sent him into a deep depression. Almost at once his body started to plague him: first the mysterious spots on his leg, then heart palpitations, then pains in his chest. Orton saw no problems with the trip. 'I hated it and came back', he explained to Peter Willes, who was aghast at the waste of £200. 'You can do that when you're rich.'[14] Orton could turn every threat into promise. His success could redeem the past. What to Halliwell was a miserable failure only enhanced Orton's celebrity. 'The publicity has been good for the play,' Orton wrote in his diary. 'The house manager tells me that the matinée was up and the evening performance was sold out except for a few seats.'[15]

The fatal pattern accelerated. 'Kenneth v. depressed. I was feeling merry', Orton wrote on 10 March. 'I'd finished cutting Entertaining Mr Sloane for Rediffusion and now have no work to do. I'm quite free. The BBC wrote asking me to do a play for their Wednesday play series. I shan't though. I don't want to do anything this year except perhaps the second draft of Up Against It and the recension of *What the Butler Saw*. If I've time on my hands at the end of the year I'd like to amuse myself by writing a bit of rubbish under an assumed name: in the nature of a joke play.'

Up Against It fizzled out quickly as a Beatles project. Orton suspected this on 7 March after Shenson found the first half of the script 'fascinating' and promised to speak to Epstein in LA about it. 'He suggested Antonioni to direct. Rubbish!' Orton could get no reply from the Beatles or Epstein about the film. The problem, Orton and Peggy Ramsay guessed, was with Epstein. 'An amateur and a fool', Orton fumed towards the end of March. 'He isn't equipped to judge the quality of a script. Probably he will never say "yes" equally hasn't the courage to say "no". A thoroughly weak, flaccid type.'

Orton was too involved in his own work to empathize with Halliwell's complaints. 'Kenneth has a pain in his chest when he doesn't take his tablets. He told me this morning', Orton wrote on 22 March. ' "They don't last eight hours", he said. "When the effect wears off the pain returns." I hope there's nothing seriously wrong. "You must go to a specialist if it doesn't get better," I said.' Squabbles started to dominate their life. On 23 March 'Kenneth H. and I went for a long trot and argued most of the way – traffic and heat aggravating the argument into a fever pitch. The argument was about Ivan the Terrible. At one point Kenneth said, "You know I'm taking these tablets. They calm me down. And you're working overtime to over-ride the effect of the tablets, aren't you." When we got home we had a cup of tea and it was smiles until bedtime.' 'Constant rowing over small things', Orton reported in his diary on 31 March about their walk on Hampstead Heath.

Their dissatisfaction with each other had begun to show: neither Orton nor Halliwell was answering the other's needs.

Kenneth has decided that what is wrong with him isn't his heart but his liver. He isn't eating. Just sipping milk every few hours. Most tiresome. I got my own lunch. There was nothing in the cupboard but spaghetti. I had spaghetti and cheese and tomatoes. As Kenneth has decided to go on a hunger strike I shall now get all my meals.

This doesn't particularly worry me, except that it means we're starting to live quite separate lives.

(2 April 1967)

On 4 April Orton learned that *Up Against It* was being returned. 'No explanation why. No criticism of the script. And apparently, Brian Epstein has no comment to make either. Fuck them.' On 10 April the *Evening Standard* reported 'the shock to Joe Orton's pride'. But two days later, Oscar Lewenstein turned Orton's disappointment to advantage by buying it for £10,000 and ten per cent of the producer's profits. Orton's almost magical resilience inevitably sank Halliwell into deeper depression. Orton's activity was a dramatic contrast to Halliwell's own constriction. Unable to compete, Halliwell instinctively tried to punish and control Orton:

Long argument with Kenneth the gist of which was 'Tell me what you want for lunch and I'll get it'. 'I'll have eggs and bacon.' 'You can't because the shops are shut.' He then began to argue over suitcases. 'I don't think we should buy new ones.' Since, as I pointed out to him, he was the one who suggested we bought new ones in the first place this rather surprised me. 'Are you going to wear your blue suit for the summer?' he said. 'No,' I said. 'Then why did you have it altered?' he said. 'If you hadn't had them altered I could've worn them.' 'But if you could wear them,' I said, 'they wouldn't've fitted me. That's why I had them altered.' 'And now they don't fit me,' he said. 'No,' I said. 'But if they'd've fitted you they wouldn't've fitted me. And as they didn't fit me I had them altered. And now I've had them altered they don't fit you.'

The knots into which Halliwell tried to twist Orton were the same painful tactics of psychic control that Orton made fun of in *What the Butler Saw*. The inspecting psychiatrist jams the mind of Geraldine Barclay, a secretary who has come for a job and finds herself certified insane:

RANCE. . . . Who was the first man in your life?
GERALDINE. My father.
RANCE. Did he assault you?

GERALDINE. No!
RANCE (*to* DR PRENTICE). She may mean 'Yes' when she says 'No'.
It's elementary feminine psychology . . .

The struggle between licence and control, between identity and invisibility, between consciousness and 'self-consciousness', is at the core of the play's desperation: the mirror-image of Orton's own struggle with Halliwell's neurotic problems. The subject of sexual and psychological exploitation which *What the Butler Saw* satirized dominated not only their lives, but also the public imagination:

Saw a poster for a film called LIBIDO MEANS LUST. It said, 'What happens when a sadistic sex-maniac falls in love!' On the way home I noticed a crit of THE DIARY OF A MADMAN which is being presented, for four weeks, at the Duchess with Nicol Williamson. I thought how fashionable madness is at the moment. The film Marat/Sade is just out. Of course it's the perennial fascination of watching lunatics. Four hundred years ago they'd have gone to Bedlam for the afternoon. Now a director and actors re-create a madhouse in a theatre. Let's look at mad people. At queer people. They have only to look in the mirrors. Kenneth H. said, 'In *What the Butler Saw* you're writing about madness.' 'Yes,' I said, 'but there isn't a lunatic in sight – just doctors and nurses.'

(14 March 1967)

'I hope I can keep up sufficient frenzy to the end of the play', Orton wrote in his diary on 24 December 1966, already halfway through *What the Butler Saw*. To simulate the schizophrenic experience Orton's plot required the kind of accelerating momentum in which at a certain speed personality starts to disintegrate. It also needed the double-binding exchanges which create suffocating psychic static. Orton typed up a long single-spaced list of exclamations and ripostes which he distributed among his characters when a situation called for a put-down or comic jolt:

The most interesting love/hate patterns it has ever been my privilege to witness.
You revolting fur-covered bitch!

And let me tell you, there is a great deal of very good chastity
in the world.
Sometimes your phraseology appals me.
You're talking like a shop-girl again!
In a pathologically elevated mood.
A word not in current use except in the vernacular.
Every sacred cow pastures in England.
Do you mind keeping your tasteless comments to yourself?
Keep the word, destroy the meaning, that has always been the
English way.
Screaming Jesus!
You shoulder-length prick!
He likes women – you know strip clubs, menstruation, mothers-in-
law.

Orton experimented with longer jokes in the same way, developing them first in a list (and sometimes in the voice of his character)
and then finding a place for the best of them when the plot war-
ranted. Many of the epigrams and laugh lines never made it into
the play; but they were kept on file to be used in future work:

I once delivered a girl child whose body was covered with sexual
openings – like a Marine's dream.

Greek paederasty was a noble ideal. I hope one day to see it practised
in this country alongside the Christian virtues of Love Thy Neighbour
and turn the other cheek.

In an age of declining faith, sir, surely it's enough for the young to
hold spiritual convictions. It's an act of pedantry to ask that they
should be the right ones.

'Hard at work on *What the Butler Saw*', Orton noted on 28
December 1966. 'I wrote a scene where Geraldine disguises herself
as an Indian nurse. Cut it though after laughing a lot. Held up the
action. And whenever anything makes me roar with laughter it's
a sure sign it must be cut out.' While working on *What the Butler
Saw* Orton paid close attention to productions of classical farces,
making sure that his own farce steered clear of the failures he saw

in others. Sardou's *Let's Get a Divorce* left him cold. 'Lots of running about, but not a single funny line. A third act that was a joke (unintentional). There wasn't a single situation of any interest. Sardou should be left where he belongs, gathering dust on the shelf of the commercial theatre.'[16] The exhilaration and impact of his jokes created an illusion of tumult, but for the jokes to register the actors had to stand still to be heard. Orton was making new demands on farce and was conscious of the delicate issue of pace. 'Last night I heard *Occupe Toi D'Amelie* on the wireless', he wrote on 27 December 1966. 'Surprisingly good. Better, by far, than that nauseating production of A FLEA IN HER EAR at the National. It has speed and managed to capture the style. At the National they gabbled the lines. Everything was taken at breakneck pace with the result that it seemed to drag. Of course the advantage of sound radio was that no idiot designer got in the way. In A FLEA IN HER EAR the sets and costumes appeared to be fantasies of a demented pervert.' Farce made the most of what Orton, quoting Shakespeare, called the theatre's 'two-hour traffic'. He preferred the vividness and astonishment of the stage to the long-winded 'two-day traffic' of the novel. Orton saw a chance for action and surprise missed in *Rosencrantz and Guildenstern Are Dead*. He admired Tom Stoppard's 'wonderful idea . . . how I wish I'd stumbled on it'. But the play disappointed him because it never seized its potential for action. 'It should've been about the futility of students – always talking, talking, talking and never doing anything. Great events, murders, adulteries, dreadful revenge happening all around them and they just talk. This is what the play should have been about but wasn't.'[17] *What the Butler Saw* attempted in its own way what Orton felt Stoppard did not. Torture, nymphomania, transvestism, incest, blackmail, bribery parade across the stage while psychoanalytic prattle twists experience into meanings all its own. 'The ugly shadow of anti-Christ stalks this house', deduces Dr Rance, hot on the trail of his case study. 'Having discovered her Father/Lover in Dr Prentice the patient replaces him in a psychological reshuffle by the archetypal Father-figure – the Devil himself . . .'

Orton fed his characters into farce's fun machine and made them bleed. Their pursuit of identity turns from the ridiculous to the murderous. Drunk, numb, bruised and bloody, they are disturbing figures who transform the landscape of farce from daydream to nightmare. Even the play's title with its evocation of Edwardian pier entertainments spoofs boulevard titillation while offering a much more unsettling spectacle to the paying customers. This reversal was the kind of mischief Orton relished. When Oscar Lewenstein later suggested teaming with Binkie Beaumont to mount *What the Butler Saw* in the West End at the Haymarket – the very bastion of escapist bourgeois entertainment – Orton was delighted.

'That'd be wonderful,' I said. 'It'd be sort of a joke even putting *What the Butler Saw* on at the Haymarket – Theatre of Perfection.' We discussed the set. 'It should be beautiful. Nothing extraordinary. A lovely set. When the curtain goes up one should feel that we're right back in the old theatre of reassurance – roses, french windows, middle-class characters . . .'

(27 July 1967)

'Why are there so many doors?' asks Dr Rance when he first stalks through the garden into Dr Prentice's clinic. 'Was the house designed by a lunatic?' Orton draws attention to the trappings of conventional farce, and then turns it to his own more serious ends. Dr Prentice's clinic, which begins as the setting for his botched seduction of the prospective secretary, Geraldine Barclay, ends as a hothouse of Freudian hyperbole and priapic pandemonium. 'Civilizations have been founded and maintained on theories which refused to obey facts', explains Dr Rance, rationalizing Miss Barclay's semi-nude presence in the clinic and Prentice's ludicrous tall story that he was attacked by her. 'As far as I'm concerned this child was unnaturally assaulted by her own father. I shall base my future actions upon that assumption.' *What the Butler Saw* satirizes analytic omniscience while making panic look like reason.

'You know what psychiatrists are like', Orton told the *Evening News* on 9 June 1967. 'They take everything you say so seriously.

Everybody is a little like psychiatrists today. They've got this enormous wish to explain everything. Religion – especially Christianity – tries to show things following a logical progression. And for all we know the whole thing may turn out to be some vast joke. There's all sorts of things that can't be explained. I don't know what we're all doing here. It all seems very ridiculous but I presume there must be a purpose.' Orton's writing gave him a sense of order and direction that Halliwell couldn't have. Like a character in Orton's farce, Halliwell was slowly going out of control and seeking medical help, which gave him psychoanalytic answers, but no cure:

Kenneth Halliwell had been to a new doctor. The doctor examined him and said he hadn't got appendicitis. He said it was nervousness and has given him tranquillizers. 'It's because your mother died when you were eleven and it was a traumatic experience. You are imagining this appendicitis out of guilt,' he said. 'Whatever are you guilty about?' I said. 'I don't know,' Kenneth said.

(14 April 1967)

What the Butler Saw is a celebration of the neurotic patterns brilliantly illuminated by Orton on stage but dismissed by him off-stage with Halliwell. Between the lines of Orton's dialogue runs the real-life terror which could not be laughed away. 'I don't want drugs', wails Mrs Prentice lurching for the whisky bottle on Prentice's desk. 'I want account taken of my sexual nature.'

If Prentice hasn't lived up to his wife's expectations, neither has she to his. Sexuality is the visible sign of a deeper inadequacy. Dr Prentice and his wife refuse to see their part in each other's problems. Instructing Geraldine to lie on the couch and think of her favourite work of fiction, Dr Prentice explains: 'My wife is a nymphomaniac. Consequently, like the Holy Grail, she's ardently sought after by young men. I married her for her money and, upon discovering her to be penniless, I attempted to throttle her. She escaped my murderous fury and I've had to live with her malice ever since.' Prentice, like Orton, is a victim of his own casual pragmatism.

In *What the Butler Saw* the air is full of legitimate demands which are never heard. As needs go unheeded, demands become more irrational, actions more outrageous.

RANCE. . . . . Were you molested by your father?
GERALDINE (*with a scream of horror*). No, no, no!
    DR RANCE *straightens up and faces* DR PRENTICE.
RANCE. The vehemence of her denials is proof positive of guilt. It's a text-book case! A man beyond innocence, a girl aching for experience. The beauty, confusion and urgency of their passion driving them on. They embark on a reckless love-affair. He finds it difficult to reconcile his guilty secret with his spiritual convictions. It preys on his mind. Sexual activity ceases. She, who basked in his love, feels anxiety at its loss. She seeks advice from her priest. The Church, true to Her ancient traditions, counsels chastity. The result – madness.

Geraldine, who is straitjacketed, sedated and shorn of most of her hair by Dr Rance in an ecstasy of analytic prognosis, wants her clothes and her identity back. So does Nick, the blackmailing pageboy who has seduced Mrs Prentice and been photographed *in flagrante delicto* with her in the linen cupboard of the Station Hotel (Mrs Prentice: 'When I gave myself to you the contract didn't include cinematic rights'). Prentice wants to salvage his reputation; and in the frantic confusion, even Dr Rance wants confirmation of his role. 'Let me cure your neurosis!' he begs Geraldine. 'It's the only thing I want out of life.' Totally self-absorbed and driven by the impetus of their own needs, nobody listens:

NICK. Have you given a thought to my predicament?
PRENTICE. No. I'm obsessed by my own.

Dr Rance is conceived as an 'inspector', the inquiring and fault-finding eye to whom everyone looks for confirmation. To Rance, life is a casebook. Under Rance's gaze, everyone in *What the Butler Saw* – even Mrs Prentice, who is in league with him against her husband's apparent malpractice – is reduced by his engulfing presence to the terrible status of nonentity. Rance tells Nick 'sternly': 'I am a representative of order, you of chaos. Unless that fact is faced I can never hope to cure you.'

Rance scrambles everyone else's picture of the world:

PRENTICE. Your interpretation of my behaviour is misplaced and erroneous. If anyone borders on lunacy it's you yourself!

RANCE. Bearing in mind your abnormality that is a normal reaction. The sane appear as strange to the mad as the mad to the sane. Remain where you are. I shall give you a capsule.

Fearing Rance's judgement, Prentice is never free to be himself. He exists in a perpetual state of 'petrified' self-consciousness. He struggles to keep his fictions in line. From the first lie about Geraldine's state of undress, he weaves a network of falsehoods in order not 'to give himself away'. But this spirals into ever-increasing mad behaviour which takes Prentice farther from the truth and from himself. Having colluded with Rance's assumption that the nude girl was not Geraldine Barclay ('She's taken my secretary's name as her "nom-de-folie" '), he has then to continue the tall story by claiming that Miss Barclay was sighted downstairs. When Rance demands to know what she was doing there, Prentice, thinking fast, answers: 'She's making white golliwogs for sale in colour-prejudice trouble spots' – an answer which from Rance's viewpoint has madness written all over it. 'These hellish white homuncules must be put out of their misery', Rance commands. 'I order you to destroy them before their baleful influence can make itself felt ... The man's a second Frankenstein.'

Prentice forgets everything but the manic needs of the moment. All his energy is exhausted in defensive manoeuvres which enslave him in impersonations intended to protect him from the judgement of others. Instead of allaying insecurity, his defences compound it. Prentice tries to hide Geraldine's dress and underwear from Mrs Prentice when she bursts into his office after her night at the Station Hotel, dressed in a fur coat and very little else:

MRS PRENTICE (in a surprised tone). What are you doing with that dress?

PRENTICE (pause). It's an old one of yours.

MRS PRENTICE. Have you taken up transvestism? I'd no idea our marriage teetered on the edge of fashion . . . Give me the dress. I shall wear it.

PRENTICE *(reluctant)*. May I have the one you're wearing in exchange?

MRS PRENTICE *(putting glass down)*. I'm not wearing a dress.

She slips off her fur coat. Under it she is dressed only in a slip. DR PRENTICE *cannot conceal his surprise.*

If he can get Miss Barclay clothed, Prentice can get her out of the clinic and resume 'being himself'. But he is labelled a transvestite when he asks again politely to borrow one of his wife's dresses: 'I find your sudden craving for women's clothing a dull and, on the whole, a rather distasteful subject.' Orton relishes Prentice's anxiety. Prentice tries to shift Geraldine's underwear, dress and shoes from sight. He never quite succeeds, and is always forced to disguise his actions in preposterous contortions when somebody catches him at it. Farce becomes a paradigm of neurotic defensiveness. Orton choreographs every move, using fear as the dynamo that drives his fun-machine:

> DR PRENTICE . . . *shakes out* GERALDINE's *underclothes, sees her shoes and stockings and picks them up.* MRS PRENTICE *enters from the hall.* DR PRENTICE *swings round, turns his back on her and walks away, bent double in an effort to conceal the clothing.*

MRS PRENTICE *(alarmed by this strange conduct)*. What's the matter? *(She approaches.)* Are you in pain?

PRENTICE *(his back to her, strangled)*. Yes. Get me a glass of water.

> MRS PRENTICE *hurries into the dispensary,* DR PRENTICE *stares about him in desperation. He sees a tall vase of roses. He removes the roses and stuffs the underclothing and one shoe into the vase. The second shoe won't go in. He pauses, perplexed. He is about to replace the roses when* MRS PRENTICE *enters carrying a glass of water.* DR PRENTICE *conceals the shoe under his coat.* MRS PRENTICE *stares. He is holding the roses. He gives a feeble smile and presents them to her with a flourish.* MRS PRENTICE *is surprised and angry.*

MRS PRENTICE. Put them back at once!

> *The shoe slips and* DR PRENTICE, *in an effort to retain it, doubles up.*

Should I call a doctor?

PRENTICE. No. I'll be all right.

MRS PRENTICE (*offering him the glass*). Here. Drink this.

DR PRENTICE *backs away, still holding the roses and the shoe.*

PRENTICE. I wonder if you'd get another glass? That one is quite the wrong shape.

MRS PRENTICE (*puzzled*). The wrong shape?

PRENTICE. Yes.

> MRS PRENTICE *stares hard at him, then goes into the dispensary.* DR PRENTICE *tries to replace the roses in the vase. They won't go in. He picks up a pair of scissors from his desk and cuts the stalks down to within an inch or so of the heads. He puts the roses into the vase and wraps the stalks in his handkerchief and puts it into his pocket. He looks for somewhere to conceal the second shoe. He gets on his knees and shoves the shoe between the space on top of the books on the lower shelf of the bookcase.* MRS PRENTICE *enters carrying another glass. She stops and stares.*

MRS PRENTICE. What are you doing now?

PRENTICE (*lifting his hands*). Praying.

Later, Mrs Prentice discovers the hidden shoe. She reports what she's found and seen to Dr Rance. From her viewpoint, she's telling the truth. Rance confronts Prentice: 'Are you in the habit of wearing women's footwear?' In hysterical desperation, the impersonation takes over Prentice. He answers: 'My private life is my own. Society must not be too harsh in its judgements.' Once begun, each falsehood compounds the need to continue the lie or face even greater humiliation. The confusion of identities is not just the traditional change of clothes, but an upheaval of consciousness where the dizzying manoeuvres and counteractions become a stage picture of the mind in retreat:

GERALDINE. We must tell the truth!

PRENTICE. That's a thoroughly defeatist attitude. (*He bundles her behind the curtain.*)

In *What the Butler Saw*, Orton's laughter dramatized the predicament it revenged: the process by which identity is discounted. Geraldine Barclay, like Halliwell, is a 'secretary' who has lost her identity. From her point of view (as from Halliwell's; he voiced the paranoid idea to his doctor), Geraldine's identity is literally stolen from her. Both Prentice and Rance refuse to admit her existence. She is cancelled out; and she becomes literally a non-entity – 'a non-existent *thing*'.

Prentice, of course, knows the truth, but for practical reasons can't tell it. In the same way, Orton knew how much Halliwell had done for him but he would never acknowledge him in public. 'Halliwell claimed that he influenced Orton and helped him in a very basic way', Dr Ismay said. '*But nobody knew.*' Like Halliwell, whose talents by Orton's admission were real but 'hidden', Geraldine's real self is manoeuvred into a position of invisibility. On stage Orton turns the anxiety of being discounted into a painfully funny and haunting situation. Geraldine can't be seen or make herself seen by the others. Despite the fact that Geraldine Barclay is flesh and blood under Rance's nose, his conviction that she is someone else of no particular importance makes it impossible for him to take her into account. 'Identity', R. D. Laing reminds us, 'requires the existence of another by whom one is known.'[18] Geraldine, like Halliwell, is hidden from view by forces outside her control. No one claims to know her.

GERALDINE. I'm Geraldine Barclay. Looking for part-time secretarial work. I've been certified insane.

RANCE (*to* MRS PRENTICE). Ignore these random reflections. They're an essential factor in the patient's condition.

Prentice sees a way to escape. He asks Nick to undress. 'I want you to impersonate my secretary. Her name is Geraldine Barclay. It will solve all our problems if you agree to my request.' Nick, who has returned Mrs Prentice's wig and dress along with the compromising negatives of their caper, becomes Geraldine Barclay. And Geraldine, already with her hair cropped short by Dr Rance, vanishes into the personality and clothes of Nicholas Beckett. Nick and Geraldine speak and act like their opposite sex. When these identities are threatened, the characters split again and proliferate.

Geraldine becomes Gerald Barclay. Nicholas Beckett, dressed in the drugged Sergeant Match's policeman's outfit, impersonates his brother on the police force in order to arrest himself and so be extricated from the proceedings. Orton makes a spectacle of their chaotic nonentity. Having engineered the hallucinatory effect, he unleashes its fragmentation on Mrs Prentice:

> NICK *hurries into the hall.* DR PRENTICE *hurries into the dispensary.* MRS PRENTICE *enters from the ward.* NICK *re-enters from the hall wearing only underpants and the helmet. Upon seeing him* MRS PRENTICE *shrieks and backs away.* NICK *runs into the garden.*
> MRS PRENTICE (*at the desk, weakly*). Oh, this place is like a madhouse!
> DR RANCE *enters from the ward.* MRS PRENTICE *turns upon him, wildly.*
> You must help me, doctor! I keep seeing naked men.
> RANCE (*pause*). When did these delusions start?
> MRS PRENTICE. They're not delusions. They're real.
> RANCE (*with a bray of laughter*). Everyone who suffers from hallucinations imagines they are real . . .

Like the others, Mrs Prentice finds herself on the verge of collapse. Her experience is continually invalidated by Dr Rance's explanations. After a flurry of half-naked bodies clutching wounded limbs and scraps of clothes again bolt across her path scurrying for safety, Mrs Prentice throws herself hysterically into the arms of Dr Rance as he re-enters the room: 'Doctor, doctor! The world is full of naked men running in all directions!' And it is.

Momentum, which Orton could never quite master in *Loot*, builds masterfully in *What the Butler Saw*. Tumult is created not only by a brilliant traffic plan, but by the brilliant play of language whose reversals send each character rebounding from scene to scene in crazed pursuit of reality. The combined velocity catches all the characters in its slipstream:

> GERALDINE. I'm not a patient. I'm telling the truth.
> RANCE. It's much too late to tell the truth.

As *What the Butler Saw* speeds up, reality for the characters becomes more frantic and violent. Hysteria threatens and shrinks their world. They are at first confused, then numb, and finally pushed in panic to the brink of insanity. The centrifugal force of events impels the characters to cling to their defences. This, in turn, creates the hilarious and hideous spectacle of people literally being 'driven out of their mind'. Act 1 ends with Sergeant Match discovering Geraldine, dressed in Nick's page-boy gear, cringing behind the curtain: 'I want a word with you, my lad.' The terror of being denied is raised to a new pitch; and the stage direction reads: 'A siren begins to wail'. Act 2 begins with Geraldine wanting to be arrested and confessing what has happened. Since she's dressed as a boy, her account of Prentice's attack is immediately misconstrued by Sergeant Match as a homosexual act. Prentice refers to Geraldine as 'she'; but Geraldine, who can be arrested only as Nicholas Beckett, must stick to her male disguise:

RANCE. . . . (*He advances on* GERALDINE.) Do you think of yourself as a girl?

GERALDINE. No.

RANCE. Why not?

GERALDINE. I'm a boy.

RANCE (*kindly*). Do you have the evidence about you?

GERALDINE (*her eyes flashing an appeal to* DR PRENTICE). I must be a boy. I like girls.

DR RANCE *stops and wrinkles his brow, puzzled.*

RANCE (*aside, to* DR PRENTICE). I can't quite follow the reasoning there.

PRENTICE. Many men imagine that a preference for women is, *ipso facto*, a proof of virility.

RANCE (*nodding, sagely*). Someone should really write a book on these folk myths. (*To* GERALDINE.) Take your trousers down. I'll tell you which sex you belong to.

GERALDINE (*backing away*). I'd rather not know!

RANCE. You wish to remain in ignorance?

GERALDINE. Yes.

RANCE. I can't encourage you in such a self-indulgent attitude. You must face facts like the rest of us.

Geraldine's predicament displaces in laughter the schizoid bind of the homosexual from which Orton tried to extricate himself. Geraldine is defined by other people's definitions of her sexuality. She is forced to live up to their unreal expectations. The situation is a recipe for madness which Orton had been trying to clarify since 1961 in *Head to Toe*. Where *Entertaining Mr Sloane* aspired, in Orton's words, 'to break down all sexual compartments',[19] the wit in *What the Butler Saw* bombards conventional sexual attitudes while its situations dramatized society's compulsion to categorize. Under the onslaught of Rance's labels, Geraldine quickly becomes mystified about herself and loses a sense of her physical identity:

> GERALDINE, *unable to stand the ordeal any longer, cries out to* DR PRENTICE *in anguish.*
> GERALDINE. I can't go on, doctor! I must tell the truth. (*To* DR RANCE.) I'm not a boy! I'm a girl!
> RANCE (*to* DR PRENTICE). Excellent. A confession at last. He wishes us to believe he's a girl in order to minimize the feelings of guilt after homosexual intercourse.
> GERALDINE (*wild-eyed, desperate*). I pretended to be a boy. I did it to help Dr Prentice.
> RANCE. How does it help a man if a girl pretends to be a boy?
> GERALDINE. Wives are angry if they find their husbands have undressed and seduced a girl.
> RANCE. But boys are fair game? I doubt whether your very personal view of Society would go unchallenged.
> *Provoked beyond endurance,* GERALDINE *flings herself into* DR RANCE's *arms and cries hysterically.*
> GERALDINE. Undress me then, doctor! Do whatever you like only prove that I'm a girl.

In the confusion, the characters no longer feel real. They lose a sense of being in their bodies. Nick and Geraldine can no longer recognize each other's gender:

NICK. Why is he wearing my uniform?
PRENTICE. He isn't a boy. He's a girl.
GERALDINE. Why is she wearing my shoes?
PRENTICE. She isn't a girl. She's a boy. (*Pouring whisky*.) Oh, if I
  live to be ninety, I'll never again attempt sexual intercourse . . .

The characters are not only disguised, they feel disembodied. In
this wild game of hide and seek, people appear to each other as
phantoms:

> NICK *supports himself on the desk and stares at the sobbing* MRS
> PRENTICE.
> NICK (*to* GERALDINE). Is she mad?
> GERALDINE. She thinks she is. She imagines you're a figment of her
>   imagination.
> NICK (*to* MRS PRENTICE, *nodding to* GERALDINE). She can see me.
>   Doesn't that prove I'm real?
> MRS PRENTICE. No. She's mad.
> NICK. If you think I'm a phantom of your subconscious you must
>   be mad.
> MRS PRENTICE (*with a hysterical shriek*). I am mad!

Caught in this web of 'mistaken identities', the characters function frantically but at an increasing distance from themselves.
'What have you done with Geraldine Barclay?' Rance asks Prentice, suspecting he's killed her and judging him 'a transvestite,
fetishist, bi-sexual murderer' displaying 'considerable deviation
overlap'. Geraldine 'feebly' replies: 'I'm here.' The timbre of her
voice indicates her uncertainty. No one in the play is certain of
being *here*. Nick: 'If the pain is real I must be real.' Mrs Prentice:
'Is the blood real?' Dr Prentice: 'I've been too long among the
mad to know what sanity is.' Since their inner world has been tor-
tured into such insecurity, the characters grope for validation
from the outside world, whose messenger is its official inspector,
Dr Rance. However, he refuses to 'get involved in metaphysical
speculation' about Nick's or anybody else's identity. But to the
characters, the establishing of their reality is now a matter of psychic

life or death. Each attempts to escape the terror of nonentity, which draws them deeper into it.

Halliwell was caught in the very psychic dilemma Orton dramatized. Like the characters, Halliwell found himself stalemated. No matter how hard he tried, he couldn't get anywhere. His future was the result of the present, the present was the result of the past and the past was unalterable. As the TV producer at Peter Willes's party told him, he was a 'middle-aged nonentity'. Orton had been part of Halliwell's defence; but Orton's success and growing independence threatened all that. Without him, any sense of direction or purpose was lost. When they were still writing together, Halliwell too had tried to find a form for his anger and turn his murderous instincts into fiction. Donelly in *The Boy Hairdresser* dreams of a peace from pain and one last laugh on the emptiness in himself and the society that helped to create it. 'He lacked the courage to die and the courage to live. He wanted a sign. Any excuse, O Lord, any excuse.' Donelly finds his excuse when his friend is murdered. 'Suicide', Donelly thinks to himself, 'is an insult to the body; it is self-hatred, which dries up energy and makes it infertile. He would be fixed forever in a dead and withered sterility. And when time ceases, will there be nothing to know but the follies and discontentments of the past.' Halliwell's life hadn't changed substantially since that self-portrait was written in 1960. 'His aloneness', as they had written of Donelly, 'was vast about him.' Murder was the perverse solution Halliwell had predicted for himself in fantasy and which came to pass. For Halliwell, as for Donelly, murder seemed to be the only way of making his presence felt, of proving to the world and Orton and himself that he could act. And that he mattered.

Annihilation as a desperate remedy for impending chaos is an idea that *What the Butler Saw* also tests when Prentice pulls a gun on Rance and threatens murder. Each declares the other mad; each desperately tries to force life to submit to his view of it:

PRENTICE (*waving his gun*). Stay where you are, doctor! Your conduct today has been a model of official irresponsibility and bloody-mindedness. I'm going to certify you.

RANCE (*quietly, with dignity*). No. I am going to certify you.

PRENTICE. I have the weapon. You have the choice. What is it to be? Either madness or death?

RANCE. Neither of your alternatives would enable me to continue to be employed by Her Majesty's Government.

PRENTICE. That isn't true. The higher reaches of the civil service are recruited entirely from corpses or madmen. Press the alarm!

DR RANCE *goes to the wall and presses the alarm. A siren wails. Metal grilles fall over each of the doors. The lights go out. The siren wails to a stop. The room is lit only by the glare of a bloody sunset shining through the trees in the garden.*

An overloading of the circuit! We're trapped.

The bars are a stunning image of emotional stalemate. They clang down with an impressive thud. The sound makes the metaphor terrifying and funny. The infernal glare of the 'bloody sunset' surrounds the characters' frantic groping to get free. Orton added this visual evocation of a living hell in July 1967, when life with Halliwell was becoming intolerable. The tantrums, the abuse, the threats of death, the whole melodramatic performance of depression were Halliwell's pleas for pity and affection. Orton was unmoved (Rance: 'Lunatics are melodramatic. The subtleties of drama are wasted on them'). The trap into which Rance and Prentice fall had snared Orton and Halliwell. Fearing engulfment, identities vied for autonomy. The situation, as Orton knew, was as painful as it was ludicrous.

The cage is the crucial image in *What the Butler Saw*. The farceur, as Eric Bentley says, 'sees man as hardly higher than the apes'.[20] Behind the bars in *What the Butler Saw*, the characters scurry for safety. Rance disarms Prentice ('I'll have you in a jacket within the hour. It's a hat trick!') and proceeds to reminisce about how he 'once put a whole family into a communal straitjacket'. With the human zoo whimpering behind him, Rance depicts himself as the Frank Buck of the insane: 'It was my own family, you see. I've a picture of the scene at home. My foot placed squarely upon my father's head. I sent it to Sigmund Freud and had a charming postcard in reply.'

When the cage descends in *What the Butler Saw*, all the boundaries and personalities have broken down. The nightmare of disorder is soon transformed into a fairytale of harmony. All the characters – even the statue of Sir Winston Churchill – are made whole. Geraldine reports to Dr Prentice the loss of her 'lucky elephant charm'. Nick then produces a similar charm. 'Oh, my heart is beating like a wild thing!' exclaims Mrs Prentice, fitting the two pieces of jewellery together and showing Nick and Geraldine that it makes a brooch – the very piece of jewellery she broke in half and gave to the illegitimate twins she was forced to abandon after being raped as a chambermaid in the Station Hotel during the war. 'It was impossible for me to keep them – I was by then engaged to be married to a promising young psychiatrist.' The hilarity of Mrs Prentice's revelation is topped by Dr Prentice. He tells them the inscriptions on the brooch and claims paternity!

PRENTICE. . . . I haven't seen it since I pressed it into the hand of a chambermaid whom I debauched shortly before my marriage.
MRS PRENTICE (*with a cry of recognition*). I understand now why you suggested that we spend our wedding night in a linen cupboard!
PRENTICE. I wished to recreate a moment that was very precious to me. If you'd given in to my request our marriage would never have foundered.
MRS PRENTICE. From this time on we'll never make love except in a linen cupboard. It's the least I can do after the years of suffering I've caused you!

'The ending works as "all is forgiven" – just as in the later Shakespear plays,' Orton wrote after rereading the play on 16 July 1967. The situation also echoes *The Importance of Being Earnest* and the baby left in the handbag at Victoria Station cloakroom. In the working out of the elaborate plot-points for Orton's happy ending, the audience momentarily forgets the implications of this harmony.

Rance brings it into focus. Rance is 'wild with delight' – not at the spectacle of human happiness but at the thought that his theory has been proved right: 'If you are this child's father . . . she *is* the victim of an incestuous assault!' Up to this point, Rance's analysis has been a fiction that twists every scrap of information into a narrative fit for a best-selling book he wants to write ('A beautiful but neurotic girl has influenced the doctor to sacrifice a white virgin to propitiate the dark gods of unreason . . .'). Fiction turns out to be fact. Mrs Prentice has also been attacked by Nick. And so Rance has a bonus of double incest for his book. He can hardly contain himself. Joyously, he embraces his case studies. 'Double incest is even more likely to produce a best-seller than murder – and this is how it should be for love *must* bring greater joy than violence.' Dr and Mrs Prentice's suffering and outrageousness have their roots in sexual guilt; in fact, the whole farce is based on covering up sexual guilt. Now the characters are magically redeemed from it. The scene builds to an exhilarating image of unity and guiltless transcendence. 'Everyone embraces one another', says the stage direction. And then, 'in a great blaze of glory', the rope ladder drops through the sky-light. The beleaguered *deus ex machina*, Sergeant Match – wearing a torn leopard-spotted dress and bleeding – clambers down. 'We're approaching what our racier novelists term "the climax" ', says Dr Rance, as Orton puns on the Greek word for ladder.

At the finale, the phallus of Sir Winston Churchill is discovered and unveiled. The comic orgy creates new fertility, and Sergeant Match 'holds up' a symbol of fertility, 'a section from a larger than life-sized bronze statue'. The penis, symbol of comedy's disruptive freedom and unrelenting sexual mischief, is waved by Sergeant Match over the proceedings like a magic wand. In what is perhaps the purest expression of the antic spirit in modern theatre, the play conjures a kind of halo around Sergeant Match, whose leopard-skin dress signifies Dionysus and who clutches in his hand the emblem of polymorphous perversity. 'The dying sunlight from the garden and the blaze from above gild Sergeant Match as he holds high the nation's heritage.' Although there was no Lord Chamberlain to censor the play in 1969, Orton's phallic fun was edited out by Sir Ralph Richardson, who turned the missing part of Sir Winston Churchill into a cigar. The change found its way into the published script (and was restored only in Lindsay Anderson's production in 1975). What was intended as one final outlandish image of triumphant stage anarchy became merely a giggle.

'Let us put our clothes on and face the world.' The play's last command is given by Prentice, the man who is responsible for getting the characters undressed. The line was reassigned to Sir Ralph Richardson; and so, in the published text, Rance has the last word. This spoils the symmetry of Orton's farce. Having brought one cover-up to a close, Prentice initiates another by getting Sergeant Match to agree to keep the 'remarkable peccadilloes' out of the paper. 'I'm glad you don't despise tradition', Prentice tells Match. Prentice has learned no moral lesson. Life is returned to 'normal', and the cycle of social hypocrisy begins again. The clothes which throughout the play are an active part of this social disguise are once again picked up by the characters. Soon, the clothes will impose on each of them a style and sexual role which farce, as a celebration of formlessness, momentarily breaks down. Clothes are part of the magical invulnerability they all seek, extensions of the psychic armour they will adopt to keep their cravings and confusions hidden from the public and themselves. This yearning to transcend the body and its demands is as brutalizing as it is profound. And the final stage picture makes this contradiction brilliantly clear: 'They pick up their clothes and weary, bleeding, drugged and drunk, climb the rope ladder into the blazing light.'

In the first production, which opened posthumously at the Queen's Theatre in London on 5 March 1969, the cage was the most grossly mismanaged moment of a notorious production. Where Orton had called for bars over 'each window', the West End director, Robert Chetwyn, lowered iron bars like a curtain across the proscenium. The bars had to be cranked down. Instead of descending with a shocking clatter, they creaked (like the rest of the production) into place. H. M. Tennent's all-star cast of Coral Browne, Julia Foster, Stanley Baxter, and Sir Ralph Richardson had to perform the last fifteen minutes of the play separated from the audience by an iron grid. The effect was puzzling and disastrous. At the back of Hutchinson Scott's set was a revolving door leading to the dispensary, inexplicable in a doctor's office. On the other side, the all-important second door leading to the hall was almost out of sight-line, and meant that the actors had to make their entrances in profile. Sir Ralph Richardson as Rance handled this problem by not coming through the hall door even when the script called for it. 'He came through the swing door,' Coral Browne recalls, 'which confused an audience and made it seem like he'd come from outer space.'

Sir Ralph, an august and lovably eccentric actor, was totally lost in the whirlwind of Orton's language. He had memorized the script, as was his custom, by writing it out on large music sheets which he put on a music stand. 'He learned it in rhythm and turned over each page as if it were a musical score,' Coral Browne explains. 'Sometimes it was difficult for him to learn because he had no idea of what the words meant. He couldn't get nymphomaniac right because I don't think he'd heard of one of those. He would refer to it as "nymphromaniac". When he had one of those long speeches with words like "transvestite" or "nymphomaniac", he was hopelessly at sea. He'd learned the rhythm of Orton but not all the words. And when he'd dry, he'd continue on saying "Di-da-di-da-di-da-di-da". Nobody in the audience seemed to take any notice.' When Peggy Ramsay was sent to Brighton to assess the production a week before its opening in the West End, her verdict was depressing. She compared it to the first production of *Loot*, 'all prose and face-pulling' . . . 'The actors aren't enjoying or expanding or feeling any zest in their parts whatsoever; most particularly Sir Ralph. Sir Ralph just seemed quite frozen in Act One . . . In Act Two, he is much better but then nobody in the cast is enjoying the play, which never flows, and which doesn't seem to have any fun about it. To me it simply struck a chill.' In Brighton, Sir Ralph found himself vociferously attacked for being in *What the Butler Saw*. 'There were old ladies in the audience not merely tearing up their programmes, but jumping up and down on them out of sheer hatred,' Stanley Baxter remembers. 'Even the house manager had to leave town.' Richardson answered every one of his letters of complaint by hand. 'Ralph got terribly, terribly depressed. He'd turned down the play a few times before finally accepting it, and he thought he'd made a terrible mistake taking part in what he came to regard as a dirty play.' Sir Ralph's delivery reflected his apprehension, as Hilary Spurling so aptly observed: 'Orton used English as she is actually spoke. But not, of course, as she is spoke at H. M. Tennents. The discrepancy is most glaring in Sir Ralph Richardson's extraordinary chanting – as though the text had been delivered to him in the form of church responses: a protective mannerism adopted, presumably, on the grounds that any close scrutiny of the meaning of these lines might well reveal disturbing implications.'[21]

Orton had discussed the choice of Sir Ralph Richardson as the manic, sharp-tongued Dr Rance with Lewenstein. 'Oscar thought of Ralph Richardson as Dr Rance,' he reported on 27 July 1967, after discussing production plans with Lewenstein on the way to Brighton for their notorious weekend. 'I'm not sure. Although I admire Richardson I'd say he was a good ten years too old for the part. And he isn't particularly noted for his comic acting. I'd like Alistair Sim. Oscar wasn't too keen. Both Kenneth and I thought Oscar misguided in suggesting Richardson. But I didn't feel inclined to argue till later.'[22] Richardson, and the rest of the star-studded cast, added an aura of respectability to Orton. 'Watching these actors is like watching cook and nanny – butler too for that matter – floundering with a vague sense of impropriety in what they dimly take to be some nursery naughtiness on the part of the young master', Hilary Spurling wrote. 'Their bland, ponderous gambolling is especially bizarre with, in this case, a young master so slippy on his feet, and one whose "naughtiness" is rather more outrageous than this fond cast envisage. So that, while they appear to feel the whole thing is plainly beneath them, it is also, for the most part, plainly quite beyond them.'

While the English muted the text, the Americans mutilated it. They cut the play's central images of death and rebirth: the cage, the blood, the penis and the rope ladder. Orton destroyed the boulevard safety of farce, only to have the Americans restore it in a campy, sloppy Off-Broadway production which the critics characterized as 'enchanting', 'sunny', 'disarming' and 'friendly'. Typically, the American commercial theatre had devoured Orton without digesting him. The production was a commercial success and an artistic disaster. *What the Butler Saw* was voted best foreign play of the year in the *Village Voice* 'Obie' Awards.

'It's no good making a show of affronting the middle-classes and then being surprised if your enemies retaliate in a nasty way,' Orton wrote in March 1967. 'That's what enemies do.'[23] On the opening night in the West End of *What the Butler Saw*, Orton's enemies retaliated. At the beginning of the second act, someone in the gallery screamed at Sir Ralph Richardson 'Give back your knighthood!' Shouts of 'Filth!', 'Rubbish!', 'Find another play!', 'Take it off!' bombarded the actors as they struggled bravely through the lines. 'At first I thought it was a drunk or someone mentally deranged. Then it became clear that it was militant hate that had been organized. An actor can feel it in his pores', Stanley Baxter who played Dr Prentice, says. 'It's the first time it ever happened to me. The first time for Sir Ralph, too. It was a battle royal. The anger really came through at the curtain calls. The gallery wanted to jump on the stage and kill us all. The occasion had the exhilaration of a fight. The auditorium was divided. The gods hating us and the rest on our side. But the gods made enough noise to destroy it. We tried to get the good lines in between the barracking. But, of course, the first-night audience in that atmosphere got no idea of what the second act was all about.'

DEAD PLAYWRIGHT BOOED BY GALLERY bannered the *Sun*. The history of theatre is the history of first nights, and no first night in the sixties was more volcanic than that of *What the Butler Saw*. The production and the premiere were a shambles. Critics mistook the flaws in the production for limitations in the script, and Orton's best work became the most grossly misunderstood and under-rated. 'The misjudgement of *What the Butler Saw* was truly reprehensible', Charles Marowitz wrote in *Confessions of a Counterfeit Critic*. Harold Hobson, who later in the *Sunday Times* described *What the Butler Saw* as 'a wholly unacceptable exploitation of sexual perversion',[24] smugly ignored the play in his initial review and used the space to portray Orton as the Devil's theatrical henchman. 'Gradually,' he wrote in the *Christian Science Monitor*, 'Orton's terrible obsession with perversion, which is regarded as having brought his life to an end and choked his very high talent, poisons the atmosphere of the play. And what should have been a piece of gaily irresponsible nonsense becomes impregnated with evil.'[25] Only Frank Marcus in the *Sunday Telegraph* appreciated Orton's achievement. Under the headline 'A CLASSIC IS BORN', he wrote: '*What the Butler Saw* will live to be accepted as a comedy classic of English literature'.[26] Not until Lindsay Anderson's brilliant revival of *What the Butler Saw* at the Royal Court in 1975 would the play's reputation be firmly established.

'I'd like to write a play as good as *The Importance of Being Earnest*', Orton said in 1966 when asked about his 'ultimate aims'. 'I admire Wilde's work but not his life, it is an appalling life. Unlike Wilde, I think you should put your genius into your work, not into your life,' he said.[27] On stage, monstrous dreams were conquered by climbing out of the chaos. In life, Orton never made it because his genius *did* go into his work, and Halliwell, the man who made it all possible, was neglected.

'How did you kill your wife? In the authorized version', Caulfield asks Pringle in an early draft of *Funeral Games*. Pringle replies 'I hit her with a hammer.' Orton had imagined his ending not only in fiction but in life. On 27 June 1967 – the day Halliwell first took aim at Orton's head – Orton had gone to a suburb of Tangier to visit the home of one of his boy-friends:

The house was lit by oil lamps . . . on the wall there was a telephone and in the second bedroom was an extension. The bedroom with the telephone extension belonged to the brother . . . Larbi suddenly produced a gun and pointed it at me. I held up my hands. 'I kill you,' Larbi shouted wildly. We all laughed as he pulled the trigger. I had the feeling that no writer with an eye for the ironic could resist having the playwright of promise falling dead beside the telephone extension.

But later in that afternoon, in the midst of a quarrel with Halliwell, Orton would survive the eerie foreshadowing of his death:

Kenneth anxious to sell his share of the boy said, 'Yes, he's very good in bed, and he'll do anything'. 'How do you know,' I said. 'You've asked him to do so little.' Kenneth said, 'Oh all boys will do anything.' 'They won't,' I said. 'There's lots of things they won't do.' It was very irritating to be told by someone who likes being masturbated that the boys 'will do anything'. 'You said yourself that he wouldn't take it. It was your excuse for having him in the first place.' Kenneth became violently angry shortly after this and attacked me, hitting me about the head and knocking my pen from my hand . . . I got back to the flat about 9.45. Kenneth was lying in his bed in a towel dressing gown, looking tight-lipped, I realized that it was no good speaking to him, the 'sore' would come sooner or later. I'd just settled down for the night when the door opened and Kenneth entered. I was selfish, I couldn't bear not to be the centre of attention, I was continually sneering at him for only wishing to be masturbated while I was 'virile' in fucking boys. 'I saw you in Nigel's car,' he said, 'and I've never seen you at a distance before. I thought what a long-nosed ponce.' The holiday had been too perfect. I was determined to spoil it somehow. 'And when we get back to London,' he said, 'we're finished. This is the end!' I had heard this so often. 'I wonder you didn't add "I'm going back to Mother!" ' I said wearily. 'That's the kind of line which makes your plays ultimately worthless,' he said. It went on and on until I put the light out. He slammed the door and went to bed.

Six weeks later, Orton was dead.

.   .   .   .   .

Douglas Orton identified his brother; and Peggy Ramsay identified Halliwell. 'It was extraordinary to see Kenneth. They do it so exquisitely. Spotlit. He looked like a Roman Emperor – relaxed, noble, serene. I looked hard and felt nothing.'

'Is this the 2.30 or the 2.45?' asked the attendant when the first of Orton's funeral party arrived at the West Chapel of Golders Green Crematorium on 18 August. Peter Willes arranged the service: and the aura of sanctimonious fiasco which Orton relished in life went with him to the grave. None of the two dozen mourners stood as the coffin, draped in maroon, was carried into the red-brick chapel and down the aisle to the tape-recorded music of the Beatles' *A Day In the Life*:

> I read the news today, oh boy
> About a man who made the grade . . .

The song was Orton's favourite. But the psychedelic references had been spliced out, and the sound was barely audible. Harold Pinter read Marion Lochhead's 'Nox Est Perpetua'.[28] Donald Pleasence read his own poem, 'Hilarium Memoriam J.O.', which began:

> Some met together when he died
> Not in the name of any god
> But in his name
> Whom they lost to the coffin,
> The box which caused him endless mirth,
> His lesson – which he could not read again
> Hilarity in death.

Orton's coffin was propped on a conveyor belt in front of the small bronze crematorium door. It was a surreal scene, made all the more macabre by being totally cosmetic. The door was merely a theatrical exit since the coffin was removed and cremated elsewhere after the service. At the conclusion of the reading, the conveyor rollers began to turn and Orton's coffin lurched slowly towards the door, which opened, by remote control, to receive it. The service was over in fifteen minutes. A professionally lugubrious attendant walked across the black and white marble altar floor and opened the doors to the Arcade. There, beside a small iron stand holding a handwritten card saying 'Floral Tributes for Mr Joe Orton', seventy wreaths were spread out on the flagstone.

Halliwell had been cremated at Enfield in Middlesex the previous day. Only Peggy Ramsay and three Halliwell relatives attended his funeral. One of them suggested that Halliwell's ashes be mixed with Orton's. Peggy Ramsay asked Douglas Orton. 'Well,' he said, agreeing. 'As long as nobody hears about it in Leicester.'

The ashes were mixed and scattered in the Golders Green 'Garden of Remembrance'. Their deaths confirmed the vision of Orton's comedy: reality is the ultimate outrage. Their epitaph was Orton's plays – a heritage of laughter created out of a lifetime's hunger for revenge.

NOTES

CHAPTER I JOKERS ARE WILD

1. See Harold Hobson, *Christian Science Monitor*, 19 March 1969; Benedict Nightingale, *New Statesman*, 18 July 1975.
2. Kenneth Halliwell to Peggy Ramsay, 3 October 1966.
3. Peggy Ramsay to Halliwell, 28 September 1966.
4. As quoted in *The Times*, 19 August 1967.
5. Halliwell to Kathleen O'Brien, 3 August 1950.
6. *Diary*, 9 March 1966.
7. Halliwell to Peggy Ramsay, 6 May 1967.
8. Ackerley, *My Father and Myself*, London: Bodley Head, 1968, p. 140.
9. Orton to Kenneth Williams, 27 May 1967.
10. Orton interview with Alan Brien, BBC Radio, 14 July 1964; transmitted 28 July 1964.
11. 'This is a story of an eruption, an explosion, an outburst . . . of inspiration', Orton wrote to Lindsay Anderson in August 1964 in an outline for what would become *The Erpingham Camp*. 'A representative group of sturdy, honest English folk, respectably pleasuring themselves at an August Holiday Camp, find themselves subjected to the influence of an intense, demonic leader. Their conventional habits – which anyway are more skin-deep than is generally supposed – are cast aside; they feel liberation; they abandon themselves under the tutelage of Don [Dionysus] to impulse . . . Propriety, in the person of the dubious Manager of the Camp, rashly attempts to intrude and to veto. But the forces of impulse are too strong; and catastrophe can be the only result . . .'
12. Although Pentheus, 'the man of suffering', persecuted Dionysus,

he was also, as his name reveals, doomed from the beginning to Dionysian suffering. The leopard-spotted dress on Sergeant Match evokes this. Dionysus had a half-female character symbolized by his long robes and almost hermaphroditic body. According to Karl Kerenyi in *The Gods of the Greeks*, 'when last heard from, Dionysos and his triumphal procession had conquered India – even more exotic animals appearing in his train, which even in earlier times had included great beasts of prey – lions, leopards, panthers – all of them tamed by wine.'

13. *Thus Spake Zarathustra*.

14. Orton, *Head to Toe* (1961), London: Anthony Blond, 1971, p. 149.

15. *Diary*, 12 July 1967.

16. Orton, *Funeral Games* and *The Good and Faithful Servant*, London: Methuen, 1970, p. viii.

17. Orton interview with Giles Gordon, *Transatlantic Review*, # 24, Spring 1967.

18. 'Orton Murder – Hammer Attack Frenzy', *Evening News*, 4 September 1967.

19. Listed as the title of the diaries in the Coroner's Report; but the title page was not returned with the diaries to the Estate after the inquest.

CHAPTER 2   SOMEBODY FROM NOWHERE

1. *The Victoria History of the Counties of England*, edited by R. B. Pugh, University of Leicester Institute of Historical Research, 1958.

2. Jack Simmons, *Leicester: Past and Present*, Volume 2: *The Modern City 1860–1974*, London: Eyre Methuen, 1974, p. 138.

3. Orton interview with Barry Hanson, Royal Court programme for *Crimes of Passion*, 6–17 June 1967.

4. *The Victoria History of the Counties of England*, op. cit., p. 302.

5. *Evening Standard*, 7 May 1964.

6. Halliwell to Kathleen O'Brien, 12 August 1950.

7. *Diary*, 28 December 1966.

8. *Adolescent Diary*, 3 May 1950.

9. Patricia Johnson, 'Money and Mr Orton', *Evening News*, 9 June 1967.

10. Orton to Peggy Ramsay, 10 June 1966.

11. *Leicester Mercury*, 22 June 1964.
12. *Adolescent Diary*, 3 April 1949.
13. *Leicester Mercury*, 10 August 1967.
14. Orton interview with Barry Hanson, op. cit.
15. Orton interview with Alan Brien, op. cit.
16. *Leicester Mercury*, 4 June 1964.
17. *Adolescent Diary*, 19 February 1950.
18. *Adolescent Diary*, 12 March 1950.
19. *Adolescent Diary*, 2 April 1950.
20. *Adolescent Diary*, 6 April 1950.
21. *Adolescent Diary*, 21 May 1950.
22–4. Interview with Barry Hanson.
25. *Adolescent Diary*, 2 July 1950.
26. *Adolescent Diary*, 5 July 1950.
27–30. Interview with Barry Hanson.
31. *Adolescent Diary*, 23 February 1950.

CHAPTER 3   UNNATURAL PRACTICES

1 and 2. Orton interview with Giles Gordon, op. cit.
3. Halliwell's statement to the police, 28 April 1962.
4. Interview with Giles Gordon.
5. *Hackney Gazette*, 18 May 1962.
6 and 7. *Islington Gazette*, 18 May 1962.
8. Patricia Johnson, 'Money and Mr Orton', *Evening News*, 9 June 1967.
9. Orton's statement to the police, 28 April 1962.
10. Alexander Connell, 'A Successful Prosecution', *Library Association Record*, May 1963.
11. Statement of Detective Sergeant Henry Hermitage, G Division, 2 May 1962.
12. Interview with Barry Hanson.
13. Rupert Croft-Cooke, *The Caves of Hercules*, London: W. H. Allen, 1974, p. 82.
14. *North London Press*, 8 May 1962.
15. Interview with Barry Hanson.
16. Halliwell to the Cordens, 21 May 1962.
17. Interview with Barry Hanson.

18. Orton to the Cordens, 29 July 1962.
19. Halliwell to the Cordens, 5 September 1962.
20. Orton to the Cordens, 29 July 1962.
21. Halliwell to the Cordens, 21 May 1962.
22. Orton to the Cordens, 29 July 1962.
23. Orton to the Cordens, 14 August 1962.
24. The Cordens were a constant source of amusement, even inspi-
    ration, to Orton. In his diary (27 February 1967) he writes: 'Mr
    Corden tried to explain to me, on the stairs, how I should fiddle
    the income tax. "You want to ring for a taxi. Go to the West
    End. Note carefully the fare and, when you come home, double
    it. And if anybody says anything, you swear blind that you came
    home by taxi when, in reality, you came home by bus. Oh,
    there are many little fiddles that the ordinary person simply will
    not take the trouble to learn". "That's quite right", Mrs Corden
    called up the stairs, "Mr Corden was in the accounting". She
    climbed the stairs and stood breathless telling me how he was in
    a firm of accountants. (He was a Commissionaire.)' Orton
    couldn't resist teasing the Cordens and wrote to them in one
    letter from prison: 'I'm writing to you using the complete works
    of Shakespeare as a writing block. I'm sure you'll understand.'
25. Halliwell attended the Wirral Grammar School from 1937 to
    1943. He obtained a School Certificate in 1941 in English
    Language, English Literature, History, German, Greek, Latin,
    Mathematics and Physics. He took his Higher School Certificate
    in Ancient History (Good), Greek (Pass), and Latin (Pass), with
    subsidiary German (Pass), in 1942.
26 and 27. Halliwell to Kathleen O'Brien, 3 January 1951.
28. Interview with Barry Hanson.
29. Halliwell to Miss C. Brown, 12 March 1953.
30. Interview with Barry Hanson.
31. Halliwell to Miss C. Brown, 8 June 1953.
32. Evening Standard, 3 October 1966.
33. Interview with Barry Hanson.
34. 'What Prison Did For This Playwright', Daily Mail, 22 June 1965.
35. Interview with Barry Hanson.
36. Halliwell to Charles Monteith, 22 September 1959.
37 Halliwell to Charles Monteith, 22 May 1959.

38. *Diary*, 25 March 1967.
39. Interview with Alan Brien.
40. Interview with Barry Hanson.
41. Charles Monteith to Orton and Halliwell, 30 November 1955.
42. Charles Monteith to Orton and Halliwell, 27 May 1957.
43. Orton to Charles Monteith, 2 June 1957.
44. Halliwell to Charles Monteith, 15 July 1959.
45. As quoted in Paul Radin, *The Trickster*, London: Routledge, Kegan & Paul, 1958.
46. *Diary*, 27 July 1967.
47. *Diary*, 13 March 1967.
48. Orton to Kenneth Williams, 6 June 1967.
49. As quoted in *The Letters of Oscar Wilde*, edited by Rupert Hart-Davis, London: Hart-Davis, 1962.
50. *Daily Telegraph*, 5 May 1964.
51. Interview with Barry Hanson.
52. Orton to Kenneth Williams, 3 April 1966.
53. *Diary*, 10 March 1967.
54. *Diary*, 29 January 1967.
55. Orton's statement to the police, 28 April 1962.
56. *Daily Sketch*, 30 November 1966.
57. *Evening Standard*, 3 October 1966.
58. *Leicester Mercury*, 4 June 1964.
59 and 60. 'The Bitter Bit: Joe Orton Introduces *Entertaining Mr Sloane*' with Simon Trussler, *Plays and Players*, August 1965.

CHAPTER 4   MONSTROUS FUN

1. See Martin Esslin's introduction to *New Radio Drama*, London: BBC, 1966, p. 7.
2 and 3. Orton to John Tydeman, 6 November 1963.
4. Orton to John Tydeman, 23 December 1963.
5. Orton to Peggy Ramsay, 16 May 1966.
6. Interview with Alan Brien.
7. Orton to Glenn Loney, 12 March 1966.
8. Orton to Glenn Loney, 25 March 1966.
9. *Diary*, 11 July 1966.
10. Harold Pinter to Orton, 15 March 1966. Pinter wrote Orton

another long, undated letter explaining his criticism of *Loot*, in which he observes: '*Ruffian, Sloane* (which production I detested) and *Erpingham* (which production I liked) seem to me to preserve a remarkable balance in themselves – they're many-layered shifting things. The great distinction and joy of your best writing is that (within a beautifully organized rhythmic structure) it possesses an inner resonance of shifting references *and* at the same time a sustained sense of dramatic momentum from one sentence to the next. (I don't apologise for that sentence!) . . .'

11. As quoted in 'The Life and Death of Joe Orton' by James Fox, *Sunday Times Magazine*, 22 November 1970.

12. Harold Pinter as quoted in Martin Esslin, *The Peopled Wound*, London: Methuen, 1970: 'The world is full of surprises. A door can open at any moment and someone will come in. We'd love to know who it is, we'd love to know exactly what he has on his mind and why he comes in, but how often do we know what someone has on his mind or who this somebody is . . .' See also the comment on Orton in the *Evening Standard*, 'In Search of Harold Pinter' by Kathleen Tynan, 26 April 1968.

13. *Diary*, 24 June 1967.

14. Eric Bentley, 'Farce', in *The Life of the Drama*, New York: Atheneum, 1964, pp. 219–56.

15. *Radio Times*, 29 August 1964.

16. *Observer*, 13 September 1964.

17. *Listener*, 10 September 1964.

18. *Daily Mail*, 22 June 1965.

19 and 20. Charles Marowitz, 'Entertaining Mr Orton', *Guardian*, 19 September 1966.

21. Patricia Johnson, 'Money and Mr Orton', *Evening News*, 9 June 1967.

22. In *The Ruffian on the Stair* Wilson haunts Joyce as he himself is haunted. Likewise, Sloane tries to spook Kemp into silence about his previous murder; *Loot* keeps the mother's corpse on stage and her invisible presence feeds the frenzy; and in *What the Butler Saw* Geraldine Barclay is visible but unseen by the others, who hunt for her and even seem like apparitions to each other in the mayhem.

23. Interview with Barry Hanson.

24. Alan Ayckbourn, Robert Bolt, Edward Bond, Howard Brenton, Christopher Hampton, David Hare, Frank Marcus, David Mercer, John Mortimer, Peter Nichols, Steven Poliakoff, David Rudkin.

25. *The Times*, 3 September 1970.

26. As quoted in *Harper's & Queen*, May 1973.

27. *Plays and Players*, August 1964.

28. Interview with Alan Brien.

29. *Diary*, 5 February 1967.

30. *Plays and Players*, August 1965.

31. Taylor, *The Second Wave*, London: Methuen, 1971, p. 140.

32. Interview with Alan Brien.

33. Orton to Peggy Ramsay, 26 May 1967.

34. Orton to Peter Gill, 22 May 1967.

35. Interview with Alan Brien.

36. Orton to Alan Schneider, 14 September 1965.

37. Peter Burton, 'I'm Not A Political Animal Says Joe Orton', *The Stage*, 6 October 1966.

38 and 39. Levin, *The Pendulum Years*, London: Cape, 1970, p. 49.

40. Interview with Giles Gordon.

41. London: Heinemann, 1970.

42–4. *Plays and Players*, August 1965.

45. Interview with Barry Hanson.

46. Orton to Michael Codron, undated (1964).

47. Orton to Alan Schneider, production note.

48. *Plays and Players*, August 1965.

49. Orton to Peggy Ramsay, 16 November 1965.

50. *Daily Telegraph*, 7 May 1964.

51. As quoted in 'What Joe Orton Saw' by Glenn Loney, *After Dark*, September 1970.

52. Orton to Glenn Loney, 25 March 1966.

53. Orton to Peggy Ramsay, 17 October 1964.

54. Interview with Giles Gordon.

55. Orton to Glenn Loney, 10 October 1965.

56. Interview with Barry Hanson. For another vitriolic response to *Entertaining Mr Sloane* and Orton, see Pamela Hansford Johnson's *On Iniquity*, London: Macmillan, 1967, in which Orton is named along with Edward Bond, John Whiting and David Rudkin as a

corrupting force in society; and her parody of the plot in her novel *Cork Street, Next to the Hatters*, London: Macmillan, 1965.

57. Hilary Spurling, 'Early Death', *Spectator*, 18 August 1967.

58–60. Orton to Peggy Ramsay, 27 September 1965.

61. Orton to Michael Codron, undated (October 1965).

62. Orton to Halliwell, 9 October 1965.

63 and 64. Orton to Halliwell, 2 October 1965.

65. Orton to Halliwell, 9 October 1965.

66. New York *Times*, 13 October 1965.

67. Orton to Glenn Loney, 26 October 1965.

68. Orton to Joy Small, 4 November 1965.

69 and 70. Interview with Alan Brien.

71. Orton to Glenn Loney, 25 March 1966.

CHAPTER 5   SCANDALOUS SURVIVAL

1. *Southern Weekly News* and *Brighton Gazette*, 'Farcical Tragedy', 5 February 1965.

2. Simon Trussler, 'Farce', *Plays and Players*, June 1966.

3. W. H. Auden, *The Dyer's Hand and Other Essays*, London: Faber, 1963, p. 158.

4. *Plays and Players*, June 1966.

5. Alexander and Margarete Mitscherlich, *The Inability to Mourn*, New York: Grove Press, 1975, p. 91.

6. Interview with Giles Gordon.

7. *Plays and Players*, June 1966.

8. Gorer, *Death, Grief and Mourning in Great Britain*, London: Cresset Press, 1965, pp. 169–75.

9. *The Stage*, 6 October 1966.

10. Auden, op. cit., p. 154.

11. *The Times*, 7 October 1964.

12. *The Times*, 12 November 1964.

13. Charles Marowitz, 'Entertaining Mr Orton', *Guardian*, 19 September 1966.

14. Interview with Barry Hanson.

15. Orton to Halliwell, 9 February 1965.

16. *Southern Weekly News* and *Brighton Gazette*, 5 February 1965.

17 and 18. Orton to Michael White, 14 July 1967.

19. Interview with Giles Gordon.
20. Orton to Halliwell, undated (February 1965).
21. *Manchester Evening News*, 13 March 1965.
22. Orton to Halliwell, 19 February 1965.
23. Orton to Michael White, 14 July 1967.
24. 'Joy through Strength', *Observer*, 28 March 1965.
25. Michael Codron to Peggy Ramsay, 8 March 1965.
26. Interview with Barry Hanson.
27 and 28. Orton to Glenn Loney, 25 March 1966.
29. Peggy Ramsay to Orton, undated (July 1965).
30. Orton to Glenn Loney, 25 March 1966.
31. Orton to Michael White, 14 July 1967.
32. *Daily Telegraph*, 12 April 1966.
33. Orton to Michael White, 11 April 1966.
34. Orton to Oscar Lewenstein, undated (July 1966).
35. London: Eyre Methuen, 1973, p. 157.
36. Orton to Michael White, 14 July 1967.
37. Charles Marowitz, 'Farewell, Joe Orton', New York *Times*, 7 April 1968.
38. Orton to Michael White, 14 July 1967.
39. *Evening Standard*, 12 January 1967.
40. Orton to Peggy Ramsay, 28 May 1967.
41. *Diary*, 4 January 1967.
42. *Diary*, 11 March 1967.
43. *Leicester Mercury*, 2 February 1967.
44. *Diary*, 24 February 1967.
45. *Observer*, 2 October 1966.

CHAPTER 6   THE FREAKS' ROLL-CALL

1. Albert Camus, *The Rebel* (1951), London: Hamish Hamilton, 1953; Penguin Books, 1962.
2. Interview with Barry Hanson.
3. Eric Bentley, 'Farce', in *The Life of the Drama*, New York: Atheneum, 1964.
4. Interview with Barry Hanson.
5. Leonie Orton Barnett to Orton, 31 March 1967.
6. Orton to Glenn Loney, undated (1967).

7. *Diary*, 25 March 1967.

8. *Diary*, 15 January 1967.

9. Oscar Lewenstein production note, undated (1967).

10. *Diary*, 23 February 1967.

11. *Diary*, 24 February 1967.

12. Oscar Lewenstein to Richard Lester, 10 May 1967.

13. Orton to Kenneth Williams, 4 March 1967.

14 and 15. *Diary*, 4 March 1967.

16. *Diary*, 31 March 1967.

17. Diary, 9 April 1967.

18. Laing, *The Divided Self*, London: Tavistock Publications, 1960; Penguin Books, 1965, p. 139.

19. Interview with Giles Gordon.

20. Bentley, op. cit. Orton wrote in his diary on 18 March 1967: 'Long walk through Regents Park . . . Sat in the blazing light and noticed how hideous the bright sunshine made everyone (including myself) appear. Like blanched and unsavoury apes.'

21. Hilary Spurling, 'The Young Master', *Spectator*, 14 March 1969.

22. Lewenstein contradicts the diary entry. 'Joe suggested two people for Dr Rance – one of them was Richardson and the other was Alistair Sim. I remember Joe telling me how he had seen Richardson in I think it was *Blandings Castle*, a series on TV, and how much he admired him in it. He may have had second thoughts but he didn't tell me. Clearly I would not have allowed someone to be cast that I knew he did not approve.'

23. *Diary*, 11 March 1967.

24. *Sunday Times*, 20 July 1975.

25. *Christian Science Monitor*, 19 March 1969.

26. *Sunday Telegraph*, 9 March 1969.

27. *Evening Standard*, 12 January 1967.

28. 'Nox Est Perpetua' by Marion Lochhead:

Perpetual night and endless sleep
Will us, and all our loving, keep.
The roman poet, long ago,
Saw all light end in shadow, so.

A little light, a fragile flame
Before the quenching darkness came.

In endless night love, scorched by hate,
Must lie, not stir of dawn to wait.

Perpetual night and endless sleep
May these not long for, who must keep
A weary vigil, wakeful lie
To watch themselves and others die.

PLAY CHRONOLOGY

The Ruffian on the Stair (1963)

London: First broadcast on the BBC Third Programme 31 August 1964; directed by John Tydeman. First stage performance in a production without decor by the English Stage Company at the Royal Court Theatre 21 August 1966; directed by Peter Gill. Produced with *The Erpingham Camp* in a double-bill entitled *Crimes of Passion* by the English Stage Company at the Royal Court Theatre 6–17 June 1967; directed by Peter Gill, designed by Deirdre Clancy.

New York: First presented at the Columbia University School of the Arts 1968–9; directed by William Garry.

Entertaining Mr Sloane (1963)

London: Produced by Michael Codron and Donald Albery at the New Arts Theatre, 6 May 1964. Transferred to Wyndham's Theatre 29 June 1964 and to Queen's Theatre 5 October 1964. Directed by Patrick Dromgoole; designed by Timothy O'Brien.

New York: Produced by Slade Brown, Tanya Chasman, and E. A. Gilbert at the Lyceum Theater 12 October 1965; directed by Alan Schneider; designed by William Ritman.

Germany: Premiere at Theater im Zimmer in Deutsches Schauspielhaus, Hamburg, 2 November 1964. Inszenierung Hans Lietzau, Buhnenbild Karl Groning.

The Good and Faithful Servant (1964)

London: First produced by Rediffusion Television on 6 April 1967; directed by James Ormerod. First staged at the King's Head, Islington, 17–28 March; directed by Frederick Proud.

Loot (1964–6)

London: Production by Michael Codron and Donald Albery first presented at the Arts Theatre, Cambridge, 1 February 1965; directed by Peter Wood, designed by Desmond Heeley. Closed at Wimbledon Theatre the week of 15 March 1965. Then produced at the University Theatre, Manchester, 11–23 April 1966; directed by Braham Murray. Finally produced by Oscar Lewenstein and Michael White with the London Traverse Theatre Company at the Jeanetta Cochrane Theatre 27 September 1966; directed by Charles Marowitz, designed by Tony Carruthers. Transferred to the Criterion Theatre 1 November 1966.

New York: Produced by Losal Productions, Inc., by arrangement with Oscar Lewenstein and Michael White, at the Biltmore Theater 18 March 1968; directed by Derek Goldby, designed by William Ritman.

Germany: Premiered at the Deutsches Schauspielhaus in Theatersaal des Unileverhauses, Hamburg, 15 February 1966; Regie, Hansgunther Heyme.

The Erpingham Camp (1965)

London: Produced in an early version by Rediffusion Television 27 June 1966; directed by James Ormerod. First staged with *The Ruffian on the Stair* in a double-bill entitled *Crimes of Passion* by the English Stage Company at the Royal Court Theatre 6–17 June 1967; directed by Peter Gill, designed by Deirdre Clancy.

New York: Produced with *The Ruffian on the Stair* as *Crimes of Passion* by Henry Fownes, Frank Bessell, Bruce Hoover, Leonard Mulhern and George Thorn at the Astor Place Theater, 26 October 1969; directed by Michael Kahn, designed by William Ritman.

Funeral Games (1966)

London: First presented by Yorkshire Television on 25 August 1968; directed by James Ormerod.

What the Butler Saw (1967)

London: Produced by Lewenstein-Delfont Productions Ltd and H. M. Tennent Ltd. at the Queen's Theatre 5 March 1969; directed by Robert Chetwyn, designed by Hutchinson Scott.

New York: Produced by Charles Woodward and Michael Kasdan at the McAlpin Rooftop Theater 4 May 1970; directed by Joseph Hardy, designed by William Ritman.

FILMS

Entertaining Mr Sloane: Directed by Douglas Hickox; screenplay by Clive Exton. Starring Beryl Reid, Harry Andrews, Peter McEnery, Alan Webb. Produced by Douglas Kentish. Distributed by EMI (1969).

Loot: Directed by Silvio Narizzano. Screenplay by Alan Simpson and Ray Galton. Starring Richard Attenborough, Lee Remick, Hywel Bennett, Milo O'Shea. An Arthur Lewis Production for British Lion (1970).

BIBLIOGRAPHY

The Ruffian on the Stair (radio version): in *New Radio Drama*, London, BBC, 1966.

Entertaining Mr Sloane: London, Hamish Hamilton, 1964; New York, Grove Press, 1964. New edition (with introduction by John Lahr), London: Eyre Methuen, 1973.

Loot: London, Methuen, 1967; New York, Grove Press, 1967.

Crimes of Passion (containing the revised *The Ruffian on the Stair* and *The Erpingham Camp*, as well as author's notes on changes for the Lord Chamberlain): London, Methuen, 1967.

Funeral Games and *The Good and Faithful Servant* (with an introduction by Peter Willes): London, Methuen, 1970.

Until She Screams (sketch for *Oh! Calcutta!*): New York, *Evergreen Review* # 78, May 1970.

What the Butler Saw: London, Methuen, 1969; New York, Grove Press (with an introductory essay by John Lahr), 1970.

Head to Toe: London, Anthony Blond, 1971; Panther paperback edition 1971.

Orton: The Complete Plays (with an introductory essay by John Lahr): London, Eyre Methuen, 1976; New York, Grove Press, 1977.

INDEX

More About Penguins
and Pelicans

Penguinews, which appears every month, contains details of all the new books issued by Penguins as they are published. It is supplemented by our stocklist, which includes almost 5,000 titles.

A specimen copy of *Penguinews* will be sent to you free on request. Please write to Dept EP, Penguin Books Ltd, Harmondsworth, Middlesex, for your copy.

In the U.S.A.: For a complete list of books available from Penguins in the United States write to Dept CS, Penguin Books, 625 Madison Avenue, New York, New York 10022.

In Canada: For a complete list of books available from Penguins in Canada write to Penguin Books Canada Ltd, 2801 John Street, Markham, Ontario L3R 1B4.

In Australia: For a complete list of books published by Penguins in Australia write to the Marketing Department, Penguin Books Australia Ltd, P.O. Box 257, Ringwood, Victoria 3134.

The Actor's Life: The Journals 1956–1976

Charlton Heston

'Here, better than any book I have read, is the feeling of what it is like
to be a filmstar . . . a goldmine'
— *Daily Telegraph*
Charlton Heston remembers it all, from the cold-water flat in a New
York slum to the top of the greatest show on earth – Hollywood.

Nijinsky

Richard Buckle

'The best biography of a dancer in the language'
— *Lincoln Kirstein*
In the history of ballet the legend of Nijinsky surpasses them all. As
light as a snowflake, as strong as steel, this was the greatest dancer, the
greatest mime artist, the most revolutionary choreographer the stage
has known.

Reel Facts

Cobbett Steinberg

Whether a trivia buff or a nostalgia freak, a film student or devoted
moviegoer, you will find this compendium of never-before-collected
material as entertaining as it is useful.

Conference of the Birds

John Heilpern

Peter Brook and his international troupe of actors left their base in
Paris to journey through the Sahara in search of new forms of theatre.
'A beautifully detailed and evocatively written account of people
embroiled in a genuine search for new values . . . the closest thing yet
written to an explanation of the phenomenon of Peter Brook'
— Charles Marowitz in the *Sunday Times*

Look out for these from Penguins

The Wolf Children

Charles Maclean

The amazing story of two girls found in a wolf's lair in the Bengali jungle. Charles Maclean found that the truth about Kamala and Amala was stranger than any fiction . . .

Orient Express

The Life and Times of the World's Most Famous Train

E. H. Cookridge

Hitchcock filmed it. Agatha Christie, Graham Greene and Ian Fleming wrote bestsellers about it. The very name of the Orient Express, with its silk and marble fittings, is redolent with fame and riches, spies and diplomats, and the mystery and romance of the East. History, comedy and tragedy were played on it – with a cast of thousands.

The Nude Male

A New Perspective

Margaret Walters

'Once you've read this book, you will never again be able to see a nude of either sex as simply a representation of the body beautiful'
– Lynne Edmunds in the *Daily Telegraph*

The Works

Beryl Cook

Introducing the world of Beryl Cook – Plymouth Argyle footballers, drag artists, transvestites, sailors on the Hoe, fish-and-chip shops, Teddy boys, fat barmaids, and all manner of wickedly funny goings on. 'Beryl Cook is the nicest thing to happen to British painting for years . . . it makes me laugh out loud'
– Edward Lucie Smith

A selection of anthologies in Penguin Plays

Open Space Plays

Selected by Charles Marowitz

Since its birth in 1968, London's Open Space Theatre has become, in the words of the *Sunday Times*, 'the leading experimental theatre' and, as the *Evening Standard* said, 'one of the liveliest fringe theatres in England'. This volume contains five of the most exciting new plays produced there.

Classic Irish Drama

Introduced by W. A. Armstrong

Yeats's *The Countess Cathleen* tells of two merchants who traffic in men's souls, and of how the Countess sells her own rather than see her people starve.

Synge's *The Playboy of the Western World* is about a peasant boy who thinks he has killed his father and so becomes a hero – until his murdered father reappears.

O'Casey's *Cock-a-doodle Dandy*, which the author considered his best play, is a satire directed against superstition, avarice and priestly authority.

Absurd Drama

Introduced by Martin Esslin

Containing Ionesco's first full-length play, *Amédée*, and three short plays: Adamov's *Professor Taranne*, Arrabal's *The Two Executioners*, and Edward Albee's *The Zoo Story*.

Three European Plays

Introduced and Edited by E. Martin Browne

In his ebullient comedy *Ring Round the Moon*, Anouilh draws vivid and entertaining portraits of human idiosyncrasies – with a total disregard for accepted moral values. Ugo Betti's reputation now rivals that of Pirandello; his concern with morality and religion is demonstrated in *The Queen and the Rebels*, a political drama of our own times written in the classical tradition. Sartre's *In Camera* involves three of life's victims who come to recognize that 'hell is other people'.

A selection of dramatists in Penguin Plays

Alan Ayckbourn

Three Plays

Containing *Bedroom Farce*, *Absurd Person Singular* and *Absent Friends*.
'Ayckbourn is witty because he can miraculously transmute the ordinary
base metal of our naturalistic speech.'
– J. C. Trewin in the *Birmingham Post*

The Norman Conquests

'A superb comic trilogy . . . Mr Ayckbourn is the most remarkable
British dramatist to have emerged since Harold Pinter'
– J. W. Lambert in the *Sunday Times*

Ben Travers

Five Plays

Containing *A Cuckoo in the Nest*, *Rookery Nook*, *Thark*, *Plunder* and
The Bed Before Yesterday. 'The single-track dirty mind, the double
entendre, the treble think, the quadruple bluff: funny names, funny
local yokels, domineering women, pretty girls and the ever-swinging
bedroom door . . . Explosively funny'
– Richard Usborne in *The Times Literary Supplement*

Peter Shaffer

Three Plays

Containing *Equus*, *Shrivings* and *Five Finger Exercise*.
'Peter Shaffer is a master of his art'
– Harold Hobson

David Storey

Home, *The Changing Room*, *Mother's Day*

'Mr Storey's farcical invention is tireless, and has the advantage of
unlimited permissiveness'
– *Financial Times*

The Expelled and Other Novellas

Samuel Beckett

'I'm working with impotence, ignorance,' Beckett once wrote.
These four stories, *First Love*, *The Expelled*, *The Calmative* and *The End*,
were written soon after the Second World War and are characterized
by this concern with the helpless individual consciousness. As well they
are rich in verbal and situational humour and offer a fascinating insight
into the work of a writer who has transformed both the art of the
novel and contemporary theatre.

Love Letters on Blue Paper and other stories

Arnold Wesker

'Integrity and a deep sense of pity are the qualities that emerge from
these thoughtful stories'
— *Sunday Times*

Focus

Arthur Miller

'I have tried to confront a man with his own hallucination', wrote
Miller when *Focus* was first published in 1945. The hallucination is
racial prejudice against the Jews, and this book is as chilling and
important now as it ever was.

Cashel Byron's Profession

Bernard Shaw

Bernard Shaw was obsessed with prize-fighting all his life – he entered
the English Amateur Boxing Association Championship as a
middleweight – and his racy, romantic adventure story superbly evokes
the bruised knuckles and raw hopes of the ringside.
'Genuine and remarkable narrative talent . . . a talent of strength, spirit,
capacity . . . It is all mad, mad and deliriously delightful . . . All I ask
is more of it'
— Robert Louis Stevenson

Recently published fiction from some of our best contemporary writers

Susan Hill

A Change for the Better

In the Prince of Wales Hotel and the shabby terraces and tearooms of Westbourne retired lives run their course – all, in their different ways, anticipating a crisis.
'A triumph' – *Daily Telegraph*

Gentleman and Ladies

Miss Faith Lavender would not have cried at her own funeral.
And indeed no one attending the service shed a tear – neither her two sisters, the handful of neighbours, not the strange man in black boots holding stolen snowdrops . . .
'A remarkable writer' – *The Times*

Alison Lurie

Only Children

Using the same stylish, tender and comic approach as in her bestselling *War Between the Tates*, Alison Lurie turns her attention to the goings-on one weekend on an idyllic Upstate New York farmhouse, when the Hubbards and the Zimmerns – plus their children – come to stay with Anna.
'It demands to be read' – *Financial Times*

Barbara Pym

Excellent Women

Mildred was quite capable of dealing with the stock situations of life. In fact her handling of births, marriages, deaths, jumble sales and garden fêtes ruined by the weather was masterly. It is the introduction of new and exotic neighbours that pulls her up short.
'I could go on reading her for ever' – A. L. Rowse in *Punch*

A Glass of Blessings

Wilmet Forsyth is fairly young, good looking, well dressed, well looked after, suitably husbanded and rather bored. Her interest wanders to the nearby Anglo–Catholic church and its three unmarried priests and on to Piers Longridge whose enigmatic overtures are rather intriguing.